Weber, Schumpeter and Modern Capitalism

This book provides the groundwork for a general theory of modern capitalism by reinterpreting Max Weber's work on the origins and institutional underpinnings of modern capitalism and Joseph Schumpeter's thought on the mechanisms and functioning of the capitalist economy. Focusing on the lesser-known works of both figures, particularly in the case of Weber, whose writings on economics and economic history are frequently overlooked, the author contends that a combination of Schumpeter's and Weber's theoretical schemas, incorporating their many valuable insights, provides the basis of a unified overall theory of modern capitalism that is comprehensive, coherent and persuasive.

With attention to the important theoretical connections between Weber and Schumpeter and the respective contributions of both with regard to the nature and workings of capitalism, the author explores the compatibility of the two approaches, arguing that the full significance of the contributions of the two writers has not been adequately appreciated.

A systematic and sympathetic comparison and synthesis of the contributions of two of the central figures in social and economic theory, which highlights the enduring relevance of their work in times of political and economic crisis, *Weber, Schumpeter and Modern Capitalism* will appeal to scholars across the social sciences with interests in social and economic theory, classical sociology and economic history.

John Love was formerly the Ashworth Lecturer in Social Theory at the University of Melbourne, Australia, and is the author of *Antiquity and Capitalism: Max Weber and the Sociological Foundations of Roman Civilization* (Routledge, 2005). He is currently a practising barrister in Melbourne.

Routledge Studies in Social and Political Thought

For a full list of titles in this series, please visit www.routledge.com/series/RSSPT

117 Elementary Forms of Social Relations
Status, Power and Reference Groups
Theodore D. Kemper

118 Groundwork for the Practice of the Good Life
Politics and Ethics at the Intersection of North Atlantic and African Philosophy
Omedi Ochieng

119 Theories of the Stranger
Debates on Cosmopolitanism, Identity and Cross-Cultural Encounters
Vince Marotta

120 Deciphering Goffman
The structure of his sociological theory revisited
Ramón Vargas Maseda

121 Planet Utopia
Utopia, Dystopia, and Globalisation
Mark Featherstone

122 Weber, Schumpeter and Modern Capitalism
Towards a General Theory
John Love

123 The Cultural Contradictions of Anti-Capitalism
The Liberal Spirit and the Making of Western Radicalism
Daniel Fletcher

124 Peter Berger on Modernization and Modernity
An unvarnished overview
Robert Bickel

125 Imaginaries of Modernity
Politics, Cultures, Tensions
John Rundell

Weber, Schumpeter and Modern Capitalism

Towards a General Theory

John Love

Routledge
Taylor & Francis Group
LONDON AND NEW YORK

First published 2017 by Routledge

2 Park Square, Milton Park, Abingdon, Oxfordshire OX14 4RN
52 Vanderbilt Avenue, New York, NY 10017

Routledge is an imprint of the Taylor & Francis Group, an informa business

First issued in paperback 2018

British Library Cataloguing-in-Publication Data
A catalogue record for this book is available from the British Library

Library of Congress Cataloging-in-Publication Data
A catalog record for this book has been requested

ISBN: 978-1-138-24238-8 (hbk)
ISBN: 978-0-367-20800-4 (pbk)

Typeset in Times New Roman
by Apex CoVantage, LLC

For Min Juan Dai

Contents

Preface

Research for the present work was commenced when I was the Ashworth Lecturer in Social Theory at the University of Melbourne. Owing to events at the university, I was obliged to change careers and subsequently became a barrister. I now practise law at the Victorian Bar. While studying to become a lawyer, I continued my keen interest in social theory and completed a PhD at Flinders University in Adelaide. From these studies I developed the ideas that have led to the present book.

Around the time I commenced writing the book, the Soviet Union had just collapsed, and the political and economic systems of the West seemed ascendant and destined to be dominant in the rest of the world. But paradoxically, in the academy the field of social theory remained under the influence of neo-Marxist and other anti-capitalist thinkers – Habermas, Offe, Baudrillard, Foucault, Bourdieu, Derrida and others. While the classic writings of figures like Weber and Schumpeter were by no means regarded as insignificant, their theories and methodologies were all too often taken to have been surpassed by later contributions.

I have taken the view that the writings of Weber and Schumpeter on capitalism remain central to the understanding of our current world, despite the changes that have undoubtedly occurred since their day. Their strength lies in the objective, penetrating and unapologetic character of the analyses they contain. In my view, these theoretical contributions are an indispensable means for coming to terms with the realities of the contemporary capitalist world without illusions. Though in recent years there has been something of a renaissance of interest in the work of Weber and Schumpeter, their key socio-economic theories remain under appreciated. I hope the book that follows will remedy this situation and form the basis for a more adequate and comprehensive theory of the modern capitalist system in all its vicissitudes.

I would like to thank my doctoral supervisor, Eduardo de la Fuente, for his support and assistance in regard to my thesis project. I would also like to thank both David Tucker and Harry Redner who read the thesis and provided many useful comments.

I have been fortunate to have had the editorial assistance and understanding of Shannon Knies, Richard Skipper and Kerry Boettcher of Routledge who have helped bring the book to its present state.

Finally, I am indebted to my loving wife Min Juan Dai who gave me invaluable support from the beginning of the project and continues to inspire me.

Abbreviations

BC	Schumpeter, Joseph, *Business Cycles; A Theoretical, Historical, and Statistical Analysis of the Capitalist Process*, McGraw-Hill, 1939.
CSD	Schumpeter, Joseph, *Capitalism, Socialism and Democracy*, Harper, 1950.
EEIBC	Schumpeter, Joseph (Richard Clemence ed.), *Essays on Entrepreneurs, Innovations, Business Cycles, and the Evolution of Capitalism*, Transaction, 1989.
EJAS	Schumpeter, Joseph (R. Clemence ed.), *Essays of J. A. Schumpeter*. Addison-Wesley Press, 1951.
ES	Weber, Max. *Economy and Society; An Outline of Interpretive Sociology*. Bedminster Press, 1968.
ESC	Schumpeter, Joseph (Richard Swedberg ed.), *Joseph A. Schumpeter: The Economics and Sociology of Capitalism*, Princeton University Press, 1991.
FMW	Weber, Max, *From Max Weber: Essays in Sociology*, Routledge, 1991.
GEH	Weber, Max, *General Economic History*, Transaction Books, 1981.
MSS	Weber, Max, *The Methodology of the Social Sciences*, Free Press, 1949.
PE	Weber, Max, *The Protestant Ethic and the Spirit of Capitalism*, Unwin, 1930.
TED	Schumpeter, Joseph, *The Theory of Economic Development; An Inquiry into Profits, Capital, Credit, Interest, and the Business Cycle*, Harvard University Press, 1934.
TGE	Schumpeter, Joseph, *Ten Great Economists, From Marx to Keynes*, Oxford University Press, 1951.

Introduction

The student of modern society is struck by the fact that in the present world capitalist economic relations and capitalist economic structures appear all but dominant.[1] This is the case not simply because Western Europe, the United States, Canada, Japan, Australia and the so-called "Asian tigers" (South Korea, Taiwan, Hong Kong and Singapore) have shown themselves to be highly prosperous and enduring capitalist economies – admittedly despite some recent difficulties – it is also indicated by the emergence of many new or emerging capitalist economies. This latter development has been largely an unexpected consequence of the end of the Cold War following the collapse of the Soviet Union and the worldwide communist movement sponsored by it. Since 1989, there has arisen in the space of the old socialist/communist systems an array of nascent capitalist economies, as well as what might be termed various quasi- or neo-capitalist systems. And these embryonic or neo-capitalisms have arisen not only in Russia itself and the states that were once under the direct control of the Soviet Union, such as Hungary or the Czech Republic, but also in other nations that were once socialist in orientation, such as India and Israel, or even avowedly communist, like China and Vietnam. Furthermore, many, if not most, of the so-called developing countries of Africa, the Middle East and South America appear to have embarked upon courses of development that are oriented in large part towards bringing about a capitalist system of some kind, such as is occurring in cases as various as Turkey, South Africa, the Gulf States, Mexico and Chile. In some instances this transformation towards a capitalist system is well under way, as with Brazil, Indonesia, Thailand and Malaysia, which have already emerged as minor economic powers.

All these developments suggest that today there is no longer a serious socio-economic alternative to capitalism – that is, if a country seeks prosperity and to develop economically – as counter examples like North Korea and Cuba seem

1 David Hale has referred to the present as the "Second Great Age of Capitalism", a phrase that refers to the fact that the world is experiencing economic change brought by entrepreneurial capitalism on a scale not seen since the Industrial Revolution. The phrase is quoted in Robert Gilpin, *The Challenge of Global Capitalism: The World Economy in the 21st Century*, Princeton University Press, 2000, p. 15.

to confirm. Even in the case of China, which remains officially a communist state, a virulent strain of capitalism has emerged, which is largely responsible for its unprecedented economic progress and the huge improvement in living standards. Of course, recognizing the evident dominance of capitalist and quasi-capitalist institutions in the modern world does not mean we are invoking an historical telos, nor are we suggesting that we are approaching "the end of history", as Fukuyama might have it. And we by no means wish to imply that capitalism as a system is immune from fundamental criticisms or does not need fundamental reform. It goes without saying that many problems and difficulties remain, some of which are probably intrinsic to this mode of arranging economic affairs.[2] Numerous aspects of the culture of capitalist modernity considered in the broad invite critical reflection and warrant investigation.[3] But here we shall not be concerned with these larger cultural, political and philosophical concerns, important though they are. Rather, in what follows we shall seek to explore the causes and structural configurations underlying the extraordinary success of the capitalist system in its modern guises, a phenomenon we submit cannot be denied. Only once we have explained why capitalism has become so dominant can we begin to show what its limits might be.

Despite recognition that the unprecedented economic progress referred to is directly connected with the phenomenon of capitalism, we think it is questionable whether either mainstream economics or, alternatively, radical Marxist or neo-Marxist approaches, adequately account for the advent of capitalism, let alone explain its present operation and future prospects. The pace of change and the complexity of developments occurring in the modern West and the newly developing nations, including Russia and China, are such that accounting for all these socio-economic formations, never mind comprehending their interrelations and the global ramifications, is clearly a considerable task. Hitherto there has been one notable theory that purported to provide a "general theory" of the rise, operation and future course of capitalism, namely Marxism. But, with the collapse of the world communist movement and the intellectual effects of this failure, Marxism can no longer be held as a convincing overall theory, let alone support a compelling worldview.[4] And mainstream economics and academic sociology have all but

2 Concerning evaluation of the present capitalist system, there are a great many such critiques. I shall only mention the recent work of Geoff Mulgan, *The Locust and the Bee: Predators and Creators in Capitalism's Future*, Princeton University Press, 2013.

3 But with a focus on Weber, we note the contributions on the character of modernity by commentators such as Wilhelm Hennis, *Max Weber, Essays in Reconstruction*, Allen & Unwin, 1988; Wolfgang Schluchter, *Paradoxes of Modernity: Culture and Conduct in the Theory of Max Weber*, Stanford University Press, 1996; and Lawrence Scaff, *Fleeing the Iron Cage: Culture, Politics and Modernity in the Thought of Max Weber*, University of California Press, 1989.

4 I make this claim recognizing that there have been worthy efforts by Marxist or neo-Marxist thinkers to "up-date" Marxist theory or to develop theories building on Marxist foundations – for example, the writings of Jürgen Habermas, *Knowledge and Human Interests*, Beacon, 1971, *The Theory of Communicative Action: Reason and the Rationalization of Society*, Beacon, 1984, or the "world systems" approach of Immanual Wallerstein, *The Modern World System: Capitalist Agriculture and the Origins of the World-Economy in the Sixteenth Century*, Academic Press, 1974. But I do not

retreated from projects of general theory, as they become increasingly specialized or focus on practical policy matters. Undeterred by this state of affairs, the present work will attempt the ambitious task of addressing the challenge of a grand theory of the contemporary socio-economic situation by offering a general framework for comprehending modern capitalism.

The range of different socio-economic systems in the contemporary era presents numerous difficulties of theory formation. For example, the economic character of post-communist societies is particularly problematic. In the case of Russia, there are complications arising from the fact that under Yeltsin an attempt was made to introduce a liberal capitalist system by direct means, "from above" as it were, but this has had very mixed results and led to the financial crisis of 1998. Then under Putin an authoritarian state re-emerged, which has revived aspects of a centrally controlled economy in association with the rise of the so-called "oligarchs". The result is that some aspects of a capitalist free market have been instituted, though in many respects the system falls well short of being fully capitalist such as we find elsewhere, say, in Europe or America.[5]

In the case of China, a quite different set of events has led to a strikingly novel outcome, namely, what appears to be a highly productive and rapidly expanding capitalist sector of the economy within a system that remains avowedly communist, at least in its political structure, state administration and ideology. Few commentators foresaw such a contradictory development, and even today, it is not easy to interpret what this means. But tendencies along these lines, wherein a socialist government embraces a capitalist-like market system, are appearing in several other former communist societies, such as Vietnam, Laos, Ukraine, Serbia and Kazakhstan.

On the other hand, recent history has also been witness to perplexing developments in the so-called advanced capitalist West. Both in Europe and America, we have witnessed events that have shaken the confidence of some as to the stability and ongoing prosperity of these economies, hitherto regarded as "bullet proof". The "sub-prime debacle" and the collapse of Lehman Brothers in America that precipitated the so-called Global Financial Crisis demonstrates not only that an economic super power has vulnerabilities but also that the world economy as a whole is not immune from a serious crisis, perhaps on the scale of the Great Depression. We have yet to see how these developments will play out, though indications are that America and the Western economies generally will cope with

regard these attempts as having saved Marxist theory as a whole from fundamental failings, which in our view remain unrectified. Marxism as a general theoretical system has not recovered from the many devastating critiques that have found it wanting, but for now we shall only mention the comprehensive critique of Weber that is contained in his methodological essays. Which is not to deny that Marxism has been a significant influence in diverse ways on both Weber and Schumpeter. It is also worth noting that to a degree, Marx's better contributions, especially in regard to his sociological insights, have been partly incorporated into their works.

5 With other former Soviet states such as Belarus, it would appear that little has changed from Stalinist times.

the present difficulties. In Europe, we have also seen extraordinary developments in the most recent past surrounding the virtual bankruptcy of Greece, Cyprus and Ireland and the demise of the economies of southern Europe. Even France and England face serious difficulties, owing in part to the exposure of their banks to the debt crisis. Finally, Japan's economy continues to lack dynamism, now made more intractable in the wake of the natural and nuclear disaster at Fukushima in 2011. For over a decade, Japan has failed to consistently register significant economic growth, in contrast to its impressive record in the 1970s and 1980s. Yet despite all these difficulties, none of these societies seems remotely likely to cease being capitalist in their basic economic institutions, and indeed the recommended "cure" for most of the supposed ills, according to many commentators, is more capitalism (free trade, privatization, deregulation, lower corporate taxes, etc.), not less.

Comprehending these developments in their multifaceted complexity, as well as grasping the future trajectory of the advanced capitalist societies, is thus a daunting task and no doubt beyond the capacity of a single theoretical achievement. Nonetheless, the present author believes that there are existing bodies of research that are available to ground such a project, and it is to these I shall turn in what follows. I shall argue that in the seminal works of Max Weber and Joseph Schumpeter one can find the fundamental elements necessary for just such an enterprise. In what follows, I attempt to explicate their key theoretical achievements and build a synthesis as the basis of a "general theory" of the worldwide phenomenon of capitalism as manifested today in its various guises.

The idea of a general theory of modern capitalism has numerous resonances within economics and social theory, but there are perhaps three thinkers who are exemplary in this regard. At the birth of modern economics is the figure of Adam Smith, whose works provided an elaborate account of the rationale of a market-capitalist system, even though his work largely predated the advent of the Industrial Revolution. A second figure that stands out is, of course, Karl Marx, who attempted to show not only why capitalism had become ascendant but also why, contrary to its apparent dominance, it would soon give rise to a "higher stage" of society, namely communism. And third, we must cite John Maynard Keynes who, as is known, employed the concept of "general theory" as a key notion in his celebrated work *The General Theory of Employment, Interest and Money*, and who sought to give his specific theses wide application in accordance with the idea. For various reasons that will become clear in what follows the present author does not regard the theories of any of these pre-eminent thinkers as adequate for the purposes of a general theory of modern capitalism today, however much they may be said to have contributed to our understanding of the issues involved. Nonetheless, the notion of "general theory" is not for that reason to be abandoned, and the effort to bring together the available knowledge in the various interrelated fields remains a worthwhile and, we believe, necessary task for social theory.[6]

6 Mention at this point should be made of the work of Talcott Parsons, which is in some ways an attempt to integrate aspects of economic theory with sociology and seeks to use Weber's work for his

The spectre of Marx

Undoubtedly, of the three thinkers just mentioned, it is Marx who has produced the most comprehensive and far-reaching account of the capitalist socio-economic system to date.[7] This is certainly the view his followers maintained and, in some cases, still maintain. Of course, much has been said and written about the validity and adequacy of Marx's claims and analyses, and here we shall only touch on a few of the many problems involved. We need to address our relation to Marx because a major concern in this work is to provide an effective alternative to Marx's theory.

Despite the recent collapse of the communist systems supported by the former Soviet Union and the evident demise of the worldwide socialist movement, Marx's account of capitalism has, to a certain extent, retained its appeal, and in some circles, it continues to be regarded as the most adequate and convincing overall theory of capitalism.[8] This is in part because mainstream economics and sociology have thus far failed to offer an effective general theory of capitalism, despite the many valuable contributions on specific issues made by these disciplines. The enduring appeal of Marx's theory of capitalism arises in part because of its comprehensive character. That is, Marx was able to combine an account of the origins and mechanism of the capitalist system with an analysis of the political and social dimensions and added to all this was a call to action. His account of primitive accumulation and the expropriation of the peasantry, which culminated in the exploitative capitalist/worker relationship, constitutes, at first glance, a persuasive overview and an indictment of the entire capitalist socio-economic system. Marx was able, through his use of his key concepts – such as the fetishism of the commodity, the mode of the production, the forces and relations of production,

---

own structural/functionalist theory. But we shall not pursue this approach in what follows because in our view, and that of other commentators, Parsons's reading of Weber is highly questionable in key respects and leads in unproductive directions. See Jere Cohen, Lawrence Hazelrigg and Whitney Pope, "De-Parsonizing Weber: A Critique of Parsons' Interpretation of Weber's Sociology", *American Sociological Review*, 40.2, (1975), pp. 229–41. For an overview of attempts to integrate economics and sociology, see the essay by Neil J. Smelser and Richard Swedberg, "The Sociological Perspective on the Economy", in Neil J. Smelser and Richard Swedberg (eds.), *The Handbook of Economic Sociology*, Sage, 1994, pp. 3–26.

7 We should note at the outset that Marx does not employ the concept of "capitalism" as such but invariably uses the concept of "the capitalist mode of production" as his key analytic tool. The term "capitalism" was not current in Marx's time and only became a commonly used sociological and economic concept after Sombart published his *Modern Capitalism* in 1902. Nonetheless, Weber employed the term prior to this in his early writings in the 1890s and then of course in *The Protestant Ethic and the Spirit of Capitalism*, and he clearly intended it to refer to the same modern industrial system that Marx had in mind. But Weber included the broader cultural and institutional supports of the industrial system in his application of the term.

8 Notable amongst recent proponents of the ongoing relevance of Marx's theory of capitalism are: David Harvey, *A Companion to Marx's Capital* (2 vols), Verso, 2010 and Moishe Postone, *Time, Labour and Social Domination: A Reinterpretation of Marx's Critical Theory*, Cambridge University Press, 1993.

surplus value, class struggle, expropriation, etc. – to accommodate the manifest complexity of the capitalist world of his day and to account for its key features. His work, as a whole, is unquestionably a brilliant intellectual achievement and quite breathtaking in its scope and vision. It is hardly surprising that generations of followers, both intellectuals and others, have been inspired and captured by the worldview and that, even today, many remain convinced of its essential validity.

But today no one can deny the massive costs in lives and other destructive consequences that have occurred in the attempt to institute communism in the twentieth century.[9] Here we shall not embark on a detailed account of the cataclysmic failures of socialist/communist societies in the twentieth century, as these failures are now abundantly clear and well established. A few aspects, however, warrant comment. Obviously, in the major communist societies that came into being in the early twentieth century, there was not only a failure to produce economic prosperity for the masses despite some industrial progress; contrary to Marx's expectations, these societies were a total disaster for human freedom and democracy. Indeed, far more than this, these societies were totalitarian and, in their worst periods, became a negative utopia based on the total subjection and sacrifice of the individual to the machinations of the state. Clearly, given such appalling outcomes conducted in the name of Marx or of Marxism, the master's theory of capitalism cannot go unscathed.

There are many specific aspects of Marx's work that cannot be accepted either in part or wholly. Some of the more obvious deficiencies of his theory that have been well noted by commentators are these: Marx failed to see that capitalism would not collapse, at least in the short term, because of its internal contradictions; economic downturns would not necessarily lead to system-wide crises. Fluctuations in economic performance would not prevent capitalism from achieving ongoing and rising prosperity for the masses. Far from industrial progress creating an "industrial reserve army" (the lumpenproletariat), Marx failed to foresee the rise of growing middle classes made up of professionally qualified and skilled workers who would be manifest beneficiaries of capitalist progress and thus supporters of the system. He did not realize the extent to which the capitalist state would expand its sphere of care and, under the influence of labour movements, redistribute at least part of the collective wealth in the form of higher wages. He did not fully appreciate the growth of bureaucracy and the advent of state-controlled mechanisms that regulate and direct national economic affairs. The advance of the corporation, and later the multinational corporation, to a large extent post-dated Marx's era, so he did not address these phenomena to any degree. Hence, he did not consider the issues arising from the separation of ownership and control and the fact of widespread share ownership by ordinary citizens. A further deficiency applies to Marx's lack of adequate appreciation of the function of stock markets and the role of banking and finance. And despite some remarkably prescient remarks in his *Grundrisse* as to the long-term prospects of technological development, Marx did not recognize

9 We shall not refer to the many treatments of the horrors of the Stalinist and Maoist dictatorships that are now widely known.

the role of technical innovation, both in facilitating the creation of new products and enabling more efficient methods of production.

Of course, some of these deficiencies are understandable, and Marx cannot be blamed for not fully anticipating future developments that were only embryonic in his time. Nonetheless, his theory suffers significantly because of these deficiencies, and we say it cannot be easily "updated" by adding qualifications to the original. In any event, there are serious theoretical weaknesses underlying Marx's account of capitalism, even as regards an account of nineteenth century capitalism.

In our view, Marx's fundamental errors arise from his methodological starting point (neo-Hegelianism) in association with the way he takes up and modifies the economic science of his day (Ricardo). This is the case even though under the influence of Fuerbach, he attempted to separate himself from the so-called idealist dialects of Hegel by "inverting" the latter and propounding a materialist dialectics (historical materialism).[10] Adapting the dialectical method of Hegel, Marx propounded a visionary philosophy of history, which differed from Hegel in particular because the end of history was conceived of as not yet at hand, as mankind still awaits the arrival of a utopian communist society in the future. To advance this vision, Marx adopted the stance of political economy as propounded by David Ricardo and others, and fashioned his key concept "the capitalist mode of production" as the lynch pin of his analysis. He considered that this notion was fully adequate to and completely coinciding with the socio-economic reality of the world he was seeking to grasp and transform. That is, the concept of "the capitalist mode of production" is not an analytical construct deployed to investigate concrete reality (à la an ideal type, as with Weber); it is rather a totalizing conception that is complete and comprehensive from the outset, and it is ultimately posited so as to disclose how the laws of history, operating through the logic of capitalist accumulation, will inevitably lead to communism.[11] Whatever occurs in the socio-economic realm is therefore always determined by the inner workings of the system; there are no accidents or contingencies to be factored in.

Marx's basic perspective is made especially clear is his *Capital*, where from the outset (Volume I, Chapter One) he claims the inner secret and inherent logic of the capitalist mode of production is revealed by dialectical analysis of the commodity. But herein lies a fundamental methodological error, for the crucial features of the capitalist economic system cannot be divined from such a starting point.[12] The well-known distinction between "use value" and "exchange value", from which Marx derives his notion of the fetishism of commodities and thereafter the idea of the extraction of surplus value, is based on highly questionable presuppositions. For a start, it wrongly assumes the production of goods for use is natural and transparent,

10 I refer to the oft-quoted remarks in Authors Preface to the Second Edition of *Capital*.

11 This aspect has been notably critiqued from a Marxist perspective by Jürgen Habermas, who admits a "latent positivism" in Marx's thinking. See his *Knowledge and Human Interests*, passim.

12 For a spirited recent defence of Marx's approach, see Postone's *Time, Labour and Social Domination*, pp. 123–85.

in contrast to production for exchange, the latter being somehow inauthentic, mysterious or opaque. A related theoretical notion that Marx utilizes here is, of course, the now discredited labour theory of value, which he attempts to show is the true measure and secret of exchange value, and which he deploys to ground his theory of exchange.[13] He attempts to construct an account of the entire edifice of the capitalist socio-economic system from these discredited elements. And despite detailed and evocative references to a wide range of historical materials – which admittedly are sometimes penetrating and insightful – Marx does not really embark on a properly empirical investigation of the available data of the capitalist economy with a view to discovering causal relations and structural configurations.

Marx's fundamental claim is that the capitalist mode of production is a system built upon the extraction of the workers' surplus labour by the capitalist bourgeoisie. The antagonistic capital/labour relation is axial, and this is linked to the idea of class struggle. To the dominance of capital corresponds the political rule of the bourgeoisie, which, however, is destined to be overthrown. This revolution will occur because of the internal logic of the capitalist mode of production, which cannot be stabilized and is unsustainable; it will be transformed into a higher stage (*Aufhebung*) of economy and society, communism. In his theory the cultural sphere, which includes political ideas, religions, law and men's beliefs generally, is regarded as entirely dependent and secondary in relation to the fundamental economic forces at work, and in accordance with the base/superstructure schema these cultural elements are relegated to mere "ideology".

Nonetheless, having stated why we reject the general approach of Marx to the theory of capitalism, we must acknowledge that some of what Weber and Schumpeter say on the topic is influenced by him. For example, to a degree, Weber accepts with Marx that the focus of theory must be the industrial system that emerged in England during the eighteenth century and matured and spread in the nineteenth century. This is "modern capitalism", as distinguished from various premodern systems where finance, mercantilism or trade constituted the forms of capitalist enterprise. And Weber also accepts much of what Marx says about the expropriation of the workers from the means of production, that this causes their deprived class situation and so on. And Schumpeter readily concedes that he owes a great deal to Marx's idea that the economic system generates fundamental change *from within*, by the machinations of the system's internal dynamics. We shall have occasion to note Marx's influence on numerous occasions in what follows.

The rationale of the present work

The underlying premise of the present work is the view that the writings of Max Weber, together with those of Joseph Schumpeter contain most, if not all, of the

13 Marx's theory of the labour theory of value never recovered, in our view, from the critique of Eugene Böhm Bawerk, *Karl Marx and the Close of His System*, Kelly, 1949, despite the efforts of Hilferding, Sraffa and numerous others to salvage it.

essential elements necessary to construct a general theory of modern capitalism. I regard both of these writers as eminently suitable for this project, owing to their unique status and outstanding achievements within the fields of social science where they practised. Of course, there are many other important thinkers on the topic of capitalism, and indeed one could argue that the entire field of economics and a good deal of sociology are addressed to this topic in one way or another. Yet many of the efforts of earlier writers are unfortunately now of limited value because of the time in which they wrote, or their contributions are already subsumed in the works of our two key thinkers. Though their legacy remains important and in some cases they cast a long shadow, we say that their accounts of capitalism are no longer adequate.

If we come to a later period and the problem of understanding contemporary capitalism, there are a number of thinkers other than Weber and Schumpeter whose contributions are of interest. Around the turn of the century in Germany, there were important theorists such as Karl Knies, Karl Bücher, Lujo Bretano, Georg Simmel, Gustav Schmoller and Werner Sombart, who in various ways addressed the issue of capitalism. In Austria we find a number of economic thinkers of note, such as Carl Menger, Friedrich Wieser, Eugene Böhm-Bawerk, Ludvig Mises, Rudolf Hilferding and later Frederick Hayek, all of whom wrote extensively on the topic. In England, there have been many economists of note, including Stanley Jevons, Francis Edgeworth, Alfred Marshall, Edward Chamberlin, Joan Robinson, F. H. Kahn and John Maynard Keynes. And in America, one can cite John Clark, Wesley Mitchell, Irving Fisher, Frank Taussig and Thorstein Veblen. Elsewhere, one might mention the eminent figures Knut Wicksell, Léon Walras and Vilfredo Pareto. But regardless of the undoubted importance of all these thinkers, it is the present work's contention that with the combination of Weber and Schumpeter we have unique contributions that are adequate for forming a satisfactory general theory of modern capitalism, as I hope to show.

It might be suggested that a better combination for such an enterprise would be, say, Marx plus Schumpeter, or Weber plus Simmel or possibly even Weber plus Marx.[14] In selecting Weber and Schumpeter, the author of the present work expresses his clear preference for those two thinkers, and it goes without saying that, if he sees in these thinkers intellectual achievements of a unique and superior kind, he correspondingly regards others as of lesser value and, in some ways, deficient. In the case of the works of both Weber and Schumpeter, one finds an extraordinarily extensive range of commentary and penetrating analyses on most, if not all, of the major aspects of capitalism about which an enquiring mind may wish to be informed. Both thinkers were steeped in historical understandings concerned with the immediate origins of capitalism and the period of pre-capitalism, and they also made contributions to the understanding of European antiquity and

14 A sympathetic, though critical, treatment of Schumpeter, but from a Marxist point of view, has been advanced by Tom Bottomore in his study *Between Marginalism and Marxism: The Economic Sociology of Joseph Schumpeter*, Harvester Wheatsheaf, 1992.

even beyond. This is very evident in the case of Weber, who wrote several works dealing with ancient Mediterranean civilizations. But it is also true of Schumpeter, who, in his *History of Economic Analysis*, discussed at some length ancient and mediaeval forms of thought in relation to the economic field and in other writings addressed the period of European feudalism and premodern conditions generally. Also, both thinkers wrote significant pieces on non-Western civilizations. This is especially the case with Weber, who wrote extensive essays dealing with the Indian and Chinese civilizations, and throughout his writings, he made reference to these cultures and to others as well. Likewise, Schumpeter offered commentaries on non-Western civilizations, and from time to time, he addressed aspects of Egyptian or Indian culture and was familiar with the broad sweep of world history. Interestingly, both Weber and Schumpeter became quite preoccupied with America and its rise as a dominant world power, even though they emerged from the heart of European civilization and were very much products of it. Of course, Schumpeter emigrated to America and lived there for most of his later years, and he naturally became extremely familiar with America, writing extensively about its economic history. In the case of Weber, there is a fascinating association with America brought about in part by his visit to America for the World's Fair in St. Louis in 1904, which gave rise to several essays dealing with religious sects in America, and reflections on American cultural phenomena appear regularly in his writings from that period onwards.[15] In some ways it is apparent that Weber saw America as marking out a future course of capitalist civilization as a whole, though this is not explicitly argued.[16]

These background features suggest that the writings of Weber and Schumpeter on the nature of the capitalism should be understood via a comparative approach to the study of socio-economic systems.[17] It is our view that there are few, if any other, theorists of capitalism who have matched the depth of socio-historical understanding of these two thinkers. As it happens, the lives of Weber and Schumpeter coincided from around 1905 until 1920 when Weber died. In this period, both thinkers were highly productive and deeply involved in interpreting and

15 On Weber's involvement with America, see the interesting book by Lawrence Scaff, *Max Weber in America*, Princeton University Press, 2011 and the penetrating analysis by Peter Ghosh, "Capitalism and *Herrschaft*: Max Weber in St. Louis", in Peter Ghosh (ed.), *A Historian Reads Max Weber*, Harrassowitz Verlag, 2008, pp. 119–70. On occasion, Weber referred to America as a case of belated "Europeanization", and compared to Germany it represented a form of "disorganized capitalism" owing to its lower cultural level.

16 The idea that America would one day become a leading power in the West was partly anticipated by Weber, who nonetheless wished for Germany to have such a role. He sensed that the centre of gravity of world civilization had shifted with the rise of America. For an extended discussion of the implications of American pre-eminence and its possible decline in the recent past for world civilization, see the detailed analysis by Harry Redner, *Totalitarianism, Globalization, Colonialism: The Destruction of Civilization since 1914*, Transaction, 2014.

17 The broad significance of Weber's work for a comparative understanding of civilizations has been the focus of Stephen Kalberg, especially his *Max Weber's Comparative-Historical Sociology*, University of Chicago Press, 1994.

understanding the capitalist order of the day. And, we believe, in this time the capitalist system had already advanced to a degree that could be said to have "matured" and even have become "high capitalism".[18] Weber and Schumpeter were both uniquely situated to comment on and interpret the capitalist system of the early and middle twentieth century, and we shall maintain that this economic system, admittedly with some changes, is in essence that which we have today. Of course, there have been important developments since the time of Schumpeter and Weber, and it will be a concern of the present work to indicate possible limitations and lacunae in the contributions of our two thinkers, especially where changes have occurred that have outstripped their purview; here we shall point to important recent contributions that are valuable additions. But at the same time, we intend to demonstrate how their thought remains vital to grasping the tendencies and trends at work in the present era of capitalist development. There are numerous topics on which Weber and Schumpeter addressed the same basic issues and came to similar conclusions. And whilst Weber is generally regarded foremost as a sociologist and not considered an economist of significance, and Schumpeter is known for his professional achievements in economics, both thinkers were in fact deeply engaged in both sociology and economics and this we believe makes their integration a more doable exercise.

In the case of Weber, as we shall see, the concept of rational economic action played an important part in his thinking about capitalism. We shall have occasion to explore at some length Weber's appreciation of the theory of marginal utility, and we argue that to a degree he builds his sociology of economic action in recognition of such principles. At least in his early self-understanding, Weber actually considered himself an economist, or perhaps a "political economist", and had a high regard for the contributions of theoretical economics, which he knew at first hand. In fact, in his earlier academic life (1894–8), Weber gave lectures on economic theory, and the notes that have been recovered recording the topics and issues dealt with show his complete familiarity with the economic science of the day.[19] Of course, he eventually became famous for his sociology and never pursued economic theory as a specialist. On the other hand, Schumpeter appears to have begun as an economist and remained such, being fundamentally preoccupied with the workings of the economic system. Yet increasingly, especially in his last

18 The concept of "high capitalism" goes back to the work of Sombart, who conceived it as a second stage of capitalism involving white-collar workers, state intervention and technical innovation. It has more recently been employed primarily by neo-Marxist theoreticians (especially the so-called Frankfurt School) in a different register, to designate the kind of capitalism that has prevailed since World War II, in light of the fact that the capitalist economic system that was Marx's focus has not been superseded by socialism as expected and continues to advance. But neither Weber nor Schumpeter use this idea.

19 The title of these lectures was apparently "General ('Theoretical') Economics", and Peter Ghosh has given a detailed account of the contents, such as can be constructed from Weber's notes, in his essay "A Situation Report *c.* 1897", in his *Max Weber and the Protestant Ethic: Twin Histories*, Oxford University Press, 2014, pp. 12–30.

writings, he felt obliged to explore the sociological dimensions of the capitalist system, and he progressively expanded his horizons to write about a number of aspects of the social world within which a capitalist economy operated. So we take it for granted in what follows that Weber and Schumpeter were each passionately interested in both the sociology and economics of capitalism. More than this, both thinkers sought to go beyond purely scholarly contributions to understanding the capitalist system. That is, they are both, in one way or another, offering interpretations of modern capitalist civilization as a whole and were even indirectly attempting to provide a kind of philosophy of modernity as such. Further, they each wrote quite extensively not just on the methodology of their respective disciplines but also on the epistemology of science, broadly speaking. A reading of Weber and Schumpeter discloses that they commented on an extraordinarily broad range of issues in relation to the world in which they lived; their writings touch on aspects of epistemology, psychology, aesthetics, statistics, ethics, religion, literature and law, to name the more prominent fields covered.

Despite the evident sharing of some perspectives, the question arises as to how a combination of the contributions of Weber and Schumpeter can be fruitful or is otherwise justified. What is be achieved by a synthetic combination of the respective achievements of Weber and Schumpeter? Are the contributions of Weber and Schumpeter perhaps antithetical? The present writer does not deny that there are some points of possible incompatibility between the two approaches. Nonetheless, we shall argue that there is more common ground between the two thinkers than what sets them apart and, as we shall see, on some topics they collaborated. Although they did not appear to have a close relationship during the time in which they were contemporaries, as I shall explain below they shared many concerns and attitudes. The rationale of the present work is that a synthetic combination of these two thinkers' works is worthwhile because their contributions are each of great individual value, yet they conveniently complement and support each other.

We shall note at the outset that in Weber's work there would appear to be no equivalence to a theory of the economic system that is an account of the *functioning* of a capitalist economy as a whole. For Weber's thesis in *The Protestant Ethic* does not amount to a general theory of the capitalist economic system as such, however insightful it might be as an account of its origins and underlying ethos.[20] And further, Weber might appear to have ruled out the possibility of a general

20 The fact that *The Protestant Ethic* did not attempt to provide a complete and comprehensive theory of capitalism appears to have left numerous issues unresolved in Weber's mind at the time. According to Peter Ghosh Weber's postponement of finding the "final *conceptual* fix" for the spirit of capitalism meant that after 1908 he did not pursue the topic of capitalism per se with the same urgency as before. This issue is taken up and developed at considerable length in the important work of Ghosh, *Max Weber and the Protestant Ethic*. Gosh argues that although in *The Protestant Ethic* Weber was focused on the issue of the origin and nature of capitalism, his treatment of this was incomplete and left unresolved in 1904–5. And though in his later *Economy and Society* he returned to the issue of capitalism and referred to it in the Author's Introduction and elsewhere, his main focus had shifted the broader issues of the rationalization and bureaucratization of bourgeois society generally.

theory of capitalism because his methodological presuppositions mean that his perspective, at least in *The Protestant Ethic*, views capitalism as an "historical individual" and not as a general concept within a typology of economic forms. But the present writer will argue that something along the lines of a general theory of modern capitalism, though not explicitly developed by Weber, is nonetheless in the background of much of his theorizing and in any event can be extracted from his work. Of course Weber clearly did not make it his task to embark on a full-scale treatment of the capitalist system from an economic theory point of view – unlike Marx, for example, who attempts to do just this in his *Capital*.[21] On the other hand, in contrast to Weber, Schumpeter provides a theory of capitalism that in many ways corresponds to and competes with the theoretical achievement of Marx, at least to the degree that it attempts to explain the long run functioning and developmental tendencies of the capitalist system. Accordingly, we shall maintain that the Schumpeterian system is an ideal complement to Weber's account of origins and institutional underpinnings of capitalism.[22]

Looking at the matter from Schumpeter's side, we note that, although he provides a rudimentary sociology of capitalism in conjunction with his economic theories, he did not develop a sociology with the depth and sophistication that one finds in Weber (which is not to say his sociological contributions are insignificant). For Weber not only gave a masterful account of social institutions and their genesis, as well as providing a sophisticated methodology for understanding and interpreting social action,[23] but he also produced detailed accounts of key phenomena like law, religion, administrative structures, political institutions and so on, all of which are extremely valuable as an interpretative framework for understanding the capitalist order, its origins and institutional supports.[24] We shall maintain that here Weber adds value to and complements Schumpeter.

Although Weber never embarked on a full-scale economic theory of capitalism, we shall argue that he largely accepted the economic theory being developed by the

21 It needs to be recognized that the term "capitalism" was not widely used before Weber, who is partly responsible for its present usage as a term referring broadly to the socio-economic system of the modern West as a whole. Marx, as noted previously, did not employ this notion, and his preferred concept "the capitalist mode of production" is not the equivalent of Weber's "capitalism". The latter concept has broader connotations, including being a descriptor of the wider cultural milieu associated with the rise of modern industrial enterprise and bourgeois man.

22 We are in complete accord with Randall Collins when he states that Weber's account of capitalism although "alone in accounting for the emergence of the full range of institutional and motivational conditions for large-scale, world-transforming capitalism. . . . is incomplete. It needs to be supplemented by a theory of the operation of mature capitalism, and of its possible demise." Randall Collins, *Weberian Sociological Theory*, Cambridge University Press, 1986, p. 44.

23 Weber's complete methodological writings are now available in English in a 563-page compendium: *Max Weber: Collected Methodological Writings*, Routledge, 2012.

24 As regards Weber's contribution to the origins of capitalism, we are also in agreement with Randall Collins when he concludes that Weber's last theory, as set out in the *General Economic History*, "is still today the only comprehensive theory of the origins of capitalism." *Weberian Sociological Theory*, Cambridge University Press, 1986, p. 44.

Austrian Marginalist School. It appears he left the field of economic theorizing, in the strict sense, to others in the emerging discipline of economics, so that when he embarked on his editorship of the *Grundriss der Sozialokönomik* (a kind of social science encyclopaedia about which we shall comment below) he engaged both Schumpeter and Wieser to provide the economic theory sections.[25]

The rationale of Weber's editorship of the *Grundriss der Sozialokönomik* and his general approach regarding the relationship of sociology to economics is the subject of a detailed and scholarly account by Richard Swedberg in his book *Max Weber and the Idea of Economic Sociology*. Swedberg is concerned to show that Weber's central task in treating economic phenomena was to set out the basis for a sociology of economic action, and that he deliberately limited himself to those aspects of economics that were relevant to this purpose. He suggests that Weber was concerned, in his own contributions to the *Grundriss*, and as regards the overall structure, to avoid the approach of the previous work to which it was a successor, namely Gustav Schönberg's *Handbuch der Politischen Oekonomie*. Weber "did not want the *Grundriss* to be either dominated by historical economics or by theoretical economics. But the *Grundriss* . . . contains no general work in economic history. He also states that the *Grundriss* will not contain more economic theory than is necessary to understand the social economy."[26]

To an extent, the rationale of the present work is at odds with Swedberg's view, because he is concerned to show that Weber was primarily focused on developing "economic sociology" as a distinct discipline, which only here and there overlaps its concerns with economics proper. In this respect, I agree with Peter Ghosh that Swedberg's attempt to read Weber's remarks on the relation of economics to sociology, especially after around 1918 following a supposed change of perspective from that of "social economics", as founding a unified economic sociology is misleading and is driven by his own project of championing "economic sociology" as a distinct field.[27] I believe that Weber's sociology can be more directly integrated with the findings of economics than Swedberg seems to allow, as we shall see.

As already noted, the question as to whether the Schumpeterian system is fully compatible with Weber's approach is a question that requires investigation, and it will be discussed at length below. There are reasons to believe that Weber would

25 At this point we must take issue with the view of Randall Collins that in inviting Schumpeter to write a history of economic doctrines for the *Grundriss* Weber was not indicating his assent to Schumpeter's point of view but merely offering a mouthpiece for the "opposing camp of economics" to that of the "Historical School" of Schmoller. *Weberian Sociological Theory*, p. 120. As we argue below, Weber embraced aspects of both schools.

26 Richard Swedberg, *Max Weber and the Idea of Economic Sociology*, Princeton University Press, 1998, p. 155. The entire Chapter Six of Swedberg's book provides a most useful account of the rationale of Weber's *Grundriss*, as well as the historical background to its production.

27 See Peter Ghosh, "'Robinson Crusoe', the *Isolated Economic Man*: Marginal Utility Theory and the 'Spirit' of Capitalism", in Peter Ghosh (ed.), *A Historian Reads Max Weber*, Harrassowitz Verlag, 2008, p. 295 n. 113.

not have accepted some aspects of Schumpeter's account of the functioning of capitalism, and indeed there are other discrepancies between their respective perspectives, especially as regards methodology and politics. Nonetheless, it is the present writer's view that, despite possible divergences, there are many points of intersection between the two approaches that warrant bringing their contributions together – hopefully to provide a solid basis for a general theory of modern capitalism.[28] Though Weber's contribution by itself does not provide a fully adequate theory of the functioning of the capitalist system, in combination with Schumpeter's work, most of the key elements for such a theory are to be found.[29]

Recent scholarship on Weber and Schumpeter

It has to be recognized that the study of Weber and also of Schumpeter has undergone a renaissance in recent times. I refer in this respect in relation to Weber, especially to the works of thinkers such as Randall Collins, Lawrence Scaff, Wolfgang Schluchter, Wolfgang Mommsen, Joachim Radkau and Peter Ghosh and in relation to Schumpeter, to Yuichi Shionoya, Esben Sloth Andersen, Thomas McGraw and Richard Swedberg, amongst others.[30] This body of work testifies to the enduring significance of the work of both Weber and Schumpeter. There has been little discussion in the secondary literature, however, of Weber's relation to Schumpeter. There have been a few analyses of Weber's relation to orthodox economic theory and with the Austrian Marginalist School in particular. Several commentators have remarked on the fact that Weber would appear to have accepted the concept of marginal utility, and some have even gone so far as to suggest that Weber basically accepted orthodox economic theory as a given. For example, Talcott Parsons claimed that, "Weber on

28 The following analogy may assist to explain the rationale underlying the present writer's intentions. I refer to the work by Julian Huxley, *Evolution: The Modern Synthesis*, Allen and Unwin, 1944, published in 1942. This book, a minor classic in its own right, sets out to provide a synthesis of the two most significant contributions to evolutionary theory of the day, the first of course being that of Charles Darwin and the second being that of Gregor Mendel. Darwin's theory predated the discoveries of genetics and thus was unable to fully account for phenomena such as variation and mutation, phenomena that became readily explicable with the understandings given by the new discoveries of genetics. Only with the combination of Darwin and Mendel is it now believed there is a complete theory of speciation, and Huxley was concerned to show just how this synthesis was possible. Huxley's work has of course been superseded and in various ways improved by further research. (A more up to date statement of the theory of evolution that incorporates recent research is Ernst Mayr's *The Growth of Biological Thought: Diversity Evolution and Inheritance*, Belknap, 1982.) Of course, I do not intend to suggest the nature of scientific advance is the equivalent in all respects as between the biological sciences and history and economics. The purpose of the analogy is simply to provide an example of how scholarly achievement can be clarified and consolidated by subsequent efforts.

29 As to the task of a "history of modern capitalism", there are many excellent works, such as Jeffrey Frieden's *Global Capitalism: Its Rise and Fall in the Twentieth Century*, Norton, 2006 and now Larry Neal's and Jeffrey Williamson's (eds.), *Cambridge History of Capitalism* (2 vols), CUP, 2014.

30 We shall be referring to these authors in detail below at which point references to their writings of relevance to the present work shall be provided.

the whole accepts the view of the functions of the competitive price system current in 'orthodox' economic theory."[31] On the other hand, others have suggested that Weber does not rely on marginal utility theory as a basis for his economic sociology at all: for example, Richard Swedberg writes, "Weber's sociology is not based on 'marginalist foundations' in any meaningful sense of this expression and Weber makes no analytic use whatsoever of the notion of declining utility in his general sociology."[32] In what follows, we shall take issue with this view.

An assessment of Weber's relation to marginal utility theory must consider his various references to it and, in particular, the discussions in his *Critique of Stammler* of 1907 and the essay "Marginal Utility Theory and 'The Fundamental Law of Psychophysics'" of 1908.[33] In both these writings it is evident that he had more than a passing acquaintance with the concept, and in fact, it would appear he accepted the basic idea of the framework. In the *Critique of Stammler*, for example, he argues that the principle of marginal utility has at least two functions. In the first place, it provides actors with a principle upon which they can regulate their action. As such, it forms what Weber calls an "ideal rule" or "norm" that an individual can adopt if they intend to act in accordance with the idea of purposive (rational) action.[34] But more than this, Weber thinks marginal utility theory can be of considerable value for theoretical investigation. In this case Weber says the notion can be used to establish how an isolated individual would behave if they followed "the principle of marginal utility". According to Weber, this is what economic theory does generally. Economic theory posits how individuals will act if they follow the principle of marginal utility to its logical end point, and it can then analyze what outcomes will result.

In discussing these issues, Weber refers, at one time or another, to a number of figures belonging to the Austrian Marginalist School, beginning with Carl Menger and including Eugene Böhm-Bawerk, Friedich Wieser and Ludvig Mises. These connections have not gone unnoticed by previous commentators. For example, Simon Clark in *Marx, Marginalism and Modern Sociology* refers at some length to the relationship of Weber to marginalism, and discusses this in a general way.[35] Other commentators who have discussed the relation of Weber to the Austrian School include Robert Holton in several of his writings.[36] But few commentators have addressed themselves specifically and in detail to the issue of the relation of Weber to either economic theory or more specifically to marginalism and the Austrian School.[37]

31 Talcott Parsons, Introduction to *Max Weber, the Theory of Social and Economic Action*, The Free Press, 1947, p. 39.
32 Swedberg, *Max Weber and the Idea of Economic Sociology*, p. 28.
33 On the nature of Weber's relation to marginal utility theory, see now the excellent discussion of Ghosh, *A Historian Reads Max Weber*, pp. 269–97.
34 Max Weber, *Critique of Stammler*, The Free Press, 1977, p. 106.
35 See his discussion in Simon Clarke, *Marx, Marginalism and Modern Capitalism: from Adam Smith to Max Weber*, Macmillan, 1991, pp. 192–229.
36 See his *Economy and Society*: Routledge 1992.
37 At this point it is worth mentioning several other commentators who have addressed Weber's writings on the sociology of economic action, some of whom we shall discuss below. From a neo-Marxist point

However, the matter has now been addressed at some length by Steven Parsons in his *Money, Time and Rationality in Max Weber*. Parsons' work is specifically concerned with the relation of Weber to the Austrian Marginalist School and the implications of this for Weber's interpretation of economic action. He argues that Weber specifically adopted the approach of the Austrian School as against that of Walras and the so-called Lausanne School. This was because he recognized, with Menger and his colleagues, the importance of the factors of time and "uncertainty" in the course of economic exchange. The former approach entails the view that market-determined prices will not necessarily give rise to equilibrium outcomes, whereas Walras had assumed that perfect knowledge and instantaneous price adjustments will generally lead the economy towards equilibrium. This is a view similar to that argued previously by Robert Holton and Bryan Turner.

> Walras had likened the market to a process of "tâtonnement" [*groping*], that is to the role of an auctioneer in clearing the supply of commodities offered in an auction. In this model equilibrium prices could be reached between utility-maximizing buyers and sellers following rational choice strategies based on perfect knowledge, such that the market reached an equilibrium end-state. For Walras there was no fundamental interest in the time dimension in market adjustments. For the Austrians, on the other hand, perfect knowledge is impossible in principle. Economic relations are characterized by uncertainty and risk-taking, with action often producing unintended consequences. From this viewpoint, the market-place is conceptualised as a dynamic process of search for equilibrium over time, rather than an entity tending to a series of equilibrium end-states."[38]

We shall argue in what follows that Weber's precise position on these questions cannot be ascertained with any confidence because he did not directly address the

---

of view, there are critical essays by Bryn Jones, "Economic Action and Rational Organization in the Sociology of Weber", in B. Hindess (ed.), *Sociological Theories of the Economy*, Macmillan, 1977 and Michael Bittman, "A Bourgeois Marx? Max Weber's Theory of Capitalist Society: Reflections on Utility, Rationality and Class Formation", *Thesis Eleven*, 15, (1986), pp. 81–91. From a conservative perspective, mention should be made of Friedrich Hayek and, in particular, his writings criticizing socialism and socialist movements, such as his *Individualism and Economic Order*, University of Chicago, 1996. The most general analysis of Weber's economic sociology, however, is the book by Swedberg, *Max Weber and the Idea of Economic Sociology*. Swedberg refers to the fact that Weber recommended to his students in the course he gave on economic theory that they should consult the works of Marshall, Walras and Jevons, a fact that invites further consideration. Of course, there are many commentaries on Weber's general approach to capitalism, both to his historical account in *The Protestant Ethic and the Spirit of Capitalism* as well as to his other contributions on the subject. The most significant are those of Anthony Giddens in his *Capitalism and Modern Social Theory*, Cambridge University Press, 1975; Karl Löwith, *Max Weber and Karl Marx*, Allen & Unwin, 1982; and Gianfranco Poggi, *Calvinism and the Spirit of Capitalism*, University of Massachusetts, 1984.

38 Robert Holton and Bryan S. Turner, *Max Weber on Economy and Society*, Routledge, 1989, p. 36 (italics added).

issues concerned. And as we shall argue below, Schumpeter takes a more complex position than that described by Holton and Turner, as he combines aspects of both the Austrian *and* the Lausanne Schools.

As Parsons is also interested in Weber's analysis and critique of socialism, much of his book is concerned with the way in which he developed an implicit critique of central planning, especially in the chapter of *Economy and Society* entitled "Sociological Categories of Economic Action". Parsons is at pains to point out how Weber advanced ideas that were already partly developed in the Austrian School's approach, particularly the ideas of Menger in regard to the superiority of a liberal capitalist economy. Parsons thus goes on to explore the way in which the Austrian School developed the critique of socialism, in part through the work of Böhm-Bawerk and then later in that of Mises and Hayek. He argues that Mises' approach in many ways can be seen to have developed ideas that were already to be found in Weber's work. But oddly, given the European intellectual milieu in which he worked, Mises did not appear to acknowledge the significance of Weber's contribution, and curiously, he thought Weber lacked crucial understandings of relevance to the key issues. Parsons wants to set the record straight on this by showing that the seminal ideas of Mises about socialism are actually very close, if not identical, to those of Weber.[39]

But surprisingly, at no point in his book does Parsons discuss or even mention Schumpeter. There is a possible connection with Schumpeter, however, in Parsons's book that comes via references to the work of Walras, who of course as we shall see was highly regarded by Schumpeter. Parsons insists there is a fundamental difference between the approach of the Austrian School as against those of Walras and the school of thought developed in England by Jevons. He argues that Weber effectively adopted a position identical to that of the Austrian School and implicitly rejected the approaches of the Walrasian and Jevonian Schools. This, in our view, is a highly questionable conclusion, however, because the difference between the approach of Walras vis-à-vis that of Menger is not one that Weber ever addressed; so one cannot presume that Weber would necessarily have rejected Walras.[40] We submit that it is unwarranted to draw any hard conclusions as to what Weber's view would have been as to the notion of equilibrium as developed by Walras and subsequently by orthodox economic theory. Nonetheless, we see no intrinsic reason why the Schumpeterian approach to equilibrium would be at odds with Weber's methodological presuppositions.

39 Mises, who was a friend of Weber, developed his ideas on socialism especially in his work *Socialism: An Economic and Sociological Analysis*, originally published in 1922, the second edition of which was published in 1932. An enlarged edition was published in English in 1951. Many of the problems he raises are touched on in Schumpeter's historical account of these issues in his *History of Economic Analysis* to which we shall refer below.

40 Weber's engagement with these writers would appear to be limited to his treatment of them in courses he gave on political economy in his early career, but there is little or no actual commentary.

The relationship of Weber to Schumpeter

As noted above, hitherto there have been few, if any, attempts to compare and contrast the work of Weber and Schumpeter; nor has there been any serious attempt to integrate their respective contributions or provide a synthesis.[41] However, there are some obvious points of contact and common concerns between Weber and Schumpeter that invite comment at the outset. First, they knew each other and collaborated on some projects in the time of Schumpeter's early career when Weber was reaching the height of his. For example, Weber commissioned Schumpeter to write the section on the "History of Economics" in the *Grundriss der Sozialokönomik* of which he was the editor.[42] Second, both were focused in their work on the phenomenon of modern capitalism, though in different and unique ways. Third, both were pioneers and leaders in their respective fields and were steeped in, and indeed masters of, the relevant scientific literature. Fourth, their approaches overlapped in important ways: Weber, though not an expert economic theorist, was deeply interested in economics; and on the other hand, Schumpeter though primarily an economist made considerable contributions to sociology in general and to "social economics" in particular. Fifth, both Weber and Schumpeter were extremely creative thinkers, and each may even be credited with being founding fathers of new disciplines – "econometrics" in the case of Schumpeter and "sociology" in Weber's case. Finally, both, in a certain sense, recognized the significance of the other, though this must be qualified by the fact that Schumpeter's major contributions were made years after Weber's death in 1920, so the latter could not have known just how significant Schumpeter was to become for economic thought. Schumpeter, on the other hand, after Weber's passing, spoke highly of him on several occasions and readily acknowledged his greatness;[43] yet it has to be acknowledged that Schumpeter did not take a great deal from Weber directly and was quite critical of him in certain respects, as we shall see.

In the remainder of this Introduction, I shall first explore the nature of the interconnections between Weber and Schumpeter, both theoretically as well as, to a degree, biographically. I shall give a brief account of the respective contributions

41 There are four notable exceptions I am aware of: "Weber and Schumpeter" in Randall Collins, *Weberian Sociological Theory*, Cambridge University Press, 1986; Jürgen Osterhammel, "Varieties of Social Economics: Joseph Schumpeter and Max Weber", in Wolfgang J. Mommsen and Jürgen Osterhammel (eds.), *Max Weber and His Contemporaries*, Allen & Unwin, 1987, pp. 106–20; Yuichi Shionoya, *Schumpeter and the Idea of Social Science: A Metatheoretical Study*, Cambridge University Press, 1997, especially Chapter 8; and Swedberg, *Max Weber and the Idea of Economic Sociology*, especially Chapter 6.

42 On the background to these events, see Swedberg *Max Weber and the Idea of Economic Sociology*, Chapter 6. According to Peter Ghosh, Weber regarded Schumpeter's contribution to the *Grundriss* as "excellent" ("'Robinson Crusoe', the *Isolated Economic Man*: Marginal Utility Theory and the 'Spirit' of Capitalism", p. 277).

43 See Schumpeter's obituary essay, "Max Weber's Work", in Richard Swedberg (ed.), *Joseph Schumpeter: The Economics and Sociology of Capitalism*, Princeton, 1991, pp. 220–29, which is, however, the only work in which Schumpeter does not offer criticisms of Weber.

of Weber and Schumpeter with regard to the theory of capitalism that is central to both. My major task is to show how an integration of the theories of the two thinkers is possible with a view to developing a better overall theory of capitalism than has hitherto been available. I do not attempt to systematically examine the empirical truth of what the two thinkers have claimed in their respective works, a task that would be beyond the scope of a single work in any event, though I hasten to add I am not indifferent to issues of empirical truth. I adopt this approach in part because the task of empirically testing the theories of Weber and Schumpeter is so vast and probably an unending one, and it is something that has engaged a veritable army of scholars over the years and continues to do so. But I am also not pursuing a detailed empirical investigation because I am of the view that the strength of the contributions of Weber and Schumpeter lies in their conceptual cogency. That is, both thinkers utilize the methods that have been classically elaborated by Weber under the rubric of the "ideal type", and this means that they have sought, in the first place, to produce conceptions of phenomena that are abstracted from reality and are "utopias", in the sense that the aspects of the world they seek to describe and analyze do not exist in a pure form in concrete actuality. Both are concerned to build models of complex social and economic structures that they well know do not correspond exactly with the world as it is. The purpose of research for them is not to directly copy the real world or even to be an approximation of it, for this is strictly not possible. Rather, the purpose of concept formation, theory construction and model building is heuristic and perspectivist, and ideally, provides a set of tools that the individual interested in knowing the world can employ for interpretation and causal explanation. Nonetheless, I do not wish to underestimate the extent to which both Weber and Schumpeter were concerned with the empirical validity of their theories. Indeed they each regarded empiricism as a foundation of modern science (*Wissenschaft*) and made considerable efforts to provide empirical evidence in support of their theories.

It has long been recognized that both Weber and Schumpeter, though Europeans and steeped in German social thought of the early twentieth century, became well known and even celebrated in the English-speaking world for their contributions on capitalism. Weber is of course best known for his work *The Protestant Ethic and the Spirit of Capitalism*, which was first translated into English by Talcott Parsons in 1930 from when it became a classic and one of the most influential works in all sociology. Schumpeter is best known for his book *Capitalism, Socialism and Democracy*, which was published in 1942, but he also had a considerable direct influence in America by virtue of his many writings published in English while he held a position as a professor at Harvard University. Clearly, both of the works just mentioned linked their respective authors very directly to the issue of capitalism, and we shall accordingly need to comment on these texts at length. But these works represent only a very small portion of the contributions the two writers made to the issue of capitalism. And, importantly from our point of view here, the significance of numerous other works of the two thinkers has hitherto not been widely recognized. Therefore, much of what I attempt in the present work is an effort to show that various other works of both

Weber and Schumpeter need to be considered to fully appreciate their respective accounts of capitalism.

To understand the relation of Weber to Schumpeter, one must begin by recognizing that, although in age they were not exact peers, their careers took off around the same time, that is, in the first decade of the twentieth century, and both became deeply immersed in the cultural and scientific milieu of the time. This meant that, inevitably, they were engaged with similar issues and moved in the same intellectual circles. After graduating at the University of Vienna in 1906, Schumpeter produced and published his first main work in 1908, *Das Wesen und der Hauptinhalt der theoretischen Nationalökonomie* (*The Nature and Essence of Economic Theory)*. By contrast, by this time Weber had already published several works in history and methodology. His main early works are: *Zur Geschichte Der Handelsgesellschaften Im Mittelalter: Nach SüdEuropäischen Quellen* (*The History of Commercial Partnerships in the Middle Ages*) of 1989, *Die Römische Agrargeschichte in Ihrer Bedeutung für das Staats- und Privatrecht* (*Roman Agrarian History: The Political Economy of Ancient Rome*) of 1891, several important essays in methodology in 1904, 1905 and 1907, and the two essays of 1904–5 that were to become the book later published as *The Protestant Ethic and the Spirit of Capitalism*. But after 1909, the two men began an association, owing to the appointment of Weber by the publisher Paul Siebeck, to edit and partly write a new handbook of the socio-economic sciences, which became known as the *Outline of Social Economics (Grundriss der Socialökonomik)*. By 1911, Schumpeter had begun to make his name with the publication of *Theorie der wirtschafttlichen Entwicklung* (*The Theory of Economic Development)*, and I assume that Weber was sufficiently impressed by his colleague's work to offer him the opportunity to contribute to the prestigious compendium he had been commissioned to edit. The work that Weber contributed to the *Grundriss der Socialökonomik* became his magnum opus and is known now as *Economy and Society: An Outline of Interpretive Sociology*; whereas Schumpeter's contribution to the *Grundriss* was a work of lesser scope entitled *Epochen der Dogmen- und Methodengeschichte* published in 1912 (now translated into English as *Economic Doctrine and Method: An Historical Sketch*).[44]

Richard Swedberg has given a detailed account of Schumpeter's relationship with Weber and the *Grundriss* in his *Max Weber and the Idea of Economic Sociology*, and he suggests that Schumpeter's approach to social economics, as developed in *Economic Doctrine and Method: An Historical Sketch*, was directly influenced by Weber. He tells us, ". . . Schumpeter more or less agreed with Weber's position on the *Methodenstreit* – that the historical-empirical approach of Schmoller was as necessary as the theoretical-analytical approach of Menger . . ."[45] He further says that Schumpeter continued to engage with the project of social economics

44 A detailed account of Schumpeter's career at this stage is contained in Richard Swedberg, *Schumpeter: A Biography*, Princeton University Press, 1991, pp. 31–45.

45 Swedberg, *Max Weber and the Idea of Economic Sociology*, p. 162.

throughout his career, and this culminated in his *History of Economic Analysis* written in the 1940s.

It is worth noting how in his *Economic Doctrine and Method* Schumpeter clearly regarded marginal utility theory as a seminal achievement of economics, and these are claims that Weber would have known and, we must surmise, largely accepted. Towards the end of an historical survey of economic theory, Schumpeter provided a detailed discussion of the emergence of marginal utility theory and its relation to the classical theory that preceded it. He refers to the contributions of Menger, Jevons, Wieser and Walras, and the thrust of the discussion is that these theorists greatly improved the coherence of economic theory as a whole and, amongst other implications, rendered Marx's economic theory and his labour theory of value obsolete.[46]

The fact that Weber saw fit to offer the writing of a significant section of the *Grundriss* to Schumpeter gives rise to at least two suppositions. First, we can say that Weber evidently acknowledged Schumpeter's competence as an economist by such an appointment; he would hardly have entrusted such a task to a scholar other than one of the first rank. It needs to be realized that just prior to this (in 1911) Schumpeter had published a major book, namely, *The Theory of Economic Development*, a work that probably made his name in academic circles, and which we must assume also impressed Weber.[47] And second, it is probable that Weber had, by this stage in his career, determined that he himself would not, in the future, be predominantly concerned with economic theory per se and that he would not contribute directly to "economics". I say this mindful of the fact that, though Weber evidently turned away from academic economics, he always considered himself a kind of economic specialist nonetheless, a point to which I shall return shortly.

In this connection it is necessary to observe Weber's position in the so-called *Methodenstreit* (or "methodology controversy") of the day and his relation to key figures such as Schmoller, Menger, Wieser and Böhm-Bawerk. First, we should not assume that Weber's apparent allegiance to the German Historical School and his admiration for Schmoller meant that he rejected the value of the contributions of the so-called Austrian School in economics or had reservations about their novel "theoretical approach". To the contrary, Weber was deeply impressed by the work of these thinkers in the field of pure economics, and what is more, evidently accepted the theory of marginal utility as axiomatic for an understanding of the price mechanism in a market economy. Thus, in his essay of 1908 dealing directly with marginal utility, entitled "Marginal Utility Theory and 'The Fundamental Law of Psychophysics'", Weber speaks very favourably of Menger and Böhm-Bawerk, both of whom regarded the theory of marginal utility as a given. Furthermore, it is significant that Weber also included in his *Grundriss* a contribution

46 Joseph Schumpeter, *Economic Doctrine and Method: An Historical Sketch*, Allen & Unwin, 1954, pp. 181–200.

47 We know that Weber's copy of the book is marked with his notes and shows that he knew it well and took it very seriously.

by Wieser entitled *Sozial Ökonomiks Wirtschaft (Theorie des Gesellschaftlichen)* ("The Theory of the Social Economy"). Wieser, who was arguably Menger's most significant pupil, made his name exploring the implications of marginal utility theory, which included developing the important notion of "opportunity cost".[48]

Weber as an economist

The question as to whether Weber was in some sense an "economist" has been obscured owing to the lopsided reception of his writings by the academy in the English-speaking world.[49] He came to be celebrated primarily as a founder of the discipline of sociology, though *The Protestant Ethic* led him to also have a lesser reputation as an economic historian. The work of Scaff has now shown that, in his early career, Weber had thought of himself as a political economist. Scaff quotes a remark made by Weber to Baumgarten around 1891 that he had "become approximately one-third political economist."[50] And a perusal of Weber's earlier writings, and the fact that he began his career as a professor of economics, suggests that he had more than a casual acquaintance with economic issues in the strict sense and that he even considered himself, at this stage at least, to actually be an "economist".[51] Furthermore, there are two early texts of Weber that make his involvement with the emerging science of economics abundantly clear.[52] One is the essay referred to above entitled "Marginal Utility Theory and 'The Fundamental Law of Psychophysics'". The other is a set of essays Weber wrote on the stock exchange and the stock market. I shall first briefly consider Weber's essay on marginal utility theory.

The 1908 essay "Marginal Utility Theory and 'The Fundamental Law of Psychophysics'" is largely concerned with the relationship between marginal utility theory – which Weber takes as a given, a fundamental notion underlying modern economic theory – and what was known at the time as the so-called Weber–Fechner

48 On the history of the Austrian School, with detailed analyses of Menger, Weiser and Böhm-Bawerk, see the excellent survey by Anthony Endres, *Neoclassical Microeconomic Theory: The Founding Austrian Version*, Routledge, 1997.

49 A typical statement that Weber was a sociologist and not an economist is that of Thomas McGraw, *Prophet of Innovation: Joseph Schumpeter and Creative Destruction*, Harvard University Press, 2007, p. 44.

50 Quoted in Lawrence Scaff, "From Political Economy to Political Sociology: Max Weber's Early Writings", in Ronald Glassman and Vatro Murvar (eds.), *Max Weber's Political Sociology: A Pessimistic Vision of a Rationalized World*, Greenwood, 1984, p. 87.

51 The story of Weber's early involvement with economics and the biographical background to his turn to "political economy" is related in detail in Scaff, *Fleeing the Iron Cage*, pp. 25–33 and in his essay "Weber before Weberian Sociology", in Keith Tribe (ed.), *Reading Weber*, Routledge, 1989, pp. 15–41. We should note at this point that Weber's initial tertiary education was in law and he also gave lectures on law in his first academic forays, though he never practised as a lawyer. Of course, this background remained with him, and legal issues continued to exercise his interest throughout.

52 The general background to Weber's relation to Austrian economics is well discussed in Holton and Turner, *Max Weber on Economy and Society*, Chapter 2.

law (the name "Weber" in this term has nothing to do with the person of Max Weber). For the time being, we need not concern ourselves with the argument that Weber was embroiled in here, suffice to say that he clearly takes for granted the validity of marginal utility theory and is largely concerned to attack the notion that the value theory of the so-called Austrian School (i.e., marginal utility theory) is psychologically based and that this aspect is adequately explained by the so-called Weber–Fechner law. Some idea of Weber's self-understanding in this essay can be gained from various statements he makes towards the end. At one point he refers to himself in as many words as an economist when he writes: "At every step and on countless particular points of interest to our discipline, we economists are and must be involved in fruitful interchange of findings and viewpoints with workers in other fields. This is something to be taken for granted as common to all economists."[53] A little later in the essay, Weber writes,

> But further, and above all, precisely as regards the point which is decisive for the peculiar quality of the questions proper to our discipline: In economic theory ("value theory") we stand entirely on our own feet. The everyday experience from which our theory takes its departure . . . is of course the common point of departure of *all* particular empirical disciplines. Each of them aspires beyond everyday experience and must so aspire, for thereon rests its right to existence as "a science". But each of them in its aspiration "goes beyond" or "sublimates" everyday experience in a different way and in a different direction. Marginal utility theory and economic "theory" generally do this not, say, in the manner with which the orientation of psychology but rather pretty much in opposite ways.[54]

Continuing the argument, which is particularly interesting for the way it links marginal utility to accounting, he says,

> Marginal utility theory, in order to obtain specific objects of knowledge, treats human action as if it ran its course from beginning to end under the control of *commercial calculation* – a calculation set up on the basis of *all* conditions that need to be considered. It treats individual "needs" and the goods available (all to be produced or exchanged) for their satisfaction as mathematically calculable in "sums" and "amounts" in a continuous process of bookkeeping. It treats man as an agent who constantly carries on "economic enterprise" and it treats his life as the object of his "enterprise" controlled according to calculation. The outlook involved in commercial bookkeeping is, if anything, the starting point of the construction of marginal utility theory.[55]

53 Max Weber, "Marginal Utility Theory and the So-Called Fundamental Law of Psychophysics", *Social Science Quarterly*, 56.1, (1975), p. 31.

54 Ibid.

55 Ibid., pp. 31–2.

Weber's main point in this discussion is that marginal utility theory does not depend on the positing of psychic forces or drives of the kind that have been advanced by various psychological theories. Rather, it accounts for the functioning of economic life on the basis of an understanding of the manner in which individuals operate, more or less rationally, in accordance with their economic interests. As he puts it further on in the essay,

> The theoretical "values" with which marginal utility theory works should in principle make understandable to us the circumstances of economic life, in a manner like that in which commercial book values render information to the businessman about the state of his enterprise and the conditions for its continued profitability. And the general theorems which economic theory sets up are simply constructions that state what consequences the action of the individual man in its intertwining with the action of others would *have to* produce, *on the assumption that* everyone were to shape his conduct toward his environment exclusively according to the principles of commercial bookkeeping – and, in *this* sense, "rationally".[56]

These remarks are of course not merely of interest in regard to Weber's self-understanding as an economist. They also indicate how far he accepted the Austrian School's approach generally and the theory of marginal utility in particular. Elsewhere Weber was especially praising of several of the individual figures of the Austrian School. For example, in 1903 he wrote a recommendation supporting the nomination of Böhm-Bawerk for an honorary doctorate at the University of Heidelberg, describing him in these terms: "Equally outstanding in logical stringency, stylistic refinement and in the elegant objectivity of his polemics, he is undoubtedly the most important representative of the abstract and deductive work done by the school of Austrian political economists."[57] But Weber reserved his highest praise for Carl Menger. According to Manfred Schön, it was Menger and not Rickert whom Weber credited with discovering the fundamental methodological distinction between law-based sciences (*Gesetzeswissenschaften*) and the sciences of concrete reality (*Wirklichkeitswissenschaften*).[58] And in a letter to Brentano, Weber wrote of Menger that he "expresses what he wants to say, to be sure in an awkward manner, but unpretentiously, simply and clearly . . . he has *very* substantial merits and was *right* on important points of the matter at *issue*, even in the dispute with Schmoller."[59]

56 Ibid., p. 32.

57 Quoted in Manfred Schön, "Gustav Schmoller and Max Weber", in Wolfgang Mommsen and Jürgen Osterhammel (eds.), *Max Weber and His Contemporaries*, Allen & Unwin, 1987, p. 60.

58 Ibid.

59 Ibid., p. 62. But in his methodological essays, Weber credits Rickert with having made important advances in this domain.

Further illustration of Weber's engagement with economics in more than a passing fashion can be gleaned from other early works, in particular the two essays he wrote in 1894 and 1896 on the stock exchange and a brief sketch of a lecture outline of 1898 that has the title "Outline of General 'Theoretical' Economics". In the works on the stock exchange, Weber provided a very detailed account of the operation of share markets and, in particular, of what is termed "futures trading". Interestingly, he was concerned not merely to produce a theoretical account of these phenomena but sought to influence policy developments in this area at the time.[60] Further, in these essays Weber not only gives an account of the way stock markets function, but he comments at some length on how markets in general operate, and much of this analysis constitutes what can only be described as "economic theory". We shall consider Weber's contributions in these areas in detail later in this work, but for the present we note that Weber was more than familiar with the economic theory relevant to these institutions and made a significant contribution to the interpretation and understanding of their operation.

The second work referred to, "The Outline of General 'Theoretical' Economics", consists of a twenty-page description of a course in economics that Weber taught at the University of Freiburg in the 1890s. According to Richard Swedberg, the work included some thirty pages of notes in which many references are made to the economic theorists of the day. Swedberg says that Part One of Weber's course dealt with fundamental concepts in economics, Part Two dealt with the relationship of the economy to nature, Part Three concerned historical developments, Part Four was devoted to the history of economic thought, Part Five dealt with the analysis of the modern market economy and Part Six concerned social and economic aspects.[61]

A fuller account of Weber's early career and his involvement with economics is contained in the essay by Steven Lestition that is the introduction to the publication of Weber's essays on the stock and commodity exchanges. Lestition points out that Weber began his career after his university studies as a lawyer in Berlin but in 1892, whilst staying in Berlin, he took an opportunity to take up a lecturing position at the University of Berlin in commercial law. Then in 1894, he was appointed to a tenured professorship in macroeconomics (*Nationalökonomie*) and finance at the University of Freiburg. During his two years at Freiberg, Weber taught courses in "general and theoretical macroeconomics", "macroeconomic policy", "money, banking and stock exchange transactions", "the history of macroeconomic analysis", and "stock and commodity exchanges and their law".[62] From all this, it is

60 Weber's explanation and partial justification of the function of the stock exchange and share trading is similar to that provided recently by Robert Shiller in his *Finance and the Good Society*, Princeton University Press, 2012. See especially Chapter 6, pp. 57–63.

61 Richard Swedberg, "Afterword: The Role of the Market in Max Weber's Work", *Theory and Society*, 29, (2000), p. 375.

62 Steven Listition, "Historical Preface to Max Weber', 'Stock and Commodity Exchanges'", *Theory and Society*, 29, (2000), p. 294. Peter Ghosh has also provided a detailed account of Weber's early career as part of his large-scale intellectual biography: *Max Weber and the Protestant Ethic*, pp. 31–57.

obvious that Weber was thoroughly familiar with the field of general theoretical economics, if not something of an expert.

Further illustration of Weber's involvement in economics at this early stage is his engagement in a project between 1894 and 1896 in which he was commissioned to review of a report of the "Exchange Enquiry Commission". Weber produced a 330-page analysis as well as essays on the stock exchange, and he also made recommendations on exchange laws. These early concerns with stock markets are particularly interesting from our point of view, because of the connection of such matters with the understanding of economic crises and economic volatility. It is noteworthy that Weber's analysis provided a kind of justification for the functioning of the stock market and futures trading in a capitalist economy, even though he recognized that the phenomenon of "speculation" is in some ways integral to the activities of traders. Weber sought to dispel the popular misconception that stockbrokers and exchange traders carry out no useful economic function. He argued that their activities, based as they are on the market value of stocks and estimations about future business performance, are necessary for the rational operation of the market system. Of course, all this relates quite directly to the work of Schumpeter, who is preoccupied with the phenomena of market fluctuations and economic crises.

But despite these early involvements with economics, Weber gradually gave up theoretical economics, though economic concerns remained a key focus in his early historical and sociological studies. After 1902, Weber shifted his interest somewhat from economics proper when he began to explore methodological/epistemological issues (the essay "Roscher and Knies: The Logical Problems of Historical Economics") and then followed the *Protestant Ethic* essays in 1904–5. But economics always remains in the background, and there is no doubt that Weber kept abreast with key developments in the field.

Affinities between Weber and Schumpeter

There are notable affinities between Weber and Schumpeter that deserve attention at the outset. As already noted, Weber and Schumpeter emerged from the same intellectual milieu and, despite important differences of perspective to which we shall return, there is an underlying compatibility between key ideas. This point has been made by Randall Collins in an essay on Weber and Schumpeter.[63] Even so, Collins says that, despite the fact that Weber and Schumpeter knew each other and were familiar with each other's work, there was little direct mutual influence. Weber does not, for example, cite Schumpeter in any of his published works, though he had invited Schumpeter to make the important contribution to the *Grundriss*, as noted above. Equally Schumpeter, though an admirer of Weber and a supporter of him in some of the academic debates of the day, does not appear to draw much directly from Weber. As we have said above, Schumpeter's interests

63 Collins, *Weberian Sociological Theory*, p. 119.

were first and foremost in economic theory, whereas Weber's were broader and in other directions.

In a sense, Weber and Schumpeter started on either sides of a rift that ran through German academic thinking in the late nineteenth century, but both eventually transcended the divide. This was the debate between the Historical School, under the leadership of Gustav Schmoller, and the Marginalist School in Austria, led by Carl Menger.[64] Schmoller had launched the so-called "Methodenstreit" by attacking the Austrian School as being too theoretical and unhistorical. Weber was greatly influenced by the Historical School but, at the same time, was not at all opposed to theory per se. Indeed, as we have seen, Weber was highly receptive to the contributions of economics in general and the marginalists in particular. In his methodological writings, he was eager to overcome this apparent division within economic-historical thought, and he went out of his way to find accommodations with the new ways of thinking in economics. And it needs to be recognized that Weber developed a form of sociology that has an elaborate theoretical architecture. Of course, Schumpeter was primarily concerned with theory from the very start and increasingly championed the purest form of theoretical economics imaginable, namely, that advanced by Walras. But Schumpeter tended to agree with Weber on the Methodenstreit issues and held that a division between history and theory was nonsense. In any event, he wrote numerous works of a sociological and historical character. His great work *Business Cycles* has very large sections of historical analysis that he considered essential to illustrate his theoretical claims.

According to Holton and Turner, Weber shared the Austrians' rejection of organicist conceptions of institutional development and analysis in terms of aggregates. Furthermore, he adopted methodological individualism as his starting point, a notion that was, according to Machlup, first coined by Schumpeter.[65] But Weber's emphasis on the role of purposive rational action and his recognition that institutions may come into being as the unintended result of individual actions owed a good deal to the work of Menger. Weber's conception of the "ideal type" was also influenced by Menger, for whom "theoretical investigation arrives at qualitative typical appearances that cannot be tested against full empirical reality (because . . . e.g., . . . an individual who pursues only economic ends . . . exist[s] only in our idea) . . ."[66]

As regards their value commitments, as we shall see, both Weber and Schumpeter shared a predilection to support the capitalist economic system of their day and both were at times highly critical of socialist movements and

64 On Schmoller and the so-called "Methodenstreit", see the essay by Schön, "Gustav Schmoller and Max Weber", pp. 59–70.

65 Holton and Turner, *Max Weber on Economy and Society*, p. 39. See Schumpeter's analysis of this notion in *The Nature and Essence of Economic Theory*, Transaction, 2010, especially Part 1, Chapter 6, "The Methodological Individualism", pp. 57–63.

66 Quoted in Schön, "Gustav Schmoller and Max Weber", p. 61.

Marxist theory. Despite their criticisms, however, both were extremely fair-minded in their assessments of socialist thought and took seriously the contributions of Marxists to political and social debate. We shall consider their respective views about socialism at length below.

Randall Collins argues that there are close affinities between Weber and Schumpeter on the general issue of monopolization. Schumpeter, on the one hand, argued that there are distinct tendencies within the capitalist system towards monopoly, and further, the concept of "monopolistic competition" is central to his economic theory. There are aspects of monopoly in the structure of markets and in the manner in which entrepreneurial innovations take place. Schumpeter talks at length about the monopolies that emerge and dissolve regularly within the economy. Monopolies contribute significantly to the general process of the capitalist organism. He argues that entrepreneurs make new combinations of the factors of production that lead to the appearance of new goods that did not exist previously. These new products are not always a response to existing demand but frequently create new demand. By this mechanism, successful entrepreneurs effectively make and appropriate market opportunities, and this gives them a kind of monopolistic power.[67]

Likewise, Weber sees various monopolizing tendencies as being common to the capitalist system, though monopolies do not always emerge from the circumstances of market competition in the strict sense. Collins quotes the following passage from *Economy in Society*:

> When the number of competitors increases in relation to the profit span the participants become interested in curbing competition. Usually one group of competitors take some externally identifiable characteristic of another group of (actual or potential) competitors – race, language, religion, local or social origin, descent, residence, etc. – as a pretext for attempting their exclusion. It does not matter which characteristic is chosen in an individual case: whatever suggests itself mostly is seized upon. . . . In spite of their continued competition against one another, the jointly acting competitors now form an "interest group" towards outsiders; there is a growing tendency to set up some kind of association with rational regulations; if the monopolistic interest persists, the time comes when the competitors, or another group whom they can influence (for example, a political community), establish a legal order that limits competition through formal monopolies; from then on, certain persons are available as "organs" to protect the monopolistic practices, if need be, with force.[68]

These monopolizations may include the establishment of licensed professions or organizations of the labour based on educational credentials. In all these cases,

67 Collins, *Weberian Sociological Theory*, pp. 127–8.
68 Ibid.

there are struggles between status groups and classes and, given the realities of the modern world, conflict is endless. In the purely economic sphere, Weber argues that modern capitalism develops from a series of monopolizations. First there is the monopolization of money capital by entrepreneurs, who make advances to labour, and then market information and sales opportunities are monopolized. Subsequently, the material means of production are monopolized by the expropriation of the workers from the means of production. And finally, there is the expropriation of the manager and even the owner, who become mere trustees of the suppliers of bank credit.

Both Schumpeter and Weber have much to say about the capitalist entrepreneur. Schumpeter does not discuss the kind of organization the entrepreneur builds in a social-psychological fashion akin to Weber, but what he says is largely consistent with Weber. As Collins puts it,

> [Schumpeter's] entrepreneur bears a strong resemblance to Weber's puritan businessman driven by the protestant ethic. Schumpeter describes the entrepreneur as being "irrational" in the sense that his motive is not hedonistic enjoyment of life but the opposite – his sheer interest in overcoming obstacles. At the same time the entrepreneur can be described as "the most rational and most egotistical of all" because of the high level of conscious rationality involved in carrying out new plans, as opposed to the routine of running an established business. Schumpeter comments that the entrepreneur breaks up traditions – economic, moral, cultural and social. "It is no mere coincidence that the period of the rise of the entrepreneur type also gave birth to Utilitarianism." This sounds like the same personality type that Weber attributed to the Calvinistic reformation. Schumpeter casts it in another light, however. Its theme is not religion but politics.[69]

Schumpeter does not investigate the bureaucratic structure of the enterprise, nor the underlying psychological motivations and their religious origins in detail, as does Weber, but the above considerations indicate that his thinking is not that far from Weber's.

The synthetic combination of Weber with Schumpeter

There are numerous reasons why integration of the work of Weber with that of Schumpeter is potentially a fruitful exercise. It is clear that Weber's work is largely oriented to explain the origins and the sociological underpinnings of the capitalist economic system. Equally, it is clear that he does not attempt to provide an account of the *functioning* of the modern economic system once established, say in the manner of orthodox economic theory. Schumpeter, however, is primarily focused on precisely this second task, of accounting for what he often refers to as the "mechanism" of the economic engine. How does the economic system,

69 Ibid., p. 134.

considered as a whole, really actually function? What are its primary dynamics and tendencies, and what is its underlying logic of development? Clearly there is an obvious sense in which these two approaches can be said to be complementary – Weber providing the historical and sociological basis, Schumpeter explaining the underlying mechanism and long-term developmental trend of capitalism – and it will be our brief to explore this.

A starting point for the comparison of the two approaches is to consider the respective definitions/characterizations of capitalism that Weber and Schumpeter respectively advance. For Weber, the operative definition of modern capitalism concerns the specific character of the capitalist enterprise. For him, the modern capitalist enterprise is essentially a peaceful operation and involves the rational organization of formally free labour with a rational division of labour and the orientation of the enterprise to the pursuit of profits offered in the market. All this is only possible where the market is extensive enough to produce for the needs of the mass of the population. For Schumpeter, the definition is similar but not identical. His emphasis is on the method of enterprise wherein the pursuit of profit is pursued using funds obtained via the credit system (i.e., banks). This feature is absolutely critical to the task of explaining the nature of the capitalist system as a whole. Further, Schumpeter is also concerned to explain the manner in which the market/price system operates and how this necessarily gives rise to cyclical features. The obvious point of difference here concerns the differing emphases on the role credit: not prominent in the case of Weber but altogether primary for Schumpeter.

It follows from Schumpeter's definition of capitalism that he will date the origin of the capitalist system by the advent of the extensive use of credit, a phenomenon associated with the development of banking. It is noteworthy that he is expressly critical of Weber's emphasis on the so-called "spirit of capitalism" and the role of the Reformation and the Protestant religions in the advent of capitalism. It is debatable, however, whether Schumpeter properly appreciated Weber's account of the origins of modern capitalism. Below we shall explain that Weber did not deny the relevance of factors other than the so-called "spiritual" ones and was in fact fully apprised of the need to take into account the full range of "materialist" factors, such as preconditions and causes.[70]

Schumpeter's focus is on the "mechanism" of the capitalist system, and he gives particular emphasis to its "creative destructiveness". This latter feature arises because the ever-recurring quest for new opportunities for profit through productive innovations and finding new markets inevitably leads to the decline and death of many hitherto viable and prosperous businesses. Weber also accepts that the course of economic life under capitalism is far from harmonious and in fact, somewhat like Marx, recognizes the chaotic character of market competition with

70 Indeed, it is debatable whether Weber accepted this distinction as such, based as it is on the crude Marxist dichotomy, for Weber's sociological conception of social action entails that the meaning of the action to the individual and its conditioning by the surrounding social environment are both integral to interpretative understanding.

the clash of interests and the struggle of man against man. But this does not quite equate to "creative destruction" with its Nietzschean overtones. Schumpeter's work on the nature of business cycles was fully developed only in the course of his later research, which was published after 1930, well after Weber's death. Insofar as an understanding of Schumpeter's "mechanism" was already present as early as his *The Theory of Economic Development*, Weber does not seem to have considered its specific theses, though he certainly knew the work.[71]

A further question arises in relation to the way in which Weber's mature writings on the nature of the capitalist enterprise and its rationality can be integrated with the corresponding discussions of Schumpeter. Related to this is the characterization of the entrepreneur in the field of economic sociology. Both Weber and Schumpeter made many contributions on these topics, and a comparison of their respective efforts is instructive and of considerable interest. For example, Weber says a good deal about the way in which the business firm operates. He emphasizes, in particular, the role of capital accounting and how the factors of production are calculated and deployed in accordance with estimates of profitability based on market prices. Schumpeter likewise emphasizes the orientation of the entrepreneur to the market situation and the impact of calculations of profitability. But are their separate contributions on this completely compatible? One of the features Schumpeter emphasizes is the way in which new production functions are created by the efforts of the entrepreneur in rationalizing the process of production. He emphasizes that this rationalization is often a revolutionary step that involves breaking new ground, doing things in a different way, seizing novel opportunities to lower costs or exploiting new markets. In Weber, by contrast, the process of rationalization appears to be more routine and mechanical on the basis of an assessment of data in the accounting records. Yet Weber also sees that there is a charismatic quality about the entrepreneur, an issue to which we shall return.

It is important to recognize that despite his various works concerning the origins of the capitalism and its essential features, Weber did not attempt to theorize the long-term functioning and developmental tendencies of capitalism, other than to imply that it will continue indefinitely into the future. Thus he did not take seriously the Marxian view that capitalism is doomed to extinction because it contains fundamental contradictions, a view that Schumpeter is inclined to believe has some merit. Weber was not overly concerned about the possibility of periodic crises of the kind that Schumpeter made the focus of his later analyses. Weber was certainly aware that economic crises do and will occur, and he thought that the state should intervene to provide welfare assistance and to promote the interests of the nation. But he did not dwell upon the kind of fundamental system crises that have emerged since his day, such as those that occurred with the Great Depression of the 1930s, about which Schumpeter had a deal to say.

71 According to Swedberg, "Weber's annotated copy of *The Theory of Economic Development* can be inspected at the *Max-Weber-Arbeitsstelle* in Munich", *Max Weber and the Idea of Economic Sociology*, p. 45.

It needs to be noted that as regards Schumpeter, his strength lay to a large extent in his ability to synthesize and systematize the contributions of fellow economists, and that his own unique contributions are perhaps more modest and limited in originality compared with Weber's. For example, apart from his thesis about credit creation and the developmental mechanism that generates capitalist progress and produces business cycles, Schumpeter makes few claims to have created fundamental new insights in regard to key phenomena such as equilibrium, marginal utility, monopoly competition or the theory of price formation. Nonetheless, he provides a rich and instructive account of these phenomena and many other aspects of economic life in the course of his quite extensive writings. In addition to this, in his *History of Economic Analysis*, a work uncompleted at his death, Schumpeter provided an encyclopaedic account of the field of economic science up until the time of his death. Thus, when we speak of Schumpeter's contributions, we are, to a degree, recognizing the achievements of economic science as a whole, and thus, we are not limiting our approach entirely to an individual perspective that is Schumpeter's own.

A final area about which Schumpeter and Weber should be compared is socialism. Both Weber and Schumpeter regarded the theory of a socialist economic system as intellectually coherent and both believed that socialism was a feasible alternative to capitalism. Both wrote essays specifically on the topic of socialism. And, both lived to see the advent of socialism in the Soviet Union. Weber made very detailed analyses of the situation in Russia in several writings that he devoted to the question of the Russian Revolutions of 1905 and 1917.[72] Schumpeter, of course, lived to see the Soviet Union and other attempts to create socialism, and addressed the question of the long-term prospect for a transition to socialism at some length, particularly in his popular work *Capitalism, Socialism and Democracy*. There he provides a very detailed argument of the pros and cons of future socialism. But, though he states that a theoretical socialism could continue to foster economic progress and be compatible with democracy, the actual gist of his argument is that socialism is likely to be authoritarian or worse and that capitalism is really superior, at least for the time being.[73]

Both Weber and Schumpeter saw socialism as not only a threat to capitalist prosperity but also as potentially destructive of individual freedom, political liberty and cultural creativity. Weber was alarmed at what he foresaw as a potential new servitude that would arise once the private entrepreneur was eliminated – the expropriation of the expropriators – and the economy was organized under the total control of a single coordinating bureaucracy. Schumpeter had the advantage of seeing the practice of socialism in the Soviet Union and therefore had no illusions

72 These are now collected and published in English in Max Weber, *The Russian Revolutions*, Cornell University Press, 1995.

73 See the discussion in McGraw, *Prophet of Innovation*, pp. 347–67. MaGraw points out that though Schumpeter pretends to see that socialism is a perfectly feasible alternative to capitalism, there are so many difficulties that may arise in instituting a socialist system that in the end it is not really a viable option at all.

that any future socialist experiment would risk producing a similar authoritarian domination of the individual.[74] The different perspectives on socialism, to a degree, hang on the differing views Weber and Schumpeter had as regards the nature of bureaucracy. Where Weber saw excessive bureaucracy as a threat to the prospects of human freedom, Schumpeter did not fear it in the same way. Below we shall address these questions at some length.

Before we embark on our attempt to synthesize Weber and Schumpeter in pursuit of a general theory of modern capitalism, we must briefly consider a fundamental methodological issue. Neither Weber nor Schumpeter sought to produce a general theory of modern capitalism, and commentators might well argue that such an enterprise is in some ways inimical to their respective methodologies. We do not agree. While neither expressly pursued such a project, I see no reason why their works are inherently antithetical to such a goal. The aim of a general theory, in our view, is to distil the basic elements of the modern capitalist system as manifest in a variety of instances, to account for its origin and subsequent worldwide expansion, to demonstrate its essential preconditions and to show its internal structural composition and functioning. Of course, this task suggests that there are common elements in some of the major economies of the present era and that there may be tendencies towards the development of this form of capitalism. Nonetheless, we do not advocate a teleological view of the matter, nor, as we have said, do we wish to posit an end of history à la Fukuyama. The rationale of a general theory is to aid in the interpretative understanding of the forces at work in the modern socio-economic systems broadly considered and to provide a framework to assist with comparative analysis.

In what follows, we attempt to build such a general theory from elements mined from the contributions of both Weber and Schumpeter. We shall present detailed accounts of the works of Weber and Schumpeter relevant to the theory of capitalism. To some degree we shall work chronologically, by first expounding Weber's early works, followed by an account and analysis of his mature writings. But the two chapters on Weber are also arranged in part by topic, between his historical account of the origins of capitalism (Chapter One) and his analysis of the institutional structure of modern capitalism (Chapter Two). After this we turn to Schumpeter and divide his oeuvre also into early work (Chapter Three) and the later period (Chapter Four), a division that also partly corresponds to different emphases. Following these chapters, we shall bring the contributions of our two major thinkers together in an attempt to synthesize them (Chapter Five) and construct the basics of a general theory of modern capitalism (Chapter Six).

74 In this regard I mention an anecdote recounted by Jaspers that depicts Schumpeter as welcoming the Russian Revolution so theorists can observe its success or otherwise, but being indifferent to the human suffering likely to be brought by it, much to the disgust of Weber. See Swedberg, *Max Weber and the Idea of Economic Sociology*, p. 90, n. 127.

1 Weber's account of the origins of modern capitalism

Weber's writings on capitalism

As we have noted, Weber began his scholarly career as a student of political economy, when he regarded himself as an economist of a kind.[1] But his first major academic publication was in the field of legal/economic history: he wrote his doctorate on *The History of Commercial Partnerships in the Middle Ages* (1898).[2] He then produced two works on ancient society, both focused on agrarian issues, with one exploring Roman socio-economic history (*Roman Agrarian History*), while the other was a comparative study of ancient civilizations (*The Agrarian Sociology of Ancient Civilizations*).[3] In both these works, the issue of the character of ancient capitalism was a major theme, in particular, whether institutions similar to those of today existed.[4] So it is clear that Weber embarked on his later treatment of modern capitalism with a considerable grounding in the history of early forms of commerce and capitalism.

The first major work Weber wrote specifically on the issue of modern capitalism is constituted by the two essays that became the book *The Protestant Ethic and the Spirit of Capitalism*. The essays, later published as the book with the celebrated title, were written in 1904 and 1905.[5] The work, as we shall see, is primarily focused on explaining the original "spiritual" basis (mentality) of

1 I myself was not fully aware of this orientation of Weber's early career when I made the claim in my *Antiquity and Capitalism: Max Weber and the Sociological Foundations of Roman Civilization*, Routledge, 1991 that Weber began his career as an ancient historian.

2 Max Weber, *The History of Commercial Partnerships in the Middle Ages*, Rowman & Littlefileld, 2003.

3 Max Weber, *Roman Agrarian History* (1891), Regina, 2008 and Max Weber, *The Agrarian Sociology of Ancient Civilizations* (1909), NLB, 1976.

4 See my *Antiquity and Capitalism* for a detailed analysis of ancient capitalism and the issues that arise in relation to the type of capitalism – "political capitalism" – that prevailed in that era.

5 The original essays that Weber published in the *Archiv für Sozialwissenschaft und Sozialpolitk* in 1904–5 were subsequently re-published in 1920 in the first volume of Weber's *Collected Writings on the Sociology of Religion*. The text of the original essays was published unaltered, but in 1919, Weber added further footnotes, some of which were probably penned much earlier, and he wrote his famous "Authors Introduction" to the entire collection.

modern capitalistic acquisition.[6] As is well known, Weber locates the origins of the capitalist work ethic in the peculiar conception of "vocation" (*beruf*) advanced by certain Protestant religions and Puritan sects, in association with positive attitudes towards the meaning of business success. The book, however, was intended to be a contribution to a larger causal analysis of the origins of modern capitalism, as Weber indicated in his concluding remarks and his debate with critics, issues to which we shall return.

Subsequent to *The Protestant Ethic*, Weber embarked on a series of further studies that involved broad-ranging investigations that some have claimed amount to a virtual comparative study of civilizations.[7] In what follows, we largely agree with Peter Ghosh that Weber's key concerns did not alter greatly, if at all, from those advanced in the original essays of 1904–5. Of course, during the period from 1905 until his death, Weber produced a tremendous body of work that included extensive historical and sociological studies of law, politics and religion, but all this largely continued the research program set out in *The Protestant Ethic*. From 1909 to 1914, he was focused on developing the work that subsequently became his magnum opus, *Economy and Society*. As already noted, this work arose following the commission by his publishers to edit the large encyclopaedic compendium on the social sciences entitled *Grundriss der Socialökonomik*. Weber not only performed the role of editor, but he also took responsibility for writing large sections of the work himself. In carrying out this task and in the course of comparative studies, Weber further developed his account of modern capitalism. What is more, he further clarified his ideas concerning the "rationalization" of modern institutions, at one point in his late lecture-essay, "Science as a Vocation", describing the fate of the times as characterized by "the rationalisation and intellectualisation and, above all, by the 'disenchantment of the world'".[8] Capitalist enterprise is not alone in being an institution infused with distinctively rational features, for extensive processes of rationalization have occurred in law, in government, in science and even in art and architecture. In *Economy and Society* and in other late writings, Weber develops these notions into a series of propositions and theses concerning

6 At the outset, we must note the important recent contributions of Peter Ghosh exploring the aims and achievements of *The Protestant Ethic*. Ghosh argues, persuasively in our view, that Weber's book contained much more than the historical thesis about the role of Protestant religious ideas in the emergence of modern capitalism and set out a research program for the remainder of his career. See his *Max Weber and the Protestant Ethic: Twin Histories*, Oxford University Press, 2014, passim.

7 I refer to the work of Stephen Kalberg, *Max Weber's Comparative-Historical Sociology*, University of Chicago Press, 1994. Other prominent commentators have argued that Weber's later work (*Economy and Society* or *The Economic Ethics of the World Religions*) is a significant development of the concerns of his early work: Wolfgang Schluchter, *Paradoxes of Modernity: Culture and Conduct in the Theory of Max Weber*, Stanford University Press, 1996. Others, such as Wilhelm Hennis, have argued that Weber's ultimate question concerned the nature of modern occidental man as such. See his *Max Weber's Central Question*, Threshold, 2000.

8 From Max Weber: Essays in Sociology *From Max Weber: Essays in Sociology*, p. 155. According to Peter Ghosh, the theme of rationality and rationalization is present throughout Weber's oeuvre and, in particular, is a fundamental notion as early as *The Protestant Ethic*.

the nature of the institutional structures of the modern world at large. We shall explore the specific nature of these contributions as they relate to our topic.

Towards the end of his life after the First World War had ended, Weber produced several works that in some ways could be said to summarize his thinking on the question of the nature of capitalism and the phenomenon of rationalization. Two of those works that we consider in what follows are: (1) the so-called "Author's Introduction" ,[9] which was originally the "Introduction" to Weber's *Collected Works on the Sociology of Religion* being readied for publication in 1919; and (2) the series of lectures delivered in 1919–20 under the title "Outline of Universal Social and Economic History", subsequently published as the *General Economic History*. This last mentioned book was not actually penned by Weber, but it was put together from notes students took of the lectures given at the University of Munich.[10] We shall have occasion to discuss both of these works, but in this chapter we shall focus on the *General Economic History* because it is a comprehensive historical account of the origins of modern capitalism. While the book was not written by Weber and did not benefit from his personal authorial guidance, there seems no doubt that it is a largely accurate rendering of the lectures he gave, and it has a status somewhat akin to what we might have if we had his own lecture notes. It is accordingly a very useful text for the interpretation of Weber's thought, despite the unusual nature of its creation. Importantly, and in contrast to *The Protestant Ethic*, Weber includes very lengthy discussions of non-religious factors. In no other work does Weber condense his thinking on the many aspects of relevance to the origins of capitalism to produce an overall statement.

Weber's approach to the theory of modern capitalism

As we have noted, Weber's approach has certain limitations from our point of view, because he does not create a complete theory of capitalism in the manner of, say, Marxian political economy; nor, apart from marginal utility and monetary theory, does he deal expressly with the theories of economics proper. Even though he was undoubtedly aware of developments in the emerging science of economics and recognized that it was producing important new explanatory theorems, apart perhaps from his early lectures and his work on the stock exchange, he does not make direct reference to this body of theory.[11] For he had begun to develop somewhat different concerns, and in effect, largely accepted the state of knowledge

9 The "Author's Introduction" is perhaps the nearest piece we have that is a summary statement in the author's own words of his overall theoretical position; in this regard, it perhaps bears comparison with Marx's famous "Preface" to *A Contribution to the Critique of Political Economy*.

10 Given the nature of this work's construction from notes taken by students in the lectures and the fact that the lectures were geared to the needs of students, it has been considered less authoritative than other writings actually penned by Weber, but I do not think this is really an issue.

11 On the importance of these early lectures on "General ('Theoretical') Economics" to estimate Weber's familiarity and engagement with economics, see Peter Ghosh's discussion in Chapter 2 of his *Max Weber and the Protestant Ethic*, pp. 13–30.

already achieved in the economics of his day, especially, the contributions of the so-called Austrian School. To a degree it could be said that he left the tasks of economic theory proper to others, those like Weiser, Schumpeter and Menger, whom he regarded as more expert than himself. Weber makes no attempt to offer theorems that address crucial economic phenomena such as the formation of prices, the function of supply and demand, the nature of the monetary system, the source of capitalist profit, the effects of monopoly or the origins of economic crises – as, for example did classic economists like Smith, Mill, Ricardo, Menger and others. Nor does Weber set out to discover the underlying "logic" or developmental tendencies of the capitalist system, as does Schumpeter.

Broadly speaking, Weber's work in relation to capitalism is concerned with two fundamental issues that are interrelated. The first is to account for the historical origins of modern capitalism. The second set of concerns is to characterize the essential nature of modern capitalism and to analyze its sociological conditions of existence. The second set of concerns is focused on the character of capitalist institutions and in particular, the phenomenon of rational calculation and the rational organization of the business enterprise. Weber places particular emphasis on the role of capital accounting and the orientation of the enterprise towards the market situation and the estimation of prospective profits.[12] We shall discuss this dimension of Weber's work at length in Chapter Three.

As we have noted, Weber does not devote effort to analyzing the way capitalism functions as an economic system once it has come into being. Nonetheless, in the course of his work, Weber occasionally comments on the workings of the capitalist system once it has emerged and is fully developed. In *The Protestant Ethic*, he refers to it resting today on "mechanical foundations", and argues that present-day capitalism no longer requires the asceticism of the early Puritans in order to maintain its ongoing functionality.[13] The ethos or spirit of modern capitalism is today largely lacking its original Puritan pathos such that the pursuit of wealth tends to have the character of "sport".[14] Weber even speculates that the ascetic basis of early modern capitalism is being undone by a counter tendency set in motion by the effects of asceticism itself. This is because the wealth created by asceticism produces temptations for indulgence and pleasurable consumption. As he puts it in his "Second Reply to Rachfahl",

> Precisely that type of amassing of wealth which was conditioned by specifically "ascetic" conduct of life was what again and again tended to break the power of asceticism . . . It would become even rarer for the self-made

12 Weber's emphasis on calculation is similar to Sombart's and is partly influenced by Simmel, who wrote in 1900: "The money economy enforces the necessity of continuous mathematical operations in our daily transactions. The lives of many people are absorbed by such evaluating, weighing, calculating and reducing of qualitative values to quantitative ones" (Georg Simmel, *The Philosophy of Money*, Routledge, 1978, p. 444).

13 Weber, Max, *The Protestant Ethic and the Spirit of Capitalism*, Unwin, 1930 (PE), pp. 181–2.

14 Ibid., p. 182.

> man – and certainly for his sons and grandsons – spontaneously to resist the "temptations" of living for the "world" (i.e. for the *pleasurable consumption* of acquired goods) . . . In fact one of the achievements of ascetic Protestantism was that it *combated* this tendency, that it steadily opposed such tendencies to "idolatry of the flesh" as the securing of "splendor familiae" through the tying up of one's fortune in real estate as rentier income, along with the "seigneurial" pleasures of the "high life," intoxication with beauty and aesthetic enjoyment, excess, pomp and circumstance. And it is these tendencies, so anathema to ascetic Protestantism, which continually evoked the danger of "capitalist tranquillisation" based on the use of assets for purposes *other* than "active capital" and which thus worked against the capitalist "spirit".[15]

It is not difficult to see in these remarks an anticipation of the thesis of commentators, such as Daniel Bell, regarding the fate of the work ethic in advanced capitalism.[16] Capitalism is now a kind of "cosmos", but is unlike the religious cosmos of the past in that it is not inwardly meaningful. It is rather an externally imposed order that, because of the requirements of specialization and bureaucracy, constrains men within an "iron cage" or "straight jacket":[17] "The capitalist economy of the present day is an immense cosmos into which the individual is born, and . . . in which he must live. It forces the individual, in so far as he is involved in the system of market relationships, to conform to capitalistic rules of action."[18]

Issues in the interpretation of Weber's work

Weber's writings on capitalism present a number of difficulties of interpretation. His first writings, which address the nature of modern capitalism at length, the essays that make up *The Protestant Ethic*, were written at the same time as two major methodological essays and a number of other discussions on epistemological questions.[19] At this time, Weber was clearly engaged by the controversy of the so-called *Methodenstreit*. He was acutely concerned with the problem of how theory can grasp the world in the light of the insights of the neo-Kantians concerning how scientific knowledge of reality can be obtained. Under the influence of Heinrich Rickert and others, Weber adopted a "solution" to these problems in part with the concept of the "ideal type".[20] The function of the ideal type in Weber's

15 David Chalcraft and Austin Harrington (eds.), *The Protestant Ethic Debate: Weber's Replies to His Critics, 1907–1910*, Liverpool University Press, 2001, p. 101.

16 I refer in particular to Bell's *The Cultural Contradictions of Capitalism*, Basic Books, 1976.

17 The German term *stahlhartes Gehäuse* has been translated in several ways. Ghosh renders it as "steel housing". See *Max Weber and the Protestant Ethic*, p. 59.

18 PE, p. 54.

19 The key methodological essays are: "'Objectivity' in Social Science and Social Policy" (1904) and "Critical Studies in the Logic of the Cultural Sciences" (1905).

20 The best account of these issues is that of Guy Oakes, *Weber and Rickert: Concept Formation in the Cultural Sciences*, MIT Press, 1998.

thought is first to provide a simplification of the complex manifold of reality; second, it facilitates a more precise and less ambiguous formulation of conceptual elements.[21] But the further purpose of the ideal type is to deal with the problem that reality can always be viewed from different points of view.[22] Thus, for example, it is possible to approach a given religious phenomenon in terms of the beliefs that certain religiously inspired individuals actually hold, in terms of the theological conceptions that have been articulated by intellectuals claiming to represent the beliefs of a group, in terms of the actual practices of persons comprising a sect or church, or again, in terms of an ideal formulation of what a particular religious meaning should be – and there are other possible angles as well. The problem is the same with all historical phenomena – such as the French Revolution, the Roman Republic, the Greek state, Islamic jurisprudence, mediaeval monasticism, Egyptian bureaucracy, the Reformation and so on. And, of course, this problem also arises in relation to capitalism: "modern capitalism", "ancient capitalism", "political capitalism", "the market system", "the Industrial Revolution", etc. Any of these phenomena can be viewed from a variety of perspectives, and the concepts to deal with them must be created by the theorist. This latter aspect is what is embraced by the so-called problem of the "hiatus irrationalis", that the world does not come already conceptualized from the everyday meaning of these terms.[23]

Weber sought to cope with these methodological issues by conceding that, in a sense, all scientific theorizing involves an inherent one-sidedness, or perhaps, to use the Nietzschean notion, "perspective". Further, there is no scientific or objective ground upon which one perspective can be said to be superior or preferred over any other. Weber approached this problem, which threatened to render all scientific endeavours subjective and relativistic, by developing Rickert's notion of "value relevance" (*Wertbeziehung*). The value relevance of a phenomenon enables a selection of features to be made from the manifold of possible aspects that imposes limits on the dimensions to be conceptualized. It follows from these presuppositions that when Weber formulates his concepts, whether of capitalism, Protestantism, the entrepreneur or whatever, he highlights certain aspects of significance from value points of view that he believes are widely shared and thus meaningful to fellow researchers. Even though he rejects the idea that such value points of view can be "objectively" given, he nonetheless maintains that some value perspectives resonate widely amongst one's contemporaries. In some cases, the values in question may have broader, cross-cultural and even "universal significance"; thus, for

21 In his key methodological essay "'Objectivity' in Social Science and Social Policy", Weber says the function of the ideal type is to offer "guidance in the construction of hypotheses," and "to give unambiguous means of expression" to descriptions of reality," and "to make clearly explicit . . . the unique individual character of cultural phenomena" (Max Weber, *The Methodology of the Social Sciences*, Free Press, 1949 (MSS), p. 90 and 101).

22 Ibid., p. 81.

23 On this concept, see the excellent discussion of Oakes in his Introduction to Heinrich Rickert, *The Limits of Concept Formation in Natural Science: A Logical Introduction to the Historical Sciences*, Cambridge University Press, 1986.

example, aspects of modern culture, especially law, science and technology, Weber believes, possess significance beyond the European context.[24]

In formulating concepts for understanding the origin of capitalism, Weber constructs what he terms "genetic ideal types". These are concepts that are capable of showing the causal connections between the phenomena to be explained and antecedent events. Hence, in his classic formulation of *The Protestant Ethic* thesis, Weber isolates certain aspects of ethically conditioned conduct associated with the religious idea of the "calling" and a methodical attitude to work in the world and relates these to the rationalization of labour fundamental to the operation of modern capitalist enterprise. This is historical method par excellence from his point of view.

But a question arises as to the relationship between these methodological theses deriving from Weber's early period and his later work, particularly *Economy and Society*.[25] Did Weber continue to operate with exactly the same method as that set out in those earlier writings? For example, are the final sections of the *General Economic History*, where he provides an account of the origins of the capitalist economic system, consistent with the earlier perspectives? This problem has been raised by Stephen Turner. Referring to Weber's *General Economic History*, Turner says in that work,

> Weber reiterated what can be found scattered throughout his later writings on the "distinguishing characteristics of western capitalism and its causes" by listing explanatory factors, including rational law, the rational organisation of labour, rational technology, rational accounting, free labour, the use of stock shares, the rational spirit, and a rationalistic economic ethic. The status of these lists is left vague: "distinguishing characteristics" and "causes" are never distinguished. The rational organisation of labour is at one moment produced by western capitalism, at another its primary cause, at another its distinctive feature. This ambiguity makes it difficult to treat the lists as explanations at all and it creates a puzzle about Weber's intent in producing them.[26]

In discussing these lists Turner goes on to say:

> In themselves they are uncharacteristically schematic and mechanical, vague as to the causal mechanisms by which the effects are produced, and lacking a framework of logic that would give sense to a notion of them as causes. As explanations, they appear to conflict with Weber's opinion on method; to the

24 The concept of value relevance is discussed with considerable acumen by Hans Henrik Bruun in his *Science, Values and Politics in Max Weber's Methodology*, Ashgate, 2007, passim.

25 Several commentators have considered the issue of such a discrepancy. For example, Thomas Burger in his *Max Weber's Theory of Concept Formation: History, Laws, and Ideal Types*, Duke, 1976, passim.

26 Stephen Turner, "Explaining Capitalism: Weber on and against Marx", in Robert Antonio and Ronald Glassman (eds.), *A Weber-Marx Dialogue*, University Press of Kansas, 1985, p. 176.

extent that they weigh factors, they conflict with the discussion of objective possibility in the early writings.[27]

In a completely different vein to Turner, the sociologist Randall Collins has taken Weber's contributions as forming the basis of a comprehensive causal explanation of the origin of modern capitalism. Collins does not see any particular methodological difficulties in reconstructing Weber's work on the origins of capitalism and assumes it contains more or less all the basic elements for an adequate causal account. Indeed, he believes that Weber's work still constitutes the most sophisticated and most convincing account of the causes of modern capitalism available, a view with which we agree. He posits the various factors that gave rise to capitalism as a series of links in a causal chain. Each element can be placed in the sequence of causes and be shown to have either been the cause of a later development or to have itself been caused by previous developments. Some causal sequences go back to the earliest period of antiquity and, even before, to factors found in primitive/tribal societies.

Somewhat surprisingly, Collins argues that Weber increasingly reduced the significance of Protestantism as his account of capitalism more and more identified various non-religious institutional structures as crucial. Collins highlights phenomena such as rational law, citizenship, rational science and technology, bureaucracy, the state and the commercialization of life as key elements that led to the advent of modern capitalism, but he says these phenomena had little, if anything, to do with Protestantism.[28] We do not accept this view, as will be made apparent below.

Contrary to the thesis of Friedrich Tenbruk, which says that there is an overall developmental logic at work underlying aspects of Weber's account of the history of religion, Collins argues that for Weber, there is no underlying trend towards ever-increasing rationality.[29] Nor does Weber posit an evolutionary model in the sense of a process of selecting more advanced forms that might be said to accumulate through a series of stages. As Collins puts it, "For Weber's constant theme is that the *pattern of relations among the various factors* is crucial in determining their effect upon economic rationalization. Any one factor occurring by itself tends to have the opposite effects, overall, to those which it has in combination with the other factors".[30] In summary, Collins concludes that "Weber saw the rise

27 Ibid., pp. 179–80. Wolfgang Schluchter has suggested grouping Weber's list of causal factors giving rise to modern capitalism into three categories relating to (1) the modern capitalist enterprise, (2) the modern capitalist economic order, and (3) the modern capitalist spirit, a solution to the problem that to us seems perfectly satisfactory. Schluchter, *Paradoxes of Modernity* pp. 200–2.

28 Collins's assessment of the causal significance of Protestantism in Weber's final version of the origins of capitalism is set out in his *Weberian Sociological Theory*, Cambridge University Press, 1986, pp. 33–4.

29 I have discussed Tenbruck's approach to this issue at length in my essay "Developmentalism in Max Weber's Sociology of Religion: A Critique of F.H. Tenbruck", *European Journal of Sociology*, 34, (1993), pp. 339–69.

30 *Weberian Sociological Theory*, Cambridge University Press, 1986, p. 34. Weber occasionally uses the term "concatenation" of factors to explain his approach to dealing with causal complexity.

of large scale capitalism, then as a result of a series of combinations of conditions which had to occur together. This makes world history look like the result of configurations of events so rare as to appear accidental."[31] Paradoxically, "Weber's account of the rise of capitalism, then, is in a sense not a theory at all, in that it is not a set of universal generalizations about economic change."[32] It is critical in Weber's theory that no one element dominates. Each element is dependent upon individuals asserting themselves in a struggle against each other. The open market depends on a continuous balance of power. The formal equality of the law depends on competition between citizens. And a non-dualistic economic ethic of tempered acquisitiveness requires compromise between the claims of in-group charity and the exploitation of those outside the group. The open market is a situation of continuous strife and struggle, which is similar to the Marxian notion of "the chaos of the market". Collins quotes the following section of *Economy and Society*, where this idea of struggle is emphasized forcefully:

> The formal rationality of money calculation is dependent on certain quite specific substantive conditions. Those which are of particular sociological importance for the present purposes are the following: (1) market struggle of economic units which are at least relatively autonomous. Money prices are the product of conflicts of interest and of compromises: they thus a result from power constellations. Money is not a mere "voucher for unspecified utilities," which could be altered at will without any fundamental effect on the character of the price system as a struggle of man against man. "Money" is, rather, primarily a weapon in this struggle, and prices are expressions of the struggle: they are instruments of calculation only as estimated quantifications of relative chances in this struggle of interests.[33]

We shall consider these perspectives on Weber at length. For the present, I shall merely indicate that I do not accept Collins's view that Weber abandoned the strong version of *The Protestant Ethic* thesis in his last writings. In this I am largely in accord with the commentary of Wolfgang Schluchter, to whose work I shall now turn.

Wolfgang Schluchter's interpretation of Weber's oeuvre

One of the most influential studies of Weber's account of the emergence of modern capitalism is that provided by Wolfgang Schluchter. Schluchter is also the managing editor of the comprehensive edition of Weber's collected works in German.[34] In what follows, I shall refer in particular to his last account of Weber's thesis on capitalist origins, which is contained in Chapter Four of his book *Paradoxes of Modernity*.

31 Ibid., p. 35.
32 Ibid.
33 Ibid., p. 36 n. 15.
34 I refer to the *Max Weber Gesamtausgabe*.

Schluchter argues that Weber's approach has both a genetic and simultaneously a comparative aspect, and he coins the expression "developmental-historical perspective" as a way of characterizing Weber's method. Schluchter locates the beginnings of a genetic explanation of the development of modern capitalism in one of Weber's early works, *The History of Commercial Partnerships in the Middle Ages.* In that work, Weber sought to show how mediaeval conditions brought about the legal separation between the private and the business sphere. This occurred even though in the mediaeval world, business corporations and in particular the limited liability firm, did not yet exist. Yet in mediaeval partnership, the idea that the private activities of the household should be kept separate from business activities and the operations of commercial firms was first established. It was partly upon this basis that Protestantism then began to work out the ethical dimensions whereby business profit could be viewed as a special form of wealth that was justifiable but subject to ascetic restraint.

Schluchter points out that, as Weber's thinking matured, he went beyond merely accounting for the genesis of certain aspects of capitalism in the West and developed a comprehensive and comparative approach directed at showing how in non-Western societies conditions were such as to inhibit or to retard the possibility of rational forms of economy. Thus, Weber's thesis about capitalism became partly an analysis of the singularity of Western cultural development in the context of universal history. Schluchter argues that the more Weber developed his comparative studies, the more he realized that there was something distinct about the West that required more intensive investigation. He traces Weber's work plans in his later years up until his death in 1920 and concludes that these indicate he intended to write further studies of the Western cultural complex. Apparently Weber had planned to write a detailed study of Western Christianity in its entirety. This would have included studies of Early Christianity, Talmudic Judaism and Eastern Christianity. The essay that Weber eventually published as the Introduction to his *Collected Essays in the Sociology of Religion*, that is, the so-called "Author's Introduction", makes it clear, according to Schluchter, that Weber now sought to focus his attention on the singularity of Western development as a whole. And the project was to include analyses of political domination, law, science and art as well as religion. Whereas the analyses of China and India were important as a way of finding points of comparison, the study of Israelite and Jewish religion was relevant because it constituted the beginning of occidental cultural development. Weber had even intended to expand his studies of occidental culture to include a short depiction of Egyptian, Mesopotamian and Zoroastrian religious ethics.[35]

According to Schluchter, "a shift had to be made from a comparative perspective that emphasizes the contrast between the Asiatic and Mediterranean-occidental world to a developmental perspective that focuses on the continuities within the Mediterranean-occidental world. . . . Questions of historical preconditions and

35 Schluchter, *Paradoxes of Modernity*, pp. 183–4.

causal attribution now move to the fore."[36] Although Weber expressly emphasized divergences between, say, antiquity and the Middle Ages, he also spoke of continuities of Mediterranean-European cultural development. But Weber rejects utterly the idea of a one-directional linear course of development.[37] Thus, in his study of *Ancient Judaism*, Weber began by noting that without the Old Testament and adherence to it of the Pauline mission, there would never have been a universalistic Christian church nor the Christian ethics of the everyday world. Thus, chance events giving rise to a religious movement have had an impact over many centuries. The world-historical significance of the Pauline mission is explained in Weber's essay on *The Religion of India* as follows:

> The elimination of all ritual barriers of birth for the community of the Eucharists as realised in Antioch, was also, in terms of its religious preconditions, the hour of conception for the "Occidental Citizenry", even if the latter was first to be born more than a thousand years later in the revolutionary "coniuratio" of medieval cities.[38]

Schluchter tells us that, at the time in 1919 when Weber was discussing with his publisher the structure of his collected works on the world religions and had the opportunity to revise his studies on Protestantism, he neither enlarged the scope of the work nor altered his original thesis. Contrary to the suggestion of Randall Collins that Weber in his later writings downplayed the significance of Protestantism and the Protestant Ethic, Schluchter argues that nothing could be further from the truth. Indeed, he says Weber in fact gave further accounts of his original thesis in the revised version being prepared for publication. Even though he anticipated a study of Western Christianity as the centrepiece of a projected Volume Four of the *Collected Essays in the Sociology of Religion*, Schluchter says this would not have changed any part of the original Protestant Ethic Thesis. The exact opposite would have occurred because Weber would have more clearly defined his argument by expanding the intra-Christian scope of comparison and by integrating Judaism and Islam into the analysis. The volume on Western Christianity would have included a more extensive discussion of the Western cultural development as a whole. It would have included analyses of Christian salvation movements, Western territorial and urban associations, Western sacred and profane law, Western science and

36 Ibid., p. 184.

37 Schluchter argues that Weber, despite some methodological reservations about the use of such terms as epoch, phase or stage, nonetheless avails himself of such conceptual devices on the assumption they are insulated from any Hegelian resonances. As Weber puts it on one occasion, "If we construct a 'cultural stage', this mental construct solely means, in terms of the judgements it implies, that the individual phenomena that we summarize conceptually by means of it are 'adequate' to one another, possessing – one would say – a certain degree of intrinsic affinity, with one another. It never entails, however, that they follow from one another according to any kind of lawfulness" (Cited in ibid., p. 193).

38 Cited in ibid., p. 179.

technology, Western organizational forms in trade and industry, Western banking and exchanges, as well as analyses of the hierocratic and political powers. Weber would thus have delivered on his projected course of study, as set out in the concluding remarks in the original *Protestant Ethic* essays, developing the other materialist side of the causal chain so to speak. In this connection, Schluchter says special attention would also have been given to the development of the city and the rise of the Western bourgeoisie.

On the basis of these preliminary considerations Schluchter proceeds to reconstruct Weber's explanatory model of the development of the modern West. He begins by emphasizing a feature of Weber's analysis of the origin of capitalism that is often overlooked but is made clear in his discussion in the so-called "Anti-critiques".[39] In those writings and elsewhere, Weber distinguishes between the spirit of capitalism and capitalism as an economic system. Schluchter explains the relationship between spirit and form this way:

> Different degrees of elective affinity can exist between them. The spirit can, as Weber expressly puts it, be more or less (or not at all) "adequate" to the form. This is the case because neither do they necessarily share a common origin, nor is one necessarily derivable from the other. Any position that makes either of these two claims is to be considered reductionist. The respective transformations of institutions and mentalities, the revolutions from without and from within, are rarely synchronised in historical realities.[40]

As regards the economic system, Schluchter notes that Weber sometimes refers to its organization or organizational form. This can be understood in two conceptually different ways. Schluchter says one can conceive of capitalism either as an ideal type of a general character or with an individual character. If one conceives of it as a general character, one extracts from the idea of capitalism certain features that are accentuated and brought to a conceptual purity. Thus, for example, if one contrasts capitalist economy with household economy, one stresses the element of profitability and the exploitation of peaceful opportunities for exchange in the market and capital accounting. However, if one considers capitalism in terms of its individual character, one would emphasize the specific character of capitalism, as it emerged in the West, and here, of course, one might emphasize the role of worldly asceticism and the way in which the capitalist spirit shaped the institutional structure of capitalistic profit-making, giving rise to the business enterprise based on the rational organization of formally free labour.[41]

39 He is referring to the series of exchanges between Weber and his critics Karl Fischer and Felix Rachfahl that are now published in English in Chalcraft and Harrington (eds.), *The Protestant Ethic Debate*.

40 Schluchter, *Paradoxes of Modernity*, p. 191.

41 Ibid., p. 190.

Schluchter says that these two aspects of analysis are reflected in various phases in Weber's work on the origin of capitalism. In early works, such as *The Agrarian Sociology of Ancient Civilizations*, Weber had sought to explore the capitalism of antiquity as an economic system, whereas the studies of Protestantism were to cover the issue of the spirit of modern capitalism. Thus the studies of Protestantism were focused on the mentality and motivation underlying the modern capitalist spirit, and the purpose was to trace the origin of this spirit back to the period of the Reformation. The period just following the Reformation, the seventeenth century, is crucial because it brought about the transformation from within, that is, of mentality and motivation. It thus created one of the key preconditions for the advent of the modern capitalist spirit, though it was not the only source of that spirit. But it did provide a pattern for that spirit, which was "specifically different from that of the Middle Ages and Antiquity."[42]

Peter Ghosh's analysis of the pivotal role of *The Protestant Ethic*

In 2014, Peter Ghosh published his large-scale study *Max Weber and the Protestant Ethic: Twin Histories* and, owing to its focus on themes of relevance to our concerns here, it warrants our consideration. Ghosh's book is a detailed intellectual biography of Weber in which he wants to explore the origin, development and proper understanding of Weber's key ideas in all their myriad interrelations and complications. Ghosh describes his approach as essentially that of a historian (as opposed to that of a sociologist or economic historian), so he is not primarily concerned with the empirical validity of Weber's various sociological and historical theses, even though he makes many acute observations in that regard.

Insofar as it is possible to reduce Ghosh's argument to a single thesis, his primary claim is that *The Protestant Ethic* is not only a masterpiece of historical scholarship, but it is seminal for the interpretation of Weber's oeuvre, because it contains all the key ideas that he subsequently developed at greater length later in *Economy and Society* and elsewhere. This is the case especially as regards Weber's arguments about the advance of rational economic conduct and the rationalization of social life generally.

Paradoxically given his obvious admiration of Weber's work, Ghosh remains sceptical as to whether Weber's express aims in *The Protestant Ethic* were achieved.[43] In other words, Weber never really completed his project of arriving at a definitive account of the spirit of capitalism, which was a project influenced, in a way, by the Marxist focus on the idea of capitalism. Rather, even in *The Protestant Ethic*, Weber was primarily developing a thesis on the ascetic origins of

42 Cited in ibid., p. 192.

43 Thus he says at one point that *The Protestant Ethic* was, "a momentous failure in the attempt to define capitalism and its 'spirit', even if its explorations of rationalizing and ascetic religiosity were broadly successful." "Capitalism and *Herrschaft*", *Max Weber and the Protestant Ethic*, p. 112.

modern rationality, of which capitalism was only one instance. Thus, although he was preoccupied with the phenomenon of capitalism in his early career and made accounting for its "spirit" the ostensible goal in *The Protestant Ethic*, after 1908, he ceased to be focused on capitalism and instead directed his analytical efforts towards the phenomena of rationalization and rationality, such as are present in modern bureaucracy and rational law. Thus Ghosh says:

> Having exited economics as a faculty by resigning his chair in 1903, he [Weber] now came "back to law", albeit in a very unusual way: that is, he used legal formalism as the principal resource for conceptual construction of an interdisciplinary "sociology" centred on formal rationality, with the institutional centre of that sociology lying in the legal-rational rule or *Herrschaft* of lawyer-bureaucrats. After 1908 a holistically conceived capitalism is never again the subject of sustained theoretical reflection by Weber, even if its contemporary historical centrality was undoubted. In broader perspective, this was a movement away from the economistic milieu associated with Marx and socialism, the *Verein für Sozialpolitik* and "the social question", back to the legal and rational roots of classical liberalism and the drive to renew this. At the same time Weber was completing a movement opened by the [*Protestant Ethic*] . . . the principal textual argument of the [*Protestant Ethic*] is not an argument about capitalism (the movement from Protestantism to capitalism), but an argument about rationality (the modern secular rationality in a rationalizing religious asceticism).[44]

Throughout his work, Ghosh explores the implications of this redirection in Weber's thought. He emphasizes that after 1908, Weber does not return to the argument of *The Protestant Ethic*, even though he had admitted its argument was "one-sided" and that a final definition of the capitalist spirit was not yet at hand. But *The Protestant Ethic*, though limited as a study of capitalism, is masterful as the history of an ethic. Which is not to say Weber does not have much to say about capitalism that is extremely insightful. According to Ghosh, "The outstanding and obviously successful component in his analysis of capitalism is not what he has to say about capitalism itself but its integration within the general theme of the rationalization of modern *Kulur*." Nonetheless, Ghosh also recognizes that Weber's writings provide an implicit sociology of capitalism, "based on the distinction between rational, industrial capitalism committed to the efficient mass production of goods and speculative, politically privileged, and opportunistic capitalism catering for luxury, where both constitute logically equal, trans-historical types."[45]

We have no difficulty in accepting these claims of Ghosh as an account of Weber's intellectual development. But whereas the idea that Weber backed-off

44 Ibid., p. 169.
45 Ibid., p. 337.

from the focusing on the issue of capitalism leads Ghosh to want to explore the cultural and political implications of Weber's later reflections, the meaning of societal and cultural rationalization for a modern occidental man, our concern remains with the project of a theory of capitalism. And whereas Ghosh is somewhat dismissive of Weber's late work *General Economic History*, a work that is clearly focused on the history of capitalism and to a degree is a response to the critics who rejected the Protestant ethic thesis as unduly idealist, we believe this text, in combination with *Economy and Society* and the "Author's Introduction", provides an invaluable overview of the character of modern capitalism and indicates Weber did not abandon the topic to the extent Ghosh claims.[46]

Idealist versus materialist approaches

Discussion of the contribution of Weber to the understanding of capitalism, as we have already indicated, has commonly focused on, and unfortunately often gone no further than, the celebrated work *The Protestant Ethic and the Spirit of Capitalism*. However, seminal it may be, this work is only one of a number of Weber's writings that address the origins of modern capitalism, and by no means does it exhaust his thinking on the subject. Indeed, it could well be said that capitalism and its origins are a reference point, and they are regularly in the foreground, throughout most of Weber's contributions to socio/historical thought. Thus, not only is capitalism discussed at considerable length in his magnum opus *Economy and Society*, but Weber also alludes to the topic frequently in many of his other writings, including those that deal primarily with religion. Arguably the most significant work apart from *The Protestant Ethic and the Spirit of Capitalism* that deals directly with capitalism is *General Economic History*. This is an interesting work for many reasons but especially insofar as it is an unambiguous corrective to the misguided impression many critics have had that Weber wished to substitute an entirely "ideological" or "idealist" theory of capitalist origins for a so-called "materialist" approach, like that of the Marx and other economic determinists. In any event, as we shall see, a perusal of Weber's writings such as *Economy and Society* shows that, not only was he *not* an "idealist", but he acknowledged the centrality of "materialistic" factors and could embrace all that Marxism was claiming in this regard.[47] Further, he could be said to have added significantly to both idealist and materialist approaches by explaining how aspects of legal,

46 Ghosh describes *General Economic History* derisorily as, "not intended for publication, being a ramshackle and hastily assembled compilation of pre-existing materials for student consumption" (Ibid., p. 165).

47 It is important to emphasize that in recognizing the role of materialist factors Weber is equally concerned to avoid the opposite error of reducing religious phenomena to a mere reflex of the former. See for instance the very clear statement in this regard in his essay "The Social Psychology of the World Religions", in Max Weber (ed.), *From Max Weber: Essays in Sociology*, Routledge, 1991 (FMW)., pp. 269–70.

political, geographic and urban features were crucial to the advent and development of modern capitalism.[48]

Weber's general approach on these matters is clarified in the various "Replies to His Critics" (i.e., Karl Fischer and Felix Rachfahl) written in response to their criticisms of the *Protestant Ethic* essays of 1904–5, and it is to these writings we shall briefly refer. At one point in his second reply to Karl Fischer written in answer to the claim that he (Weber) has provided, or is concerned to provide, an idealist interpretation of capitalism as against the approach of Sombart, Weber says, on the contrary,

> it is precisely this part of Sombart's account – his discourse on the significance of "calculativeness" (*Rechenhaftigkeit*) and the techniques it involves – that is relatively the least disputed and as far as Sombart's central question of whence arose the modern economic importance of capitalist *industrial* and *commercial* forms, I consider his account completely correct in all crucial respects. . . . It goes without saying that for his own central question Sombart considers *technical* "calculativeness" the decisive characteristic of the *spirit of capitalism*. . . . We have both been concerned with the same phenomena, but from different angles and with myself necessarily focussing on different features. So it is a matter of terminological differences, not substantive disagreements, at least not on my side. Indeed, as far as I can see, we are entirely at one in our attitude to historical materialism.[49]

In other words, Weber is claiming to have addressed only one aspect of the question of the character of early capitalism in *The Protestant Ethic*, and he is openly endorsing Sombart's more general account of the origin of capitalism as being equally valid and perfectly compatible with his own thesis.[50]

A useful clarification of the idealist versus materialist issue is provided by Ghosh, who points out that, while Weber was not a naïve idealist as has often been claimed, he nonetheless did

> allot an ultimate priority to ideal factors, always bearing in mind that what many would see as simple materialism is for him a cast of mind: "material *Kultur*", a set of values that allocated value to material things, or "the economic way of looking at things". Hence the "transcendental presupposition" set down in 1904 that all human beings were "*beings with Kultur*"; or the famous dictum from 1919–20 that it was quasi-Platonic "Ideas" (*Idean*) and not material "interests" that determined the turning points in the tracks of world history.[51]

48 Weber's most elaborate methodological discussion of the issue of materialist versus idealist approaches in history is the discussion in his *Critique of Stammler*, The Free Press, 1977, especially the section "Stammler's Account of Historical Materialism", pp. 62–70.

49 Chalcraft and Harrington, *The Protestant Ethic Debate*, p. 50.

50 It has to be said that these remarks give a somewhat misleading view of Weber's appreciation of Sombart's work, for he is elsewhere highly critical.

51 Ghosh, *Max Weber and the Protestant Ethic*, pp. 234–5.

Weber's earliest explorations of the origins of modern capitalism

We have already referred to Weber's work on the stock exchange and his early interest in economic theory. It is not well known, however, that Weber wrote his doctoral thesis on mediaeval economic history, a work in which he raised a number of concerns that are absolutely central to his understanding of modern capitalism and to the question of its origins.[52] *The History of Commercial Partnerships in the Middle Ages* interests us because it raises questions about the specific character of capitalism in the mediaeval period and whether this capitalism was the same type as modern capitalism. Further, it addresses the issue of what, if any, were the causal connections between the capitalism that had emerged in the Middle Ages and subsequent developments. Weber is particularly interested in the legal structures that facilitated the development of commercial partnerships, and it is obvious from his discussion that he sees these as being important because such commercial arrangements could be regarded as precursors to a form of economic enterprise that later emerges, namely, the corporation. Weber wants to know whether there is a possible course of development between such mediaeval partnerships and the economic structures that emerged later in the form of the industrial corporation.

Weber takes as his starting point the development of the mediaeval enterprise devoted to sea trade known as the *commenda*, which he distinguishes from the form known in antiquity. Throughout his discussion of the *commenda* and partnership law he makes comparisons with the limited liability corporation of the modern era. In the case of the modern type of enterprise, one finds a fund of capital reserved and deployed exclusively for the operation of the business at hand. Such businesses are in continuous operation, and liability is restricted to the capital fund referred to along with the assets deployed in the enterprise. Weber is acutely aware that these corporate-like structures have not been common throughout history, but approximations towards such arrangements may well have occurred prior to the modern era in the period of the Middle Ages.

Weber argues that the most primitive condition of maritime trade is that in which a ship owner (or *patronus navis*) provides the ships, purchases goods from a producer and sells them in a foreign market by accompanying the goods in person on these ships. In this way, the shipowner already acts in the role of a merchant and possibly shares the proceeds of the sale with the producer. But from early in the mediaeval period, a division of labour had developed so that the grand merchant typically sent a *fattore*, who was an employee, on the voyage instead of going himself. Other possibilities were that a commission agent was employed who had

52 See the Introduction by Lutz Kaebler to Max Weber, *The History of Commercial Partnerships in the Middle Ages*, Rowman & Littlefileld, 2003, especially pp. 36–8. Actually, Weber's dissertation formed only a part of the book that is now available in English because he added important sections to his original dissertation published as a pamphlet. This later version became the book that has the German title *Zur Geschichte Der Handelsgesellschaften im Mittelalter* and was published in October 1898.

knowledge of the foreign markets and received a commission or fixed remuneration for his services or possibly a share of the profits. Where there was a share in the profits, Weber says we have the *commenda* in the strict sense.

The simplest form of *commenda*, referred to as the unilateral *commenda*, occurs where the managing partner invests no capital of his own, the risk of loss being entirely on the other partner. According to Weber, this type of partnership does not correspond to the limited partnership of modern German law where one partner invests money but does not participate in the venture otherwise. It is rather a form of agency. More significant for Weber is the *societas maris* or bilateral *commenda*. Here both parties contribute capital but are not always equals. Owing to the different contributions, the arrangement necessarily requires some form of accounting to keep track of the contributions and the proportions of profits that will be distributed at the end of the venture. However, Weber says, at least for the case of Genoa, there are only the beginnings of a separate fund that could be treated as such for the partnership's relations with third party creditors. In these early forms of *commenda*, the personal liability of the partners is unlimited. In the later part of his work, however, in a detailed case study of Pisa, Weber is able to show that the city's commercial stipulations show the existence of a separate fund, as well as business undertaken in the name of a firm. Nonetheless, there is no solidary liability amongst all partners, as the liability of each *socius* is limited to his contribution. This is akin to the modern form of limited partnership.

What particularly interests Weber is the case of a partnership where there is solidary liability and the operation of the business on the basis of a separate fund. He focuses on the legal status of the family household and contrasts the mediaeval situation with that of the Romans. In mediaeval law, all members of the household could lay claim to the household's assets. The household is a community of production as well as consumption. Weber emphasizes that kinship is not the foundation of the household but rather it is joint residence and acquisitive activity. The relations of the household thus go beyond the immediate kin, and this gives rise to a need to formalize relations between all those who are members. This is especially the case when commercial acquisition is the basic activity of the household, because some income or expenses belong to the entity as a whole while others are merely personal. Thus, there must be some form of "accounting", and this need contributes to the general trend towards formal sociation. Sociation becomes, in effect, a contract that binds the parties. Weber says, "the family household . . . found it necessary, if it also intended to be the basis for a commercial enterprise, to set up its bookkeeping system and to represent itself towards third parties – in short: to cover all aspects relevant to the law of property – the same way a commercial company did. Thus in both cases the legally relevant aspects coincide."[53] The distinction between the business assets of the household and personal assets facilitates treating the business assets as a separate fund, and this raises the issue of the extent to which liability for debts incurred by the association extend to those

53 Ibid., p. 93.

assets and whether members are jointly or merely individually liable. Finally, Weber discusses the situation in Florence, where he finds that the concept of the firm and of a separate fund representing the joint equity of the partners is well established. Here are the beginnings of modern general partnership. These ideas about the separation of the enterprise from the household and the need for monetary accounting were background to Weber's major exploration of the question of the origins of capitalism in *The Protestant Ethic* to which we now turn.

The role of the Protestant ethic

According to Gordon Marshall, Weber actually produced two complementary arguments in *The Protestant Ethic and the Spirit of Capitalism*. The first is an argument about the origins of what could be said to be the capitalist ethos. Weber argues that the neo-Calvinist ethic of the seventeenth century was crucial to the development of a capitalist spirit or ethos. However, Weber also developed, in response to his critics, a further argument about the role of the capitalist spirit in the advent of the capitalist economic system. This second argument required Weber to relate the capitalist spirit to the range of other factors that are implicated in the rise of capitalism.[54]

To depict the *spirit* of modern capitalism, Weber cites Benjamin Franklin's famous text offering advice to those who seek wealth with this famous admonition – one should not waste time, for to do so is to lose money, one must cultivate an ability to raise credit and put it to good use, one should not misuse money, which would be to lose a potential fortune, punctually repay loans, be vigilant in the maintenance of accounts and be frugal in consumption. This set of attitudes is prototypical of the spirit of capitalism. The question then becomes how did it first come into being; for Weber is insistent that such dispositions are not natural and certainly do not occur universally, nor are they typical in societies prior to the seventeenth century, when Protestantism emerged. Weber says that in order for a manner of life such as that implied by Franklin, so well adapted to the peculiarities of capitalism, to be selected and come to dominate others, it had to originate somewhere, and it had to be spread as a way of life common to whole groups of men. It is the origin and dissemination of this way of life that Weber wants to explain.

The problem for Weber is neither to explain the pursuit of profit per se nor to explain why greed and the pursuit of unlimited gain appear in history and are of significance. Such attitudes are found widely distributed throughout the ages, both in the mediaeval and ancient periods, not to mention in non-Western societies, but they are not Weber's concern. His problem is to explain the origins of the historically peculiar form of the pursuit of gain typical of modern capitalism. The latter is characterized by the pursuit of profit and ever-renewed profit by the means of continuous rational enterprise in close association with disciplined restraints on personal consumption.

As is well known, Weber concentrates his argument on the notion of the "calling" as advanced by Luther. But the concept underwent further development

54 Gordon Marshall, *In Search of the Spirit of Capitalism*, Hutchinson, 1981, p. 15.

under the impact of the teachings of Calvin and finally as a result of the religious practices of the Puritans, Pietists, Methodists and Baptists. All these religious movements placed specific demands on their believers to act purposefully in their worldly callings (or "vocations"), to practice strict self-control in the way they consume material goods, and to resist the temptations of worldly pleasure. In different ways, they placed strong psychological pressure on the individual to adhere to a range of ethical standards that encouraged involvement in the world but deterred indulgence in the fruits of success. The critical idea that Weber claims as his own novel contribution is stated as follows:

> The essential point is that an ethic based on religion places certain psychological sanctions (not of an economical character) on the maintenance of the attitude prescribed by it, sanctions which, so long as the religious belief remains alive, are highly effective . . . Only in so far as these sanctions work, and, above all, in the direction in which they work, which is often very different from the doctrine of the theologians, does such an ethic gain an independent influence on the conduct of life and thus on the economic order.[55]

According to Weber, this ethic originated in two sources: in the first place in the doctrine of predestination, as this was developed by the neo-Calvinist religions, and in the second place, in the structure of the ascetic Protestant sects. In both cases there was a necessity of proof: in the first case to prove oneself before God, in the second before men.

The major issue of empirical research for Weber concerns the relationship between the ethos that he says was developed by ascetic Protestantism and the operation of the capitalist enterprise.

> To be sure the capitalist form of an enterprise and the spirit in which it was run generally stayed in some sort of adequate relationship to each other, but not in one of necessary interdependence . . . the two may well occur separately. Benjamin Franklin was filled with the spirit of capitalism at a time when his printing business did not differ in form from any handicraft enterprise . . . the management for instance of a bank or wholesale export business, a large retail establishment, or a large putting out enterprise dealing with goods produced in homes, is certainly only possible in a form of a capitalist enterprise. Nevertheless they may all be carried on in a traditionalistic spirit.[56]

Weber is well aware that the Fugger's and North Italian merchant princes during the Middle Ages were highly successful in business, but these were not the equivalent of modern capitalists. First, such individuals were not systematically generated by the social system. They were idiosyncratic cases of financial success

55 Quoted in Ibid., p. 16.
56 Quoted in ibid., p. 17.

that were not typical of the world in which they lived. And second, they accumulated their wealth for purely selfish motives: greed and avarice. Those who created the modern capitalist system, on the other hand, acquired their wealth to a certain extent as a duty or an end in itself. As Weber puts it, "The peculiarity of this philosophy of avarice appears to be the ideal of the honest man of recognized credit, and above all the idea of a duty of the individual towards the increase of his capital, which is assumed as an end in itself. Truly what is here preached is not simply a means of making one's way in the world, but a peculiar ethic."[57]

The nature of the personality that was required to underpin the new capitalist era is set out in the following passage, which we shall see bears remarkable closeness to the corresponding analysis of Schumpeter:

> A flood of mistrust, sometimes hatred, above all moral indignation, regularly opposed itself to the first innovator. . . . It is very easy not to recognize that only an unusually strong character could save an entrepreneur of this new type from the loss of his temperate self-control and from moral and economic shipwreck. Furthermore, along with clarity of vision and ability to act, it is only by virtue of a very definite and highly developed ethical qualities that it has been possible for him to command the absolutely indispensable confidence of customers and workmen. Nothing else could have given him the strength to overcome the innumerable obstacles, above all the infinitely more intensive work which is demanded of the modern entrepreneur. . . . they were men who had grown up in the hard school of life, above all temperate and reliable, shrewd and completely devoted to their business, with strictly bourgeois opinions and principles.[58]

Now as we have seen, Weber's initial thesis, which focused on the development of the spirit of capitalism, led to attacks by Rachfahl, Fischer and others who accused him of advancing an unduly idealist interpretation of history. One can surmise that it was this state of the critical debate that led Weber to address the second issue, namely, what was the role of the spirit of capitalism in the development of the modern economy. That is, amongst the various factors that caused the emergence of the modern capitalist economy, how crucial was the role of the spirit of capitalism? Of course, Weber was not naïve enough to assume that the mere existence of the "spirit" of capitalism was sufficient to conjure up the entire capitalist world. Nonetheless, he maintained that the spirit of capitalism, that is, the subjective motive complex denoted by this term, was causally necessary for the development of modern capitalism: "[capitalist] enterprise has derived its most suitable motive force from the spirit of capitalism."[59]

Weber in part addressed the issue of the adequacy of the spirit of capitalism to capitalist enterprise in an exchange with Sombart over the question of what is

57 Quoted in ibid., p. 19.
58 PE, p. 69.
59 Quoted in Marshall, *In Search of the Spirit of Capitalism*, p. 23.

unique about modern capitalism. In defining capitalism and its economic system as essentially bound up with rationality and calculability, Weber brings the spirit of capitalism and the economic system of capitalism into close conceptual relation. Thus, he at various points refers to the spirit and form of capitalism developing an "adequacy" for each other. Elsewhere he employs the term "elective affinity", adapted from Goethe's novel of the same name, to indicate the nature of the relation. In the years between his early studies of the Protestant ethic and his later comparative studies in the *Economic Ethics of the World's Religions*, Weber was able to explore, in more detail, his position concerning the role of the religion in the rise of capitalism, in particular, and of Western modernity in general. In his study of China, for example, Weber was concerned to point out that in many of the material conditions of that society, the structural elements that might have led to a form of capitalism were just as favourable, if not more so, than in the West, yet capitalism did not appear. He attributes this in no small way to the belief systems of China, specifically Confucianism and Taoism, which encouraged attitudes that were hostile to the form of capitalism that emerged in the West. Elsewhere Weber made similar claims about the import of ideological conditions for the prospect of rational capitalism in the cases of India and the ancient world.

Weber's final account of the rise of modern capitalism

As we have seen, contrary to the commonly accepted view that Weber's theory on the origins of capitalism focuses largely on its religious origins in the Protestant Ethic, a more comprehensive and seemingly "materialist/institutional" account is to be found elsewhere in his oeuvre, especially in his *General Economic History*.[60] This work could be said to complement that of *The Protestant Ethic* insofar as it provides a very detailed account of non-religious factors. But in suggesting that in his *General Economic History* Weber is concerned to give due weight to so-called materialist factors, one should not assume he is intent on only registering the impact of "economic" factors in the strict sense, for he is at the same time interested in assessing the interaction of a wide range of causal elements, which include law, science and technology, the city and citizenship as well as, once again, the "spirit of capitalism".

In the *General Economic History*, Weber begins his analysis of the development of modern capitalism with a consideration of features occurring first in remote antiquity. He notes that many of the institutional arrangements of capitalism, such as markets, profit-making, workshop production, monetarization, free labour, technical innovation, trade, merchant classes and even share ownership, existed in some form well back into ancient times, and they often achieved a quite high degree of development. But there are no continuous lines of development from

60 For an account of the background to Weber giving the lectures and to the production of the text Weber, Max, *General Economic History*, see the Introduction to the 1981 Transaction edition by Jere Cohen, pp. xv–lxxxiii.

these ancient institutions to the present. Weber locates the more immediate factors of causal significance for the rise of modern capitalism in the late mediaeval period and shortly thereafter. But again, there is no suggestion of a line of development that can be traced as a continuous process of unfolding progress.

Weber notes that in countries that became capitalist first, such as England and later Germany and France, the socio-economic structure that had to be overcome was the manorial system. The manor involved a system of mutual dependence between the landowner and the peasant. This relationship bound them together in such a fashion that both were prevented from becoming suitable agents for the promotion of individual economic action. The rupturing of these relationships of dependence took various forms in different countries, but in some cases, it led to the emancipation of the peasants and the freeing of the land from the restraints of peasant rights and other encumbrances. Of course, the most well-known case of this, as classically described by Marx, was England, where the expropriation of the peasants occurred.[61] The dissolution of the manor meant the destruction of the pre-existing agrarian communism, and this was followed by the advent of private property. The organization of the household shrunk to only the father, his wife and children, who constituted the basic social unit, and this ceased to have a productive function.

The commercialization of economic life

Weber says that in early societies commerce is an affair between ethnic groups and does not occur between members of the same tribe. However, individuals and groups who specialize in trade with foreign tribes may arise. Trade may be in goods produced by the trading individual's own tribe, and trading may at first only be a secondary occupation conducted seasonally. In some societies, such as India, a specialized group or caste may be primarily responsible for the conduct of trade. In feudalism, the manorial lord may seek to trade their agricultural surplus, for which purpose they may engage professional merchants. Political authorities may also engage in trade on their own account, either in the form of gift exchange or to acquire luxury goods not otherwise available to them. In order for commerce to become an independent occupation, Weber says that suitable means of transport are a prerequisite.

Private sea trade was well developed in antiquity, especially by the Phoenicians and the Greeks. In the case of the latter, we know that quite elaborate legal arrangements arose, such as the maritime loan (*foenus nauticum*), which set out the obligations and entitlements of the contracting parties (financier, trader and ship owner). But sea trade always remained risky owing to the dangers of piracy and shipwreck.

Trade by land routes was very limited in antiquity and the Middle Ages, despite the existence of the famous Roman roads. This was in part because of the nature

61 Ibid., p. 92.

of the roads, which were built primarily for military purposes, and also because wheeled transport was not capable of carrying heavy loads. Trade was also subject to the danger of robbery, so the ancients used the caravan to deal with this. But inland sea transport, initially on rivers but later on man-made canals, became increasingly important as a means of carrying large quantities, as barges could carry bigger payloads, and this made the movement of goods more reliable.[62]

As traders invariably found themselves in foreign lands, they needed some form of legal protection. A typical means of protection was to acquire a patron in the foreign city. In the mediaeval city, protection was greatly enhanced with the advent of guilds of merchants that were granted permission by the city rulers.[63] These developments led to the development of warehouses and sales rooms in foreign lands that were able to conduct more regular forms of commerce. Sometimes merchants were required to reside in the towns and even to locate their trading houses on particular streets, a development that concentrated trade and enhanced the growth of a market. Weber explains the course of development from these beginnings as follows:

> The resident merchant is to begin with an itinerant trader. He travels periodically in order to market products at a distance or to secure products from a distance and is a peddler who has acquired a fixed residence. The next stage is that in which he has the travelling done for him, either by an employee or a servant or by a partner; the one arrangement goes over into the other. The third stage is formed by the system of factors. The trader has increased in capital power to a point where he founds independent settlements at distant pints, or at least maintains employees there . . .[64]

But mediaeval trade was at first focused on retailing, as the merchant generally sold directly to the consumer.[65] In this role, they often had to contend with local urban interests that sought to maintain a monopoly of trade or production. But the conflict of interest between local and foreign merchants over regulation of the market eventually led to the separation of retailing from wholesale trade.

Importantly, Weber locates the beginnings of rational calculation in trade rather than in production.

> Rational commerce is the field in which quantitative reckoning first appeared, to become dominant finally over the whole extent of economic life. The necessity of exact calculation first arose wherever business was done by companies. In the beginning commerce was concerned with a turnover so slow and a profit so large that exact computation was not necessary. Goods were bought at a

62 Ibid., p. 199.
63 Ibid., p. 212.
64 Ibid., p. 216.
65 Ibid.

> price that was fixed traditionally, and the trader could confine his efforts to getting as much as he could in sale. When trade was carried on by groups it was necessary to proceed to exact bookkeeping in order to render an accounting.[66]

Weber says that the first books of accounting came into use in the fifteenth century, a development that required an understanding of position notation that was not available previously. Weber again emphasizes his argument about the importance of the separation of the household from the business. The key factor promoting this separation was the need for credit. Exact calculation first arose where business was carried on by companies. Initially, goods are bought at a price that is traditionally fixed and the trader simply seeks whatever he can get above the purchase price.[67] Later, prices become variable and are subject to the effects of market competition.

The role of the city

The role of the city in the emergence of capitalism is an aspect that has not been as widely recognized by scholars as it deserves, but it is an issue to which Weber devoted considerable attention.[68] Of course, the city is a phenomenon that dates to earliest antiquity, and cities have existed in civilizations other than the West. But Weber's thesis is that the occidental city, especially the city as it came into being in the later Middle Ages, was crucial for the development of modern capitalism.

The mediaeval city, which is the focus of Weber's attention, was not a development of the ancient city (*polis*). For Weber had already explained in earlier writings, such as the essay "The Social Causes of the Decline of Ancient Civilization" of 1896, that ancient culture and its urban infrastructure went into significant decline in the late Roman Empire. The mediaeval city is rather an outcome of the dissolution of what Weber calls the *Ständestaat*, which was a political formation that arose as a consequence of the growth of corporate bodies (estates or *stände*) that emerged with feudalism. When the estates degenerated in the later Middle Ages, certain corporative powers remained intact, and these became significant for mediaeval urban development.[69] The mediaeval city developed as a corporation, which included rights to impose laws, appoint officials, raise taxes and regulate commercial relations. Some of these features existed in antiquity, but the medieval city was distinctive in its autonomy and the structure of its political authority. In the classical *polis* of antiquity, rule was based on either military factors or religious exclusivity, whereas in the mediaeval case, especially in the producer cities of inland Europe, the concept of the corporation became crucial and was the basis of the political association. Nonetheless, mediaeval cities were not the

66 Ibid., p. 223.
67 Ibid., p. 226.
68 A general discussion of Weber's account the city in the context of later scholarship is Robert Holton, *Cities, Capitalism and Civilization*, Allen & Unwin, 1986.
69 On these developments see Gianfranco Poggi, *The Development of the Modern State: A Sociological Introduction*, Stanford University Press, 1978, pp. 36–60.

immediate occasion for the growth of modern capitalism, because not all mediaeval cities were economically based, and even those that were did not become capitalist in the modern sense.

Over time, mediaeval cities grew in autonomy and in autocephaly because of the weakness of the feudal lords who sought to control them. As the producer cities gained commercial and industrial power, the non-urban feudal authorities increasingly granted them concessions in the form of legal privileges. The cities that had gained a degree of autonomy sought to develop self-government and exploited the rivalries between the various contending seigniorial authorities. This had the consequence of undermining the existing relation between the town and the countryside. Weber is at pains to point out how the economic orientation of the burghers living in the cities produced a lifestyle totally at odds with that of the feudal knights. The burghers lacked all concern with honour and heroic asceticism and had more in common with life in the Church. Christianity played an important role in the way these cities evolved because of its devaluation of ritual barriers of birth, a product of the Paulian victory over Jewish Christianity. This is not to say the city became a part of the Church, but membership in the city community was restricted to those who were Christians. Strangers were not prevented from gaining membership, however, but those who could not participate in the Christian Eucharist, such as the Jews, were unable to gain acceptance and they thus remained "guest peoples" or pariahs. Of course, fraternization between Christian burghers did not impede the organization of various sub-associations and the emergence of status differences that eventually became highly significant.

The mediaeval city was by no means homogenous, but importantly for Weber the associations that formed within it were formally free and in the course of time, many religious, social, occupational and political groupings of various kinds developed. Although there were tendencies towards democracy and although citizenship rights were disseminated to a degree throughout the population, certain groups, such as the guilds, commonly came to have a dominant position as they sought to monopolize economic power. There were two important consequences of the guild system: although it was a system of inequality based on occupation, it nonetheless ignored status differences outside the city; and it constituted an impersonal associational grouping, unlike the lineage or sib group. The ultimate effect of all this from the point of view of the development of modern capitalism was that the mediaeval city dominated by the upper guilds meant the dominance of an urban stratum that was wholeheartedly engaged in largely economic activities including trade and industry. In this way they formed the germ of the modern bourgeois class. Subsequently, under pressure from the competition of the putting-out system the closed guild system was forced to increase its rationality by orienting itself more and more to the open market. A further consequence of the emergence of the bourgeoisie was that a new principal of organization and legitimization was born, namely the corporate form of secular association with its democratic ethos.

Aside from these political developments, the mediaeval city made important contributions to industry and forms of commerce. Weber says it gave rise to new legal institutions – such as the annuity bond, the stock certificate and the bill of exchange – that were important for later economic developments. It created the accounting practices that became crucial for the later evolution of double-entry bookkeeping. It also provided a precursor to the corporate form of business association in the form of the unlimited partnership. A further stage was reached in the evolution of society when the activities of the bourgeoisie were extended beyond the sphere of the immediate city and its surrounds. For this to occur it was necessary for the *Ständestaat* to be replaced by some kind of national state, the first form of which was the absolutist state. Under these circumstances, state policy first developed in the form of mercantilism, whereby economic policies were driven by the compromise in economic interests between the dominant bourgeois groups and the absolutist monarchs. This, however, was not conducive to market-oriented capitalism of the modern kind. But it did facilitate the increasing pursuit of profits of monopoly through the means of war and the provision of luxury goods. The latter phenomenon was gradually subject to a democratizing influence with the advent of mass production. In this way the urban bourgeoisie was transformed into a national bourgeoisie. Weber explains how the national bourgeoisie arose out of the unique situation of the European state system:

> The modern city was deprived of its freedom . . . [as it] came under the power of competing national states in a condition of perpetual struggle for power in peace or war. This competitive struggle created the largest opportunities for modern western capitalism. The separate states had to compete for mobile capital, which dictated to them the conditions under which it would assist them to power. Out of this alliance of the state with capital, dictated by necessity, arose the national citizen class, the bourgeoisie in the modern cense of the word. Hence it is the closed national state which afforded capitalism its chance for development – and as long as the national state does not give place to a world empire capitalism also will survive.[70]

The immediate preconditions of modern capitalism

Weber turns his attention specifically to the immediate causes of modern capitalism around Chapter 22 of his *General Economic History*. He embarks on his account with another definition of capitalism that at first sight appears straightforward and uncontroversial: "Capitalism is present wherever the industrial provision for the needs of a human group is carried out by the method of enterprise, irrespective of what need is involved."[71] This definition with its reference to "enterprise" appears to coincide with that of Schumpeter, though this agreement is not as complete as

70 GEH, p. 337.
71 Ibid., p. 275.

use of the term suggests, as we shall see. For Weber adds a qualification that is characteristic of his later concerns. "More specifically, a rational capitalistic establishment is one with capital accounting, that is, an establishment which determines its income yielding power by calculation according to the methods of modern bookkeeping and the striking of a balance. The device of the balance was first insisted upon by the Dutch theorist Simon Stevin in the year 1698."[72] We note that this definition coincides with that of the "Author's Introduction" of 1920 that will be discussed below. Weber notes that economies can be conducted along capitalistic lines to varying degrees; parts may be organized capitalistically and other parts on handicraft or manorial patterns. However,

> Today, in contrast with the greater part of the past, our everyday needs are supplied capitalistically. . . . A whole epoch can be designated as typically capitalistic only as the provision for wants is capitalistically organized to such a predominant degree that if we imagine this form of organization taken away the whole economic system must collapse.[73]

This penetration of the provision of everyday needs by capitalism, a characteristic that is given emphasis also in Marx's theory, is therefore a defining feature of the modern form of capitalism: "Such capitalistic beginnings as are found in earlier centuries were merely anticipatory, and even the somewhat capitalistic establishments of the sixteenth century may be removed in thought from the economic life of the time without introducing any overwhelming change."[74]

The advent of the factory

Marx made what he thought was an important distinction between the "factory" and "manufactory". Manufactory was described as shop industry with free labour without the use of mechanical power but with the workers grouped and disciplined. Weber claims this distinction is casuistic and of doubtful value. He says that a factory is shop industry with free labour and fixed capital. The nature of the fixed capital is indifferent; it may consist of horsepower or a water mill. The critical factor in the advent of the factory proper is that the entrepreneur operates with fixed capital and he says for this to happen capital accounting is required. Thus, the factory, in this sense signifies the capitalistic organization of the process of production, that is, an organization of specialized and coordinated work within a workshop using fixed capital and capital accounting. Weber says the economic prerequisite for the existence of the factory is mass and steady demand: that is, a certain development of the market. A highly volatile market is totally unfavourable for the entrepreneur owing to his location at the conjuncture between supply and

72 Ibid.
73 Ibid., pp. 275–6.
74 Ibid., p. 276.

demand; he cannot take the risk of embarking on a process of production oriented to mass demand if there is no reasonable prospect of the effort being fruitful. The entrepreneur must be especially mindful to cover the costs of his fixed capital, which will only be discharged over a period of time when the proceeds generated by the operation of the enterprise are sufficient to lay down those costs. Thus, the market must be large enough to sustain a sizable scale of production and relatively constant. These market conditions require a certain level of monetarization of the economy and adequate purchasing power in the hands of consumers, all of which depend upon the reliability of the monetary system. A further prerequisite is that the technical process of production should be relatively inexpensive, because in order to establish himself and find a steady market, the capitalist must produce more cheaply than traditional methods of household production. Hence, at the advent of capitalism, the goods produced were generally simple items of mass consumption; only later did a more extensive capitalist system enable sophisticated innovations to occur that enabled forms of production that would have been unthinkable before the capitalist era.

A further prerequisite for the development of capitalism is the presence of a sufficient supply of free labour. Weber is adamant that rational capitalism is not possible on the basis of slave labour. Only in the West was a sufficient supply of free labour available. In this regard Weber seems to agree, at least in part, with Marx that it was the eviction of the peasantry from their rural holdings in the seventeenth century England that provided the quantities of free labour required. Weber suggests that the peasantry suffered expropriation in England in part because of the country's insular geography, which meant it did not need a standing army and thus did not require social policies designed to protect the peasantry as the basis of a national army. As early as the sixteenth century, he points out the supply of free labour from the eviction of the peasantry was of such a scale to cause policies to be implemented to deal with poor relief.

According to Weber, the industry of the craft guilds did not form a direct antecedent to factory production because it was largely carried on without fixed capital. The first forms of fixed capital of note were mills owned by lords or sometimes owned communally. There were various types – saw mills, water mills, oil presses, grain mills, fulling mills – but these were not directly related to capitalist developments, because they were not owned by the participating groups, and unlike the stock company they were leased out as sources of rent. Similar arrangements have applied to ovens and breweries. Iron foundries were initially owned municipally because of their significance for the production of artillery cannons. The municipal foundries were not capitalistic but produced directly for the military requirements of the princes who owned them. Only in the sixteenth century do we find the beginnings of industrial production operating capitalistically, in the sense that there were establishments of a private economic character in which a single owner had possession of the work place, tools and raw materials. At that time there arose the first establishments that involved the concentration of workers in a single room with some specialization of function. As such, they appear in many respects similar to the *ergasterion* of ancient times.

In the *ergasterion* the workers are slaves, whereas in the early factory the workers, though not bound formally, are nonetheless subject to forces that oblige them to work. Labourers attach themselves to these establishments from a compulsion generated out of poverty, having no other choice in fear of the absolute impossibility of finding other sources of livelihood. Weber refers to the organization of a workshop in England in the sixteenth century in which there were two hundred looms in one room, all belonging to an enterpriser who furnished the raw materials. The workers worked for wages and children were also present. Interestingly, in 1555, at the behest of the guilds, the king forbade such concentrations, but by the early eighteenth century suppressing such large establishments was no longer considered. The concentration of work in a single workplace was important because it made control over the uniformity of the product and the quantity of output possible. But concentrating in one place increased the risk that the entire fixed capital could be lost in a single catastrophe, and it was vulnerable to violent reaction on the part of the employees. At the start, workshops are really little more than a concentration of a number of small productive units within a single premise. But after the sixteenth century, these establishments are progressively transformed into factories.

Weber tells us a new stage in the evolution of capitalism occurred when technical specialization and the systematic organization of work began to be combined with the use of non-human sources of power. Non-human sources of power had traditionally been available in the form of primitive animal power, and there had been prior uses of some natural forces such as water and wind. Windmills had been an early use of air power for the pumping of water, but the real impetus for the use of non-human power came with developments in mining, in particular the use of devices for pumping water out of deep mines. As we have already said, a prerequisite for the transition from shop industry to the factory was the development of an extensive demand for the goods produced. For this reason Weber says one of the first places in which one finds an internal division of labour with fixed capital was in the political domain, the minting works of mediaeval princes, but of course, this was supplying only one type of good. The political demand for mass-produced goods was also felt in the military area in the manufacture of weapons and uniforms for the army. The first occasions where there appeared a demand for mass consumer goods of the kind we are familiar with today, that is, of goods for use by ordinary people in their everyday lives, was for various kinds of "luxury" goods. Weber points to the mass production of tapestries that became common after the crusades to cover the bare walls and floors of luxury houses. There were also establishments for the production of glass, mirrors, silk, velvet, fine cloth, soap and sugar. Only subsequently were goods produced for the broader masses, and these were, in the first place, imitations of luxury goods previously destined only for the rich. Also in this category were items such as glues, starch and chicory. When production was destined for the rich, the market was not sufficiently extensive to sustain a series of enterprises competing and producing on a very large scale. Hence, production was monopolistic, for the arms factories and tapestry works of the early industrial period began as a series of privileged manufacturers under royal tutelage. The legal position of these early enterprises was complicated because of the antagonism of the guilds. In order to be established, exemptions were required from the guilds whose privileges did not always cover the entire town. Consequently, factories had to be established in special domains outside guild jurisdiction. In England the guilds were municipal bodies, which meant guild law had no sway outside town boundaries; therefore, many early factories were established in places that were not in towns.

According to Weber, the factory did not at first develop out of simple craftwork or at the expense of it but existed alongside it. Factories developed new forms of production and new products like cotton, porcelain and coloured brocade – goods that substituted for luxury consumption items. Only later did factories enter into the domains of the guilds. Factories did not develop out of the domestic system either but again grew up alongside it. Where fixed capital was not needed the domestic system endured, but where and when it was required factories arose. Originally communal institutions operating with fixed capital were gradually taken over by entrepreneurs and used for the mass production of consumer goods. The factory was not at first, in its earliest stages, spurred on and developed because of the invention of machines. Machines originally made use of horsepower, but the specialization of work and labour discipline were predisposing conditions that greatly aided the use of machines – a classic example is the use of steam power.[75] Weber's point here is that the rationalizing of the process of production was the decisive development, not the fortuitous invention of useful devices – a point that both complements Schumpeter's views about innovation but also partly distinguishes Weber's approach because of the latter's emphasis on the rationalizing element.

The role of the state

To highlight the significance of the modern state for the rise of capitalism, Weber at one point contrasts the state in the West with the Chinese state of the old regime, based on the rule of a stratum of officials called mandarins. Mandarins were primarily humanistically educated *literati* who enjoyed the position of a benefice but were not trained for administration. Everything was based on magical theory, so that the virtue of the empress and the merits of the officials would keep society in order. Essentially things were left to take care of themselves. Clearly rational capitalism cannot exist under these conditions. It is only under a rational state that an expert officialdom can provide the preconditions for rational capitalism.

The state is initially crucial for Weber's theory because it is the state that breaks down the feudal system with its patrimonialism and traditionalism. It is the modern state, further, that pacifies large areas to make them suitable for trade and industry

75 A good account of this era of European economic history from the perspective of a contemporary historian is Jan De Vries, *The Economy of Europe in an Age of Crisis, 1600–1750*, Cambridge University Press, 1976.

and eliminates internal barriers to market exchange. It creates predictable circumstances in its standardization of taxation and in its promotion of a reliable monetary system. But Weber does not believe that the advent of a bureaucratic state of just any kind is sufficient to bring about capitalism, because in societies such as China and Ancient Egypt a bureaucratic structure emerged that in effect stifled the development of a free market economy. The kind of bureaucratization Weber says is favourable to capitalism is that which incorporates a formalistic legal code based on citizenship. Citizenship means membership of a city, and eventually membership of a state, and this means individual political rights.

Weber explains that formal citizenship rights originally applied to only the local elites when such rights were attached to the existence of small city states; however, when these cities were incorporated into large states, they provided the basis for more widely inclusive system of adjudication. This is what had begun to emerge in the case of Rome, which introduced universal citizenship under the emperor Caracalla, but it did not survive the decline of the Empire. Citizenship emerged again later in the Middle Ages when the cities in alliance with kings lost their independence but contributed their legal structures to the constitution of these states.

The modern state, which is governed by rationalized rules and related norms of conduct as the basis on which the officials make decisions, arose, at least on the formal side, with the revival of Roman law. Roman law then played a role in the development of the modern state because classical ideas about the legitimacy of the state were influential throughout Europe and America from the Renaissance onwards. But Weber is quick to point out that most of the substantive legal requirements of modern capitalism were not Roman in origin. The Roman and Greek courts administered what Weber terms a "petty justice": the litigants worked on the judge with pathos, tears and the abuse of their opponents. But in civil trials, the praetor appointed a *iudex* or judge, and strict instructions were given requiring a judgement against the accused or acquittal. Eventually, Weber explains, "Under Justinian the Byzantine bureaucracy brought order and system into this rational law, in consequence of the natural interest of the official in a law which would be systematic and fixed and hence easier to learn."[76] Later, around the twelfth century, Roman law came into the hands of Italian notaries. These individuals and secondarily the universities are responsible for the revival of Roman law, which led to the subsequent influence of Roman law on European Law and the transformation of the latter into Civil Law. Roman law was progressively reinterpreted according to the needs of the time, and the universities developed systematic legal doctrine. An essential feature of all this was the rationalization of legal procedure. German law picked up on the formalism of Roman law, which had an affinity with its own primitive trial procedure. The French borrowed the idea of the representative or advocate. The Catholic Church was also attracted to many of these features, and out of its association with Roman institutions it developed Canon Law. The Church

76 GEH, p. 340.

utilized strict Roman forms for disciplinary matters in relation to the laity and its own internal order. But the businessman could not permit his claims to be decided by a rigidly formal procedure involving reciting formulas. Weber says that businessmen sought and were often granted exemption from formalistic legal contests and ordeals everywhere. The Church also eventually abandoned its excessively legalistic procedure.

Paradoxically given the rationalism of Roman law, Weber downplays its significance for the development of modern capitalism, because in England, which he designates the birthplace of capitalism, Roman law was never accepted – though it did have some influence as is known in legal education and legal theory.[77] The reason Roman law was not taken up in England was because in the royal courts there existed a class of advocates who protected the national institutions against corruption and who controlled the development of legal doctrine. From its ranks were chosen, and still are chosen, the judges. The dominance of the Common Law advocates prevented Roman law from being taught in universities, and this meant an academic form of recruitment to the judiciary never developed. The crucial point is that all the characteristic legal institutions of modern capitalism have origins other than in Roman law: the annuity bond came from mediaeval law; similarly, the stock certificate rose out of mediaeval law; and the bill of exchange was developed from Arabic, Italian, German and English influences. The commercial company is also mediaeval in origin, only the *commenda* sea loan has an ancient origin. Likewise, the mortgage with security registration and deed of trust, and the power of attorney are all derived from mediaeval times.

Thus the key role of the state in fostering modern capitalism was its function of guaranteeing the performance of contractual obligations. This issue has given rise to numerous works on the topic in recent years in relation to what has been termed the "credible commitments" problem.[78] Weber does not address this issue directly but seems to take it for granted that modern states one way or another gradually came to deal with this.

In what follows we shall briefly explore Weber's account of how law, in particular contract law, developed so as to facilitate capitalist enterprise proper.

The legal preconditions of modern capitalism

Weber's complete account of the role of law for the development of capitalism is complicated and involved. It is largely expounded in Chapter Eight of *Economy and Society*, "The Sociology of Law", though this chapter treats the

77 This is what some commentators have referred to as the "England problem", an issue that arises because the most rational system of law was evidently not conducive to the development of rational law. See David Trubeck, "Max Weber on Law and the Rise of Capitalism", *Wisconsin Law Review*, 3, (1973), pp. 720–53.

78 See the discussion in Ron Harris, "Spread of Legal Innovations Defining Private and Public Domains", in Charles Camic, Philip S. Gorski, and David M. Trubek (eds.), *Max Weber's Economy and Society: A Critical Companion*, Stanford University Press, 2005, pp. 127–68.

field of law broadly and is at the same time an historical inquiry concerning the development of law as an institution. In what follows, we shall attempt to limit our discussion to those aspects that are of significance for the theory of capitalism that is our focus.

A key presupposition of Weber's approach to law is that he resolutely rejects the idea that economic circumstances could, by their own force, give birth to new legal forms, as implied by much Marxist thought that construes law as a superstructural reflex of underlying economic conditions. For Weber, the rationality of law and the rationality of economic affairs, though related, are nonetheless distinct phenomena. The history of law must be treated as having its own unique course of development, however much economic interests have from time to time influenced legal ideas.

At the outset Weber distinguishes public law and private law. He defines public law as the total body of those norms that regulate state-oriented action. In contrast, private law is crucial for capitalism because capitalist economic activity, particularly the sale and purchase of goods and inter-business relations, are facilitated and smoothed by the rules of private law.[79] Obviously contracts in a general sense, meaning voluntary agreements constituting the basis for claims and obligations, have become very widely diffused. In business, exchange is typically construed as a legal transaction, namely, the acquisition, transfer, relinquishment or fulfilment of a legal claim. Weber insists that while the extensive development of freedom of contract has largely coincided with the advance of capitalist institutions of the modern kind, this outcome cannot be reduced to the effect of economic factors, as in Marxist theory. Even so, with every extension of the market, legal transactions become more numerous and intricate, and the development of the market and capitalist economic arrangements have generally greatly facilitated expansion of the scope of contractual relations per se. Weber notes that it is entirely natural that bourgeois strata should have demanded an unambiguous and reliable legal apparatus that functions calculably and have thus promoted such developments. As he points out, "Every rational business organization needs the possibility of acquiring contractual rights and of assuming obligations through temporary or permanent agents. Advanced trade moreover needs not only the possibility of transferring legal claims but also and quite particularly a method by which such transfers can be made legally secure and which eliminates the need of constantly testing the title of the transferor."[80]

79 Weber contrasts the dichotomy between public and private law in modern societies with the situation in primitive societies where crime and tort are not distinguished; procedure does not vary whether the suit is about a piece of land or a homicide. In these societies there was often no official machinery to enforce judgements, it being sufficient simply that a judgement has been determined. The assumption is that magical forces will do whatever is necessary to enforce the judgement. It is only with the advent of the state as a compulsory association with a staff to carry out enforcement that the legal order becomes routine and reliable.

80 Weber, Max, *Economy and Society: An Outline of Interpretive Sociology*. Bedminster Press, 1968 (ES), pp. 681–2.

In discussing the origins of modern contract law, Weber posits a key distinction between "status contracts" and "purposive contracts". In early times, all contracts were status contracts, and contracts were of little or no significance in economic affairs. The distinction between status contracts and purposive contracts is based on the fact that primitive contracts involve a change in what Weber calls the total legal situation and social status of the persons involved. Such primitive contracts are typically secured by the threat of the imposition of magical sanctions, but, as the notion of the divinity replaces animism, the oath appears as a person's conditional self-surrender to evil magical forces.

Despite its origins, the oath was important for the rise of purposive contracts. This is because the oath was technically suited as a guarantee that obligations entered into would be honoured. Insofar as economic barter existed, this was usually confined to transactions with persons who were not members of one's own household or were outsiders. Weber claims that a formal legal construction of barter did not begin to occur until goods such as metals took on a monetary function. Prior to this stage, the various forms of contract were all oriented towards the total social status of the individual and his integration within an association. Such contracts with their all-inclusive rights and duties and special attitudinal qualities are in marked contrast to the money contract that is quantitatively delimited and is quality-less.

Weber says that primitive contracts were gradually transformed from obligations of a delictual nature, as disputes over land became more common. Initially, in the early military associations like the ancient polis, disputes about ownership of a farm (*fundus* or *kleros*) assumed the form of a bilateral dispute. Typically such disputes turned on the rights of an individual by virtue of their membership of a group. Nobody could steal a farm because nobody could steal from a person his status as a member of the group. Hence, disputes about land and disputes about status emerged alongside unilateral tort action, such as the Roman *vindicatio*, which was an action concerned to establish one's legitimate claim over a parcel of land against a competing claim. Gradually, out of such disputes the concept of contractual obligation emerged. One of the earliest forms in which an obligation was acknowledged as arising from a purposive contract was the obligation to pay a debt arising from a loan. The loan was originally an interest free form of emergency aid amongst brothers. At first there was no way of enforcing a loan other than by magical means, by shaming or by other forms of social pressure such as the boycott. But gradually a unified law of obligations arose from the action of tort. Weber says the entry of money into economic life was decisive for contractual development. Both primitive forms of contract in Roman law, the debt contract *per aes et libram* and the debt contract by the symbolic pledge *stipulatio*, were money contracts, but the development of contract law in Roman times was cut short by the demise of ancient capitalism and the collapse of the Empire.

Weber explains that before the emergence of the purposive contract and the advent of the doctrine of freedom of contract, any action that represented something akin to a lawsuit would take place only in the form of proceedings between different groups. Subjection to special law was, in these circumstances, a strictly personal quality, a "privilege" acquired by usurpation or grant.[81] Roman law was at first the law solely for Roman citizens (*ius civile*). Only later did it develop *ius gentium* owing to the need for common legal principles in the relations between Roman citizens and their neighbours. Law was not truly *lex terrae* until after the Norman conquest, when English law became the law of the king's court and Common Law came into being. The situation changed with the development of the modern state that rests on formal legal equality. The two great rationalizing forces that fostered this change were the extension of the market economy and bureaucratization of public administration.[82]

As trial procedure became more and more formal and fixed, the occasions on which incidental transactions could create contractual obligations increased. Originally, the liability for a contracted debt was not a personal liability of one's assets but a liability of the debtor's physical body and it alone. There was no execution upon the debtor's assets, but execution could be had upon the person, who could even be killed or imprisoned as a hostage or held as a bond-servant or slave. Economic contracts at first related only to changes in the possession of goods. Hence, all legal transactions were connected to legal forms of a transfer of possession, often resting on magical conceptions. Legal thought did not recognize intangible phenomena such as promises but was interested only in the wrong, that is, a misdeed against the gods or a person's life and wellbeing. To be legally relevant the contract had to involve tangible goods.[83] An important way in which new contractual actions arose was out of actions *ex delicto*. By this action the non-performance of a promise was characterized as a harm requiring compensation. Thus, in England the royal courts increasingly construed non-performance as a trespass to be dealt by the writ of assumpsit. Out of these beginnings, Common Law gradually developed the extensive system of contract law that we know today.

Weber's final statement on the role of Protestant ethic

As mentioned earlier, Randal Collins has questioned whether, in his later work, Weber still retained his view regarding the role of Protestantism in the origins of capitalism. In what follows, we shall briefly consider the final chapter of his *General Economic History* where the issue of the spirit of capitalism is again addressed, some fourteen years after the original thesis was elaborated in 1904–5.

In this section of the book Weber again argues that the mere release of economic interest from traditional or religious restraints cannot explain the rise of the modern economic order. He refers to Cortez and Pizarro as classic embodiments of the unchaining of the pursuit of riches, but these individuals were only exemplars of

81 Ibid., p. 696.

82 Ibid., p. 698.

83 Thus arose the principal that only purposive contracts involving payments could be binding, and this remains, to this day, the basis for the English doctrine of consideration as being an essential element of all contracts.

irrational adventure capitalism. He says that early societies typically maintained two contradictory attitudes to wealth. Internally, there are traditionalistic and pious relations with fellow members that prohibit an unrestricted pursuit of gain between the members of the clan or household community; however, externally there is an unlimited pursuit of gain, every foreigner being treated as effectively an enemy to whom there is no ethical restraint in taking advantage.[84] But with the course of development there are fundamental changes in this dualistic in-group and out-group morality.

On the one hand, when accountability for household income and expenses arose, calculation entered into the traditional brotherhood and displaced the old communistic relationships. Simultaneously with this, there was a moderation of the unrestricted pursuit of gain, and this led to a regulated economic life that operates within boundaries. Weber says the beginnings of a change are first registered around the fifteenth century, in Renaissance Florence. Up to this point, the typical attitude of Catholic ethics was hostile to any acquisitive activity because of the impersonality such relations implied, meaning they could not be regulated by ethical dictates. But the obverse of this was that Catholicism placed economic affairs largely outside the influence of the Church. Thus, whereas the relationship between a master and a slave could be ethically regulated, the relations between the mortgage creditor and the mortgagee or between the endorser and the bill of exchange could not be subject to moralization.[85]

Following ideas he had developed about religious institutions in *Economy and Society*, Weber sets out a difference between "virtuoso" and "mass" religiosity. Virtuoso religious practice is only significant as an example, for its demands are too high for conduct of the masses. In Catholicism, this problem between the two realms led to a division between the monks and priests vis-à-vis the laity. But this had the consequence that the more worthy individuals who lived most in accordance with the teachings of Christ, namely the monks, had necessarily to withdraw from the world in separate communities. Thus their impact on the world in which the masses carried on their everyday affairs was, as a necessity, very limited. Even so, monks rationalized their lives in various ways, often by working methodically and by pursuing their goal of a holy life through systematic means of an ascetic character. However, the Church's effect on the average individual of the Middle Ages was merely to domesticate them by channelling their concerns about sin through the release gained by the confessional. But it had no rationalizing effect and merely enforced traditional attitudes to life and work. In its desire to maintain authority, the Church spread its grace over both the just and the unjust. The

84 This issue is the subject of Benjamin Nelson, *The Idea of Usury: From Tribal Brotherhood to Universal Otherhood*, Princeton University Press, 1949.

85 The impact on capitalist development of this enabling of prohibited economic activity cannot be attributed to the role of the Jews, as Sombart had claimed. Sombart's theory concerning the role of the Jews is set out in his *The Jews and Modern Capitalism*, Collier, 1962. Weber's most thorough discussion of the relation of Judaism and the Jews to capitalism is contained in his "Sociology of Religion" in ES, pp. 611–15.

Reformation brought by Luther changed all this. The Reformation meant the elimination of the dualistic system of ethics and of the distinction between a universally binding morality of low ethical demands and a special, more demanding code for the virtuosi. The asceticism oriented to other-worldly concerns typical of the monasteries was also ended: "The stern religious characters who had previously gone into monasteries now had to practice their religion in the life of the world."[86]

The Reformation allowed no flight from the world but regarded working in the world in a disciplined and methodical way as a basic religious task for the individual believer. From these ideas came the notion of the "calling", which expresses the importance of rational activity carried on within a capitalistic world as fulfilling God's directions. As Weber summarizes,

> This development of the concept of a calling quickly gave to the modern entrepreneur a fabulously clear conscience – and also industrious workers; he gave to his employees as the wages of their ascetic devotion to the calling and of a co-operation in his ruthless exploitation of them through capitalism the prospect of eternal salvation, which in an age when ecclesiastical discipline took control of the whole of life to an extent inconceivable to us now, represented a reality quite different from any it has today. . . . such a powerful, unconsciously refined organisation for the production of capitalistic individuals has never existed in any other church or religion and in comparison with it what the Renaissance did for capitalism shrinks into insignificance.[87]

From the above, it is clear that Weber did not alter his position about the role of Protestantism in the rise of capitalism, as he restates the original argument without any apparent alteration. Of course, further proof of this, if it were needed, is given in the fact that Weber authorized the republication of the *Protestant Ethic* essays of 1904–05 without substantial change, though he added further footnotes and the important "Author's Introduction", which provided broader context.

In the next chapter, we shall turn to Weber's account of the institutional structure of modern capitalism and his construction of various ideal types that he posits as a way of comprehending the phenomenon. We bear in mind that in constructing his ideal type of rational capitalism the account of origins that we have just surveyed is always in the background and in a sense is a subtext to the theory.

86 GEH, p. 366.
87 Ibid., p. 368.

2 Weber's later account of modern capitalism

Having surveyed Weber's writings that deal with the origins and ethos of modern capitalism, we shall now address his later work concerning the structural characteristics of capitalism once it has emerged into its mature phase. In theorizing modern capitalism, we presume Weber generally has in mind the capitalism he knew from his familiarity with developments in England, America and Europe in the late nineteenth and early twentieth century. But though his account of the origins of capitalism was based primarily on the case of England, and to a lesser extent America, his account of fully developed capitalism seems to rely as much on the example of the Germany of his day.[1] Below we shall focus primarily on Weber's major work *Economy and Society*, especially the sections in which he advances his economic sociology.

Given his definition of modern capitalism as profit-making activity oriented to the exploitation of opportunities offered by the market, the question arises as to how this type of action is possible on a scale that enables mass production and the creation of a capitalistic social system at large. In what follows we shall attempt to describe and analyze the matrix of sociological factors that Weber argues must exist in order for a rational capitalist system to reach its ultimate possibility of development. We shall need to consider his various analyses of the business enterprise, the market system and capitalist profit-making. These basic institutions form a complex structure in which the elements are intimately interconnected. And clearly Weber's account of the origins of capitalism remains in the background, as his thinking about contemporary phenomena is never detached from awareness of the historical antecedents.

1 Weber appears to have partly relied on his familiarity with the business of his uncle Carl David Weber for insights into modern business practices. His uncle was an industrialist who ran a linen weaving factory at Oerlinghausen near Bielefeld. On the influence of this association on Weber's thinking, see Peter Ghosh, *Max Weber's Protestant Ethic: Twin Histories*, Oxford University Press, 2014, pp. 69–75. Curiously, given the centrality of England in *The Protestant Ethic*, Weber does not appear to have based his analysis in *Economy and Society* on the case of the Industrial Revolution in England.

Marginal utility theory

Before we embark on a detailed exegesis of Weber's economic sociology, we shall first consider his relation to Marginal Theory Utility. We have already alluded to his recognition of this as a fundamental principle of modern economics, but to what extent did he accept it? At the outset there is clearly one aspect where he disagreed: he did not accept that the principle was a universal law valid for all times. But as a tool for analyzing contemporary capitalism, he regarded it as indispensable. How was this so?

Weber's acceptance of marginal utility theory was a part of his broad recognition that modern economics is necessary for the mastery of socio-historical reality and that, against Schmoller, history could not progress if it remained "untheoretical". He thus rejected Schmoller's insistence that history did not require theory because the facts "speak for themselves". Weber believed that without theory historical understanding would be lost in an infinite chaos of unorganized empirical data.

At least from the time of the "Objectivity" essay of 1904, Weber considered that marginal utility theory could be readily absorbed into his own methodological procedures by considering it an ideal type. Indeed, the theory and its use by economists is an exemplary illustration of the method of ideal type analysis. The idealized conduct described by the theory need not be presumed to correspond precisely with real phenomena, but it was eminently useable as a model with which to compare and describe empirical reality.

The essence of marginal utility theory lies in the counterintuitive idea that the values at which goods and services are exchanged in a modern capitalist economy do not depend on the amount of labour, land and capital embodied in them but on the subjective estimates individuals make of their needs in the context of their perception of the scarcity of available resources.[2] In Weber's analysis of marginal utility theory in his 1908 essay "Marginal Utility Theory and the Fundamental Law of Psychophysics" he echoes Menger and the other Austrians when he states:

> Men – be it in ever so varying degrees – are able to act "expediently", that is, in the light of "experience" and of "prior calculation". This means to act in such a fashion that they allocate the quantitatively limited "goods" and "labour powers", which they can dispose of or obtain, to the particular "needs" of the present and of the foreseeable future according to the importance they attach to this present and future.[3]

2 The term "marginal utility" was first coined by Friedrich Wieser and then adopted by Menger and Bohm Bäwerk: see Anthony Endres, *Neoclassical Microeconomic Theory: The Founding Austrian Version*, Routledge, 1997, pp. 41–59. It is noteworthy that Wieser's lengthy article on "Social Economics" was placed at the beginning of Weber's *Grundriss*.

3 Ibid., p. 29.

More than this, rationality underlies the conduct so described:

> Marginal utility theory . . . treats human action as if it ran its course from beginning to end under the control of commercial calculation – a calculation set up on the basis of all conditions that need to be considered. It treats individual "needs" and the goods available . . . for their satisfaction as mathematically calculable "sums" and "amounts" in a continuous process of bookkeeping.[4]

Of course Weber does not assume that all needs are naturally given, and notes how they are regularly subject to influence by producers. Consumption desires can be "awakened" and may be significantly manipulated by entrepreneurs – and as we shall see, in the work of Schumpeter this is an absolutely necessary and regular feature of capitalism flowing from the drive of entrepreneurs to achieve new and ever more lucrative avenues of profit.[5]

The theory of marginal utility suited Weber's predilection to interpret social phenomena in terms of the subjective meaning individuals give their actions; at the same time it could explain how complex socio-economic phenomena come into being from such individualistic presuppositions – such as price formation through market exchange. Further, as Ghosh argues, the theory also dovetailed with the thesis of *The Protestant Ethic* in that "Protestant restraint is consonant with the marginalist model because both represent a sophisticated, individual calculation of value."[6] But Weber went to considerable lengths to insist that the validity of the theory owes nothing to psychology, nor does it constitute a fundamental immutable law; that after all was the main point of his essay. As long as it was not treated as an immutable law, the theory that could greatly assist historical research, which must always remain cognizant of the unique individuality of its objects of study.

Now, contrary to the gist of these considerations, according to Weber the marginal utility theory had become more and more pertinent to the interpretation of socio-economic phenomena in the modern era because the conduct of the capitalist entrepreneur and the modern consumer increasingly coincide with the idealized action schematized in the principle. Indeed Weber argued that,

> The historical distinctiveness of the capitalist epoch, and thereby also the significance of marginal utility theory . . . for the understanding of this epoch, rests on the circumstance that . . . under today's conditions of existence the approximation of reality to theoretical propositions of economics has been a *constantly increasingly* one. It is an approximation to reality that has

4 Max Weber, "Marginal Utility Theory and 'The Fundamental Law of Psychophysics'", *Social Science Quarterly*, 56.1, (1975), pp. 31–2.

5 ES, p. 92.

6 Peter Ghosh, "'Robinson Crusoe', the *Isolated Economic Man*: Marginal Utility Theory and the 'Spirit' of Capitalism", in Peter Ghosh (ed.), *A Historian Reads Max Weber*, Harrassowitz Verlag, 2008, p. 278.

> implicated the destiny of ever wider layers of humanity. And it will hold more widely, as far as our horizons allow us to see. The heuristic significance of marginal utility theory rests on this *cultural-historical* fact.[7]

Weber goes on to suggest that stock exchange represents a particularly telling case where theory and realty almost completely coincide.

> It is, for example, no accident that an especially striking degree of approximation to the theoretical propositions of price formation (as Böhm-Bawerk, connecting his work with that of Menger, developed them) has been represented by the fixing of the Berlin market rate . . . This Berlin situation could serve directly as a paradigm for the theoretical propositions.[8]

But having recognized the relevance of marginalism in modern economics and in economic reality, Weber does not consider it sufficient for his theory of capitalism, for there are distinct limitations on the extent to which capitalism is entirely rational and can be understood in accordance with the schema. This is the case especially as regards entrepreneurial conduct and profit-making, as we shall see.

The theory of modern capitalism in *Economy and Society*

Whether or not one considers *Economy and Society* to be Weber's magnum opus, the work undoubtedly contains much of his mature thinking on the nature of capitalist enterprise and the market system generally. In the section entitled "Sociological Categories of Economic Action", he expounds an extensive array of concepts and ideal type theories that are ostensibly designed to provide the framework for a general sociology of economic life. Yet the nature of modern capitalism is a central concern of the entire section, as we shall see. And throughout other parts of *Economy and Society*, in "The Sociology of Law", in the sections dealing with class and status, and in the chapters on "The City" and "Bureaucracy", the issue of capitalism is never far from his concern.

Starting out from his general concept of "social action", Weber first develops a series of ideal types that deal specifically with "economic action" and its vicissitudes. It is apparent that he seeks to show that capitalist economic activity is economic action par excellence owing to the fact that in its ideal typical form it embodies rational features of a distinctive kind. But at the same time, he wants to explain the sociological preconditions and essential elements of this type of action. He builds up a series of concepts and distinctions that explores the extensive ramifications of the capitalist type of action and, at the same time, he seeks to explain what capitalism opposes or supplants and what its human costs might be.

7 Weber, "Marginal Utility Theory and 'The Fundamental Law of Psychophysics'", p. 33.
8 Ibid.

A recent introduction to the treatment of economics and economic sociology in *Economy and Society* is an essay by Richard Swedberg entitled "Max Weber's Economic Sociology: The Centrepiece of *Economy and Society*?"[9] Swedberg argues that the section on economy in Chapter II is the key to Weber's magnum opus. Perhaps this is overstating the case, as the hypothetical question mark suggests, though the proposition is certainly arguable. Swedberg emphasizes the large scope of the discussions in Chapter II of *Economy and Society*, which he says constitutes the core of Weber's economic sociology. In what follows we shall review and discuss the various sub-sections of "Sociological Categories of Economic Action" with a view to show how they, in effect, form the basis for an elaborate ideal type theory of modern capitalism.

Formal and substantive rationality

Pivotal to Weber's sociology is the fundamental distinction he makes between "formal rationality" and "substantive rationality", so the origins of this distinction warrant a brief discussion. According to Ghosh, the concept of the "rational" is found in Weber's earliest thinking about economics, even prior to *The Protestant Ethic*, but there it was employed mainly to describe economic theory. But in *The Protestant Ethic* the concept of "rationalism" is taken up and reworked, such that, in Ghosh's view, it even begins to displace "capitalism" as Weber's pivotal concept.[10] From his earliest writings, Weber had recognized that in the capitalist orientation of conduct there was a pre-occupation with "calculation", a feature that has distinctive "formal" properties. At the same time, being a trained lawyer, Weber was aware of the promotion of "formalism" in modern law, especially by the Pandectist legal movement, which emphasized system and logical consistency. These ideas seem to have led Weber to the recognition that any area of human conduct might be guided by, or adapted to, formal schemata of some kind – that is, where action is guided by the intellect following rules that have been constructed in accordance with a formal procedure of some sort. Importantly, Weber's use of the term "rational" does not overlap with the liberal notion of "reason", with its naïve assumption of normative goodness or rightness; rather what is rational is a purely technical matter that can be "perfected" only in a formal or logical sense and is thus devoid of ideal content.[11] Yet, on the other hand, Weber is aware that rationalism of a kind is also prominent in religious thought, especially in the creation of values connected to worldviews and theological conceptions (theodicies). But today there is no prospect of returning to a world in which a unified worldview

9 Charles Camic, Philip S. Gorski and David M. Trubek, *Max Weber's Economy and Society: A Critical Companion*, Stanford University Press, 2005, pp. 127–42. Swedberg notes that the section contains some 150 pages of text divided into forty-one sections, and in some sense, it could be said to be a work in its own right.

10 Ghosh, *Max Weber and the Protestant Ethic*, pp. 15–17.

11 Weber specifically rejects the idea that capitalist rationality can be deduced from a general rationalization of society arising from the "reason" of the Enlightenment. See PE, pp. 76–7.

such as existed in the past, because religious (and now secular) rationalizing processes are undertaken according to the most varied ultimate values and lead in different directions. To deal with the apparent contradictions between the various values posited by rationalized worldviews and the divergent requirements of the rational structures in the world, Weber advances the distinction between "formal" and "substantive" rationality.

This distinction is of considerable significance in Weber's account of the nature of modern capitalism (not to mention his approach to modernity in general). He defines the "formal rationality" of economic action as "the extent to which quantitative calculation or accounting is technically possible and is actually applied". By contrast, "substantive rationality" is "the degree to which the provisioning of a given group of persons (no matter how delimited) with goods is shaped by economically oriented social action under some criterion (past, present, or potential) of ultimate values (*wertende Postulate*), regardless of the nature of those ends."[12] As regards formally rational economic action, Weber says the extent of formal rationality will be dependent upon the degree to which the provision of needs in the economy "is capable of being expressed in numerical calculable terms and is so expressed."[13] The technical form in which these calculations take place, whether in money or in kind, is not decisive; however, the highest degree of rationality requires the use of money. As regards substantive rationality, Weber emphasizes the fact that there are many value points of view from which an economy or an economic action can be evaluated; and there is no scientific/objective way to determine which is best.

Thus, even though in *The Protestant Ethic* Weber highlights the rationality of conduct engendered by Puritan asceticism, he also recognizes that the resulting extreme acquisitiveness – whereby man exists for his business and not the other way round – is, at the same time, "irrational" (from a "natural" point of view). Weber clearly saw modern capitalism as involving very serious negative effects, at least from certain value points of view, as can be gleaned from the famous concluding remarks in *The Protestant Ethic*: "This nullity imagines it has attained a level of civilization never before achieved."[14] Or consider the following statement: "There is not the shadow of plausibility in the view that the economic development of society, as such, must nurture the growth either of inwardly 'free' personalities or of 'altruistic' ideals."[15] In principle formal and substantive rationality are always in conflict, and this means that insofar as the economy tends towards the maximization of formal rationality, it must necessarily require a greater sacrifice or curtailment of certain substantive values. It is significant for our purposes here that Schumpeter deploys a notion with a

12 ES, p. 85.
13 Ibid.
14 PE, p. 182.
15 From Max Weber (Walter Runciman ed.), *Weber: Selections in Translation*, Cambridge University Press, 1978, p. 283.

meaning that bears comparison; he uses the concept of "creative destruction" to characterize the contradictory effects of capitalist progress, a notion we discuss in later chapters.

The concept of economic action

A key distinction Weber makes at the outset of the section on "Sociological Categories of Economic Action" is that between what he calls "economically oriented action" and "economic action" per se. "Economically oriented action" he defines as action that is concerned in some way with the satisfaction of a desire for utilities – that is, it takes that desire into account (for example, political action that recognizes the need for economic prudence). By contrast, "economic action" in the strict sense is the use of an actor's control of resources that is *rationally oriented* by deliberate planning to economic ends. Thus, any action, which though primarily oriented to other than economic ends, takes account of economic considerations is to that extent "economically oriented"; whereas action that is primarily directed to the satisfaction of economic ends, and is essentially peaceful, is what Weber calls "economic action" in the pure sense. Importantly, "economic action" is inherently rational. Further, it only exists in the context of "scarcity", which suggests Weber is concerned to relate his definition directly to known principles of economic theory: "We shall speak of economic action only if the satisfaction of a need depends, in the actor's judgement, upon relatively *scarce* resources and a *limited* number of possible actions."[16] The purpose of this restriction of the scope economic action is to avoid the consequences of allowing any activity oriented to satisfying needs to be included (such as breathing). But it is also a clarification of the way actors pursue economic interests, because, for example, action directed to obtaining success in competitive market struggles needs to be distinguished from, say, political action designed to secure favourable labour relations, property rights, etc., a distinction not properly recognized, for example, by Marxist commentators.

Weber also distinguishes economic action from mere "technical action". What he says about the essential characteristics of "economic action" vis-à-vis "technical action" agrees with what Schumpeter says on the same subject. Both agree that economic action is a discrete form of activity that gives rise to specific features fundamental for demarcating the field of economics as such. As Weber explains,

> As long as the action is "purely technical" in the present sense, it is oriented only to the selection of the means which, with equal quality, certainty, and permanence of the result are comparatively most "economical" of effort in the attainment of a *given* end . . . The end itself is accepted beyond question and a purely technical consideration ignores other wants. . . . But once consideration is extended to take account of the relative scarcity of [means of

16 Ibid., p. 339.

> production] . . . in relation to their potential uses, as today every technician is accustomed to do even in the chemical laboratory, the action is no longer in the present sense purely technical, but *also* economic. From the economic point of view 'technical' questions always involve considerations of "costs."[17]

The typical measures of rational economic action according to Weber are:

(a) the systematic allocation between present and future of utilities, the control of which the actor feels he can count on, that is, "saving";
(b) the systematic allocation of utilities for various potential uses in the order of their estimated relative urgency and ranked according to the principle of marginal utility, that is, "consumption";
(c) the systematic procurement through the production or transportation of such utilities for which all the necessary means of production are controlled by the actor himself, taking into account the irksomeness of the requisite labour services as well as other potential uses to which the requisite goods could be put, that is, "production"; and
(d) the systematic acquisition by agreement with the present possessors, or with competing bidders, of assured powers of control and disposal over utilities, that is, "appropriation".[18]

Each of these dispositions is brought to a particularly high level of development under modern capitalist conditions, as we shall see.

The rationality of monetary calculation and capital accounting

Weber's analysis of monetary accounting is crucial to his account of modern capitalism. He says that from a purely technical point of view, money is the most "perfect" means of economic calculation: "it is formally the most rational means of orienting economic activity."[19] A completely rational monetary accounting has a number of consequences. First, it means the possibility of valuing in numerical terms all the means of carrying out a productive purpose, including all types of utilities, means of production and other economic advantages that the economic actor may think it useful to control. Second, it means the possibility of a quantitative statement of the prospects of any projected course of action, and once completed, the actual results can be calculated in monetary terms. Third, it means the possibility of a periodical estimation of all the goods and assets controlled by

17 ES, p. 66. Schumpeter's similar view of the distinction between "technical" versus "economic" activity is brought out especially in his discussion of the difference between "invention" and "innovation", topics to be subsequently discussed at length.
18 Ibid., p. 71.
19 Ibid., p. 86.

a given economic unit at a given point with those at a previous period and a comparison made in monetary terms. Fourth, it allows before and after consideration of the receipts and expenditures that are likely to be available for the use of an economic unit in a given period. And finally, it allows through the orientation of consumption to these data for the requisite utilities to be acquired in accordance with the principle of marginal utility.[20] Obviously, the profit-making enterprise of the modern type is unthinkable without the use of this type of monetary accounting, but a non-profit budgetary unit can equally utilize monetary accounting in a rational way if it chooses to do so.

Fundamental to the phenomenon of rational capitalism is for monetary accounting to be taken a step further to include considerations of the value of all means of production and their potential use in market-oriented enterprise. As we have seen, Weber emphasizes the means of capital accounting that is peculiar to rational economic enterprise, namely "double-entry bookkeeping".

> Capital accounting is the valuation and verification of opportunities for profit and of the success of profit making activity by means of a valuation of the total assets, goods and money of the enterprise at the beginning of a profit making venture, and a comparison of this with a similar evaluation of the assets still present and newly acquired at the end of the process; in the case of a profit making organization operating continuously, the same is done for an accounting period. In either case a balance is drawn between the initial and final states of the assets. "Capital" is the money value of the means of profit making available to the enterprise at the balancing of the books; "profit" and corresponding "loss", the difference between the initial balance and that drawn at the conclusion of the period.[21]

As we noted in the previous chapter, according to Weber, the technically most advanced form of business accounting double-entry bookkeeping was first developed in the late Middle Ages and gradually became universally applied in capitalist business operations.

What Weber says about the role of capital accounting suggests that his approach owes much to the theories of competitive enterprise, as developed by the Austrian School of economics. He says, "In a market economy every form of rational calculation especially of capital accounting is oriented to expectations of prices and their changes as they are determined by the conflicts of interest in bargaining and competition and the resolution of these conflicts."[22] The monetarization of the economy facilitates the use of the principle of marginal utility by both producers and consumers.

But for Weber the process of exchange also involves inherent conflict, for money prices are in effect weapons in a continual and ineluctable struggle for

20 Ibid., pp. 86–7.

21 Ibid., p. 91. The substance of this definition is repeated in similar terms in the "Authors Introduction", p. 18.

22 Ibid.

economic advantage. Weber is especially concerned to dispel any illusions that the competitive market is an arena of largely benign interactions between participants, as might be suggested by conventional accounts – there is no "hidden hand" promoting the general welfare.

> In an economy that makes use of capital accounting and is thus characterized by the appropriation of the means of production by individual units, that is by "property", profitability depends on the prices which the "consumers", according to the marginal utility of money in relation to their income, can and will pay. It is possible to produce profitably only for those consumers who, in these terms, have sufficient income. A need may fail to be satisfied not only when an individual's own demand for other goods take precedence, but also when the greater purchasing power of others for *all* types of goods prevails. Thus the fact that the battle of man against man on the market is an essential condition for the existence of rational-monetary accounting further implies that the outcome of the economic process is decisively influenced by the ability of persons who are more plentifully supplied with money to outbid the others, and if those more favourably situated for production to underbid their rivals on the selling side. The latter are particularly those well supplied with goods essential to production or with money.

In this passage Weber alludes to several of the elements that he describes in more detail elsewhere, such as the expropriation of the workers from the means of production and the monopolization of capital. But he goes on to emphasize that the use of money in the market struggle has a crucial effect as regards prices:

> Rational-money accounting pre-supposes the existence of effective prices and not merely of fictitious prices conventionally employed for technical accounting purposes. This in turn, presupposes money functioning as an effective medium of exchange, which is in demand as such, not mere tokens used as purely technical accounting units.[23]

We note that Weber does not deem the prices generated by the market contest "rational" as such but says they must be "effective". By this term he implies that the prices have been arrived through a course of competitive bargaining, which suggests the idea that they reflect relevant economic realities. It is also worth noting that in his remarks about pricing, Weber is pointing to the very serious difficulties a socialist transformation of the economy would face in the event it were to abolish money, the market or both.[24]

23 Ibid., p. 93.

24 These are issues that were taken up subsequently in particular Mises, Hayek and others in their various critiques of socialism.

Economic exchange

Weber wants to show that exchange in the market is a unique kind of social phenomenon, because on the one hand, it arises out of the separate and essentially incommensurable interests of individuals and yet it secures, when completed, a resolution that momentarily avoids or at least suppresses ongoing hostility. So even though there is contest – the struggle of man against man never disappears – there is also a potentially satisfactory outcome in the form of the mutual benefits gained.

> The opposition of interests, which is resolved in the compromise, involves the actor in potentially two different conflicts. On the one hand there is a conflict over the price to be agreed upon with the partner in exchange; the typical method is bargaining. On the other hand, there may also be competition with actual or potential rivals, either in the present or in the future who are competitive in the same market. Here the typical method is competitive bidding and offering.[25]

This analysis of Weber warrants comparison with Marx on the same issue. Whereas for Marx the exchange process is opaque and conceals the fact that, in particular, the price of wage labour does not reflect its true value and thus facilitates the extraction of surplus value, for Weber the exchange process does not have such mystifying connotations. Which is not to say that Weber regards the exchange system based on money prices etc. as "natural" or unproblematic – indeed much of his work is devoted to explaining how such a system has arisen historically. And Weber by no means thinks that the ordinary worker is on equal footing with their employer in wage bargaining of the labour contract; but the exploitation of the workers by capitalists is recognized simply for what it is, the dominance of stronger economic players over the weaker: "The fact that the maximum of *formal* rationality in capital accounting is possible only where the workers are subjected to domination by entrepreneurs, is a further specific element of the *substantive* irrationality of the modern economic order."[26]

Weber defines what he calls "the market situation" for any object of exchange as being all the opportunities of exchanging it for money that are known to participants in the exchange situation. "Marketability" he defines as the degree of regularity with which an object tends to be an object of exchange. "Market freedom" is the degree of autonomy enjoyed by the parties in the market relationship in the price struggle and in competition. Clearly, under certain modern conditions, marketability and market freedom are raised to a level that approaches a maximum possible, and this is conducive to "rational" pricing.[27] Conversely, where barriers to market entry exist that derive from traditional cultural norms, from monopolistic

25 Ibid., p. 72.
26 Ibid., p. 138.
27 See discussion at Ibid., pp. 82–4.

practices or political interference, prices will be "distorted" and diverge from what would otherwise be an effective optimum.

The concept of capitalistic profit-making

Capitalistic profit-making, Weber says, "is activity which is oriented at least in part to the opportunities of profit-making and it is economic if it is oriented to acquisition by peaceful methods. It may be oriented to the exploitation of the market situation."[28] In the latter case, of course, it constitutes "market capitalism", and if formally rational, we have fully "modern capitalism". Importantly, Weber emphasizes the peaceful character of capitalistic profit-making, because he is well aware that numerous forms of profit-making in the past, and even today, depend on violent or coercive means of various kinds – he lists a range of various types of what he terms "political capitalism", such as tax farming, the sale of offices and the imperialistic exploitation of dependent territories (plantations), as well as "adventure" or "booty" capitalism (piracy, slaves).[29]

Weber also distinguishes several forms of formally peaceful profit-making that are part of the complex of types that make up the modern capitalist system. He says capitalistic profit-making may entail the orientation to the profit possibilities in continuous buying and selling on the market with free exchange ("trade"), the orientation to the profit possibilities in continuous production of goods (industrial enterprise), it may entail purely speculative transactions in standardized commodities or in the securities (futures and stock trading), the promotional financing of new enterprises (promoters), or finally, the speculative financing of capitalistic enterprises (merchant banking).[30] Each of these obviously plays a role in the fully functioning modern capitalist system and each has distinctive modern features.

The concept of the enterprise

Even though, as we have just noted, Weber lists a variety of forms of profit-making as constitutive of the modern capitalist system as a whole, he places special emphasis on the case of continuous production of goods in enterprises, that is, industrial production in factories. He notes that institutions akin to the factory have existed previously in antiquity and elsewhere, but these lacked a rational division of labour and were not controlled with the use of rational accounting.[31] He uses the terms "establishment" and "enterprise" (*Betrieb*) to refer to the physical premises in which

28 Ibid., pp. 90–1.

29 Ibid., pp. 164–5.

30 Ibid.

31 Ibid., pp. 116–17. Weber notes that the "workshop" (*ergasterion*) was a common characteristic of Greek and Byzantine economic life, and he also discusses the similar Roman *ergastulum*. But these never approached the equivalent of the modern factory. In many such cases, even where the means of production were owned by an individual, labour was not hired but invariably that of slaves, or some other form of forced labour was in use. In addition, such premodern workshops seldom used

productive activities occur and notes that the economic concept of the "firm", by contrast, does not necessarily entail that a premises exists (for example, a putting-out operation). He therefore reserves the expression "profit-making enterprise" for the case where the technical (the premises) and economic (the firm) units coincide.[32] The uniqueness of the factory arises from its being a productive establishment under the control of a profit-making firm operating with fixed capital. It takes the form of an organized workshop with internal differentiation of function, all non-human means of production are appropriated, and there is a high degree of mechanization.[33] It follows that the development of the market system, mass production and a consumer society etc. are all intimately bound up with the advent of the factory.

Expropriation of the workers from the means of production

In considering the earliest stages of the modern factory, Weber refers to workshops such as that of "Jack of Newbury" of the early sixteenth century, which had hundreds of handlooms that were the property of the workers. However, in that case, each worker worked independently as if he was at home and there was no internal division of labour and combination of functions. The factory system and the industrial type of production oriented to profit-making presuppose "the expropriation of the workers from the means of production". In using such phraseology, Weber is evidently in agreement with Marx on this aspect.[34] He says the expropriation of the workers in general, including clerical personnel and technically trained persons, from ownership of the means of production has important economic consequences because it facilitates the achievement of higher levels of economic rationality. This follows from the fact that management has extensive control over the selection of workers and the modes of use to which their labour is put. Thereby management is not hampered by traditional claims of workers to their position or by their working in their own way. Capitalist management operations are oriented predominantly to the requirements of efficiency and profitability.[35]

The expropriation of the individual worker from the means of production can be driven by purely technical factors, such as where production requires many workers working cooperatively at the same time or where there are complex production processes that require specialized training and stringent disciple and control. Where the

---

any form of machinery or mechanical power, nor did there come into being internal differentiation of labour.

32 Ibid.

33 Ibid., p. 135.

34 It is not clear how far Weber endorses the Marxist account of the expropriation of the peasantry, in particular as regards Marx's celebrated account of "naked and bloody class struggles" graphically described in the famous Chapter 24 of his *Capital* Volume 1. Weber certainly acknowledges the "enclosure" movement of the eighteenth and nineteenth centuries but has a more nuanced account. See GEH, pp. 84–6.

35 These are issues made well known by Harry Braverman in his *Labor and Monopoly Capital: The Degradation of Work in the Twentieth Century*, Monthly Review Press, 1974.

workers have been completely separated from the means of production, it is usual for management to appropriate all managerial functions. Owners of a business can in this situation exercise control personally, as entrepreneurs do or by appointing professional managers.[36]

Weber's account of the way in which labour is organized in the setting of the modern factory appears to coincide with Frederick Taylor's theories of "scientific management" though without the latter's apparent endorsement of the technique. As we have seen already, Weber noted the early forms of discipline in large organizations in slave plantations, ancient *ergastula* and military barracks and expressly contrasted these with the modern factory. In the latter, organizational discipline has a rational basis.

> With the help of suitable methods of measurement, the optimum profitability of the individual worker is calculated like that of any other material means of production. On this basis, the American system of "scientific management" triumphantly proceeds with its rational conditioning and training of work performances, thus drawing the ultimate conclusions from the mechanization and discipline of the plant. The psycho-physical apparatus of man is completely adjusted to the demands of the outer world, the tools, the machines – in short, it is functionalised, and the individual is shorn of his natural rhythm as determined by his organism; in line with the demands of the work procedure, he is attuned to a new rhythm through the functional specialization of muscles and through the creation of an optimal physical effort.[37]

Business bureaucracy

Weber's account of the internal structure of the business enterprise has not been extensively discussed in the secondary literature. This is in marked contrast to the reception of his general theory of bureaucracy, which is focused on the state's bureaucracy.[38] Weber's well known account of bureaucracy in *Economy and Society* is largely concerned with governmental bureaucracy. It is clear, however, that many of the features he saw as central to the operation of governmental bureaucracy are also found in the larger business firms. In both cases, we find the separation of the workers from ownership of the means of administration (the files and office equipment). In the business organization, one also finds such phenomena as quasi-judicial rules of conduct, an hierarchy of powers, distinct jurisdictions of competence, lifetime employment, payment by salary and so on.[39] It would

36 ES, p. 137.

37 Ibid., p. 1156.

38 Weber's best known account of "bureaucracy" is that contained in Chapter XI of *Economy and Society*.

39 For recent accounts of the business firm and its preconditions of existence advanced from an economics perspective, see Oliver Williamson, *The Economic Institutions of Capitalism*, Free Press,

appear that individuals employed in bureaucratized firms become oriented to the organization and its norms in an analogous way to what happens in governmental bureaucracies.[40] However, according to Weber, it is only the very large enterprises that are "unequalled models of strict bureaucratic organization. Business management throughout rests on increasing precision, steadiness, and, above all, speed of operations."[41]

But for Weber, the most important effect of bureaucracy in the sphere of business is specialization and matter-of-factness, features highlighted earlier in *The Protestant Ethic.*

> Bureaucratization offers above all the optimum possibility for carrying through the principle of specializing administrative functions according to purely objective considerations. Individual performances are allocated to functionaries who have specialized training and who by constant practice increase their expertise. "Objective" discharge of business primarily means a discharge of business according to *calculable rules* and "without regard for persons." "Without regard for persons," however, is also the watchword of the market and, in general, of all pursuits of naked economic interests. . . . The peculiarity of modern culture, and specifically of its technical and economic base, demands this very "calculability" of results. . . . Bureaucracy develops the more perfectly, the more it is "dehumanised," the more completely it succeeds in eliminating from official business love, hatred and all personal irrational and emotional element which escape calculation. This is appraised as its special virtue by capitalism.[42]

Weber does not argue that the advance of the administrative bureaucracy of the state is entirely positive for capitalism and indeed it is in some ways inimical to it. Thus he notes that England, where capitalism first became dominant, "was the slowest of all countries to succumb to bureaucratization or, indeed, is only partly in the process of doing so."[43] What capitalist interests require is a calculable legal order and a state that is predictable and does not impose onerous burdens on private enterprise.

1985 and Oliver Williamson and Sidney Winter (eds.), *The Nature of the Firm: Origins, Evolution and Development*, Oxford, 1993. It is noteworthy that Weber does not attempt to provide a strictly *economic* theory of the firm.

40 Apart from Swedberg's work, there are few detailed commentaries on Weber's sociology of the capitalist business enterprise. But mention should be made of Talcott Parsons, "Introduction" to Talcott Parsons (ed.), *Max Weber: The Theory of Economic and Social Organization*, The Free Press, 1947, pp. 30–55. A critique from a Marxist point of view is Bryn Jones, "Economic Action and Rational Organization in the Sociology of Weber", in Barry Hindess (ed.), *Sociological Theories of the Economy*, Macmillan, 1977, pp. 28–65.

41 ES, p. 974.

42 Ibid., p. 975.

43 Ibid., p. 987.

The possibility of socialism

In his remarks on the rationality of pricing under competitive market conditions, Weber alludes to the possibility of a socialist system in which prices are fixed by a central authority. He is clearly highly sceptical that an economy that dispenses with money can achieve a level of formal rationality equivalent to that of a capitalist economic system. "A socialist regime might issue vouchers, in payment for a given quantity of socially useful 'labour', valid for the purchase of certain types of goods. These might be saved or used in exchange, but their behaviour would follow the rules of barter exchange, not of money."[44]

As already noted, Weber is acutely aware of the issues raised by the socialist critique of capitalism, and indeed, despite his rejection of socialism, he made significant contributions to the development of the theory of the planned socialistic economy.[45] Highlighting the inevitable negative consequences of a thoroughgoing socialization of the economy, he explains how the socialistic provision of individual needs must inevitably weaken the incentive to labour. For, "it would be impossible to allow workers' dependents to suffer the full consequences of a worker's lack of efficiency in production. Hence it would be impossible to retain capital risk and proof of merit by a formally autonomous achievement.... Where a planned economy is carried out, it must further accept the inevitable reduction in formal, calculating rationality which would result from the elimination of money and capital accounting. Substantive and formal (in the sense of exact *calculation*) rationality are, it should be stated again, after all largely distinct problems."[46] It follows that enhancement of substantive rationality along socialist lines must come at the cost of formal rationality.

Weber does not argue that formal rationality is superior to substantive rationality, and in any event, judgements about this are not a matter that can be decided scientifically. Personally, he advocated a compromise between the two forms of rationality – in other words, he saw the necessity of a trade-off between the efficiency gains of formal rationality and the satisfaction of substantive values such as equality, individuality, freedom and the like. It bears noting that Weber was a passionate advocate of many of the social reforms being advanced in Germany in his day, and he was genuinely concerned for the welfare of the working classes.[47] Equally, however, he was wary and at times highly critical of attempts to eliminate the market and to overthrow capitalism as a system. If these efforts were finally successful, he feared the effect would be to so reduce the efficiency of the economy

44 Ibid., pp. 79–80. Since Weber's time there have been a number of socialist economists, most notably Oskar Lange and A. P. Lerner, who have argued that via the mechanism of "indicative prices" the central authority can achieve a rational allocation of resources.

45 We shall consider these issues further in Chapter 5.

46 ES, pp. 110–1.

47 On Weber's involvement with the Verein für Sozialpolitik, which was an association of academics that supported various social reforms, see Dieter Krüger, "Max Weber and the Younger Generation in the Verein für Sozialpolitik", in Wolfgang J. Mommsen and Jürgen Osterhammel (eds.), *Max Weber and His Contemporaries*, Allen & Unwin, 1987, pp. 71–87.

as to lead to an unacceptable reduction in the standard of living of the masses along with other consequences that would be undesirable. But importantly, Weber had no illusions that the inevitable outcome of a capitalist system is the subjection of the workers to the domination of capitalist entrepreneurs.[48] We shall have occasion to return to these issue at some length in Chapter Five.

The capital market

Given that profit-making has reached the level of the modern enterprise with mass production, the financing of such operations creates further avenues of enterprise and this leads to the creation of a "capital market". By this concept Weber indicates that certain "goods" such as money are in demand to be used as capital goods, and specialist financial institutions, namely banks, come into being that derive their profit from the business of supplying these goods.[49] Here Weber is alluding to the significance of the provision of credit, a point of obvious intersection with the work of Schumpeter. Weber distinguishes the lending of money for purposes of consumption and non-economic uses from the lending of money with the object of profit-making. The latter is a crucial precondition of modern capitalist enterprise.

> In a rational profit-making enterprise, the interest, which is charged on books to a capital sum is the minimum of profitability. It is in terms of whether or not this minimum is reached that a judgment of advisability of this particular use of capital goods is arrived at. . . . It is one of the fundamental phenomena of a capitalist economy that entrepreneurs are permanently willing to pay interest for loan capital. This phenomenon can only be explained by understanding how it is that the average entrepreneur may hope in the long run to earn a profit, or that entrepreneurs on the average in fact do earn it, over and above what they have to pay as interest on loan capital. . . . Profit-making enterprises will be founded and operated continuously (capitalistically) *only* if it is expected that the minimum rate of interest on capital can be earned. Economic theory . . . might then very well say that this exploitation of the power distribution (which itself is a consequence of private property in goods and the means of production) permits it only to this particular class of economic actors to conduct the operations in accordance with the "interest" criterion.[50]

These remarks show that Weber recognizes that the financial sector is integral to the operation of the industrial system. We shall see later that Schumpeter also has a highly developed theory of finance as the basis of entrepreneurial activity.[51]

48 ES, p. 138.
49 Ibid.
50 Ibid., pp. 97–8.
51 Weber was highly cognizant of the Marxist critique of capitalism and was familiar with his argument that characterized the market situation as one which allows for the "exploitation" of the workers who, having been separated from the means of production, are obliged to sell their "labour

The concept of economic order

According to Richard Swedberg, the concept of "order" (*ordnung*) is a concept that has been unduly ignored by Weber commentators, but it is one of his most important concepts for it complements his notion of social action:

> A social relationship may turn into an order when the maxims that infuse a social relationship acquire an independence of their own, so that actors may orient their actions to the order. Orders of this type, based on maxims that are either obligatory or exemplary, also exist in economic life, for example in the form of conventions. They are also at the core of organisations which Weber in all brevity defines as orders policed by a staff. . . . The most important economic organisation in modern capitalism is obviously the firm, whose impact on economic life Weber describes as revolutionary. A firm typically consists of an order, maintained by three types of actors; the entrepreneur, the staff (the bureaucracy), and the workers.[52]

Weber also says that the market system and the distribution of property form an "economic" order. In a later section of *Economy and Society* entitled "Legal Order and Economic Order", he defines the concept "economic order" as follows:

> Sociological economics (*Sozialökonomie*) . . . considers actual human activities as they are conditioned by the necessity to take into account the facts of economic life. We shall apply the term economic order to the distribution of the actual control over goods and services, the distribution arising in each case from the particular mode of balancing interests consensually: moreover, the term shall apply to the manner in which goods and services are indeed used by virtue of these powers of disposition, which are based on *de facto* recognition (Einverständnis).[53]

It is unfortunate that this section of *Economy and Society* is almost entirely devoted to the concept of legal order and nowhere else does Weber develop the concept of economic order at any length. This may be because, in fact, he often uses the concept "economy" as equivalent to that of "economic order." But the significance of the concept is surely analogous to that of a legal order. It is designed to explain

---

power" to the capitalists at under its true value. While he does not accept the labour theory of value, and many other aspects of Marx's theory, Weber was sympathetic to the condition of the working class and did not think the unequal distribution of wealth in capitalist society was inherently justified. For an analysis of Weber's relation to Marxist class theory and his treatment of the idea of class domination, see the essay by Erik Olin Wright, "The Shadow of Exploitation in Weber's Class Analysis," in Charles Camic, Philip S. Gorski and David M. Trubek (eds.), *Max Weber's Economy and Society: A Critical Companion*, Stanford University Press, 2005, pp. 204–36.

52 Richard Swedberg, "Max Weber's *Economy and Society*: The Centerpiece of Economy and Society?" in Charles Camic, Philip S. Gorski and David M. Trubek (eds.), *Max Weber's Economy and Society: A Critical Companion*, Stanford University Press, 2005, p. 130.

53 ES, p. 312.

that, once a certain stage has been reached in the development of market relations – with property relations and routines of economic conduct in production and consumption well established – social actors come to accept this state of affairs as legitimate and orient themselves to it.

The dependence of modern capitalism on the state

As we have already seen, Weber regards the modern state as crucial for the advent of modern capitalism, and he sees the state in the West as having achieved a unique degree of rationality compared with other instances. Weber claims that a "rational state" has only existed in the modern West. By "rational" he first means that the basis of the state's legitimation is grounded through rational justifications, that is, through notions of legitimacy that are subject to reasoned exegesis: "Rational grounds – resting on a belief in the legality of enacted rules and the right of those elevated to authority under such rules to issue commands (legal authority)."[54] Typically, rule in modern states is subject to a constitutional settlement of some kind that set limits to the power of governing bodies and secures rights. This may or may not involve a written constitution.

Second, rationality means that the state is governed with the means of a rational bureaucratic administration. In its purest form, authority is exercised via the principle of appointment, because in contrast to where officials are elected, this attains the highest possible level of obedience to commands. Appointment must also be, by virtue of free contract and free selection, based on specialized competence, increasingly measured by formal qualifications. Normally the bureaucratic official is a full-time employee and remunerated by a fixed salary paid in money, and has no other ownership of, or rights to, the benefits of office.[55]

We have already explored Weber's view of the crucial role of the modern legal order for the development of capitalism of the modern type and this necessarily entails the enforcement role of the state. Law is central primarily because present-day business transactions rely entirely on opportunities acquired through contracts.

> The tempo of modern business communication requires a promptly and predictably functioning legal system, that is, one which is guaranteed by the strongest coercive power. . . . The universal predominance of the market consociation requires on the one hand a legal system the functioning of which is *calculable* in accordance with rational rules. On the other hand, the constant expansion of the market which we shall get to know as an inherent tendency of the market consociation, has favoured the monopolisation and regulation of all (legitimate) coercive power by one *universalist* coercive institution through the disintegration of all particularist status-determined and other coercive structures which have been resting mainly on economic monopolies.[56]

54 See Ibid., p. 217.
55 Ibid., p. 221–2.
56 Ibid., pp. 336–7.

A final function of the state in facilitating modern capitalism concerns its role in relation to the monetary system. On monetary theory, Weber was largely influenced by Georg Knapp and takes up his theory that the use of paper tokens to symbolize money is made possible only by the state's function as guarantor. Weber notes that "the modern state has universally assumed the monopoly of regulating the monetary system by statute; and . . . the monopoly of creating money, at least for coined money."[57] Money is not accepted because of its apparent function as a kind of commodity but because of the backing of the state through certain legal ordinances. The fact that money circulates shows that transactors accept and hold it, not because of its intrinsic value but because they trust its future re-exchangeability: it is not mere possession but possession with the prospect of future use as payment that explains money's acceptance. But the state also provides an economic basis for money's acceptance, and that concerns the requirement for taxes to be paid with money. As this fiscal function dominates the payment system of the economy, there arises a secondary basis for money's widespread acceptance.

Weber notes, in addition to this, that the state in a capitalist society engages in financial transactions itself on a tremendous scale. As he says, "the state needs money to a large degree, sometimes even entirely, as a means of exchange to cover future purchases of goods and supplies in the market."[58] Weber conceptualizes these different aspects of money's acceptance by positing a distinction between money's function as a means of payment guaranteed by statute, which he terms its "formal validity", and its use as a means of exchange, which he terms its "substantive validity". The latter he defines as "the exchange possibility of money against other specified goods, which rests on its valuation in relation to marketable goods . . ."[59] The two types of validity may, according to Weber, empirically coincide, an outcome that is likely where validity as a means of payment and formal acceptability as means of exchange in private transactions are made compulsory by state law.[60] However, under certain circumstances, radical changes in the substantive validity of the currency (debasement) may be so disruptive of people's expectations as to "produce a chronic tendency towards social revolution", an outcome state monetary policy seeks to avoid for obvious reasons.[61]

The significance of rational law

Having discussed the role of the state in facilitating a legal order that supports capitalism, we shall now consider some further specific effects of law. Weber says that a legal system in its structure can be based on either formal (legalistic) or material principles. And a system of law can be "rational" in different ways,

57 Ibid., p. 166.
58 Ibid., p. 160.
59 Ibid., p. 169.
60 Ibid., p. 79.
61 Ibid., p. 193.

depending on which legal doctrines are dominant. By material principles he means utilitarian and economic considerations, such as those to which the Islamic *Kadi* pays attention in his conduct of a case. This is often the case with bureaucracies and absolutist systems of justice. According to Weber, Roman law is particularly significant because it was a way of resisting the material or substantive orientation of legal thought in favour of "formalization".[62] Formalization is notable for the way it tends to promote a calculable legal order.

Weber gives, as an example, what happens in a situation like that of traditional China when a man who has sold his house to someone later comes back and asks to be taken in because, in the meantime, he has become impoverished. If the purchaser refuses to heed the ancient Chinese command to aid a brother, the spirits will be disturbed; hence, the impoverished seller ends up in the house as a non-paying renter. Capitalism cannot exist with such as system. It requires a law that can be counted on like a machine: from particular inputs a definite outcome is more or less certain and can be relied upon. As Weber puts it on one occasion, "industrial capitalism must be able to count on the continuity, trustworthiness and objectivity of the legal order, and on the rational, predictable functioning of legal and administrative agencies."[63] Such a body of law was achieved in the West through an alliance between the modern state and the jurists for making good the state's claims to power.

But paradoxically, capitalism arose first in England where the rule of officials was minimized.[64] This could occur in part because of the role of the bourgeoisie, whose practical need for a calculable law was decisive in developing the tendency towards a formalized law.[65] But this did not culminate in a highly formalized gapless system as advanced by the Pandectists in Germany, because a formal, empirical case law was more apposite to the situation in England.[66]

Modern contract law is the most perfect realization of the purposive contract in Weber's sense. "Today it is fundamentally established that any content whatsoever of a contract in so far as it is not excluded by limitations on the freedom of contract creates law amongst the parties, and that particular forms are necessary only to the extent that they are prescribed for reasons of expediency, especially for the sake of the unambiguous demonstrability of rights, and thus of legal security."[67] As we have seen, the purposive contract first arose gradually in ancient Rome by

62 Ibid., p. 342.

63 Ibid., p. 1095.

64 Ibid., p. 1109.

65 Peter Ghosh has noted that Weber recognized that in the case of England a third strain of legal development derived from neither Common Law or Roman Civil Law, namely "Natural Law", was significant in seventeenth century England. Natural Law became influential in the period of the English Revolution and was supported by the Puritans who, however, were not in the end able to overcome the dominance of Common Law. See Ghosh, *Max Weber and the Protestant Ethic*, pp. 125–7.

66 ES, p. 855. On the whole issue of the so-called "England problem", see Swedberg's excellent discussion in Richard Swedberg, *Max Weber and the Idea of Economic Sociology*, Princeton University Press, 1998, pp. 105–6.

67 ES, p. 855.

virtue of the internationalization of law with the Empire, and in modern times, it was reinvigorated under the influence of Civil Law doctrine. But as we have seen, contract law also arose independently in England from early in the Middle Ages with the growth of the Common Law.

The role of corporations law

Weber argues that, as the internal relations between group members of business partnerships and the power of officials became more fixed and rule-governed, contracting required special arrangements. It became necessary to establish unambiguously the significance of every action of the members of the firm and of the role of every official and to legitimize them. The technical solution found to this problem was the concept of the "juristic person".

> The most rational actualisation of the idea of the legal personality of organizations consists in the complete separation of the legal spheres of the members from the separately constituted legal sphere of the organization; while certain persons are designated as alone authorized to assume obligations and acquire rights for the organization, the legal relations thus created do not at all affect the individual members and their property and are not regarded as their contracts, but all these relations are imputed to a separate and distinct body of assets. . . . The concept of juristic personality can be extended even further to contain the control over economic goods the benefit of which is to accrue to a plurality of persons who, while they are determined in accordance with rules, are not to be associationally organized. . . . [A consociation of persons] can be organized as a *corporation*. . . . the body of members is constituted as a fixed group of persons.[68]

Weber here is clearly describing the modern corporate structure that, by virtue of the unique legal institution of the legal personality, facilitates the transformation of the business partnership into a body that has both a bureaucratic element that operates the enterprise and an ownership structure that is in principle completely separate.

> Such an organization thus requires that, at least as a general rule, that membership be closed and that the purposes be fixed in a relatively stable way; also that the membership rights be formally inviolable and transferable upon death and, at least usually *inter vivos*; that the management be carried on bureaucratically; that the members participate either themselves or through proxies in an assembly that is *de iure* organized democratically but in fact plutocratically, and that adopts its resolutions, after discussion, by a vote proportionate to capital shares. The special aim of such organizations, furthermore, does not

68 Ibid., p. 707.

require personal liability of the members externally, since it is irrelevant to the credit standing of the enterprise."[69]

Clearly, this is the legal framework that came to underpin the modern business corporation, typically today structured as a joint-stock company with limited liability. Such corporate legal arrangements are not found in ancient Western society or elsewhere in premodern societies. Their predominance today is a key element in the structural matrix of modern capitalism.

To summarize this account of legal aspects, we note that Weber does not merely highlight the dependence of the capitalist system on the legal and political structures of modern society; he also suggests a mutually reinforcing relationship: not only is the capitalist economic order dependent on a legal system with specific characteristics, capitalism itself partly fashions the legal order.

The ideal type of rational capitalism

In Section 30 of the "Sociological Categories of Economic Action", Weber provides an analysis of what he terms "The Conditions of Maximum Formal Rationality of Capital Accounting". We argue that this section, in effect, advances a condensed and comprehensive description of an ideal type of highly rational capitalism and can be seen as a synthetic summary of those sections of *Economy and Society* that deal with the modern capitalist system. Here Weber outlines the principal social, legal and other conditions necessary to raise the level of peaceful and continuous capitalist acquisition to a state that is the highest conceivable. Like all ideal types, this is a "utopia", not in the sense of being ethically ideal, but because these conditions, if institutionalized, would create a capitalist economic system with the greatest formal rationality. The conditions necessary for maximizing formal rationality may from time to time be approached or approximated in concrete reality, and Weber implies that this has been the case at various points in the recent history of Europe and possibly elsewhere. Weber does not say the maximization of formal rationality is inevitable or even a definite trend, but he recognizes distinct tendencies towards this level of capitalist acquisition in the modern West.[70] In the following, we note Weber's principal conditions and comment on them.

The first condition is the appropriation of the means of production, which means, "complete appropriation of all material means of production by owners and the complete absence of all formal appropriation of opportunities for profit in the market, that is, market freedom." In other words, the distribution of assets is such that the major means of production are held by discrete business entities (companies, partnerships). The interests of these entities stand opposed to those

69 Ibid., p. 719.

70 At times Weber seems to have envisaged there would in the future be a retreat from laissez-faire and a pure free market and thought a return to something akin to mercantilism might occur given the agonistic political situation of the world powers Weber's account of the conditions of maximum formal rationality of capitalism is contained in ES, pp 161–64.

of the majority of the populace, who are correspondingly without such means and to survive economically must sell their labour services to the owners of the means of production. Weber does not specify the absence of monopoly, but it is likely he has in mind the situation modern economists describe with the concept of "perfect competition". The phenomenon of appropriation is of course central to Marx's theory and Weber uses it largely in line with the former's usage. Of course, Weber knows that the economic order of modern capitalism is more complicated than this division between propertied and property-less would suggest owing inter alia to the growth of professional middle classes.

Weber's second condition is autonomy in the selection of management, that is, "complete autonomy in the selection of management by the owners, thus complete absence of formal appropriation of rights to managerial functions." Business skills and managerial competence must alone be the criterion for selecting managers. No group can monopolize the managerial function, and this means that religious, ethical or other non-economic criteria should not influence the selection of the personnel of management. The leadership of the business firm is "appointed", which means that managers are not self-selected nor arise charismatically. This seems to exclude the case of the self-made man who becomes an entrepreneur.

The third condition is free labour, that is, "complete absence of appropriation of jobs and opportunities for earning by workers and conversely the absence of appropriation of workers by owners." This rules out situations in which guilds or unions can determine which individuals are employed and in what positions. In other words, management must have the freedom to employ whichever workers they deem suitable and conversely have the ability to dismiss those not competent or superfluous. The absence of appropriation of workers by owners means the absence of various forms of unfree labour. The reason this is important is that, contrary to what is often thought to be the tendency of capitalism, it is not in the interests of a rational profit-making enterprise to hold its workers as slaves or to operate other types of indentured labour. For such ownership places an excessive burden on the enterprise to maintain its workers and their dependents, even in situations where they may not be fit, proficient or otherwise needed. As Marx was keen to emphasize, a capitalist enterprise requires only the workers' labour power and not their persons.

The fourth condition is freedom of contract, that is, "complete absence of substantive regulation of consumption, production, and prices or other forms of regulation which limit freedom of contract or specify conditions of exchange. This may be called substantive freedom of contract." The terms of the economic transactions that occur between consumers and producers and between producers in a capitalist economy must be largely unregulated by outside forces, such as religious or political powers that oblige compliance with their values. Where there is freedom of contract, the parties to exchange transactions will be primarily oriented to the prices set by the market mechanism. Weber accepts that the theory of marginal utility gives the most adequate account of how those prices are typically formed.

The fifth condition Weber specifies is rational technology. This means "complete calculability of the technical conditions of the production process; that is, a mechanically rational technology". Only where modern science has become established and the field of industrial technics is developed is it possible to maximize the calculability of the economic enterprise. As Swedberg explains, "by 'rational science' Weber means natural science with a mathematical foundation, which is developed through experimentation by a specifically trained staff in laboratories. Western science united with capitalism in the eighteenth century . . . and this meant the production of goods could be liberated from economic traditionalism."[71] Insofar as industrial technique is restricted by traditions, religious taboos or other non-economic restraints it is not possible to maximize productivity.

Weber's sixth condition is rational law and administration, which entails the "complete calculability of the functioning of public administration and of the legal order and a reliable purely formal guarantee of all contracts by the political authority. That is, a formally rational administration in law." Only under the conditions of a relatively stable and predictable political system and a relatively rational legal system is it possible for the enterprise to pursue its economic interests in the security that efforts will be rewarded as expected. Weber does not specify the precise type of legal system, whether that of England with its Common Law or that of Continental Civil Law, that is most conducive to rational capitalism.

The seventh condition listed by Weber is separation of the household from the enterprise, that is, "the most complete separation possible of the enterprise and its conditions of success and failure from the household or private budgetary unit and its property interests". Here Weber has in mind the historical process by which the economic enterprise has emerged as a distinct entity. It has been further transformed with the advent of the corporation. Today the enterprise typically takes the form of the limited liability company wherein the interest of shareholders and the actions of management and employees are formally separated from the substantively oriented needs of households.

The final condition mentioned by Weber is a rational monetary system, that is, "a monetary system with the highest possible degree of formal rationality". The condition Weber thinks most supports capitalism is where there is "state money", that is, media of exchange that have been coined or printed by the state, and where these instruments are guaranteed by that authority.[72]

The model of capitalism described in the elaboration of these eight elements clearly coincides to a degree with the actual reality of many of modern economies with which Weber was familiar, such as those of England, Germany, Holland and America, but none are "perfect" exemplars. Weber's theory is also similar in obvious ways to the accounts of competitive capitalism typical of modern economic theory, though it is not presented as a contribution to economics proper. Weber's theory is basically sociological in contrast to what we find in economics proper. Below we suggest ways in which Weber's ideal type of modern capitalism can be employed in the interpretation of contemporary capitalist systems that approximate the model more or less and in varying degrees.

71 Swedberg, *Max Weber and the Idea of Economic Sociology*, p. 147.
72 ES, pp. 161–2.

The tendency to monopoly

Now contrary to the specifics of his ideal type model of modern capitalism, Weber points out that while it is typical for capitalist interests operating under modern market conditions to favour the continuous extension of the free market, this may occur only up to the point where some players succeed. An initial effect of intensive business competition was to break up the status-based monopolies that constituted an impediment to the unlimited pursuit of profit. Hence, the early monopolies based on a grant of rights from the state were challenged by the rising bourgeoisie who fought against such privileges based on claims of status. But free competition, which ensues when the older monopoly situation is undermined, persists only so long as new monopolies are not created based on the machinations economic forces per se.

> Those monopolies, on the other hand, which are based solely upon the power of property, rest, on the contrary, upon an entirely rationally calculated mastery of market conditions which may, however, remain formally as free as ever. The sacred, status, and merely traditional bonds, which have gradually come to be eliminated, constituted restrictions on the formation of rational market prices; the purely economically conditioned monopolies are, on the other hand, their ultimate consequence. . . . the rational-economic monopolist rules through the market."[73]

The exercise of monopolistic power represents a pure type of economic domination from Weber's point of view. This is the situation in which those with a monopoly position can impose their will on the behaviour of others without a legitimizing basis. Monopolistic domination arises from a "constellation of interests".

> In its purest form . . . [it] is based on influence derived exclusively from the possession of goods or marketable skills guaranteed in some way and acting upon the conduct of those dominated, who remain, however, formally free and are motivated simply by the pursuit of their own interests. . . . Any large central bank or credit institution, for instance, exercises a "dominating" influence on the capital market by virtue of its monopolistic position. . . . The credit banks do not, however, pretend that they exercise "authority", i.e., that they claim "submission" on the part of the dominated without regard to the latter's own interests; they simply pursue their own interests and realize them best when the dominated persons, acting with formal freedom, rationally pursue their own interests as they are forced upon them by objective circumstances.[74]

Of course these remarks partly agree with the thrust of Marx's view that capitalism becomes increasingly dominated by big business and monopolies, but

73 Ibid., p. 639.
74 Ibid., p. 943.

importantly, Weber does not see these tendencies are leading inevitably to socialism. We shall have occasion to return to this issue of monopoly at length in relation to Schumpeter, for whom monopoly is also a common outcome of the free market and not necessarily negative from the standpoint of economic progress.

The ethical character of the market under capitalism

According to Weber, the advent of the modern corporation has important ethical implications. This is especially the case as regards the possible regulation of business activity in accordance with substantive ethical norms of the kind that have been typically advanced by the world religions. He explains that the separation in the West of the powers of the Church from those of the state has allowed the realm of profit-making to remain relatively immune from interference by antipathetic ethical regimes. The reasons underlying this he locates in the extreme impersonality of capitalist relations under modern conditions.

> It is possible to advance ethical postulates and to attempt the imposition of substantive norms with regard to household head and servant, master and slave, or patriarchal ruler and subject, since their relationship is personal and since the expected services result therefrom. Within wide limits, personal, flexible interests are operative here, and purely personal intent and action can decisively change the relationship and the condition of the person involved. But for the director of the joint-stock company, who is obliged to represent the interests of the stockholders as the masters proper, it is difficult to relate in this manner to the factory workers; it is even more difficult for the director of the bank that finances the joint-stock company, or for the mortgage holder in relation to the owner of property on which the bank granted the loan. Decisive are the need for competitive survival and the conditions of labour, money and the commodity markets; hence matter-or-fact considerations that are simply non-ethical determine individual behaviour and interpose forces between the persons involved. From an ethical viewpoint, this "masterless slavery" to which capitalism subjects the worker or the mortgagee is questionable only as an institution. However, in principle, the behaviour of any individual cannot be so questioned, since it is prescribed in all relevant respects by objective situations. The penalty for non-compliance is extinction . . . such economic behaviour has the quality of *service* toward an *impersonal* purpose.[75]

By these remarks Weber emphasizes the ethical dilemma facing the critic of the individual capitalist. By suggesting the only meaningful route of ethical criticism is to reject the institution of capitalism as a whole, he is not advocating revolution but implying that criticism has first to acknowledge the inescapable reality that

75 Ibid., pp. 1186–7.

confronts the critic. For the institution of capitalism cannot be fundamentally reformed or significantly modified without risking many adverse effects. As we have noted above and will comment further below, Weber was intimately involved in various reform movements of the day, some concerned with ameliorating the undesirable effects of full-fledged capitalism. But his political stance eschewed the pursuit of absolute justice, and he insisted it is simply not possible to achieve an ethically satisfactory regulation of capitalism.

This problem is the focus of the profound reflections contained in Weber's late essay "Religious Rejections of the World and their Directions". There he again notes the agonistic and impersonal and character of economic relations under modern capitalist conditions and insists that, "The more the world of the modern capitalist economy follows its own immanent laws, the less accessible it is to any imaginable relationship with a religious ethic of brotherliness."[76] Salvation religions have not only failed to achieve complete distance of men from attachment to goods and money and have inevitably made compromises with the material needs of their own institutions and society at large, they have never been able to "overcome the tension between their own religiosity and a rational economy."[77]

But is capitalism completely unconnected to ethics of any kind? Weber suggests that paradoxically capitalist relations engender an ethic of a peculiar type. Included in *Economy and Society* is a section entitled "The Market: Its Impersonality and Ethic" in which Weber addresses the nature of the market and its ethical meaning.[78] Weber begins his discussion with a statement of the character of the market from a purely sociological point of view:

> The market represents a coexistence and sequence of rational consociations, each of which is specifically ephemeral in so far as it ceases to exist with the act of exchanging the goods, unless a norm has been promulgated which imposes upon the transferors of the exchangeable goods the guaranty of their lawful acquisition of warranty of title or of quiet enjoyment. The completed barter constitutes a consociation only with the immediate partner. The preparatory dickering, however, is always a social action (*Gemeinschaftshandeln*) insofar as the potential partners are guided in their efforts by the potential action of an indeterminately large group of real or imaginary competitors rather than by their own actions alone. The more this is true, the more does the market constitute social action. Furthermore, any active exchange involving the use of money (sale) is a social action simply because the money used derives its value from its relation to the potential action of others.[79]

76 "Religious Rejections of the World and Their Directions" FMW, p. 331.

77 Ibid., p. 332.

78 This section is described as a "fragment" and was included by Weber's wife Marianne Weber after his death and published even though it was evidently uncompleted.

79 ES, pp. 635–6.

Weber goes on to argue how the use of money necessarily implies not only social action but group formation as well, because its use requires a community of interest between the potential participants in the market in the reliability of monetary payments. He explains the market community is the result of a peculiar set of orientations by social actors to the potential action of others, even though those others may not be physically present and even though a particular act, such as the purchase or sale of a good, may bring them into association with the others only momentarily.

> Within the market community every act of exchange, especially monetary exchange, is not directed, in isolation, by the action of the individual partner to the particular transaction, but the more rationally it is considered, the more it is directed by the action of all other parties potentially interested in the exchange. The market community as such is the most impersonal relationship of practical life into which humans can enter with one another. . . . the reason for the impersonality of the market is its matter-of-factness, its orientation to the commodity and only to that. Where the market is allowed to follow its own autonomous tendencies, its participants do not look towards the persons of each other but only towards the commodity; there are no obligations of brotherliness or reverence, and none of those spontaneous human relations that are sustained by personal unions. . . . Market behaviour is influenced by rational, purposeful pursuit of interests.[80]

In this description of the market community Weber in effect provides a sociological complement to the capitalist mechanism as described in the classical equilibrium theory. In both cases it is assumed that the behaviour of the individual is oriented to the exchange of goods in terms of the estimated values or prices. The prices of goods are not determined by single exchanges but ultimately by the behaviour of *all* those pursuing interests in the market. As Weber puts it,

> any active exchange involving the use of money (sale) is a social action simply because the money used derives its value from its relation to the potential action of others. Its acceptability works exclusively on the expectation it will continue to be desirable and can be further used as a means of payment.[81]

Later we shall see in detail how this aspect is crucial to the understanding of economic equilibrium, because it is the interplay of individuals in the course of exchange that generates prices, and this, in turn, causes the balancing of supply and demand.

Weber is interested in the possibility of a normative grounding of market behaviour, despite its impersonality. Thus he says,

80 Ibid., p. 636.
81 Ibid.

> The partner to a transaction is expected to behave according to rational legality and, quite particularly, to respect the formal inviolability of a promise once given. These are the qualities which form the content of market ethics. . . . Violations of agreements, even though they may be concluded by mere signs entirely unrecorded, and devoid of evidence, are almost unheard of in the annals of the stock exchange. Such absolute depersonalisation is contrary to all the elementary forms of human relationship. . . . It is normally assumed by both partners to an exchange that each will be interested in the future continuation of the exchange relationship, be it with this particular partner or some other, and that he will adhere to his promises for this reason and avoid at least striking infringements of the rules of good faith and fair dealing. It is only this assumption which guarantees the law-abidingness of the exchange partners. In so far as that interest exists, "honesty is the best policy."[82]

Nonetheless, Weber has no doubt that this minimal ethic of the market falls far short of any ethic that would be defensible on typical religious grounds: "The 'free' market, that is, the market which is not bound by ethical norms, with its exploitation of constellations of interest and monopoly positions and its dickering, is an abomination to every system of fraternal ethics."[83] He notes how in the early period of modern capitalism market relationships stabilize and trading activity frees itself from unlimited dickering and the exploitation of momentary interest situations. This has the effect of limiting fluctuation in prices and brings about greater predictability of the general trading situation.

The 1919 "Author's Introduction"

Weber's "Author's Introduction" is significant for a number of reasons but in particular because it points to the broad thematic concerns of Weber's full maturity.[84] It is of relevance to our concern here because it presents, in summary form, his attitude to and conceptual understanding of what he means by the concept of "modern capitalism". But it also relates the issue of modern capitalism to other rational or rationalizing aspects of Western society.[85] The celebrated opening sentence of the

82 Ibid., pp. 636–7.

83 Ibid., p. 367. Perhaps Weber is here echoing aspects of the Marxian critique of capitalism, as expressed classically in *The Communist Manifesto* where capitalism is derided for reducing all human relationships to nothing other than "the cash nexus".

84 It has this short title because the essay formed the Introduction to Weber's collective works on religion that were published under the title "The Economic Ethics of the Worlds Regions". The first two essays in this three volume collection are *The Protestant Ethic* essays of 1904–5, and these are followed by book-length essays on Judaism and other world religions.

85 Mention at this point should again be made to the work of Peter Ghosh, who argues that Weber's late work seems to have shifted the focus from the Marxist problematic of "capitalism" to his own problematic of the "rationalization of culture". Regardless of whether this is correct, in this work we are concerned primarily with the theory of capitalism and to that extent we remain focused on Weber's original problematic.

"Author's Introduction" gives a clear indication of the broader perspective from which Weber now understands the nature of his ultimate task: "A product of modern European civilization, studying any problem of universal history, is bound to ask himself to what combination of circumstances the facts should be attributed that in Western civilisation and in Western civilisation only, cultural phenomena have appeared which (as we like to think) lie in line of development having universal significance and value."[86]

Weber goes on to itemize a series of cultural achievements that he believes are unique to Western civilization and have only reached their full maturity in the modern West. He refers first to systematic theology and then to science, rational scholarship and rational jurisprudence. He even cites the development of music, in particular, rational harmonious music with counterpoint and harmony, which he says was only developed in the West. Weber also lists architecture, the press, education, bureaucracy and even feudalism, or at least its later stages. Of course the rise of the modern state is a crucial rational development with its legalistic constitutional basis, rational law and an administrative system carried on by trained officials bound by rules.

Finally, Weber refers to capitalism and sets out, in some detail, what he means by the concept of "rational capitalism". He again raises the problem of whether capitalism can be explained simply on the basis of reference to the pursuit of gain or money and the impulse to acquire as much of it as possible, concerns that go back to the key problematic of *The Protestant Ethic*. He again emphasizes that "capitalism is identical with the pursuit of profit, and forever *renewed* profit, by means of continuous, rational, capitalistic enterprise. For it must be so: in a wholly capitalistic order of society an individual capitalistic enterprise which did not take advantage of its opportunities for profit making would be doomed to extinction."[87] However, he points out, in line with his earlier thesis concerning the worldly asceticism of the Puritans, that modern capitalism is paradoxically connected with an opposite motive force, with restraint and a tempering of the impulse for gain. Having emphasized that capitalism must be associated with the pursuit of profit, he limits the scope of capitalistic acquisition in the modern setting defining it as action "that rests on the expectation of profit by the utilization of opportunities for exchange, that is on (formally) peaceful chances of profit. Acquisition by force (formally and actually) follows its own particular laws, and it is not expedient however little one can forbid this to place it in the same category with action which is, in the last analysis, oriented to profits from exchange."[88] There follows an extended discussion of how it is possible to fully exploit the opportunities for profit in a rational way, using the most technically rational available means. What Weber says then repeats the elements of the theory of rational capitalism elaborated in *Economy and Society* that we have expounded in this chapter.[89]

86 PE, p. 13.
87 Ibid., p. 17.
88 Ibid., pp. 17–18.
89 Ibid., pp. 18–19.

Weber again discusses various premodern forms of enterprise in trade and industry that he insists must be distinguished from the form of capitalism that has appeared in modern times in the Occident.[90] He finally goes on to relate the rationalizations he has been discussing to the forms of rationalism found elsewhere. He allows that other cultures have rationalized their institutions or rationalized conduct in various directions often to a considerable degree. He notes that the rationalization of mystical contemplation had been taken to a high level by the Yogi in India, and elsewhere, he refers to the rationalism of Confucianism, which entails the rational adaptation of conduct practised in the world. But only in the West has economic rationalism become central and dominant. This form of rationalism, whilst partly dependent on external structures of rationality, is at the same time determined by the ability and disposition of people to conduct themselves in a practically rational fashion. In other cultures there have been profound spiritual obstacles to the emergence of such dispositions, but in the West, ascetic Protestantism was able to clear a path to this general rationalization of everyday life.

90 Ibid., p. 25.

3 Schumpeter's theory of capitalist development

Introduction to the work of Schumpeter

In this chapter we explore the contributions of Schumpeter that complement and contrast with those of Weber in a number of ways. An obvious difference is their respective starting points: for whereas Weber begins and remains within the outlook of the historian, even as much of his work might be said to belong to sociology, Schumpeter is first and foremost an economist. Accordingly, we shall not expect their work to follow similar lines of inquiry, even if the focus for each was the phenomenon of modern capitalism.

Schumpeter is best known for his work *Capitalism, Socialism and Democracy*, a book he produced as a "popular" exposition of his theory of capitalism, whereas his larger writings, such as *Business Cycles: A Theoretical, Historical and Statistical Analysis of the Capitalist Process* and *The History of Economic Analysis*, are not well known outside a limited circle of academic followers. This is partly parallel to the reception of Weber, whose *The Protestant Ethic and the Spirit of Capitalism* became his best known work at the expense of an appreciation for his other writings. But whereas Weber became the most cited and probably the most lauded of all scholars in the social field in the twentieth century, Schumpeter did not achieve the same measure of notoriety. This in not to say Schumpeter has not been well recognized; some commentators have noted the large number of citations of Schumpeter in the literature of economics, even suggesting he tops the list.[1]

The comparative lack of appreciation of Schumpeter's work can perhaps be attributed to the timing of the writings, for his early works were published in German just prior to the First World War. This meant that they did not receive an "airing" in the English-speaking world until many years later – *The Theory of Economic Development*, originally published in 1911, was not published in an English version until 1934. Another reason is that, in the period prior to this point in time, the Western economies were in the grip of the Great Depression, and as

1 For example, see Peter Senn, "The Influence of Schumpeter's German Writings on Mainstream Economic Literature in English", in Jürgen Backhaus (ed.), *Joseph Schumpeter: Entrepreneurship, Style and Vision*, Kluwer, 2003, pp. 142–9.

a consequence, socialist views were widely accepted, so much of the political commentariat was unreceptive to a thinker as apparently sympathetic to capitalism as was Schumpeter. By the time Schumpeter produced his most mature writings, in particular, *Business Cycles* in 1939, the Keynesian perspective on the woes of capitalism, as set out in *The General Theory of Employment, Interest and Money* of 1936, had come to dominate economics. A further factor is that much of Schumpeter's work is written as a contribution to economic science, viewed at a high level of theoretical sophistication. That is, many of his writings are directed exclusively to the professional economic theorist and are rather inaccessible to the general reader. This is particularly true of his two great master works, *Business Cycles* of 1939 and *The History of Economic Analysis*, the latter published posthumously in 1954. Both are large, extremely complex and difficult to master – though it has to be said they are probably no more demanding than many of Weber's works. The subsequent reception of the works of our two thinkers is clearly relevant to their wider influence – for, as we have noted, Weber gradually came to be recognized as the seminal sociologist of his day, largely through his incorporation into American academic sociology (Parsons and Mills), whereas Schumpeter's star was somewhat eclipsed by the success of Keynes, and this remained the case for some time thereafter. Schumpeter's reputation probably was built most on his "popular" work, *Capitalism, Socialism and Democracy* as against his more scholarly writings. More recently, however, his works have been the subject of renewed interest because of what they offer in understanding the economic ups and downs of the last two decades.

As has been noted by various commentators, Schumpeter was a unique kind of eclectic thinker whose special talent lay in his ability to take up, digest and synthesize ideas from all manner of sources. For example, he eagerly incorporated the best elements of the theories of classical economic thought as it had been developed by major innovators like Alfred Marshall, Léon Walras and Carl Menger. But as well as these thinkers, he was open to the influence of a diverse range of others, including Karl Marx, Vilfredo Pareto, Wesley Mitchell, Irving Fisher and Frank Taussig.[2] Whilst Schumpeter's approach owes most to the influence of Walras and the Austrian School, it is also the case that he sought to introduce an entirely new paradigm inspired partly by Marx.[3] The impact that Marx's approach had on

2 To gain an idea of the full scope of Schumpeter's interest in, and engagement with, the whole gamut of economic theory of the day, one should consider his early discussions in *The Nature and Essence of Economic Theory*. Useful background and interesting personal anecdotes are recorded in the first part of Paul Samuelson, "Schumpeter as an Economic Theorist", in Helmut Frisch (ed.), *Schumpeterian Economics*, Praeger, 1981, pp. 1–9.

3 Although Schumpeter frequently mentions Marx as an important influence on his thinking, Paul Samuelson argues this has to be taken with a grain of salt, because "Schumpeter was of all my teachers the one whose *economics* was essentially farthest from Marx's: The labour theory of labour he considered a joke" (Paul Samuelson, "Schumpeter's Capitalism, Socialism and Democracy." Arnold Heerjie, *Schumpeter's Vision*, Praeger, 1981, p. 17).

Schumpeter is especially apparent in the latter's theory of economic fluctuations and his idea of the role of "vision" in theoretical work.[4]

Though recognizing and accepting many of the achievements of the Austrian School, Schumpeter's attitude to it was nonetheless equivocal, as is reflected by an article on Menger of 1921. There he writes that, on the one hand, "Menger's theory of value, price and distribution is the best we have up till now" – yet, on the other hand, he says, "No economic sociology or sociology of economic development can be derived from Menger's work. It makes only a small contribution to the picture of economic history and the struggle of social classes . . ."[5] This ambivalence is reflected throughout Schumpeter's work where he accepts and builds on equilibrium analysis yet at the same time emphasizes how the economy is in constant flux and undergoes periodic crises, often with far-reaching consequences.

We shall not explore in any detail Schumpeter's early writings such as *The Nature and Essence of Economic Theory* or *Economic Doctrine and Method.* This is not because they are unimportant but because many of their themes are repeated in his later work, and it is not our purpose here to provide a complete intellectual biography.[6] Nonetheless, it will be useful to refer briefly to *Economic Doctrine and Method* owing to its connection with Weber's *Grundriss*. In *Economic Doctrine and Method* we find a survey of economic theory that is in many ways a curtain raiser to the later and more substantial *History of Economic Analysis*. It is worth noting that towards the end of the book Schumpeter discusses the rise of marginal utility theory, and it is clear that he regards this as a theoretical achievement of utmost significance. "Marginal utility was the ferment which has changed the inner structure of modern theory into something quite different from that of the classical economists."[7] He goes on describe the general features of marginal utility theory and how it differed from what went before:

> The theory of marginal utility . . . places the main emphasis on the complex of problems which the classical economists passed over too lightly, namely, the foundations for the determination of value and price. . . . It placed the explanation of the nature of price determination and of the various forms of income into the forefront . . . Thus a different and much "purer" economics

4 For a full understanding of Schumpeter's appreciation of Marx, see the extensive discussions in *Capitalism, Socialism and Democracy*, Harper, 1950 (CSD), Part 1 and in *History of Economic Analysis* (HEA), Oxford University Press, 1954 especially at pp. 383–92.

5 Joseph Schumpeter, "Carl Menger", in *Ten Great Economists: From Marx to Keynes*, Oxford University Press (TGE), 1951, p. 86.

6 For a thorough overview of the entire corpus of Schumpeter's writings on capitalism, which persuasively argues that his works can be separated into an early and later "trilogy", see Esben Andersen, *Joseph A. Schumpeter: A Theory of Social and Economic Evolution*, Palgrave, 2011, pp. 139–41.

7 Joseph Schumpeter, *Economic Doctrine and Method: An Historical Sketch*, Allen & Unwin, 1954, p. 181.

> originated which contains much less concrete and factual material . . . but is immeasurably more firmly founded.[8]

Now even though Schumpeter is fully aware of the fact that marginal utility was developed independently by Menger in Austria and Jevons in England, he regards Léon Walras as having brought the notion to its highest level of theoretical sophistication. And despite his concern to address the issue of the irregular character of capitalist progress and his scepticism as to its long-term prospects, he strongly endorses the general approach of the great equilibrium economist. Indeed, there is hardly a figure in the history of thought that Schumpeter admires more. For not only does he attribute to Walras a profound achievement in his account of the mechanism of equilibrium, he also credits Walras as having placed economics, as a whole, on a secure scientific footing. For a long time, Walras's work was not well known in the English-speaking world, due to its availability only in French and owing to the complex mathematics that underlay its theorems. This situation has been decisively changed since the 1950s when William Jaffé began to champion his works in the English-speaking world, and figures such as Kenneth Arrow developed the so-called "general equilibrium theory".[9] So in what follows, we must first discuss Schumpeter's relation to Walras.

Schumpeter's appreciation of Walras

In Schumpeter's oeuvre, there are several detailed accounts of Walras and he refers to him frequently throughout. He gives his most detailed appraisal of Walras's theories in *The History of Economic Analysis*. There he is concerned to explain the nature of Walras's system of equations and why it was so path-breaking. According to Schumpeter, Walras' achievement lay in his ability, at least in theory, to explain the equilibrium values of all economic variables: "the prices of all products and factors and the quantities of these products and factors that would be bought in perfect equilibrium and pure competition, by all households and firms."[10] Walras conceived equilibrium prices to be the level around which actual prices oscillate in the real economy; though he was aware that this was to some degree an approximation because there are always disturbing factors of a non-economic nature in the real world.[11]

According to Schumpeter, the Walrasian entrepreneur operates as follows: he buys raw materials from other entrepreneurs, leases land from landowners, acquires the personal aptitudes of workers, buys capital goods from other capitalists, and sells the products that result from a creative combination of these factors for his

8 Ibid., p. 188.

9 See in particular Donald Walker (ed.), *William Jaffé's Essays on Walras*, Cambridge University Press, 1983.

10 HEA, p. 999.

11 Walras's key description of the economic pattern that is expressed by his equations is set out in Lessons 17–19 of his *Éléments d'économie politique pure, ou théorie de la richesse sociale*.

own benefit. Walras set out to construct a theory of the various markets through which all this economic activity must occur, the interaction of which comprises the economic system. A key notion in the theory is the concept of *tâtonnement* or "groping", which he introduces in the following terms:

> What must we do in order to prove that theoretical [that is, mathematical] solution [of the determination of equilibrium prices] is *identically* the solution worked out by the market? Our task is very simple: we need to show [in the case of pure exchange] that upward and downward movement of prices solves the system of equations on offer and demand by a process of groping [par *tâtonnement*].[12]

Walras identifies the markets through which the economic mechanism operates, the interaction of which make up the object of analysis – those for products and those for productive services – but in addition, he points to the existence of markets that determine the prices of capital goods and other elements of the system. He places considerable emphasis on the inventories that economic agents have at their disposal. As Schumpeter explains,

> There are inventories of new capital goods, consumers goods inventories held by households and by firms, raw material inventories held by both their producers and their users, and also as we have seen stocks of money (cash holdings of various types). Since the existence of these inventories presuppose a certain past behaviour of the people concerned and since their current reproduction presupposes certain expectations, the system – even if perfectly stationary – still depicts a process in time and might therefore be called "implicitly dynamic".[13]

However, in the Walrasian system, households do not strictly purchase consumer goods or sell their services as such. Nor do entrepreneurs purchase productive services and offer their products outright.

> They all merely declare what they *would* respectively buy and sell (produce) at prices *criés au hazard*, that is, announced experimentally by some agent in the market, and are free to change their minds if these prices do not turn out to be the equilibrium prices: other prices are thereupon announced, other

12 Quoted in *William Jaffé's Essays on Walras*, p. 222. Jaffé explains that, by "groping", Walras means a process of "blindly feeling its way, since no one in the actual world is presumed to know in advance the parameters or the solution of the equations." However, Jaffé argues that Walras actually failed in his attempt to prove his thesis, because, "Though he allowed for trading at 'false prices' in his preliminary description of the operation of the mechanism of competition in the real market, he overlooked it completely in his analytical discussion of *tâtonnement*." (pp. 222–3). The question of whether Walras "solved" his fundamental theoretical problem is complicated and remains controversial to this day. See Jaffé's further discussion of the issues involved at pp. 223–42.

13 HEA, p. 1002.

> declarations of willingness to buy or sell (and to produce) are written down on *bons* [tickets] – pieces of paper that do not carry any obligation – until equilibrium values emerge, namely prices such that no demand willing to pay them and no supply willing to accept them remain unsatisfied. And the only mechanism of reaction to these variations of experimental prices that Walras recognises is to raise the prices of commodities of services, the demand for which at these prices is greater than the supply, and to reduce the price of commodities or services, the supply of which at these prices is greater than the demand.[14]

Importantly, Walras conceives a "system of exchange relations", rather than a theory of competitive exchange of just two commodities, for his theory of equilibrium requires the existence of a significant number of commodities in order for unique prices to emerge. According to Schumpeter, Walras assumes something like this: that a certain number of players, endowed with definite tastes and possessing at the start arbitrary quantities of a range of commodities, enter the market in order to see what advantages trade will bring.[15] He takes for granted that there is a tendency for all participants to maximize their satisfaction. If the number of people is n and the number of commodities is m, then there must be $m(n - 1)$ behaviour equations expressing for all n participants the quantities that they will give away or acquire in any given system of exchange relations. They will go on trading at prices in terms of a standard commodity or *numéraire* until no further exchange will increase their level of satisfaction. Further, there must be m equations for every commodity. The total amount of a commodity given away must equal the total amount of the commodity acquired for the market as a whole. There are therefore $m(n + 1)$ conditions or equations. Without going into the further technical/mathematical aspects of Walras' system, the thrust of his argument is that the system of equations is able to produce a solution that is an approximation of the actual price level.

Now the key problem that arises from all this is: given the possibility that there can be a unique solution, is there in fact a tendency of the economic system to actually produce this solution? In other words, what is the relationship between the strict logic of the theory wherein a mathematical solution to the equations is possible and the process of price formation in the actual marketplace? Walras "solved" this problem, according to Schumpeter, by arguing that "the people in the market, though evidently not solving any equations, do by a different method the same thing that the theorist does by solving equations; or, to put it differently, that the 'empirical' method used in perfectly competitive markets and the 'theoretical' or 'scientific' method of the observer tend to produce the same equilibrium configuration."[16] In the Walrasian system, as we have said, people appear

14 Ibid.

15 The following account of Walras relies on Schumpeter's exegesis in HEA, pp. 998–1026.

16 Ibid., p. 1008. This problem of whether Walras actually solved the problem of how an economy arrives at equilibrium prices is discussed at length by William. Jaffé in his essay "Walras's Theory of *Tâtonnement*: A Critique of Recent Interpretations", *Journal of Political Economy*, 75 (1967), pp. 1–19.

in the market with the commodities they possess and with definite marginal utility schedules, and they are confronted with the prices as *criés au hazard* (random price calls). They offer to give away certain commodities to acquire certain others at the prices called. But actually, they do not complete the transactions, because they only note on *bons* (tickets) what they would buy and sell at those prices should they persist. If, however, no recontract proves necessary and the *bons* are redeemed, then the conditions of the equations are in fact fulfilled. If they are not able to agree to the prices and recontract at different prices, which are higher or lower than those initially offered, then, accordingly as they experience positive or negative excess demand, the prices offered will be adjusted until they are equated in all cases. Schumpeter says, "whatever we might have to say about this on the score of realism, it seems at first sight to be intuitively clear that, *so long as no other mechanism of reaction is admitted than the one exclusively considered by Walras*, equilibrium will be attained under these assumptions: that, in general, this equilibrium will be unique and stable; and that the prices and quantities in this configuration will be those we get from our theoretical solution."[17]

Walras' theory of production has direct parallels with his theory of consumption. It is a theory in which the mechanism of pure competition allocates the services of the different types of natural agents – labour and produced means of production. The theory of allocation effectively amounts to the same as a theory of the pricing of those services, because the price mechanism brings the services into the arena of the marketplace in just the quantities necessary to satisfy demand. A question that must now be raised is whether or not there exists a unique set of solutions for a system of equations that covers both consumers' and producers' behaviour. Schumpeter answers in the affirmative and argues that Walras' solution is as follows:

> The households that furnish the services have in *Walras' set up* definite and single valued schedules of willingness to part with these services. These schedules are determined, on the one hand by their appreciation of the satisfaction to be derived from consuming their services directly and, on the other hand by their knowledge of the satisfaction they might derive from the incomes in terms of *numéraire* that they are able to earn at any set of consumers' goods and service "prices". For the "prices" of consumers' goods are determined simultaneously with the "prices" of the services and with reference to one another: every workman, for an instance, decides how many hours of work per day or week he is going to offer in response to a wage in terms of *numéraire* that is associated with definite prices, in terms of *numéraire*, of all the consumers' goods that would be produced with the total amount of work being offered at that wage rate. Mathematically, we express this by making everybody's offer of every service he "owns" a function of all prices (both of consumers' goods and the services) and, for the same reason, everybody's

17 HEA, p. 1008.

> demand for every commodity another function of all prices (both of services and the consumers' goods). Everybody's demand for the *numéraire* commodity follows simply from everybody's balance equation . . .[18]

Schumpeter points out that for a mathematical solution, the number of variables to be determined must be equal to the number of equations and, though Walras did not reach the standards of modern mathematics in arriving at his view that a solution is obtainable, his computations were not far from that level: "It may be averred that, *so far as this part of the Walrasian analysis is concerned*, our result is, or it comes near to being the common opinion of theorists."[19]

But Schumpeter goes on to point to a fundamental difficulty in the Walrasian system, as regards the tendency of the economic system to move towards the establishment of equilibrium prices. This arises because of the way Walras sets up the process of *tâtonnement* with the requirement that there be experimental *criés* to be followed by recontracting when parties do not accept those prices. The problem is that it would appear that the process of "groping" must occur amongst all the participants in the market at the same instant, which cannot be the case in actual reality. "Even if all firms and all owners of productive services did succeed in this task, they would still have to carry out this production program which takes time, during which nothing must be allowed to change."[20] The issue of time is thus critical, and the question of how equilibrium can be a product of a dynamic system becomes all the more pressing. Schumpeter saw the task of dealing with this problem, which leads to the problem of crises and ultimately cycles, as his own special task. So Schumpeter did not accept Walras' approach in toto but engaged with his system with a view to improving it.

Just as Marx saw the essence of the capitalist system as leading inevitably to system-wide crises, Schumpeter also sees that there are inherent tendencies in the system towards serious instability. As with Marx, grasping this requires in-depth analysis of the capitalist mechanism. Innovations, the credit mechanism and the process of carrying out new combinations in the form of enterprise – all these not only create cyclical effects (to be described in detail later in *Business Cycles*), but they also eventually lead to outcomes that may even change capitalism itself into something fundamentally different. Schumpeter at times tends to agree with Marx about the fundamental limit of the capitalist era: both suggest it is the very productivity of capitalism that threatens its ongoing existence. But whereas Marx foretold that the tendency to over-production would culminate, and not long into the future, in the collapse of the capitalist system as a whole, Schumpeter generally sees cycles as being manageable short of total system failure – at least for the

18 Ibid., p. 1012. These remarks about the disposition of workers to adjust their labour services in accordance with expectations about wages bears comparison with Weber's remarks about the role of tradition in conditioning workers' attitudes in *The Protestant Ethic*: see pp. 59–63.

19 HEA, p. 1014.

20 Ibid.

time being. Nonetheless, Schumpeter regards socialism as more than a remote possibility, as we shall see.

Schumpeter's theory of the wave-like fluctuations of business activity and his account of the tendency of the system towards crises in part derives from his view that entrepreneurial activity typically manifests in the form of "clusters". Economic booms are triggered when one or a few branches of industry are witness to the success of a few entrepreneurs, and this attracts other innovators into the same field. The initial players may simply remove obstacles that allow others to take up the opportunities unleashed by the first wave, and this creates a swarm-like effect or rush.

A starting point for understanding Schumpeter's work in this regard must be his classic study *The Theory of Economic Development*, published in 1911.[21] This is one of the works that gave him his early standing as a major thinker in the field of economics, and it contains many of his essential ideas in basic form. In what follows we shall rely on this work as the primary statement of Schumpeter's theory of capitalism, though his previous works to some degree anticipate the argument of the work. Unfortunately, it is not possible to gauge the precise extent of Weber's appreciation of this work, though the timing of Schumpeter's appointment by Weber to write the section on the history of economics for the *Grundriss* suggests that he was certainly aware of it; but Weber does not appear to have commented expressly on the book.[22]

The "circular flow" and the basic elements of economic activity

In a nutshell, in *The Theory of Economic Development*, Schumpeter sets out to build a framework for grasping the entire capitalist system and its dynamics on the basis of the economic theories advanced by Walras and the marginal utility School.[23] That is, he wants to combine the marginalist account of how an economy typically sets prices and operates under competitive conditions with an evolutionary

21 It is worth noting that the English edition of this work and the subsequent German editions are different from the original, as an important section, namely Chapter Seven, was omitted in the later versions. Chapter Seven is now available in German and English with a full bibliographical account and commentaries in the collection edited by Jürgen Backhaus, *Joseph Alois Schumpeter: Entrepreneurship, Style and Vision*, Kluwer, 2003. The fact of the two versions of Schumpeter's *Theorie der wirtschaftlichen Entwicklung* has led Andersen to consider they deserve separate treatment in assessing Schumpeter's work as a whole. See his discussion in *Joseph A. Schumpeter*, pp. 5–11.

22 According to Jürgen Osterhammel, "The *Theory of Economic Development* . . . was widely discussed and studied, also by Max Weber, whose annotated personal copy has survived." Jürgen Osterhammel, "Varieties of Social Economics: Joseph Schumpeter and Max Weber", in Wolfgang J. Mommsen and Jürgen Osterhammel (eds.), *Max Weber and His Contemporaries*, Allen & Unwin, 1987, p. 106.

23 The most significant early attempt to give an overall account of Schumpeter's theory of capitalism is Richard V. Clemence and Francis S. Doody, *The Schumpeterian System*, Addison-Wesley Press, 1950.

perspective where change is seen as endemic involving continual innovation and system disruption. It is remarkable, given his conservative political value stance, that Schumpeter expressly takes up the perspectives of Marx, especially certain aspects of his *Capital*, as being fruitful for the understanding of capitalism as an evolutionary system – though his overall approach, as already noted, is definitely at odds with the political thrust of Marx's thought.

Schumpeter begins his account of the capitalist economy by proposing a conceptual simplification along the lines of a theoretical device also employed by numerous others.[24] Such an approach, Schumpeter believes, is the only way the theorist can build a theory that is capable of grasping the full complexity of the reality that is the capitalist economy. Largely following the lead of Walras, Schumpeter, piece by piece, builds a model of a simplified economy in pure form. The model has only some of the features of an actual exchange economy and lacks important dynamic phenomena that are associated with such a system. He adopts this approach to show at a further stage how dynamic elements are crucial to and constitutive of actually existing capitalism. As he puts it later in *Business Cycles*, "Obviously, such a model will present the fundamental facts and relations of economic life in their simplest form, and it is hardly possible to bring them out satisfactorily without it. Implicitly and in a rudimentary form it has, therefore, always been present in the minds of absolutely all economists of all schools at all times, although most of them were not aware of it."[25]

Schumpeter's model of a simplified economy posits the idea of an unchanging economic process that flows in a regular fashion without ever growing. The model is clearly influenced by Walras' theory of how an exchange economy functions so as to create prices that enable an equilibrium outcome. Schumpeter adopts this approach to establish a kind of foundational structure upon which he can subsequently build the complications of an economy that continually expands in the fashion of real capitalism. In the model of an unchanging economy, there are no technological innovations, no surplus or profits and no growth in output – therefore, there are none of the typical features of mature capitalism such as capitalists, entrepreneurs, banks, inflation, unemployment, the stock market or business fluctuations. But, the simplified economy is otherwise akin to an actually existing market economy insofar as it has certain systemic features in common with it – such as exchange, money, prices, production and consumption. "We shall primarily think of a commercially organised state, one in which private

24 For example, just as Marx begins his exegesis of the capitalist mode of production with a preliminary account of a simplified economic system based on the extraction of what he calls "absolute surplus value" and then proceeds to explain the more complex situation of the actual capitalist manufacture with its labour-replacing machinery allowing the extraction "relative surplus value", so Schumpeter begins by outlining a simplified model of an economy that does not correspond to the realities of the actual capitalist economy and then adds in the crucial real-world elements.

25 Joseph Schumpeter, *Business Cycles: A Theoretical, Historical and Statistical Analysis of the Capitalist Process*, McGraw-Hill, 1939 (BC), p. 36.

property, division of labour, and free competition prevail."[26] From these assumptions, Schumpeter proceeds to build an elaborate model of the working of this economy in which all factors promoting fundamental change are absent. In effect, he is conducting a protracted thought experiment to bring out, as graphically as he can, the nature of a perfectly static economy. In all this, we suggest Schumpeter is employing the method of ideal types similarly to Menger and consistently with Weber's ideal type approach. Just as Weber explains that the theoretical schemas of the historian or economist do not exist in reality, so Schumpeter knows his unchanging exchange economy has never actually existed, nor could it.

Schumpeter wants to emphasize the routine and repetitive character of his static economy, which he describes with the phrase the "circular flow of economic life".[27] (He later calls this, somewhat contradictorily, the "stationary flow".[28]) In the course of this exercise, he provides a commentary on a series of theoretical problems that are current in economic science, some of which have been issues since at least the time of Adam Smith. He refers to issues such as: the ultimate source of wealth creation; the difference between various types of labour; the distinction between consumer goods and producer goods; the role of money in exchange; and so on. Much of what Schumpeter says is not particularly novel and might even be considered the conventional view. But, typically, he gives things his own unique twist.

Schumpeter asks the reader to consider the following hypothetical situation:

> If someone who has never seen or heard of such a state were to observe that a farmer produces corn to be consumed as bread in a distant city, he would be impelled to ask how the farmer knew that this consumer wanted bread and just so much. He would assuredly be astonished to learn that the farmer did not know at all where or by whom it would be consumed. Furthermore, he could observe that all the people through whose hands the corn must go on its way to the final consumer knew nothing of the latter, with the possible exception of the ultimate sellers of bread; and even they must in general produce or buy before they know that this particular consumer will acquire it. The farmer could easily answer the question put to him: long experience, in part inherited, has taught him how much to produce for his greatest advantage; experience has taught him to know the extent and intensity of the demand to be reckoned with. To this quantity he adheres, as well as he can, and only gradually alters it under the pressure of circumstances.[29]

26 TED, p. 5.

27 The term "circular flow" in English is a rendering by the 1934 translator of Schumpeter's German term "Kreislauf". We do not know if Schumpeter agreed with this translation. The later term "stationary flow" referring to the same phenomenon is Schumpeter's own term as employed in *Business Cycles*, which he wrote in English.

28 BC, p. 35.

29 TED, pp. 5–6.

Schumpeter says the same holds good for other items in the farmer's calculations. He ordinarily knows the prices of the things he must pay when he buys inputs, how much of his own labour will be needed and the method of cultivation that is best – all from years of experience. Also all those from whom he buys will be familiar with the extent and intensity of his demand. In every economic period more or less the same things occur. The experience of previous economic periods governs the activity of the individual in the present. This is the case not only because experience has taught him what he has to do, but also because during every period the farmer must live either directly upon the physical product of the preceding period or upon what he can obtain with the proceeds of this product. All the preceding periods have, furthermore, entangled him in a web of social and economic relations that have bequeathed him definite means and methods of production.

Schumpeter then says the case of the farmer can be generalized. All producers are in the position of the farmer. They are all simultaneously buyers – for the purposes of their production and consumption – as well as sellers. In general, all products will be disposed of, for they will only be produced with reference to known market possibilities. Thus, how much meat the butcher sells depends upon how much his customer the tailor buys and at what price. That depends, however, upon the sales from the latter's business, these proceeds again upon the needs and the purchasing power of the shoemaker, whose purchasing power again depends upon the needs and purchasing power of those for whom he produces, and so on. This concatenation and mutual dependence of the quantities of which the economic system consists are always transparent, in whichever direction one may choose to move. Analysis never discovers an element that does more to determine other elements than it is determined by them.[30]

Schumpeter wants to press his ideal typical conception of the "circular flow" to its logical conclusion. He says we can imagine that, year in and year out, there is an ever-recurring employment of productive powers designed to reach the same set of consumers, the outcome of which is similar in each case. Hence, somewhere in the economy every demand is matched by a corresponding supply, and nowhere are there commodities in the hands of people who will not exchange them given the right conditions. It follows that in the "circular flow", economic life is a closed system in that the sellers of commodities are also buyers in sufficient measure to acquire those goods that will maintain their present level of consumption as well as their productive equipment into the next period, and vice versa.

> Obviously this does not mean that no changes can take place in their economic activity. The data may change, and everyone will act accordingly as soon as it is noticed. But everyone will cling as tightly as possible to habitual economic methods and only submit to the pressure of circumstances as it becomes necessary. Thus the economic system will not change capriciously on its own

30 Ibid., p. 8.

> initiative but will be at all times connected with the preceding state of affairs. This may be called Wieser's principle of continuity.[31]

Schumpeter points out that economic activity in the "circular flow" may have *numerous possible* motives, even spiritual ones, but its ultimate *meaning* is always the satisfaction of wants.[32] Hence, the fundamental importance of concepts that are derived from the fact of wants, the foremost of which is the concept of utility and its derivative marginal utility. From this he argues that certain theorems follow about the distribution of resources to possible uses, about complementariness and rivalry amongst goods, and about ratios of exchange, prices, and the "law of supply and demand." Finally, one reaches a system of values and the conditions of the system's equilibrium.

The fundamental sources of wealth creation

Schumpeter asks: What is the underlying purpose of production? The goal that economic man pursues in producing goods, and which explains why there is any production at all, he says, puts its mark on the method and volume of production. This end determines the "what" and the "for why" of production within the framework of given means and objective necessities. The end can only be the making of useful things, of objects of consumption. Therefore, production follows needs; it is pulled after them. But this characteristic of production creates a problem that is essentially economic in nature and must be distinguished from a purely technological question. For there are changes in the productive process recommended by the technician that are rejected by management; for example, the engineer may recommend a process that is rejected with the argument that it will not pay. What concerns the businessman is commercial advantage, for he may well say that the resources that the provision of a machine requires can be employed otherwise to better effect. The business leader is correct in *not* following the engineer's recommendations. Clearly these views clearly coincide with Weber's on the same topic.

Schumpeter points out that technologically, as well as economically, production "creates" nothing physically. Production can only control things and processes. It is always a question of changing the existing state of the satisfaction of our wants or of changing the relations of things. To produce means to combine things and forces. Different methods of production can only be distinguished by the objects combined or by the relation between their quantities. Schumpeter places considerable emphasis on this feature and see the fortunes of business as being much effected by such "combinations". He argues that "production coefficients" represent the quantitative relation of production goods contained in a unit of product, and they are therefore specified for any combination. The economic point of view does not only decide between different methods of production, but it also

31 Ibid., pp. 8–9.

32 This assumption would appear to correspond to Weber's concept of "rational economic action".

determines the coefficients, since the individual means of production can, to a certain extent, be substituted for one another. That is, deficiencies in one means can be compensated for by increases in another without altering the method of production: for example, a decrease in steam power by an increase in hand labour. Schumpeter's concept of combination is very important to his subsequent theory of development, as we shall see. Under the conditions of developed capitalism, "new combinations" are the driving force of technological innovation. But in the stationary state, new combinations are in principle not present.

According to Schumpeter, the basic ingredients that are required in the production of all goods are land and labour. Much of what he says here is linked to debates that have engaged economists intensively over the years concerning the ultimate source of wealth creation. Like Marx, Schumpeter agrees that labour is a fundamental source, but contrary to Marx, he says nature/land is also a source of wealth, and entrepreneurial and managerial work must equally be counted as a type of labour. He explains, "It is usual to classify goods into 'orders' according to their distance from the final act of consumption. Consumption goods are of the first order, goods from combinations of which consumption goods immediately originate are of the second order, and so on, in continually higher or more remote orders."[33] It follows from this that labour is a good of the highest order, because it enters at the very beginning of production. In successive stages each good matures into a "consumption good" through the addition of other goods belonging to the various orders. Schumpeter imagines a hierarchy of orders such that at the lowest level are specialized consumption goods and the highest goods that are increasingly amorphous and lack any precise qualities that predestine them for particular uses. The higher up in the orders of goods, the more they lose their specialized character. As we ascend in the hierarchy of goods, we eventually come to the ultimate elements, namely labour and the gifts of nature or land.[34]

Having broached the issue as to the essential role of labour, Schumpeter comments on the question as to the role of managerial activities. This means he must clarify the distinctions between so-called "directing" and "directed" labour, and between independent and wage labour. Importantly, he proposes definitions that are particularly at odds with the Marxist approach. What distinguishes directing and directed labour is fundamental. Directing labour stands higher in the hierarchy of the productive organism. Supervision of the "executing" labour places directing labour in a different order to ordinary labour. While executing labour is similar to the uses of land and, from the economic standpoint, has the same function as these, directing labour occupies a governing position. Schumpeter thereby suggests that it forms a third productive factor. And another characteristic separating it from directed labour is that it has something creative about it in that it sets its own ends. The important fact about directing labour is that it determines the method and quantity of production.

33 Ibid., p. 16. Here Schumpeter is closely following Menger. See Roger Garrison, "Austrian Capital Theory: The Early Controversies", *History of Political Economy*, 22, (1990), pp. 135–9.

34 TED, p. 17.

Under the assumptions Schumpeter has set down as basic constituents of the "circular flow" there is no leader of the productive process in general – or rather, the real leader is the consumer. The people who direct business activity only execute what is required of them by the expressed wants and by the available means of production. Every individual takes part in the direction of production, not only the director of the business firm, but everyone including the workers. The data that have governed the economic system till then remain unchanged, and the system will continue in the same way indefinitely into the future. To anticipate a little, Schumpeter wants to emphasize the importance of consumer sovereignty and the lack of leadership in the state of the circular flow because in the real world of dynamic capitalism these features are reversed.

Schumpeter says that in his imagined stationary economy, the quantity of labour is set by the given circumstances. Assuming that the best possibilities of employing the labour of all individuals are known, then the anticipated utility of every concrete employment of labour is compared with the disutility accompanying that employment. The burden of work ensures that no labour is undertaken that is not required out of necessity. These considerations determine the amount of work that each worker performs. At the beginning of each working day, it is clear what work is to be undertaken. But the more one achieves in the satisfaction of wants, the more the impulse to work declines and at the same time the more the disutility of work, increases; so that eventually the moment comes when increasing utility and increasing disutility of work balance each other.[35]

Imputation and the theory of value

As the services of labour and of land are the only productive powers, the issue arises as to how the system is stabilized in the "circular flow". The measurement of the quantity of labour and the measure of the services of land, however complicated in practice, are not in principle insoluble. This leads to the problem of values. Schumpeter wants to explain how the economic system generates the price mechanism from the valuations that must be placed on the ingredients that go into production. He relies here on the groundbreaking work of his fellow Austrians and especially the work of Wieser and the notion of "imputation":[36]

> What the individual wishes to measure is the relative significance of quantities of his means of production. He needs a standard with the help of which to regulate his economic conduct; he needs indexes to which he can conform. In short, he requires a standard of value. But he has such a thing directly only for his consumption goods; for only these immediately satisfy his wants, the

35 Ibid., pp. 22–3.

36 On Wieser's contribution see his seminal essays "On the Relationship of Costs to Value" Chapter 8 and "The Austrian School and the Theory of Value" Chapter 9 in Israel Kirzner (ed.), *Classics in Austrian Economics*, Vol 1, Pickering, 1994.

> intensity of which is the basis of the meaning of his goods to him. For his stock of services of labour and land there is in the first instance no such standard, and likewise none, we may now add, for his produced means of production.[37]

So how do means of production or producer goods acquire value and how are they costed in accordance with the theory of imputation? It is clear that these goods also owe their importance to the fact that they likewise satisfy wants, because they contribute to the realization of consumption goods. The value of the consumption goods, as it were, radiates back to them and is "imputed" to them.

> In contrast to use value of consumption goods this value of production goods is "return value" (*Ertragswert*), or as one might also say, productivity value (*Produktivitätswert*). To the marginal utility of the former corresponds the marginal productive use (*Produktivitätsgrenznutzen*) of the latter, or, following the usual term, the marginal productivity; the significance of an individual unit of the services of labour or land is given by the marginal productivity of labour or land, which is therefore to be defined as the value of the least important unit of product so far produced with the help of a unit of a given stock of the services of labour or land. This value indicates the share of every individual service of labour or land in the value of the total social product, and can hence be called in a definite sense the "product" of a service of labour or land. . . . In this sense also we say that the prices of the services of land and labour in an exchange economy, that is rent and wages, are determined by the marginal productivity of land and labour, and therefore that under free competition landlord and labourer receive the product of their means of production.[38]

But how does knowledge of correct values arise in practice? Schumpeter says that, although once in operation the individual relies on previous experience, one must disregard the existence of this experience and start from the point where the individual is not yet clear about the existing possibilities of employment. He says the individual will first employ his means of production in the production of those goods that satisfy his most urgent needs, and thereafter pursue less pressing needs. And at each step he will consider what other wants must go unsatisfied in consequence of the decisions he makes. Each step is only economical provided that the satisfaction of more intensive wants is not rendered impossible. To each contemplated option of employment of resources, there corresponds a particular value of every increment. If no choice is made, the means of production will have no definite value. Schumpeter assumes that, if no given want is satisfied before more intensive wants have been satisfied,

37 TED, p. 24.

38 Ibid., p. 25. It is noteworthy that, in contrast to Marx and his attitude to the idea of exchange value, the imputed value of goods is not derided as mysterious or "unnatural".

then the result must be that all goods will be so divided amongst their different possible uses such that the marginal utility of each good is equal in all its uses. In this arrangement the individual has found the circumstance that is the best possible. He will strive after this state of want satisfaction until it is achieved. If necessary, he must feel his way to the optimum step by step. If previous experience is already available, he will use this to avoid having to employ trial and error. And if the conditions change, he will submit to the new conditions and adapt his conduct accordingly. In all cases, according to Schumpeter, there is a definite way of employing every good, hence a definite satisfaction of wants. As a result, one can arrive at a utility index for the individual increments of the goods involved. If a new possibility of employment of a good occurs, it must be considered in the light of this value. There finally emerges a definite utility scale for every good, and this reflects the utilities of all its possible uses and gives rise to a definite marginal utility. With means of production, the same applies through their "productive contribution."

Schumpeter now comes to the issue of "costs". All production involves a choice between various possibilities and always entails the renunciation of producing other goods. This is where the element of cost arises.

> In the final analysis what the production of a good costs the producer is those consumption goods which could otherwise be acquired with the same means of production, and which in consequence of the choice of production cannot now be produced. Therefore the outlay of means of production involves a sacrifice, in the case of labour just as in the case of other means of production. To be sure, in the case of labour there is also another condition which must be fulfilled, viz., that every expenditure of labour must result in a utility which at least compensates for the disutility attaching to that expenditure of labour. This, however, in no way alters the fact that within the limits of this condition the individual behaves towards the expenditure of labour exactly as towards the expenditure of other productive resources.[39]

Schumpeter points out that unsatisfied wants are by no means without significance, for every productive decision must contend with them. The further the producer goes in a given direction, the harder this battle with unsatisfied wants becomes: "that is the more a particular want is satisfied, the less the intensity of the desire for more in the same line, hence the less the increase in satisfaction to be achieved through further production."[40] Further, the sacrifice associated with production in a given direction also increases at the same time. For the means of production for such products must be taken away from ever more pressing wants. The key theorem of the theory of marginal utility is thus stated as: "The gain in

39 Ibid., p. 28.
40 Ibid.

value from the production in one direction becomes therefore continually smaller, and finally it vanishes. When that happens, this particular production comes to an end. Thus we can speak here of a law of decreasing returns in production."[41] Here also the concept of "opportunity costs" arises.

The concept of equilibrium

Schumpeter takes up the further implications of the classical theory of marginal utility with a discussion of the related notion of equilibrium that he takes over largely from Walras. He maintains that the system of the "circular flow" tends to always be in balance or "equilibrium". This is a necessary consequence of the way he has constructed the model; for he has built it precisely to show the conditions under which equilibrium must in theory be the normal and constant result of economic activity. But of course he does not accept that equilibrium is the usual state of an actually existing capitalist economy – though he maintains there is a tendency *towards* equilibrium, as we shall see. The state of equilibrium in the "circular flow" arises essentially because of the nature of costs. Costs are an expression of the value of other potential employments of means of production and, as we saw, this is the deepest significance of the cost phenomenon:

> It follows from [economic equilibrium], first of all, that the last increment of every product will be produced without a gain in utility above costs. . . . But further, it follows that in production generally no surplus value above the value of producers' goods can be attained. Production realises only the values foreseen in the economic plan, which previously exist potentially in the values of means of production. Also in this sense . . . production "creates" no values, that is in the course of the productive process no increase in value occurs.[42]

Following the Austrian School's approach to the problem of value, Schumpeter argues that the imputation process refers us back to the ultimate elements of production, namely, the services of labour and land. It cannot stop at any particular produced means of production, for these can be further reduced to more basic elements themselves. Hence, no product can show a surplus of value over the value of the services of labour and land embodied in it. In the "circular flow" the prices of all products will, where there is free competition, be equal to the prices of the services of labour and nature embodied therein. For the price obtainable for the product after production has occurred must have been obtainable at the outset for the complete set of required means of production. Each producer must give up his total receipts to all those who supplied him with means of production, and insofar as the latter are also producers of some product or other, they must in their turn

41 Ibid.
42 Ibid., pp. 29–30.

pass on their receipts until the whole original price falls to the providers of the services of labour and of nature.[43]

Now the question arises as to whether profit can exist under these conditions. This is a crucial issue because profit is an essential element of any real capitalist system. So if profit does not exist in the "circular flow", how does it come into being? Considering the situation the "circular flow", Schumpeter says that, if the businessman takes into consideration the costs he must pay for his inputs in order to produce goods for sale and adds in a sum equivalent to the money value of his own efforts, this total must equal the total price for the services of labour and nature, so there can be no profit. As he explains:

> That the economic system in its most perfect condition should operate without profit is a paradox. If we remember the meaning of our statements, the paradox vanishes, at least in part. Of course our assertion does not mean that if it is perfectly balanced the economic system produces without result, but only that the results flow entirely to the original productive factors. . . . Consequently, net profit cannot exist, because the value and price of the original productive services will always absorb the value and price of the product, even if the productive process is parcelled out among ever so many independent firms.[44]

In Schumpeter's schema the value system set up in the "circular flow" exhibits a special kind of stability. For in every economic period there is a tendency to follow well-worn tracks and thereby to realize the same values. Even when this constancy is disrupted, some continuity always remains; it is never a question of doing something completely new, but only of adapting the previous approach to new conditions. The established value system and the combinations once given are always the basis of the values of a new period. Such continuity is crucial for the economic life of individuals who could not readily do the mental labour necessary to create their economic world anew each day. And in any event, experience teaches that the rules of behaviour previously followed have stood the test of time and that one will not do better than go on acting by following them. According to Schumpeter, there must be one unique set of economic behaviours which, under given conditions, establishes the equilibrium between the means available and the wants to be satisfied in the optimum way. The value system outlined corresponds to a state of economic equilibrium whose constituent parts cannot be changed without the individual believing he is worse off than before.

Importantly, in the organization of the "circular flow", Schumpeter says there is no class of people whose special characteristic is that they *are the owners of* means of production. Unlike the real world capitalistic economy, no such group has a claim to a surplus or profits:

43 Ibid., p. 30.
44 Ibid., p. 31.

> If we choose to call the manager or owner of a business "entrepreneur", then he would be an *entrepreneur faisant ni bénéfice ni perte*, without special function and without income of a special kind. If the possessors of produced means of production were called "capitalists", then they could only be producers, differing in nothing from other producers, and could no more than the others sell their products above the costs given by the total of wages and rents.[45]

Exchange value and money

In the theory of the "circular flow", Schumpeter sees a stream of goods being produced continually in a repetitive sequence of productive efforts. Only for an instant is there anything like a stock of goods. In one sense the "circular flow" ends here; in another sense, however, it does not cease, for consumption generates the desire to repeat the process, and this fosters renewed economic activity. But Schumpeter must now explain how transactions can take place in a system where many exchanges of different commodities occur on a regular basis, and for this purpose he introduces the concept of "exchange value". He says the exchange value of a commodity depends upon the value of the goods the individual can procure and in fact intends to procure with that outlay. When the best employment for a good is found, the exchange value remains at one and only one definite level, given that conditions remain unchanged. The exchange value of any unit of one and the same commodity varies for different individuals, in part, because of the differences of their tastes and their differing economic situations as a whole, but also, quite independently of these aspects, because of differences in the goods which the individual exchanges. But he argues that the relation of the quantities in which any two goods are exchanged in the market, that is, the "price" of each good, is the same for all individuals. For the price of every good is connected with the prices of all other goods.

At this point Schumpeter introduces his account of the role of money.

> At first sight money appears as a general order upon different quantities of goods or as we may say as "general purchasing power." Every individual regards money first of all as a means of obtaining goods in general; if he sells his services of labour or land, he sells them not for definite goods but, as it were, for goods in general. If one looks more closely, however, things take on a different aspect. For every individual values his money income really according to the goods which he actually obtains with it and not according to goods in general. . . . In general, a definite plan of expenditure is adhered to as being the best, and it does not change quickly. This is why, in practice, everyone can normally reckon with a constant value and price of money and he need only gradually adjust them to changed conditions. Therefore, . . . for

45 Ibid., pp. 45–6.

> every part of the existing purchasing power there lies ready somewhere in the economic system a demand for it, a supply of goods for it, and that the bulk of the money . . . goes the same way year I year out.[46]

Thus far Schumpeter has not had to refer to any employment of money that would necessitate an accumulation beyond the amount sufficient for the individual to pay for his current purchases. And for similar reasons, he has not had to speak of credit instruments. Clearly, when he later comes to explore the reality of an actually existing capitalist economy, the accumulation of money and credit will become absolutely central. But in the "circular flow" they are not essential. For the exchange process could in theory do without money altogether and rely on something like the bill of exchange. All that is necessary to put money in a fixed relation to the values of other goods is that it should have a connection with something of definite value, thus there is no inherent need for metal money. Schumpeter's argument also entails that interest does not appear in the economic system under the assumptions of the "circular flow". In summing up, he says, "Thus, corresponding to the stream of goods there is a stream of money, the direction of which is opposite to that of the stream of goods, and the movements of which, upon the assumption that no increase of gold or any other one-sided change occurs, are only reflexes of the movement of goods. With this we have closed the description of the circular flow."[47]

The causes of "development"

Schumpeter's unique and original contribution to economic theory really begins with his concept of "development". By this term he means something special that causes progressive change but that, importantly, is intrinsic to the economy as such.[48] An account of economic development cannot be merely a description of historical events as they have unfolded and contributed to the shaping of the economy. Schumpeter may well have Weber in mind when he sets out to distinguish his approach from that of the historian. That is, he wants to focus exclusively on the nature of the economic process in pure form, no matter how much this may be influenced by non-economic factors from time to time, concerns that are,

46 Ibid., pp. 51–2.

47 Ibid., p. 55.

48 Andersen adopts the labels of Christopher Freemen in denoting the model of economic evolution described in *The Theory of Economic Development* as Schumpeter's innovation theory "Mark 1" to distinguish it from his later conception, "Mark II", where there is a strong feedback loop arising from the further inventive activity that occurs with intra-firm research and development and market concentration. Andersen develops this dichotomy into two full-blown models of the economy corresponding to the early and later historical stages of modern capitalist development. We shall not follow Andersen completely in this regard, though it makes the obvious point that Schumpeter modified his views over time and had to accommodate the rise of big business. See Andersen, *Joseph A. Schumpeter*, pp. 141–5.

by contrast, the abiding preoccupations of Weber. As Schumpeter puts it: "No historical evolutionary factors will be indicated, whether individual events like the appearance of American gold production in Europe in the sixteenth century, or 'more general' circumstances like changes in the mentality of economic men, in the area of the civilized world, in social organization, in political constellations, in productive technique, and so forth – nor will their effects be described for individual cases or for groups of cases."[49] Rather, Schumpeter intends to build on his account of the "circular flow" as expounded above and to demarcate a field of enquiry that is purely "economic".

As we have seen, the theory of economic life from the standpoint of the "circular flow" shows economic activity running on in channels essentially the same year after year. Now, by contrast, Schumpeter wants to focus on certain changes that occur otherwise than as a result of the routine and regular working of the economy, as do normal adaptive changes in the ordinary functioning of the "circular flow". For some occurrences alter the basic framework of the economy as such. These, he says,

> cannot be understood by means of any analysis of the circular flow, although they are purely economic and although their explanation is obviously among the tasks of pure theory. Now such changes and the phenomena which appear in their train are the object of our investigation. But we do not ask: what changes of this sort have actually made the modern economic system what it is? nor: what are the conditions of such changes? We only ask, and indeed in the same sense as theory always asks: how do such changes take place, and to what economic phenomena do they give rise?[50]

It is crucial to Schumpeter's approach to rigorously exclude the impact of non-economic factors; which he does not deny or ignore but which he claims constitute a fundamentally different category of causation. He seeks a source of change that is endogenous to the working of the economic system itself. As we shall see, his approach has numerous parallels with that of Darwin in developing his theory of the origin of species. Just as Darwin sought to find within the very processes of living nature itself factors that explain the creation of new species, a principle encapsulated in the notion of "natural selection", in a similar manner, Schumpeter wants to claim that the capitalist economy "evolves" as a result of forces at work within the structures of the system as such. "If the change occurs in the non-social data (natural conditions) or in non-economic social data (here belong the effects of war, changes in commercial, social, or economic 'policy'), or in consumers' tastes, then to this extent no fundamental overhaul of the theoretical tools seems to be

49 TED, p. 61.
50 Ibid., pp. 61–2.

required. These tools only fail – and here this argument joins the preceding – where economic life itself changes its own data by fits and starts."[51]

Schumpeter gives as a classic illustration of "pure" economic change the case of the building of a railway and all that flows from this. But he also he mentions the situation where many small, continuous changes, which though small steps can, for example, create a great department store out of a small retail business. Crucially for Schumpeter the "static" analysis of the "circular flow" is not only unable to deal with discontinuous change in the accepted way of doing things; it cannot account for the occurrence of such productive revolutions as are caused by "railroadization" or the phenomena that are associated with them. It can only describe the equilibrium position after the changes have taken place. Thus he says, "It is just this occurrence of the 'revolutionary' change that is our problem, the problem of economic development in a very narrow and formal sense. . . . By 'development,' therefore, we shall understand only such changes in economic life as are not forced upon it from without but arise by its own initiative, from within."[52]

In summary, Schumpeter's main focus is the process of change that arises from *within* the economy. If major changes in the economy were only the result of exogenous factors affecting it from the outside, there would be no "economic" development as such and thus no need for economic theory to explain the changes. Hence, the mere growth of the economy, as occurs due to the increase of population, is not part of the process of development in Schumpeter's sense: "For it calls forth no qualitatively new phenomena, but only processes of adaptation of the same kind as the changes in the natural data."[53] As he adds in a footnote:

> Development in our sense is a distinct phenomenon, entirely foreign to what may be observed in the circular flow or in the tendency towards equilibrium. It is spontaneous and discontinuous change in the channels of the flow, disturbance of equilibrium, which forever alters and displaces the equilibrium state previously existing. Our theory of development is nothing but a treatment of this phenomenon and "the processes" incident to it.[54]

And he goes on to explain: "what we are about to consider is that kind of change arising from within the system which so displaces its equilibrium point that the new one cannot be reached from the old one by infinitesimal steps. Add successively as many mail coaches as you please, you will never get a railway thereby."[55]

But precisely how do endogenous changes in the economy arise? For Schumpeter it is a fundamental assumption that, contrary to what may be intuitively

51 Ibid., p. 62.
52 Ibid.
53 Ibid., p. 63.
54 Ibid., p. 64.
55 Ibid., footnote 1.

thought, major economic changes manifest themselves first in the sphere of industrial and commercial activity and not in the wants of the consumers:

> Yet innovations in the economic system do not as a rule take place in such a way that first new wants arise spontaneously in consumers and then the productive apparatus swings round through their pressure. We do not deny the presence of this nexus. It is, however, the producer who as a rule initiates economic change, and consumers are educated by him if necessary; they are, as it were, taught to want new things, or things which differ in some respect or other from those which they have been in the habit of using.[56]

Schumpeter argues that producing means combining materials and forces within the power of the individual actor. Insofar as a "new combination" may over time grow out of the old by incremental steps of adjustment there is certainly change, and possibly growth, but not a new phenomenon. But, if the new combinations appear discontinuously, then "development" in Schumpeter's sense can be said to have occurred.[57] The concept of development may involve any of the following:

> (1) The introduction of a new good – that is one with which consumers are not yet familiar – or of a new quality of a good. (2) The introduction of a new method of production, that is one not yet tested by experience in the branch of manufacture concerned, which need by no means be founded upon a discovery scientifically new, and can also exist in a new way of handling a commodity commercially. (3) The opening of a new market, that is a market into which the particular branch of manufacture of the country in question has not previously entered, whether or not this market has existed before. (4) The conquest of a new source of supply of raw materials or half-manufactured goods, again irrespective of whether this source already exists or whether it has first to be created. (5) The carrying out of the new organization of any industry, like the creation of a monopoly position (for example through trustification) or the breaking up of a monopoly position.[58]

56 Ibid., p. 65. It is hard to underestimate the significance of this phenomenon of the producer "educating" the consumer, given the ever-expanding role of advertising in today's society. Indeed the impact of this manipulation of consumer needs has grown to such an extent that some theorists suggest it has changed the fundamental nature of capitalist society as such. An early but radical critique of this directing control of the individual's consumption habits is Herbert Marcuse's celebrated book *One-Dimensional Man*, which argued that modern technological society is notable for its imposition of "false needs" in place of "true needs", such is the level of its psychic domination of the individual. Of course in recent times there has grown up a significant subsection of sociology that is focused on the topics of consumerism and consumer society. I here mention only Judith Williamson, *Consuming Passions: The Dynamics of Popular Culture*, Marion Boyars, 1986.

57 TED, pp. 65–6.

58 Ibid., p. 66.

Having defined his notion of development and explained how it is crucial to understanding the dynamics of the capitalist economy, Schumpeter proceeds to unpack the further implications of his approach. He explores various themes that are to become significant in his later work. In the first place, he says, it is not necessary for new combinations to be carried out by the same people who control the existing productive or commercial processes. On the contrary, new combinations are to be typically found in new firms and do not arise out of established ones – it is not the owner of stagecoaches who builds railways. Schumpeter points to how this is confirmed by the fact that in a capitalist society it is a normal feature that individuals and families rise and fall both economically and socially – that is, there is high volatility in the fortunes of businesses as well as high social mobility. A further aspect of development, he insists, is that the carrying out of new combinations does not take place by employing means of production that happen to be unused. Rather, the new combinations must draw the necessary means of production from existing combinations. The carrying out of new combinations means, therefore, a different employment of the system's existing productive means.

Capitalists, banks and the creation of credit

The next stage in Schumpeter's argument is to consider how command over the necessary means of production is achieved in the carrying out of new combinations. Procuring the means of production is not a problem for established firms operating within the "circular flow", for they have already procured them or else can procure them with the proceeds of previous production; there is no fundamental gap between receipts and disbursements, which necessarily correspond to one another. The problem of procuring the means of production does not exist if those who wish to develop new combinations can get them in exchange for others that they have. But do all those who wish to establish new combinations already possess the wherewithal to purchase the means of production they require? The instructive case that interests Schumpeter is that where an individual must resort to credit if he wishes to carry out a new combination, because he does not control an established business that could finance its new operations by returns from previous production.

> To provide this credit is clearly the function of that category of individuals which we call "capitalists". It is obvious that this is the characteristic method of the capitalist type of society – and important enough to serve as its differentia specifica – for forcing the economic system into new channels, for putting its means at the service of new ends, in contrast to the method of a non-exchange economy of the kind which simply consists in exercising the directing organ's power to command.[59]

59 Ibid., pp. 69–70.

While the process of production within the "circular flow" does not require borrowing as a necessary ingredient, this feature is crucial in the creation of new combinations: that is, "'financing' as a special act is fundamentally necessary, in practice as in theory."[60]

A key mechanism whereby existing means of production are detached from their previous uses so as to be available for novel productive purposes is via the use of credit. More specifically, this is achieved by the individual who wishes to carry out new combinations outbidding the producers remaining within the "circular flow" for the desired means of production. But from where do the sums needed to purchase the means of production necessary for the new combinations come if the individuals concerned do not happen to possess them already? For in the "circular flow" there is no source out of which sufficient funds can be saved to finance new combinations, and in any event there is essentially little, if any, incentive to save.

At this point in his argument Schumpeter introduces his unique account of how the financing of new combinations is achieved under the conditions of modern capitalism. The key method is the creation of purchasing power by banks.

> The issue of bank-notes not fully covered by specie withdrawn from circulation is an obvious instance, but methods of deposit banking render the same service, where they increase the sum total of possible expenditure. Or we may think of bank acceptances in so far as they serve as money to make payments in wholesale trade. It is always a question, not of transforming purchasing power which already exists in someone's possession, but of the creation of new purchasing power out of nothing – out of nothing even if the credit contract by which the new purchasing power is created is supported by securities which are not themselves circulating media – which is added to the existing circulation. And this is the source from which new combinations are often financed, and from which they would have to be financed always, if results of previous development did not actually exist at any moment."[61]

These credit means of payment can serve as ready money because they can be converted immediately into payments to individuals such as wage earners or to purchase existing stocks of productive means. In this way the role of the financier of new combinations acquires special significance, because without this credit-creating service development in the operative sense would simply not occur.

> The banker, therefore, is not so much primarily a middleman in the commodity "purchasing power" as a *producer* of this commodity. However, since all reserve funds and savings to-day usually flow to him, and the total demand

60 Ibid., p. 70.

61 Ibid., p. 73. For a detailed account of the historical origins of the development of capitalist credit-money that largely follows Schumpeter's analysis see Geoffrey Ingram, *The Nature of Money*, Polity, 2004, pp. 107–33.

> for free purchasing power, whether existing or to be created, concentrates on him, he has either replaced private capitalists or become their agent; he has himself become the capitalist par excellence. He stands between those who wish to form new combinations and the possessors of productive means. He is essentially a phenomenon of development, though only when no central authority directs the social process. He makes possible the carrying out of new combinations, authorizes people, in the name of society as it were, to form them. He is the ephor of the exchange economy.[62]

It is not clear from these remarks whether Schumpeter is placing the financier ahead of the entrepreneur as the true leader of the capitalist economy, but he is clearly giving prominence to his role. At this stage we shall not comment further on the role of finance and the question whether "financial capitalism" is a further development or transformation of industrial capitalism; but Schumpeter evidently sees finance/credit as an integral feature of capitalism from its earliest stages.

The function of the entrepreneur

Thus far Schumpeter has analyzed two of the essential elements of development: new combinations and credit. But a third ingredient is possibly the most important of all and this is the "entrepreneur" and his "enterprise", which bring the first two elements together in such a way as to transform the "circular flow" into modern capitalism proper.

> The carrying out of new combinations we call "enterprise"; the individuals whose function it is to carry them out we call "entrepreneurs." These concepts are at once broader and narrower than the usual. Broader, because in the first place we call entrepreneurs not only those "independent" businessmen in an exchange economy who are usually so designated, but all who actually fulfil the function by which we define the concept, even if they are, as is becoming the rule, "dependent" employees of a company, like managers, members of boards of directors, and so forth, or even if their actual power to perform the entrepreneurial function has any other foundations, such as the control of a majority of shares. As it is the carrying out of new combinations that constitutes the entrepreneur, it is not necessary that he should be permanently connected with an individual firm; many "financiers," "promoters," and so forth are not, and still they may be entrepreneurs in our sense.[63]

Schumpeter says that the modern idea of the "captain of industry" corresponds fairly closely to what he means. But whatever the type, a person is an entrepreneur only when he actually carries out new combinations, and he possibly loses that

62 TED, p. 74.
63 Ibid., pp. 74–5.

character as soon as he has built up his enterprise and settles down to running it along conventional lines.

Schumpeter does not acknowledge that entrepreneurs form a class as such. His view as to whether entrepreneurs constitute a class makes an interesting contrast with the approach of Weber, who is quite explicit that entrepreneurs do occupy a distinct class position. Schumpeter may be thinking primarily of the concept "social class", in which case he is not necessarily at odds with Weber. Weber defines a social class as "the totality of those class situations in which individual and generational mobility is easy and typical", and accordingly, he does not include entrepreneurs in his listing of major social classes.[64] Schumpeter's explanation of why he thinks entrepreneurs do not constitute a class is as follows:

> Because being an entrepreneur is not a profession and as a rule not a lasting condition, entrepreneurs do not form a social class in the technical sense, as, for example, landowners or capitalists or workmen do. Of course the entrepreneurial function will lead to certain class positions for the successful entrepreneur and his family. It can also put its stamp on an epoch of social history, can form a style of life, or systems of moral and aesthetic values; but in itself it signifies a class position no more than it presupposes one. And the class position which may be attained is not as such an entrepreneurial position, but is characterized as landowning or capitalist, according to how the proceeds of the enterprise are used.[65]

Weber's analysis on these issues is somewhat cryptic and underdeveloped. In a brief section of *Economy and Society*, he sets up a dichotomy between positively and negatively privileged classes. He explains that the one of the advantages enjoyed by a "positively privileged commercial class" is their "the monopolization of entrepreneurial management for the sake of its members and their business interests", and the safeguarding of those interests through influence on the economic policy of political and other organizations. But here Weber conflates entrepreneurs with managers, a construction that ignores the gravamen of Schumpeter's analysis of the entrepreneur.

But regardless of whether the two approaches to class are commensurable, what especially concerns Schumpeter is to bring out the significance of the entrepreneur for "development". He raises the question of whether the carrying out of new combinations is a special process and constitutes a special function. He points out that business people in general are eager to do the best they can and are prepared to adopt new methods or change their modus operandi if they can see advantages in doing so. But while the individual in the "circular flow" will act rationally and

64 ES, pp. 302–5.
65 TED, pp. 78–9.

expediently given his usual circumstances, he will be uneasy when confronted with the prospect of a completely new task.[66]

> While he swims with the stream in the circular flow which is familiar to him, he swims against the stream if he wishes to change its channel. What was formerly a help becomes a hindrance. What was a familiar datum becomes an unknown. Where the boundaries of routine stop, many people can go no further, and the rest can only do so in a highly variable manner. . . . Therefore, too, the carrying out of new combinations is a special function, and the privilege of a type of people who are much less numerous than all those who have the "objective" possibility of doing it. Therefore, . . . entrepreneurs are a special type . . .[67]

Having sketched his concept of the entrepreneur, Schumpeter proceeds to characterize this individual in detail. First, he wants to insist that the entrepreneur should not be confused with a manager, for the two roles are significantly different. Whereas the manager remains wedded to the situation of the "circular flow" and is oriented to maintaining the existing mode of operation of his business, the entrepreneur is focused on a non-existent reality, which has to be imagined and created sometime in the future. This visionary quality of an individual is not common and amounts to a special psychological disposition. To a degree, the entrepreneur is similar to a manager, for he must set people their tasks, keep up discipline and so forth; but these skills are relatively easy to find and learn. According to Schumpeter, even the directing of other people is just like any other task and is comparable to the labour of tending a machine. In any production process everyone learns their daily tasks and carries them out more or less well, including the manager. Even so, the demands on the individual remain considerable because the burden of work is never slight and most manage to just cope. But to go beyond the level of work competence required in the ordinary circumstances of the "circular flow", a person needs something extra and rare, and this is "leadership."

At this point it is worth noting some possible parallels and synergies with the thought of Weber on leadership, especially political leadership, as he expounds this in his celebrated essay "Politics as a Vocation." In that text Weber seeks to characterize the nature of genuine political leadership and distinguishes it, in particular, from the mere administration of the bureaucratic official. Weber's ideal politician

66 Andersen designates the model of the circular flow, consistently with his adoption of the Mark I and Mark II labels, as Mark 0; and he refers to the entrepreneur in Mark 0 as the "w-entrepreneur", in contrast to the entrepreneur of Mark I as the "s-entrepreneur", "w" standing for Walras and "s" for Schumpeter. While this may make some sense of the differences involved, it is also potentially misleading, because the so-called Mark 0 model is merely an ideal type constructed for heuristic purposes and is not on a par with the so-called Mark I or Mark II that are meant to correspond to actual realities. Further, strictly speaking, there are no entrepreneurs in Schumpeter's circular flow. See Andersen, *Joseph A. Schumpeter*, pp. 39–42.

67 TED, pp. 79–81.

requires a genuine calling for politics and possesses moral qualities; he may also possess charisma, an aspect that does not at first glance seem relevant to economic enterprise. But there are definite affinities between the type of leadership Schumpeter describes in the case of the business leader and Weber's ideal politician, especially insofar as they both involve the capacity for vision and require a capacity to chart new courses. For Schumpeter, leadership in business must deal with the special challenges of market competition: outside accustomed channels, the individual is without data for his decisions and lacks rules of conduct that are tried and tested. Many things are uncertain, and others can only be guessed at. Weber's ideal politician must be capable of dealing with extraordinary circumstances that require much more than administrative skills; what is needed inter alia is "trained relentlessness in viewing the realities of life, and the ability to face such realities and to measure up to them inwardly."[68]

Schumpeter also says that the entrepreneur needs to be rational. In comments that also bear comparison with Weber on the same issue he says, "There will be much more conscious rationality in this than in customary action, which as such does not need to be reflected upon at all; but this plan must necessarily be open not only to errors greater in degree, but also to other kinds of errors than those occurring in customary action."[69] And Schumpeter further claims that, "In one sense, [the entrepreneur] may indeed be called the most rational and the most egotistical of all. For, as we have seen, conscious rationality enters much more into the carrying out of new plans, which themselves have to be worked out before they can be acted upon, than into the mere running of an established business, which is largely a matter of routine."[70] Here is a possible correlation with Weber's account of the increasing prevalence of "instrumentally rational action" under the conditions of modern capitalism. But Weber's formal rationality in the sphere of business seems to correlate more with the routine calculations of ordinary business management rather than with the extraordinary skills of Schumpeter's entrepreneur. Weber's concern with capitalist rationality highlights the historical contrast with traditional forms of economic action, whereas Schumpeter's rationality contrasts the entrepreneur's dispositions with the routine and customary orientation of contemporary business managers.

Schumpeter's entrepreneur is rational because he must calculate and estimate, as best he can, all the elements of a proposed course of action in advance without being able to rely on customary arrangements. Even so, it is impossible to survey exhaustively all the effects and counter-effects of a projected venture. In economic life decisions must be taken without having at hand all the details of what is to be done; that is, one must proceed with "imperfect knowledge". Much depends upon intuition, the capacity of seeing things in a way which afterwards proves to be true, and discarding the non-essential. The temptation always remains to revert to

68 FMW, pp. 126–7.
69 TED, p. 85.
70 Ibid., p. 91.

habits of thought and traditional ways of doing things. An effort of will is therefore necessary, Schumpeter says, "in order to wrest, amidst the work and care of the daily round, scope and time for conceiving and working out the new combination and to bring oneself to look upon it as a real possibility and not merely as a day-dream. This mental freedom presupposes a great surplus force over the everyday demand and is something peculiar and by nature rare."[71] To be able to make the kind of effort Schumpeter says is needed, the entrepreneur must also possess a special kind of psyche. The habits of the mind are very fixed and have an energy-saving function, and as such, they become drag-chains when no longer useful. The entrepreneur must somehow break free from the accustomed tracks of thought if he is to bring on his novel enterprise. He must also resist the negative reaction of the social environment and if necessary conquer any political or legal impediments:

> Surmounting this opposition is always a special kind of task which does not exist in the customary course of life, a task which also requires a special kind of conduct. In matters economic this resistance manifests itself first of all in the groups threatened by the innovation, then in the difficulty in finding the necessary cooperation, finally in the difficulty in winning over consumers.[72]

To clarify his view, Schumpeter refers to the relation of entrepreneurship or innovation to "invention." Economic leadership he insists must be distinguished from invention. If inventions are not developed into products, then they are economically of no consequence. The crucial task is that of bringing an invention to fruition in the form of a saleable product, which is entirely different from invention per se. Of course, some entrepreneurs are also inventors just as they may also be capitalists, but the role of entrepreneur has no necessary connection with that of the inventor or the capitalist. Besides, as Schumpeter points out, many innovations do not depend on inventions at all.

Schumpeter argues that the entrepreneur possesses an exemplary role, which has wider implications, for the entrepreneur in effect "leads" the system of production into new channels. He leads by drawing other producers after him, even though they are his competitors, who at first set out to limit and then annihilate him. This means that the entrepreneur is a crucial driving force behind the constant progress that capitalist societies experience. For all this the entrepreneur is not generally revered by his society, as are leaders in other fields like politics or war. Further, the precariousness of the economic position of the entrepreneur, and the fact that despite his economic success he has no cultural tradition or social standing to fall back upon, means that he appears in society as an upstart and gains relatively little status for all his efforts.

71 Ibid., p. 86.
72 Ibid., p. 87.

> And the typical entrepreneur is more self-centred than other types, because he relies less than they do on tradition and connection and because his characteristic task – theoretically as well as historically – consists precisely in breaking up old, and creating new, tradition. Although this applies primarily to his economic action, it also extends to the moral, cultural, and social consequences of it. It is, of course, no mere coincidence that the period of the rise of the entrepreneur type also gave birth to Utilitarianism.[73]

There are numerous aspects in this discussion that warrant further comparison with Weber. Schumpeter notes that the rationality of the entrepreneur is antithetical to dispositions of the hedonistic kind. For the specific motivation of the entrepreneur has no connection, in Schumpeter's view, with a desire to increase the level of his own want satisfaction: "Experience teaches, however, that typical entrepreneurs retire from the arena only when and because their strength is spent and they feel no longer equal to their task. . . . And activity of the entrepreneurial type is obviously an obstacle to hedonist enjoyment of those kinds of commodity which are usually acquired by incomes beyond a certain size, because their 'consumption' presupposes leisure."[74] These remarks have obvious resonances with the ideas of Weber regarding the ascetic disposition of early modern capitalists. Not only do they suggest that the entrepreneur is subject to ascetic restraint and that he rationally tempers his enjoyment of the wealth he creates, they also imply something along the lines of a work ethic.

A further issue that is touched upon at this point in Schumpeter's work is the question of whether the dynamism that flows from the innovative activity of the entrepreneur can be provided in some other way that through the drive of individuals. Of course, this issue is connected with the question of the impact of a possible socialization of the economy and the elimination of private enterprise. Weber was especially perturbed at this prospect and, as we shall see, argued forcefully against a radical transformation of the capitalist system. Schumpeter, paradoxically given how much he appreciates the role of the entrepreneur, was more open to the idea that social arrangements could be engineered to replace the private entrepreneur. The extent to which we can say Schumpeter's approach here is at odds with Weber's approach must await our more extensive discussion in our final chapter.

In the next chapter, we shall address Schumpeter's later writings and in particular, his account of the long-term tendency of capitalist development. This is discussed primarily in his magnum opus *Business Cycles: A Theoretical, Historical and Statistical Analysis of the Capitalist Process* and his more popular book *Capitalism, Socialism and Democracy.*

73 Ibid., pp. 91–2. Weber likewise sees utilitarianism as typical of the stage of capitalism once religious belief has lost its hold over the masses.

74 Ibid., p. 92.

4 Schumpeter's account of the long-term trend of capitalism

It is not surprising that having explored the irregularity and instability of the capitalist engine Schumpeter should turn his attention to a consideration the long-term implications of these features. Indeed, as early as *The Theory of Economic Development*, he had addressed the issue of the business cycle at some length, especially in the chapter on business cycles that was Chapter VI of the revised and downsized second edition. Schumpeter argues that business cycles are ultimately the result of the effects of "swarms" of innovation. These account for the upswing in economic performance, whereas the downswing occurs when the increased activity can no longer be sustained. Schumpeter noted that, even though Marx had recognized the phenomenon of economic crises, he had failed to see how these were generated by entrepreneurial activity and had a cyclical character. Schumpeter argues that business cycles are fundamental to the very nature of capitalist evolution. Thus in a paper published in 1927, he claimed that "the recurring periods of prosperity of the cyclical movement are the form the progress takes in capitalistic society."[1] This line of thought eventually gave rise to *Business Cycles: A Theoretical, Historical and Statistical Analysis of the Capitalist Process*, arguably Schumpeter's magnum opus. In what follows we shall first consider the argument of that work published in 1939. After this, we shall consider Schumpeter's more well-known and controversial work published in 1942, *Capitalism, Socialism and Democracy*, with its important reflections on the contemporary economic situation of the day.

Introduction to Schumpeter's *Business Cycles*

As the title suggests, *Business Cycles* is focused on the phenomena of economic fluctuations and crises. In Chapter VI of *The Theory of Economic Development*, Schumpeter did not advance a fully worked-out theory, contenting himself with some comments on the relation of fluctuations and crises to the conduct of entrepreneurs. However, he did advance ideas that were subsequently to become the basis of his major work *Business Cycles*. The work contains enormous detail on the

1 Cited in Esben Sloth Andersen, *Joseph A. Schumpeter: A Theory of Social and Economic Evolution*, Palgrave, 2011, p. 116.

early growth and flowering of business in Britain, Germany and the United States and focuses on five areas of industry: cotton textiles, railroads, steel, automobiles and electric power. In what follows, we shall provide a discussion of this theory in relation to Schumpeter's work as a whole. It will become apparent that much of the framework that Schumpeter utilizes in *Business Cycles* was already present in *The Theory of Economic Development*, especially the opening theoretical section, which actually restates what he first advanced in the earlier work.

Schumpeter notes at the outset that a fundamental issue for a theory of business cycles concerns causation. This is the case because fluctuations in economic activity can be attributed to a large variety of causes, both economic and otherwise. Essentially, Schumpeter's theory of business cycles is attempting to establish that there is a set of conditions *internal* to the economy that is responsible for the generation of cyclical phenomena. But the difficulty with any such theory is that economic phenomena are never present without the influence of other factors that are fundamentally non-economic. Schumpeter thus fully recognizes the difficulty of dealing with the effects of "external factors". External factors include phenomena such as wars, social upheavals, geography, climate and other influences of a religious or political nature. Clearly, in the course of economic development these non-economic phenomena frequently, in fact regularly, interfere with the conduct of economic affairs. Nonetheless, the aim of Schumpeter's work is to show that, despite the undoubted impact of external factors, it is possible to divine the workings of a cyclical process determined by purely economic phenomena.

In order to achieve his goal, Schumpeter sets out to construct a model of the entire economic process as it functions over time and, just as with any other science, attempts to compare this with concrete reality to see whether the model is justified by the observable facts. In contrast with his theory of the "circular flow" with its focus on the static state of affairs, his theory of business cycles will be essentially dynamic in character. In what follows, we shall first give an account of Schumpeter's overall theory, which culminates in his theory of business cycles. We shall to some degree need to repeat aspects of the theory as set out in *The Theory of Economic Development*, as his later work relies on and develops ideas first set out in that work. After this we shall consider his *Capitalism Socialism and Democracy* that discusses political implications.

Schumpeter sets out his fundamental question thus:

> When we behold one of the familiar graphs of economic time series – such as the graphs of the US Bureau of Labour Price Index, the commercial paper rate, bank clearings or debits, numbers of unemployed – or one of the business barometers, for example, that of the American Telephone and Telegraph Company, we undoubtedly have, as our businessman had, the impression of an "irregular regularity" of fluctuations. Our first and foremost task is to measure them and describe their mechanism.[2]

2 BC, p. 33.

But more than this, Schumpeter wants to explain the underlying causes. Of course, he is aware that there will never be a single factor or prime mover that accounts for all the phenomena of crises, booms and depressions that are observed. To get at the primary causes of the individual phenomenon, the facts of each case and their background must be explored in detail. But a further question arises, in Schumpeter's view, which is: Even if we can succeed in describing the economic system by means of a general schema, does the system by its own working produce the various crises and depressions, and if so, under what circumstances? Schumpeter refers to the analogy of the human body and says that, while it may not be of interest scientifically to explore why a particular man dies, there is a very great scientific interest in explaining why human beings die just because of the working of the human organism or the cells of which it consists.

Equilibrium and the theoretical norm

Schumpeter's starting point is again his analysis of the "circular flow" or what he now terms the "stationary flow". His approach here repeats and develops the framework originally set out in *The Theory of Economic Development*. He says "the analytic treatment of the facts of autonomous change in a closed domain of which it is our task to give account, begins conveniently with the construction of the model of an unchanging economic process which flows on at constant rates in time and merely reproduces itself."[3] Such a model will present the fundamental facts and relations of economic life in simplified form, but Schumpeter says there is no other way to proceed. Here of course he again effectively employs the methodological device of the "ideal type", where there is a necessary simplification and idealization of the facts for heuristic purposes.[4] The most fruitful example of a model of such closed economy was first created, in Schumpeter's view, by the physiocrats, but it was then definitively elaborated by Léon Walras. Following Walras, Marshall built his theory on the basis of the same idea and economists ever since have used similar devices of one kind or another.[5]

3 Ibid., p. 35.

4 There may be differences in the manner of applying ideal types in historical analysis, as is Weber's focus, and in theoretical economics. In the case of the latter, the expectation may be stronger that the models constructed are not only heuristically useful but describe laws operating in concrete reality. This could be the case with Schumpeter's cycles theory, though not his theory of the "circular flow".

5 In anticipation of the objection that building a model of a static exchange economy has fundamental limitations, Schumpeter elsewhere responds to just such a criticism by Marshall directed at John B. Clark in a footnote in an essay of 1928. Schumpeter gives the following riposte: "Now if it were true that reasoning by means of [the static apparatus] is 'too removed from life to be useful,' then the greater part of the analysis of the *Principles* would be useless – as would be the greater part of any exact science: For Marshallian analysis rests just as much on static assumptions as Prof. Clark's structure. But it is not true. There is nothing unduly abstract in considering the phenomena incident to the running of economic life under given conditions taken by themselves." Joseph Schumpeter, "The Instability of Capitalism", in Richard Clemence (ed.), *Essays of J. A. Schumpeter*, Addison-Wesley Press, 1951 (EJAS), footnote 2, p. 54.

In developing his notion of the "stationary flow", Schumpeter says one can visualize an economic process in which the system merely reproduces itself at constant rates. There is a given population that is static and organized for the purpose of consumption in households and for the purpose of production in firms. The population lives and works in a static physical and social environment. The wants and needs of households are given and do not alter over time, and the ways of producing things and the means of commerce are already at maximum efficiency and cannot be further improved. The ways in which the quantities of the factors of production are linked together, such as the labour, the services of natural agents and the means of production, constitute a "production function".

In this stationary economy, the production function itself is a given datum and is invariant in form. The coefficients of production are therefore all fixed so that, if, for example, a bushel of wheat is required to be produced, land, labour, seed, fertilizers and so on must be combined in given and unalterable proportions. In this system nothing more than ordinary work by managers and workers is required. It is not necessary to pursue efforts in the area of production other than the repetition of orders and operations based on previous experience: "The production process is entirely "synchronized", which means there is no waiting for the results of production, all of which represent and replace themselves at the moment they are wanted, according to a plan in which everything is perfectly adapted. Everything is financed by current receipts."[6] In the pure version of his system, Schumpeter says it is convenient to exclude savings, since anyone who saves does something with a view to changing his economic situation into the future. The income stream consists of wages, which are payments for productive and consumptive services rendered, and rents, which are payments for natural agents. In such a system, year after year, the same kinds of goods and the same quantities of consumers and producers goods would be produced. Every business would employ the same quantities of inputs every year, and finally, all these goods would be bought and sold at the same prices every year. The question of what prices would be, of course, necessarily depends on the relations between prices and quantities. This relationship is one of interdependence and forms a system.

A first task for Schumpeter is to establish how the relations between various elements of the system determine prices, for he maintains along with Walras that the system is only "logically self-contained" if this is possible.

> We can be sure that we understand the nature of economic phenomena only if it is possible to deduce prices and quantities from the data by means of those relations and to prove that no other set of prices and physical quantities is compatible with both the data and the relations. The proof that this is so is the magna charta of economic theory as an autonomous science, assuring us that its subject matter is a cosmos and not a chaos. . . . The values of prices and quantities which are the only ones, that data being what they are in each case,

6 BC, p. 40.

> to satisfy those relations, we call *equilibrium values*. The state of the system which obtains if all prices and quantities take their equilibrium values we call the *state of equilibrium*. . . Equilibrium that is unique and stable is, of course, the only perfectly satisfactory case."[7]

Here Schumpeter is referring to the concept of what is also known as *general* or *Walrasian equilibrium*. This means that every household and every firm is in equilibrium: that is, for households, no unit feels itself able to improve its present situation by transferring any of its income from the commodities that it has actually purchased to other commodities; for firms, it means that under the existing circumstances no firm believes it is able to increase its returns by deploying its capital resources from one factor it has actually acquired to any other. For Walrasian equilibrium to exist, prices and quantities must be adjusted accordingly. Every household and every firm must have its budget perfectly balanced. This entails that all quantities of goods produced by firms must be purchased by households or by other firms. All existing factors must be employed as far as their owners wish them to be and at the prices they can obtain, and no demand effective at the given prices must go unfulfilled. It follows also that there can be no effective unemployment. A further presupposition is that there is perfect competition between the various economic entities and agents and thus no monopoly.[8]

The proof that there is one and only one set of values of the variables that satisfies the given data does not mean that firms and households will consciously behave so as to arrive at that set of values or return to them if there is some disturbance. But there is a tendency of the *system* to move towards the ideal set of values and thus to reach the state of equilibrium. Schumpeter credits Walras with having first properly addressed this problem:

> [Walras's] solution starts from the observation that disequilibrium, which means deviation of at least one price or quantity from its equilibrium value, necessarily spells profits or losses to somebody at the spot or spots in which it occurs. And the argument is that this somebody can, under conditions of perfect competition get out of that loss or fully reap that profit in no other way than decreasing or increasing the quantity of his commodity. This will drive him toward equilibrium, and if all firms and households simultaneously react in the same manner, it will eventually bring the whole system to equilibrium, *provided that all actions and reactions are performed within the bounds of familiar practice that has evolved from long experience and frequent repetition.*[9]

7 Ibid., pp. 41–2.

8 Schumpeter describes the situation of perfect competition as having the following conditions: "(a) that no seller or buyer is able to influence the price of any commodity or factor by his own action and that there is no concerted action; and (b) that there is perfect mobility of commodities and factors all over the economic field" (i.e., amongst all possible uses). Ibid., p. 46.

9 Ibid., p. 47.

In a subsequent discussion, Schumpeter goes on to point out that in reality there is always an inevitable lag in the system adapting to disturbances because there are always elements in the setup of a firm or in the structure of an economic system that prevent immediate and complete adaptation to bring the system to equilibrium. Further, the fact that perfect equilibrium takes time to be reached means that it may fail to come about at all, as new disturbances may impinge on an already imperfectly equilibrated system. Schumpeter emphasizes, however, that the lags that occur because of "friction" in the system and which make it not always possible for equilibrium to be reached do not mean that there is no *tendency* towards perfect equilibrium. He gives as an example of the problem the case where producers' reactions to changes in price do not take effect immediately. In such cases, supply does not work up to equilibrium in small gradual steps and having reached equilibrium stops. The change in supply may outrun equilibrium in one jerk, and then the price reacts with a corresponding jerk back in the opposite direction. In fact it is quite conceivable that adaptation will never stop at any given point and that under conditions of perfect competition, prices and quantities will fluctuate indefinitely around equilibrium values without ever coinciding with them exactly.

The causes of economic fluctuations

For Schumpeter, what causes economic fluctuations to occur must either be individual shocks, which impact on the economy from the outside, or a distinct process of change that is generated by the system itself. In either situation it is the theory of equilibrium that supplies the most effective explanation of how the system will react, for it is "a description of an apparatus of response."[10] A further feature of the concept of equilibrium is that, although no such state is ever found to have been perfectly achieved, use of the notion is indispensable as a means to measure the actual states of the economy; for these can be measured by their distance from the theoretical norm. Economic fluctuations must be movements around something, and that something must be the equilibrium state. But the most important feature that theory has for Schumpeter concerns the fact that movement towards or away from equilibrium is always to be understood as a tendency to be considered the result of an actual force; the concept of equilibrium is not just an ideal state or a mere point of reference. He explains this as follows:

> We take our stand on the fact that the values of economic variables fluctuate in the course of business cycles between figures which roughest practical common sense recognises as abnormally high and figures which it recognises as abnormally low and that somewhere between these two lie values or ranges of values which that same commonsense would recognise as normal. We wish to distinguish definite periods in which the system embarks upon an excursion away from equilibrium and equally definite periods on which it draws towards

10 Ibid., p. 68.

> equilibrium. In order to harness our equilibrium concept to this service, which is fundamental for our analytic technique, we will not postulate the existence of states of equilibrium where none exist, but only where the system is actually moving towards one. . . . Hence, we will, for our purpose, recognise existence of equilibria *only at those discrete points on the time scale at which the system approaches a state which would, if reached, fulfil equilibrium conditions* and since the system in practice never actually reaches such a state, we shall consider instead of equilibrium points, ranges within which the system as a whole is more nearly in equilibrium than it is outside of them.[11]

Thus, contrary to the situation of the "stationary flow", an actually existing economic system is never in perfect equilibrium and is always either moving from or towards an equilibrium state. There are two obvious possibilities why this is so. One is that external factors impinge on the economy, but Schumpeter wants to put these to one side so he can grasp the deeper causes. What interests him most are factors of change that are internal to the economic system as such, that is, changes in the quantity or quality of factors of production or changes in the methods of supplying commodities. But before he explores these factors, Schumpeter must explain why some phenomena that may appear to generate fundamental change do not really do so.

Schumpeter maintains that consumers' initiative in changing tastes are of little consequence for economic development because changes in consumer tastes are really incident to and brought about by the action of producers. In other words, it is the producer or entrepreneur that elicits the change in taste of the consumer and not the consumer changing his needs and creating new demand. This assumption is consistent with the fact that in modern economies the role of product promotion and brand advertising would appear to be crucial in creating and maintaining the demand for particular consumer goods. Schumpeter gives as an example the advent of railroads and tells us they did not come into being because consumers took the initiative and demanded the service railroads provide in preference to that of coaches. Nor do consumers demand that electric lamps, rayon stockings, motorcars, aeroplanes, radios or chewing gum be invented and produced cheaply in large quantities because they suddenly have a need for such things. So, precisely how does internal economic development generate fundamental change in the system?

One possibility that Schumpeter considers is that there is an increase in productive resources. Given that the physical environment is constant, an increase in productive resources boils down to either an increase in population or an increase in the stock of producers' goods, but these are not independent variables. In any event, increase in population does not by itself cause a change in the economic system as such, for population increases can be absorbed without any variation in the economic system. Similar considerations apply, according to Schumpeter, to increases in the stock of goods. This could mean saving, but "saving" in the

11 Ibid., pp. 70–1.

requisite sense does not mean the assembling of a sum of goods for the purpose of buying durable consumer goods. Saving in order to buy a motorcar for non-business use or a house to live in is not true saving but merely rearranging consumption expenditure. What is crucial is the carrying into effect of a decision to acquire titles to income in the future. In the case of households, this often involves the acquisition of shares and bonds or land or buildings intended for business purposes. In the case of firms, it will mean spending on all kinds of producer goods beyond replacement, and this is what is designated by the term "real investment." In any event, in the stationary flow the level of saving is very small, if it exists at all, so that it cannot give rise to fundamental change. (This fact explains why third world economies find it so difficult to finance a "take-off" to capitalist industry from their own resources.) Thus, saving cannot be a major factor giving rise to economic change, as this would include in the premises a part of what has to be explained.

Innovation and economic evolution

To explain economic change, Schumpeter, as we know, turns his attention to innovative changes in the methods of production and supply of commodities. He focuses on a range of phenomena wider than what this might at first imply. He includes, as the standard illustration, the introduction of new commodities. But there are numerous other ways in which changes may arise:

> Technological change in the production of commodities already in use, the opening up of new markets or of new sources of supply, Taylorization of work, improved handling of material, the setting up of new business organisations such as department stores – in short, any "doing things differently" in the realm of economic life – all these are instances of what we shall refer to by the term innovation. It should be noted at once that the concept is not synonymous with the term "invention."[12]

We have already referred to Schumpeter's view of the relationship of innovation to invention. In *Business Cycles* he again emphasizes that innovation does not necessarily require a scientific novelty, as the concept of invention implies. Of course, many innovations will depend on inventions, but new ways of doing things may simply mean new methods of organizing existing techniques and involve no new invention as such. It is to innovation proper that Schumpeter wants to devote his attention, because when distinguished from invention it shows itself as a purely internal factor.

> We immediately realise that innovation is the outstanding fact in the economic history of capitalist society or in what is purely economic in that history, and also that it is largely responsible for most of what we would at first sight

12 Ibid., p. 84.

> attribute to other factors. . . . The changes in the economic process brought about by innovation, together with all their effects, and the response to them by the economic system, we shall designate by the term Economic Evolution.[13]

Schumpeter begins his detailed analysis of innovation by referring to his definition of the "production function." He states that this is the way in which the quantity of product varies if quantities of factors vary. If, instead of variation in the quantities of factors, it is the form of those factors that varies, we have innovation. Innovations break the trajectory of the normal curve of productivity. There is a transition from an old to a new curve or, to refer to the Ricardian law of decreasing returns, innovation interrupts the action of this curve, which means that it replaces the law that has so far described the effects of additional increments of resources by another one. The old total or marginal costs curve is undone, and a new one takes its place. "What dominates the picture of capitalistic life and is more than anything else responsible for our impression of a prevalence of decreasing cost, causing disequilibria, cut throat competition and so on, is innovation, the intrusion into the system of new production functions which incessantly shift existing cost curves."[14] Schumpeter notes that major innovations, and also minor ones, invariably involve the construction of new plants and equipment or the rebuilding of old plants. The carrying out of innovations always means time lags and requires significant outlays of resources. This feature has manifold implications for the modern economy where the vast bulk of new plant beyond mere replacement either embodies some innovation or is in response to situations connected with innovations of some sort. Every innovation potentially gives rise to a new firm founded for this purpose only, for most new firms are founded on the basis of a new idea of some kind and for a definite purpose. Life goes out of these firms when their purpose has been fulfilled and they become obsolete. Of course, many new firms are failures from the start, whereas others fall by the wayside for various accidental reasons. But importantly, no firm that merely runs along established lines, however well managed, can indefinitely remain as a source of profit in a capitalist society.

Schumpeter says there is an inevitable contradiction between the novel production function that arises through the action of new firms and the hitherto existing production function. The new firms, if successful, prosper and, for a time, outdo their rivals and are very profitable. On the other hand, the older firms continue on for a time and then react in various ways, adapting as best they can, to the new state of affairs brought on by the pressure of competition. They either absorb the new ways of doing things by adapting effectively to the competitive environment or their profitability declines and they may collapse and disappear as viable entities. These general features correspond, in Schumpeter's view, to what we observe empirically in the various disequilibria and fluctuations. It also explains

13 Ibid., p. 86.
14 Ibid., p. 91.

the incessant rise and fall of firms, whole industries and even national economies, all of which are a hallmark of the capitalist era.

A further feature Schumpeter highlights is that innovations are always associated with the rise to leadership of "new men." New men are required because new production functions typically do not grow out of old businesses, and it takes new men to act creatively in bringing about the new firms through which innovations thrive. Schumpeter notes that where large companies are involved, innovations may arise within an existing firm such as when a new leader takes hold. He is aware of course that some firms today have massive size, so he introduces the concept of "trustified capitalism" to cope with this. But he maintains that the growth of company size does not fundamentally alter his theoretical assumptions, because even giant concerns still have to react to others' innovations and so forth. "Even in the world of giant firms, new ones rise and others fall into the background. Innovations still emerge primarily with the 'young' ones and the 'old' ones display as a rule symptoms of what is euphemistically called conservatism."[15] This perspective about the role of leadership is critical to Schumpeter's theory, for it explains why innovations are not carried into effect simultaneously and automatically in all firms and in the same manner everywhere. It also accounts for the "lumpiness" of various economic data that show uneven development and fits and starts of progress. The nature of innovations is such that they inherently cause disequilibria that cannot be absorbed easily and smoothly but only as a result of awkward and painful processes. "Only some firms carry out innovations and then act along new cost curves, while others cannot and have merely to adapt themselves, in many cases by dying."[16] This aspect is what Schumpeter elsewhere describes with the dramatic phrase "creative destruction."[17]

Relevant to the idea of innovation is the concept of novelty. Schumpeter points out that the ability to favour untried possibilities or to choose between tried and untried options is a quality that, whilst not exceptional, is not universally distributed. It is common sense to say that it is much more difficult to do something that is not part of everyday routine, and Schumpeter mentions three reasons why choosing to do novel things is difficult. In the first place he says doing something novel comes up against the fact that the environment resists it. Resistance may consist of disapproval of machine-made products or may be manifest in prohibitions on the use of certain types of new machinery or even their smashing ("luddites"). Second, acts of a routine nature are often supported by the environment in special ways; for example, lenders readily loan for established purposes, labour of the required kind is plentiful, or customers will prefer what they are used to consuming. Third, new arrangements for the operation of a business confront the individual manager with the difficulties of conducting their affairs in an entirely new fashion compared

15 Ibid., p. 97.

16 Ibid., p. 98.

17 See Chapter VII of *Capitalism, Socialism and Democracy* entitled "The Process of Creative Destruction," pp. 81–6.

to familiar ways. In the new frame the task itself may change its character. Major elements in a new undertaking simply cannot be known and irrational inhibitions enter. These types of considerations mean that, whenever a new production function has been finally adopted, it then becomes easier for other people to do the same thing and even to improve upon it. In fact there is often a tendency for copying or imitating. It is obviously easier not only to do the same thing but also to do similar things in similar ways. Thus Schumpeter maintains that innovations seldom remain isolated events and, as we have already noted, they are not evenly distributed in time but, on the contrary, tend to appear in "clusters". He argues this is because first a few and then most firms follow in the lead of a successful innovation.

> Industrial change is never harmonious advance with all elements of the system actually moving, or tending to move in step. At any given time, some industries move on, others stay behind; and the discrepancies arising from this are an essential element in the situations that develop. Progress – in the industrial as well as in any other sector of social or cultural life – not only proceeds by jerks and rushes but also by one sided rushes productive of consequences other than those that would ensue in the case of co-ordinated rushes. In every span in historic time it is easy to locate the ignition of the process and to associate it with certain industries and, within these industries with certain firms, from which the disturbances then spread over the system.[18]

All this leads Schumpeter to conclude that economic evolution is necessarily "lop-sided, discontinuous, disharmonious by nature", and of course he makes many references to the history of capitalism, which is replete with examples of both bursts of progress, crises and depressions; hence the further problem to enquire as to whether they have a cyclical character.

Entrepreneurial profit

As we have seen, the entrepreneur is more than the mere head or manager of a business that is run along conventional lines, though of course many entrepreneurs will also carry out the mundane tasks of management day-in day-out. Schumpeter points out that nobody is ever an entrepreneur all the time. This is because a person who introduces a new combination invariably also carries out non-entrepreneurial tasks in the course their work. And many innovations, once they are established, are then exploited in a routine fashion with no other logic to their operations than those typical of the management of an existing firm. But in periods of high intensity in competitive capitalism, the entrepreneur will be found amongst the heads of firms and will often be an owner as well. Typically he will be the founder of a firm and possibly also of an industrial family. Sometimes, the entrepreneur is the

18 BC, pp. 101–2.

controlling owner of the shares of a company, though company promoters are not generally entrepreneurs in Schumpeter's sense.

The entrepreneur need not necessarily be either the person who provides the capital nor of course the person who is the inventor of the good or process that is being introduced. Often an entrepreneur will have very little of the necessary means at his disposal to begin with. In this respect Schumpeter criticizes figures like Marx who made ownership of capital the decisive feature of the individuals that are the driving force of capitalism. Of course, ownership of goods and assets which may serve as collateral or of money that can be expended in setting up a new production system make it easier for capitalists to become entrepreneurs but this is not an inevitable transition. One consequence of this separation of ownership from the entrepreneurial function is that the entrepreneur, strictly speaking, does not bear the risks of investment and, in fact, typically uses other people's money.

Schumpeter is especially concerned to account for the nature of profit under capitalism, an issue that had famously been a focus of Marx's critique. He first considers the situation in which an entrepreneur operating in a perfectly competitive economy carries out innovations that consist of producing commodities already in circulation at a total cost per unit that is lower than that of existing businesses. In this case, the entrepreneur will buy the producer goods he needs at existing prices based on the conditions under which the pre-existing firms are operating. And he will sell his product also at the prevailing prices, which are adjusted to the costs of the old firms. As a result, his receipts will be greater than his costs. This difference Schumpeter calls entrepreneur's profit or simply "profit." This profit is the premium that capitalist society places upon successful innovation, though it is inherently temporary and disappears as soon as subsequent competition and adaptation produce the tendency towards equalization of the premium.

In a stationary economy, both the entrepreneurial function and profit are totally absent, for in that situation, although there are rents and quasi-rents of factors owned by firms, the manager's earnings or his wages are merely a return paid for his managerial services. But in a real capitalist society, in order for private fortunes to amass, they must result from the process of innovation and not merely from the return of earnings of management. Profit thus understood is a *functional return* in the sense that it does not necessarily return to the entrepreneur as such. Whether it accrues to the entrepreneur or to the firm is a matter merely of the institutional structure involved. In corporations, profits accrue to the firm as such and their distribution is not automatic; it is a matter of policy – shareholders, executives and employees receive dividends, bonuses and other benefits in accordance with contractual and other arrangements. Struggles over the share of profits are simply one feature of the social arrangements of capitalism. More important from the economic point of view, however, is the effort to conserve the stream of profit as such. Schumpeter refers to secrecy regarding processes, patents, judicious differentiation of products, advertising and aggression directed against competitors as illustrative of familiar strategies designed to preserve the profit advantage of one firm vis-à-vis others. He even considers the possibility that, at times, the mere prospect of competition from innovations produces efforts of sabotage on the part of the old industries aimed at undermining the success of the new.

> Taking industry as a whole, there is always an innovating sphere warring with an "old" sphere, which sometimes tries to secure prohibition of the new ways of doing things – as the artisans congresses did in Europe as late as the eighteenth and nineteenth century – or to discredit them – the "machine-made product", for instance – or to buy them off – which is sometimes the real rationale of cartelisation – or to penalise them, by fiscal legislation or in other ways, including public planning of the type sometimes resorted to in depressions.[19]

Thus, in Schumpeter's view, entrepreneurial profit is not a result of the extraction of surplus labour, as with Marx, nor does he seek to justify it as an entitlement of private property or reward for abstinence. As he says, insofar as it is not comprised of moneys that can be categorized as "wages of management", it is a "functional return" that occurs because it is successful innovation that generates the increase in wealth.

The function of credit and banking

Schumpeter points out that the idea of credit creation is often difficult to understand because many think that bankers can only lend what is entrusted to them by depositors. This view, however, rests on a misconception. In considering the role of money in the setting up of new businesses under the direction of entrepreneurs, Schumpeter notes that would-be entrepreneurs do not generally already happen to own part or all the assemblage of goods that they need to carry out their projects, nor do they have assets that they can readily exchange for such goods. Existing firms, by contrast, have the option of financing their plant and equipment from current receipts. Assuming that old firms are so financed, Schumpeter says that it follows that the entrepreneur creating a new combination must borrow virtually all the funds they need both for starting up and operating a new venture, namely their fixed and working capital. Those funds are made up of means of payment created *ad hoc* by the banks.

To explain the role of credit creation, Schumpeter makes a comparison with a hypothetical socialist economy and points out how in such an economy, in order for new production functions to be set up, it would be necessary to issue orders to those in charge of productive resources to withdraw part of them from the employments in which they have hitherto been engaged and apply them to new purposes. This is also a problem for a capitalist society; the issue to the entrepreneur of new means of payment created *ad hoc,* that is out of nowhere, corresponds to the order issued by the central bureau in socialist society. In both

19 Ibid., p. 108.

cases, innovation involves the shifting of existing factors from old deployments to new ones, but there is one crucial difference. In the case of the socialist system, the new order involves cancelling old uses. But innovation in capitalist society is financed by credit creation, so the shifting of the factors is not affected by the withdrawal of funds cancelling the existing orders from old firms. The new orders for factors come on top of the old ones that are not cancelled as in socialism. This is an crucial feature of the capitalist system. In the socialist system the decision as to which innovations to carry out is made by the central bureau. However, under capitalism this function is effectively fulfilled by the banks, which provide the entrepreneurs with the means to buy the factors of production that they need. The banks thereby constitute a new type of firm whose economic function it is to produce means of payment.[20]

Schumpeter is fully aware that this is not the only way credit can be created. Firms themselves may issue of bills of exchange and central banks create money in other ways too, but these are secondary from the point of view of the creation of credit on the scale needed to finance the capitalist engine. Schumpeter notes that loans to entrepreneurs need not necessarily be repaid in full, and in fact they are often renewed and cause a corresponding amount of means of payment to be permanently part of the circulating medium. At any given time, the bulk of bank credit outstanding will be what has become current business and has lost its original connection with innovation or its adaptations, although the history of each loan must lead back to one or the other.

The function of the banks is ideally much more than to simply provide the funds in question. Commercial banking means that the banker should know and be able to judge for what his credit is going to be used. The banker must not only be familiar with the transaction he is asked to finance but also be mindful of how it will turn out. He must also have knowledge of the customer, his business and even his personal dispositions in order to be certain of the nature of the risk he is undertaking. Of course, to fulfil this function the banks must be completely independent agents. They cannot act like the equivalent agency in a socialist economy where the officials will have concerns as to the social value of a new enterprise. This independence means that banks and their officers must not have a stake in the gains of the entrepreneur's project, beyond what is entailed in the loan contract itself. Banks ought also to be independent of politics. That is, they cannot be subservient to a government's public policy objectives such as might jeopardize the rationality of their lending decisions.

We shall not, for the present, explore Schumpeter's theory of money, which is related to the role of banking. We note that he did make several attempts to develop a theory consistent with his general account of the capitalist mechanism. These

20 Schumpeter distinguishes *member banks* from *bankers' banks* or *central banks. Member banks* are those which keep the accounts of and manufacture balances for firms and the households of entrepreneurs, whereas *bankers' banks* keep accounts of and manufacture balances for *member banks.* See Ibid., p. 112

efforts issued first an essay published in German around 1918 that was called in English "Money and the Social Product". Subsequently, until the late 1920s, Schumpeter worked on a monograph on the topic, which was never completed; though a German edition was published in 1970 as *Das Wesen des Geldes*. Some commentators have suggested that Schumpeter was upstaged in his effort to make a major contribution on the monetary theory by the publication of Keynes's *Treatise on Money* of 1930. Be that as it may, Schumpeter continued to work on his own theory but was never satisfied with his results and declined to authorize publication of his manuscript. The gist of his approach was to see the economy as a whole as a system of flows of money expenditure and of goods sold against such outlays. The Walrasian system of inter-dependent markets is held together by the flow of money. These flows enable the link between successive disbursements of money by entrepreneurs and the payments made for the goods produced by industry to be established through time.[21]

The effects of disequilibrium

On the basis of the analysis of innovation and credit creation we have surveyed above, Schumpeter proceeds to lay out his theory of business cycles. Because of the complexity of the phenomena to be explained, he proceeds by a series of approximations, each time adding additional features to arrive at an overall theory only at the end. His first approximation starts with the fact that at any given point in capitalist society, there exist possibilities for new combinations. The ability to take advantage of these is necessarily unequally distributed, and this has important implications. The motivation for taking up these opportunities derives from the possibility of obtaining profit. In the usual situation, certain individuals make plans for their new combinations and carry them out with varying degrees of proficiency, in anticipation that they will make profits in the future. The ability to take the lead in doing this Schumpeter refers to as the "entrepreneurial aptitude". As a new firm is set up, it constructs new plants or purchases new equipment from existing firms. The money to do this is acquired from banks. In order to acquire the goods, which otherwise would be purchased by existing firms, the entrepreneur must outbid the existing purchasers of producer goods, and this has an inflationary effect. Upon the lead of some entrepreneurs, others follow in increasing numbers and, because of the path-breaking work of the initial innovators, the way is smoothed for those that follow. Because within the stationary state there are no unemployed resources,

21 For a fuller account of Schumpeter's monetary theory, see Arthur Marget, "The Monetary Aspects of the Schumpeterian System", in Seymour Edwin Harris (ed.), *Schumpeter, Social Scientist*, Harvard University Press, 1951, pp. 62–71. There is also a useful discussion of the second chapter of *Das Wesen des Geldes* by Ulrich Busch, "Joseph A. Schumpeter's 'Soziologie des Geldes'", in Jürgen Backhaus (ed.), *Joseph Alois Schumpeter: Entrepreneurship, Style and Vision*, Kluwer, 2003, pp. 191–202. On the general topic of the nature and role of money in a capitalist society, see Geoffrey Ingham, *The Nature of Money*, Polity, 2004 and Nigel Dodd, *The Sociology of Money*, Continuum, 1994.

prices of factors of production will tend to rise as entrepreneurs attempt to outbid the old firms in order to acquire resources. As prices of goods rise, so necessarily do the costs for all firms, but this of course also means that those industries that are able to sell goods at these higher costs receive greater receipts. There are clearly gains and losses, but as a whole taken together, all old firms together should show a net surplus.

The general effect of new entrepreneurial activity spread over the system as a whole is that it disrupts the equilibrium that existed before. Clearly some firms and industries will experience gains of a windfall nature and others will have losses, but at this stage there is no net increase in total output. This is because in the preceding period where there was perfect equilibrium, firms produced their optimum output using all their plants up to the point at which the total cost was at a minimum, but as soon as entrepreneurial activity breaks with the previous state, factors of production previously used by the old firms must be withdrawn to be deployed by innovating entrepreneurs. This means that the production of consumer goods must necessarily be sacrificed in the interest of making producer goods. Even though the net quantity of consumer goods may decline in this period, this does not mean that the demand for consumer goods will decline, and in fact, it is likely to increase because of the increased purchasing power brought about by the increased payments flowing into the hands of the consumers. All this continues until the first entrepreneur's plant becomes operative, at which time an entirely new situation comes onto being. The new commodities that have been produced now enter the market. All things being equal, these goods are readily taken up by consumers at the price the entrepreneur anticipates they can be sold. On the assumption that the entrepreneur continues to produce the new consumer goods without any further changes in his operation, he begins to receive receipts from the sale of these goods that are sufficient to repay the loans with which he has purchased his plant and equipment. Given that entrepreneurial activity in its first phase has been successful and that numerous entrepreneurs have achieved similar successes, the result is that the new firms are able to place a larger quantity of consumer goods into the market than had previously been the case. This increase in consumer goods is what amounts to the experience of prosperity and gives rise to the appearance, and indeed reality, of "economic progress."

The new goods that enter into the market will, as Schumpeter has previously explained, not be easily absorbed without disruptions. The first wave of new products entering the market will not alter the total business situation but will clearly affect those firms that are in immediate proximity to the productive area of the new firm. But as the process continues, the effects create disequilibrium and force a course of adaptation. Whilst the effect on old firms is initially not necessarily negative because they may benefit from increased prices for their goods, eventually the competition of the new firms forces a much more difficult adaptation. For some old firms new opportunities may arise for expansion and they may be able to prosper for a while, but for others the emergence of new methods and products ultimately leads to a situation in which it is impossible for them to compete. This latter situation spells their economic death. Still others are only partially able to adapt and find themselves in decline.[22]

Schumpeter claims that eventually a time arises when entrepreneurial activity slackens and innovation ceases. Why should this be so? First, he says entrepreneurial activity characteristically begins in a particular direction. It does not distribute itself equally over all industries. Its possibilities are inherently limited. As more industries develop in the wake of the initial innovations, the point is reached at which the costs of producing the new commodity become equal to the price at which it will sell. Profits are thereby eliminated and hence the impact of the innovation will have spent itself. This then completes the cycle of entrepreneurial innovation and its exploitation. Schumpeter provides the following general overview of the process of economic evolution:

> Our theory of the mechanism of change stresses discontinuity. It takes the view that, as we put it, evolution proceeds by successive revolutions, or that there are in the process jerks or jumps which account for many of its features. As soon, however, as we survey the history of any sector of social life, we become aware of a factor which seems, at first sight, to be incompatible with that view; every change seems to consist in the accumulation of many small influences and events and comes about precisely by steps so small as to make any exact dating and any sharp distinction of epochs almost meaningless. Evolution of productive technique may serve as an example. What we designate as a big invention hardly ever springs out of the current events, as Athene did from the head of Zeus, and practically every exception we might think of vanishes on closer investigation. . . . The decisive step in bringing about a new thing or ultimate practical success is, in most cases, only the last straw and relatively insignificant in itself. . . . What is technically called a revolution never can be understood from itself, i.e., without reference to the developments that led up to it; it sums up rather than initiates.[23]

How business cycles begin

A major concern of Schumpeter is to show how an evolutionary mechanism underlies the apparent performance of modern economies from their inception down to the present. For he is certain he has discovered convincing evidence of cyclical phenomena operating as early as the time of the Industrial Revolution and perhaps earlier. This claim about pre-industrial capitalism is controversial, because the consequence of adopting this view would seem to be to deny that there is a fundamental epochal change with the advent of industrialization and the various modern institutions associated with it – such as the corporation, the stock market,

22 BC, p. 134.
23 Ibid., pp. 226–7.

mechanization of production, a regulated monetary system, the rational division of labour, and so on. Schumpeter wants to say that his mechanism of capitalist evolution can be divined well back into the pre-history of the modern era. Clearly this position is fundamentally at odds with the position of Weber, amongst others. For Weber, the advent of the modern market economy constitutes a unique and unprecedented development and created rational economic phenomena not found previously in world history.

Let us consider Schumpeter's definition of capitalist enterprise, as set forth in *Business Cycles*. He defines capitalism as, "that form of private property economy in which innovations are carried out by means of borrowed money, which in general, though not by logical necessity, implies credit creation."[24] He is aware that his definition is in a sense nominalistic. That is, he has chosen to define capitalism in this way for purely heuristic/scientific purposes. In placing the idea of credit creation at the very centre of his definition, Schumpeter is in some ways at odds with many, if not most, other theorists. He distinguishes his own position, for example, from those of Marx, Sombart and Böhm-Bawerk – and we can add Weber. But he insists that the phenomenon of credit creation, whilst not necessarily implying a direct causal relation, nonetheless does suggest all manner of institutions that are typical of the setting in which modern capitalism appears. But the critical thing about credit creation is that it introduces elements that are determinative of the cyclical character of the capitalist phenomenon. "The only thing that could be controversial about this [definition] is our proposition that the economic process of capitalist society is identical with the sequence of events that give rise to the business cycle."[25]

As a result of this definitional starting point, Schumpeter says that the beginnings of capitalism can be seen as far back as the phenomenon of credit creation itself and can be traced to where there have been negotiable credit instruments, the presence of which gave the possibility of credit creation. Schumpeter at times appears to want to go back in time further than this, for he even says that we must take in the era of non-negotiable instruments, which preceded the imperfectly negotiable ones. So it is his view that the practice of credit creation may be as old as deposit banking as such. He specifically takes issue with those thinkers such as Wesley Mitchell and Arthur Spiethoff, who were strongly resistant to the idea that one can speak of business cycles in the requisite sense before the end of the eighteenth century. He concedes that the smaller the capitalist sector is in an otherwise pre-capitalist world, the less the fluctuations characteristic of the capitalist process will assert themselves, and the more other causes of fluctuations, such as external factors, will tend to dominate. Thus the impact of innovations will be felt differently in a small-scale capitalist environment than it would in one in which modern corporate capitalism is dominant. Schumpeter admits that it may be difficult to discern phenomena of a cyclical nature in these early periods, but nonetheless, he claims they are in principle detectable. In this connection he

24 Ibid., p. 223.
25 Ibid., p. 224.

refers to the bursting of the South Sea Bubble, which he suggests bore a striking resemblance to the crises of 1873 and 1929. "While proof must wait upon future research, there is certainly no reason to expect that those 'crises' will eventually turn out to have been anything else but incidents of a cyclical movement, distorted no doubt by the action of external factors, exactly as they are today. All evidence from such material as we have points in our direction, certainly as far back as the sixteenth century, down to details of financial practice."[26]

At this point in his exegesis, Schumpeter alludes to the history of banking and refers to the fact that the non-negotiable bill of exchange came into existence in the second half of the fourteenth century, an important factor in the credit business of banks.[27] He also refers to the use of the cheque, which was prohibited in Venice as late as 1526, and then refers to the gradual elimination of the prohibition on interest.[28] These developments in banking and commercial culture, he wants to say, are not merely incidental elements in the history of economic life but may well partake in the operation of a cyclical mechanism. To illustrate the point, he refers to an iconic industrial development – the electrification of the household – and notes the many discontinuities incidents upon the setting up of the new production function associated with electrification. He admits that it is true that, if we look at western European economic life in the sixteenth century and compare it with the tenth, we cannot but note an enormous difference. However, even in the tenth century, he says, there were rudimentary forms of capitalism – for example, quite definitely in Venice at that time.[29]

Schumpeter's critique of cultural theories of the advent of capitalism

Now it is of more than passing interest that, at this point in his argument, Schumpeter sets out to criticize those theorists who have argued that with the advent of industrialization there came into being a new "spirit" or *Geist*, and he makes specific reference to Sombart and Weber in this regard. He says that these thinkers have argued that somewhere between the fourteenth and the sixteenth century there arose an economic system fundamentally different to the preceding one.

26 Ibid., p. 225.

27 For an account of the economic role of the early bill of exchange, see the excellent analysis of Larry Neal, *The Rise of Financial Capitalism*, Cambridge University Press, 1990, pp. 5–9.

28 It is worth noting that Weber does not regard relaxing the prohibition on charging interest as having been significant for the growth of capitalism, as this did not require supplies of money but a positive incentive to gain wealth.

29 It is disappointing that Schumpeter nowhere refers specifically to Weber's several discussions of mediaeval and Renaissance capitalism where he is able to show that even the most acquisitive and lucrative business operations did not amount to a truly modern form of capitalism. See for example the long essay-length footnote (Ch 2. no. 12) on Alberti in *The Protestant Ethic*, pp. 94–8. Schumpeter likewise makes no mention of Weber's concept of political capitalism, which, for example, more adequately accounts for the banking activities of the great Florentine houses of the Peruzzi and Medici that were partly built on the financing of war. See also GEH, p. 259.

With Weber specifically in mind, Schumpeter explicitly rejects the idea that the "rationalization" of life generally, or of economic life in particular, was a new phenomenon with far-reaching consequences for the way in which the economy developed. Somewhat provocatively, he says, "In particular there is no need to trace what that group of authors entirely unrealistically considers as a new rationalism on the one hand and as a new attitude towards profits on the other hand to religious changes (M. Weber) – which is a way of arguing hardly superior to the economic interpretation of history which it is intended to improve or replace."[30] Evidently, Schumpeter here has in mind some version or other of the Weber's Protestant ethic thesis and is assuming that Weber was attempting to establish that religion was the key to the rise of modern capitalism. He is adamant, on the contrary, that his own position is superior and warns against approaches akin to that of Weber:

> The historical sequence of the forms of enterprise, in particular, appears in a different and much more promising light as soon as we drop the attempt to look at each of them as a world of its own incomparable with all other such worlds. The type of mediaeval artisans organization, their organization and behaviour, are fully accounted for by the conditions of their environment and particularly of their market. The way in which they succumbed to what then was a commercially superior method, the putting out system, whilst, as will be seen, illustrating well what we mean by the process of new things "competing old ones out of existence," does not stand in need of an extraneous principle of explanation.[31]

In other words, Schumpeter is saying that the transition from the putting-out system to full-fledged capitalist enterprise is to be explained as yet another manifestation of the impact of innovation, of better methods of production competing out obsolete ones that are not as efficient. It is this mechanism that largely explains the victory of the novel organizational forms associated with the factory system and modern management.

As we have seen in previous chapters, Weber has a good deal to say about the way in which the traditionalistic methods of production, such as the putting-out system, were overtaken by modern capitalist forms. Weber acknowledges that the domestic system goes back well before the Reformation and was important for the economic development of England. But it remained centred in the household, even when tools and some equipment were provided by the factor. And there was no simple transition to workshop production and factories, because these required fixed capital, rational division of labour and numerous other preconditions.[32] We shall not repeat those considerations here, which we say remain unshaken

30 Ibid., p. 228.
31 Ibid.
32 See GEH, pp. 153–77.

by Schumpeter's criticisms. Schumpeter insists that the transition from small-scale production to that typical of the more advanced modern forms of enterprise required no new mentality to emerge. He refers to the early commercialization of life and claims profits created in premodern forms of enterprise were sufficient to bring about later forms: "The entrepreneur of the commercial type imperceptibly shades off into the entrepreneur of the industrial type and the transition of the one to the other does not constitute a problem *sui generis*."[33] But this bald claim is unconvincing when compared to the detailed and exhaustive discussions of Weber on this question. We say that Schumpeter overstates the case for the early appearance his capitalist mechanism, as we shall explain in the next chapter.

The theory of waves and cycles

Thus far we have seen how, according to Schumpeter, it is entrepreneurial innovation that generates the expansion of economic activity. Whilst output may decrease in the initial stages of the innovating period, consumption may in fact increase as innovators pay higher wages to attract workers to new modes of production. This may give rise to an inflationary period and may also lead to a tendency for economic actors to speculate on prospects for the intensification of economic activity to continue into the future. Further borrowing takes place as wholesalers, anticipating increased sales and in order to finance larger orders, take out bigger loans. This phase of economic activity Schumpeter refers to as the "secondary wave." It means that there is a cumulative process of additional economic activity that is dependent on the "igniting mechanism" of the initial entrepreneurial phase. In this secondary wave, however, entrepreneurs may overshoot and take on more debt than they can effectively repay. There may be a series of liquidations, as a result of reckless and speculative ventures that fail, and these may be greater in number than those of the primary wave. In this stage there may even occur a kind of panic culminating in a crisis, though this is not inevitable. But every liquidation contributes to a fall in values, which further undermines confidence, and a pessimistic attitude may gradually engulf the economic environment as a whole.

Events then go seriously in a reverse direction and the process of adjustment just described may overrun the point of equilibrium towards which it was tending and enter a state of depression. Schumpeter describes this as "abnormal liquidation" – this is where a downward revision of values occurs and a reduction of operations causes the economy to operate at below-equilibrium levels. Whereas a recession involves a mechanism drawing the system towards equilibrium, if the crisis develops to a point where a new disequilibrium is developing, there is the possibility of "depression". But if a depression has developed, eventually a new mechanism comes into play wherein the depressive phase runs its course. The system will eventually track back towards the point of equilibrium again; this is the phase of recovery or revival. Whereas recession, according to Schumpeter, is

33 BC, p. 229.

an inevitable part of the cyclical process of business evolution, depression is not, and whether it occurs depends on accidental circumstances such as the mentality of businessmen, the moral character of the community and the individuals that make it up, along with other circumstances of the day. The spiral into depression, if it occurs, may be accentuated by the influence of external factors, such as warfare or natural disasters. But when the depression phase eventually ends, reversion towards the neighbourhood of equilibrium occurs, leading sooner or later to a further phase of innovation – and thus the cycle continues again repeating the stages as before. When booms in business bust, there will generally follow a decline in the general level of prosperity as investors lose confidence and businesses enter a phase of contraction.

Schumpeter tells us the impact of innovations is highly variable because their effects may be rapid in one field but very slow in others.

> One railroad or a few lines may be all, and more than all, that can be successfully built in a given environment at a given time. Reaction and absorption may have to follow before a new wave of railroad construction becomes possible. . . . In such cases, innovation is carried out in steps each of which constitutes a cycle. But these cycles may display a family likeness, and a relation to one another which is easy to understand and which tends to weld them into a higher unit that will stand out as a historical individual.[34]

There may also be cumulative effects from the commercial and industrial implications of innovations over a long period. For example, in the case of railroadization,

> expenditure on, and the opening of, a new line has some immediate effects on business in general, on competing means of transport, and on the relative position of centres of production. It requires more time to bring into use the opportunities of production merely created by the railroad and to annihilate others. And it takes still longer for population to shift, new cities to develop, other cities to decay, and, generally, the new face of the country to take shape that is adapted to the environment as altered by the railroadization.[35]

These complications suggest there are many and perhaps an indefinite number of separate cycles for each innovation and its related adaptations. However, Schumpeter argues that it happens to be the case that the business cycle can be fully understood on the basis of a three-cycle schema. The shortest cycle, he says, is the forty-month or Kitchin, the next cycle of a ten-year duration he terms the Juglar, and the final and longest cycle is the Kondratieff with a time span of sixty years. Schumpeter claims that within each Kondratieff there are a set number of

34 Ibid., p. 167.
35 Ibid., p. 168.

Juglars and within each Juglar a set number of Kitchins. He claims there is nothing inherent in reality that causes these specific periods to be the case, but nonetheless they provide the most adequate theoretical schema available with which to analyze the cyclical processes of the capitalist system. In his analyses of time series, Schumpeter found that as a matter of fact there were three Kitchins to each Juglar and six jugulars to each Kondratieff. We shall now turn to a detailed exegesis of Schumpeter's first major cycle, the long wave from 1787 to 1842.

The first Kondratieff

In what follows, to illustrate the nature of his approach to the business cycle phenomenon, we shall briefly survey one of Schumpeter's key examples, the period 1787 to 1842. This is significant for Schumpeter because it is possibly his best case of a long cycle or "Kondratieff" and coincides with the era in which the economies of England and America began the process of "railroadization".[36] Whilst he does not necessarily see this period as being the first such Kondratieff, it is the first occasion on which he believes there is sufficient data to establish the clear existence of such a cycle.

At the outset, Schumpeter wants to guard against what he sees as a possible misunderstanding with respect to the relationship between the conventional notion of the Industrial Revolution and this first identifiable Kondratieff. As we have just seen, he rejects the idea that the Industrial Revolution, or indeed the term of revolution per se, provides an adequate description of the developments he is seeking to identify and explain. He wants to argue that each business cycle is created out of the wreckage of a previous one, so that it is misleading to locate what appear to be singular economic developments in the conditions immediately preceding them. For many of the elements that are part of the so-called Industrial Revolution have antecedents many years before and are part of a much larger schema of economic evolution. Schumpeter says he has no particular quarrel with Usher, who locates the Industrial Revolution as occurring as early as 1700, except there is no reason even to stop there if the term is to designate the whole process of the emergence of modern industry. Schumpeter claims "it is in recession, depression and revival that the achievements initiated in the prosperity phase mature and fully unfold themselves, thus bringing about a general reorganization of industry and commerce, the full exploitation of the opportunities newly created, and the elimination of obsolete and inadaptable elements, which is exactly what happened and what accounts for what everyone admits to have been a prolonged, though often interrupted, 'depression' . . ."[37] Thus, the innovations that were relevant to the upswing of economic activity in the eighties and nineties of the eighteenth century, in many respects, have their origins much earlier, and likewise, the twenties and the thirties

36 Nikolai Kondratieff's seminal paper is "Die langen Wellen der Konjunktur", *Archiv für Sozialwissenschaft und Sozialpolitik*, 56, (1926), pp. 573–609.

37 BC, p. 254.

of the nineteenth century already manifest the innovations that will contribute to the next Kondratieff.

If one is to locate a starting point for the Industrial Revolution, Schumpeter says the relevant innovations must have begun some time before 1793, at the time when England had declared war on France. In discussing the situation of England he then refers to the fact that agriculture was by far the most important single industry and the main site of innovation. Enclosure acts were still being enacted as late as 1810. Intensive cultivation in the neighbourhood of cities had first developed in Flanders, but this had begun to occur in England in places like Norfolk, where drainage by the use of steam pumps and the more scientific use of fertilizers had become common. English colonial and commercial enterprise exploiting the opportunities of political power was also important in this period. Later, the cotton textile industry became a leader. Production and trade in cotton goods had been common previously; however, several new innovations can clearly be distinguished. The first of these was the introduction of Indian cotton fabrics by the East India Company. By 1721, the success of this new cotton material threatened the old firms based on wool and silk. There were efforts to prohibit the sale as well as the wearing of printed or painted dyed calicoes. Eventually, English industry began using cotton as weft in woollen warp as the industry gained an exemption from the prohibition on the production of mixed fabrics. Schumpeter says many steps led up to the elimination of restrictions on the production of pure cotton fabrics. "Experimentation, resistance, failure, and local success (Arkwright's, about 1760, was the outstanding one) are what we observe before. Spread, induced improvements, dislocation and absorption, copying, following and competing are what we observe afterward, in the down-grade and revival, when the real avalanche of products came."[38] Many of the most important textile inventions, such as the Flying Shuttle, the Jenny, Barker's Loom and Cartwright's Loom, had been made much earlier, but their true impact was not felt till a subsequent period. A really successful power loom only evolved later from the efforts of Austin, Horricks and Roberts in the early nineteenth century. Schumpeter emphasizes again that invention and innovation are entirely different things and not directly related to each other. Of course, they interact, and sometimes invention is an incident in the entrepreneurial achievement. The figure of Arkwright was exemplary in this regard. Again and again, Schumpeter insists that the evidence shows that the actual setting up of a new production function is a distinct achievement. "We readily see how every step conditions other steps – yarn and cloth, for instance, alternating in offering new demand to each other and in running up against bottlenecks, the removal of which then makes the next achievement. We see how demand for cotton conditions Whitney's ginning machine and so on. But we also see that these conditions . . . lead up to other innovations . . ."[39]

38 Ibid., p. 271.
39 Ibid., pp. 272–3.

Schumpeter notes that other historians have often discounted the importance of innovation because the actual extent of industrial change brought by it up to the beginning of the nineteenth century was rather small. But to form an idea as to the quantitative adequacy of the innovations of this period, he says one has to consider their effect as "ignition."

> What we see on the surface is largely the effect of what we have called the Secondary Wave, the phenomena of which can in fact be sufficiently expressed in terms of general conditions, growing commercial sectors, independently given demand conditions, and so on. To that ignition we must, hence, always apply a multiplier before confronting it with statistical findings about social aggregates. Looked at in this manner the development in the cotton trade alone would be adequate to explain a Kondratieff upswing.[40]

In general terms, what Schumpeter stresses is that the jerkiness and unevenness of economic progress is to be explained in terms precisely of the cyclical process. This process was connected with shorter cycles centred on cotton, textiles, coal, iron and transportation. The course of economic progress was manifested in the spread of improvements in these areas, especially as regards the steam engine, the iron machine, machine tools and mechanical engineering generally. Schumpeter notes that Watt and his partner Boulton eventually achieved success in 1782, but it is not correct to say that the alliance between them is best described as that between an entrepreneur and a capitalist. Before Wilkinson, who had improved the boring of cannons, came to Watt's aid, his condenser was unworkable because the pistons did not fit his cylinders. Watt's early machines were wasteful, quickly wore out and broke down. Even by 1800, the total volume of horsepower from installed steam engines was relatively small compared with other sources of power.

During the period under discussion, Schumpeter says steam ships did not rise to great importance; however the locomotive, particularly after Stephenson's success, put the alternative forms of railway traction, horses and stationary engines, out of business. The Liverpool and Manchester railroad was the first entrepreneurial achievement of national importance and induced the greater part of Schumpeter's secondary wave. Then followed the spate of railroad construction that he classifies as part of the Jugular prosperity that preceded the crash of 1837. Up to 1838, roughly 490 miles of rail track had been added to the English network. But the really important development in quantitative terms came later in the 1840s when almost the entire English rail system was created. This railroadization, Schumpeter says, belongs to the second Kondratieff, even though the essentials of railroad enterprise already existed in the 1830s. Here railroad entrepreneurs stand out particularly in sharp relief. Given that the joint-stock company did not become the normal means of enterprise prior to the Act of 1856, it was not used as the main means of enterprise prior to that time. Of course, the advances referred to

40 Ibid., pp. 274–5.

had the effect of crowding out those firms and individuals tied to the older forms of industry. Even so, the impact of the machine, according to Schumpeter, was not to reduce total employment or even to reduce it in the areas that were being revolutionized.

As regards to the impact of the joint-stock company, Schumpeter notes that in banking the spread of the corporate form was barred until 1826.[41] However, from the beginning of the eighteenth century, promotion of companies with a quasi-corporate character became quite common. This was the period of the Bubble Act following the mania of 1807 and 1808. But throughout the early 1800s, despite the difficulties of incorporation, many companies were formed, particularly in mining, insurance, gas, canals and a wide variety of trading, building and other industries. Many, of course, did not last and failed almost immediately or within a few years. No less than fifteen banks, based on joint-stock deposits, were founded between 1826 and 1830, and a further twenty-five were founded in the next three years. But by 1844, when there were nearly a thousand companies in existence, only one was a cotton manufacturing establishment. Railroads, gas, water and shipping were the major areas of corporate development.[42]

We shall not consider further historical illustration of the business cycle phenomenon, which Schumpeter provides in abundance, as this would involve a lengthy discussion of the rich detail of Volume Two of his book and take us beyond our key concerns here.

Criticism of Schumpeter's theory of business cycles

The most controversial aspect of Schumpeter's theory of business cycles and the areas which have received the most criticism concerns two related problems: Why is it that innovations occur in clusters, and why are there business cycles with regular wave-like characteristics?[43] The main objection raised against clusterings follows from the proposition that there can only be clusterings if there is discontinuity in the distribution of entrepreneurial activity, but there is no obvious reason why this should be so. A related objection concerns Schumpeter's view that innovations are concentrated in the neighbourhood of equilibrium. It is argued that in maintaining this view, Schumpeter relies too much on the principle that increased risk will deter innovations occurring in boom periods.

41 Schumpeter relies considerably on the classic account of the development of the corporation by Bishop Hunt, *The Development of the Business Corporation in England: 1800–1867*, Harvard University Press, 1936.

42 We note here that Schumpeter seems to have no appreciation of the fact, crucial in Weber's account of origins, that the development of institution of the joint-stock corporation involved an historically unique course of development that cannot be reduced to an instance of innovation.

43 For a general introduction to the issue of finding empirical support for business cycles, see Robert Gordon, "Current Research in Business Cycles", *American Economic Review*, May, (1949), pp. 47–63.

A classic exponent of the first criticism is Simon Kuznets, who argues that Schumpeter's theory requires discontinuity over time in the manifestation of entrepreneurial ability: It "implies cycles in the supply of entrepreneurial ability, whether the supply be conceived in terms of individuals or phases in the life of various individuals."[44] Kuznets thinks this is improbable:

> Given an infinite supply of possible innovations . . . why need entrepreneurial genius defer the next pioneering step until his preceding one has been so imitated and expanded that the upsetting of the equilibrium stops him in his tracks? . . . Why should we not conceive these applications of high entrepreneurial ability, whether represented by one man or several, as flowing in a continuous stream, a stream magnified in a constant proportion by the efforts of the imitators.[45]

This criticism is somewhat misplaced, however, as Schumpeter does not account for innovation exclusively in relation to the presence of the entrepreneurial aptitude, as it is the combination of this with the objective economic conditions that facilitates innovation at a given point in time. For example, unless there are capitalist promoters prepared to finance new combinations, and this entails that the business cycle is at a stage that is opportune for investment, no amount of entrepreneurial drive will suffice.

Kuznets has advanced a further criticism of Schumpeter's theory in suggesting that there are fundamental methodological problems.

> One cannot escape the impression that Professor Schumpeter's model in its present state cannot be linked directly and clearly with statistically observed realities: that the extreme paucity of statistical analysis in the treatise is an inevitable result of the type of theoretical model adopted: and that the great reliance upon historical outlines and qualitative discussion is a consequence of the difficulty of devising statistical procedures that would correspond to the theoretical model . . . The cycle is essentially a quantitative concept. All its characteristics such as duration, amplitude, phases etc., can be conceived only as measurable aspects, and can be properly measured only with the help of quantitative data. To establish the existence of cycles of a given type requires first a demonstration that fluctuations of that approximate duration recur, with fair simultaneity, in the movements of various significant aspects of economic life (production and employment in various industries, prices of various groups of goods, interest rates, volumes of trade, flow of credit,

44 Simon Kuznets, "Schumpeter's Business Cycles", *American Economic Review*, 30.2, (1940), p. 263.

45 Ibid., pp. 262–3. For a general review of the reception of Schumpeter's *Business Cycles*, see Charles Staley, "Schumpeter's Business Cycles", *New York Economic Review*, Spring, (1986), pp. 3–16.

> etc.); and second, an indication of what external factors or peculiarities of the economic system proper account for such recurrent fluctuations.[46]

Schumpeter's response to this type of criticism is to partly concede that such correlations are not always possible. For, strictly speaking, he does not believe that the business cycle is a purely quantitative phenomenon. At one point in *Business Cycles* he says "it is absurd to think that we can derive the contour lines of our phenomena from our statistical material only. All we could ever prove from it is that no regular contour lines exist." And he goes on: "General history (social, political and cultural), economic history and more particularly industrial history are not only indispensable but really the most important contributors to the understanding of our problem. All other materials and methods, statistical and theoretical, are only subservient to them and worse than useless without them."[47] In discussing the nature and use of a time series Schumpeter explains that "the time sequences we observe are, of course, part of our material from which we have to start and for which we have to account. And we have to bring every new factual finding into accord with the rest of the facts of the economic process and not with any poetry of ours. But no statistical finding can ever either prove or disprove a proposition which we have reason to believe by virtue of simpler and more fundamental facts."[48] His view is perhaps best summarized in this statement: "Analysing business cycles means neither more nor less than analysing the economic process of the capitalist era."[49] Thus, Schumpeter is saying that statistical and historical data must be analyzed together in unison in order to establish the reality of cyclical phenomena. It follows that the criticism that he has not based his theory entirely on the analysis of the quantitative time series data is not to the point.

Related to the Kuznets's criticisms of Schumpeter's business cycle theory are those of Angus Maddison in his study of the phases of capitalist development. In a review of the major theorists of business cycles, Maddison is especially critical of Schumpeter's account of the business cycle. He refers to his three types of cycle, the Kondratieff, the Juglar and the Kitchin, and raises doubts as regards the empirical regularity of the schema. He maintains it has not been well established by the empirical data. And he doubts the relevance of some of the theory that underlies Schumpeter's analysis.

> Kitchin's paltry contributions to the literature is lean meat indeed compared with that of NBER [the National Bureau of Economic Research of the USA], and Juglar never claimed to have demonstrated the existence of an eight to nine year rhythm. In fact, the NBER had already demonstrated rather wide variance in the length of cycles, so that there was little ground for distinguishing Juglars

46 Ibid., pp. 266–7.
47 BC, p. 13.
48 Ibid., p. 33.
49 Ibid., Preface.

and Kitchins. Furthermore, Schumpeter distinguished only the length of these three types of cycles and said nothing about their amplitude.[50]

Maddison goes on to argue that Schumpeter's use of statistics is rather cavalier and by modern standards not sufficiently rigorous. He says that judged on the statistical evidence alone, the theory would long ago have been discredited. However, somewhat at odds with the criticisms, he admits the theory underlying it is highly imaginative and illuminating. Nonetheless, he says Schumpeter significantly misread certain key events, such as the significance of the 1929–33 US recession. Schumpeter said this had been more or less consistent with a pattern of depressions occurring every 55 years and referred to the 1873–77 recession as being the previous case. But Maddison claims this is not a genuine parallel and is quite misleading because the earlier depression saw a fall in production of only 14.8% whereas the 30s depression saw production fall 44.7%.[51] Maddison seems to accept that as far as the long wave Kondratieff is concerned, Schumpeter is on stronger ground than otherwise; however, his theory still has three fundamental weaknesses.

> 1) He does not provide a persuasive explanation why innovation (and entrepreneurial drive) should come in regular waves rather than in a continuous but irregular stream, which seems a more plausible hypothesis for analysis concerned with the economy as a whole; 2) He makes no distinction between the lead country and others, but argues as if they were all operating on a par as far as productivity level and technological opportunity is concerned. Thus his waves of innovation are expected to affect all countries simultaneously; 3) He greatly exaggerates the scarcity of entrepreneurial ability and its importance as a factor of production.[52]

In his defence, it has to be said that Schumpeter anticipated the criticism about the clustering of innovations. One reason why innovations do not occur as a continuous stream is that those who have the ability to make them usually take a long time to bring them to fruition. Often an innovative venture involves founding a new firm through which the innovation is developed. This can take many years of determined effort, and in order to gain success, the entrepreneur must stick at his original project to the exclusion of others. So it is usually not practical for him to move onto further innovations of a different kind. As to why innovations occur in the neighbourhood of equilibrium, Schumpeter argues that this is because equilibrium conditions are the most suited for their introduction. In the neighbourhood of equilibrium, the risk of failure is reduced to its minimum. The other aspect of why there are clusters concerns the way innovations impact the field of economic

50 Angus Maddison, *Dynamic Forces in Capitalist Development: A Long-Run Comparative View*, Oxford University Press, 1991, p. 102.

51 Ibid., p. 103.

52 Ibid., pp. 103–4.

activity. According to Schumpeter, the first breakthroughs have the effect of eliminating resistances that had hitherto prevented progress, and in doing so, they smooth the way for others that come after. The initial innovators show that profits can be gained in the new domain of action. Bankers also participate in the matrix of causes that lead to clusters, because they are more likely to lend to ventures that are showing promise than to those that have been completely untested.

The question nonetheless arises as to why, given that innovations have begun in the neighbourhood of equilibrium, they do not continue when the enterprise starts to take off and disequilibrium emerges. In the boom, the prospect of larger than normal profits may be said to compensate for the increasing risk of a possible downturn and failure. Schumpeter's answer seems to be that innovations slacken as the boom proceeds because the entrepreneurs become satisfied with the above average returns they are already receiving and prefer to stay where they are. What does happen in the boom phase of the cycle is speculation, which is a different phenomenon altogether, and this increases because of the prospect of higher than average returns, but with these of course go greater risks of failure.

A criticism of Schumpeter from a different direction is that innovation should occur in periods of depression, because at these times, because of the decline in profits, business managers will be even more than normally eager to develop new measures of cutting costs and of maintaining profits and will develop innovations as a means of survival. This argument, however, is somewhat misleading because, strictly speaking, it refers to the reactions of old firms to the circumstance of a downturn in profitability, rather than to the creation of new firms that is what Schumpeter's innovation is all about. If old firms develop strategies of survival during a recession, this is mere adaptation and does not amount to innovation in Schumpeter's sense.

Despite the above criticisms, Schumpeter's theory of the business cycle has received significant support in recent years from a number of commentators. Gerhard Mensch has claimed that around the years 1825, 1886 and 1935, new clusters of innovations can be identified, and these generated completely new product sectors. Around those years, new markets came into being that allowed these sectors to grow and to improve products and production processes. He argues that competition and rationalization raise the efficiency and output of the new industries until a saturation point in the domestic market is reached. Over capacity may stimulate exports, but less developed countries have limited means with which to buy the goods in surplus and a limit is eventually reached, at which time a decline sets in and the long wave is ended. "Basic innovations tend to cluster in periods of discontinuity, when changes in the marginal efficiency of capital (amongst other things) lead to disappointing depreciation in the operative value of installed capital goods in stagnating industries, thus inducing investors to seek alternatives, and so making the economic system ready for new technologies."[53]

53 Gerhard Mensche, Charles Coutinho and Klaus Kaasch, "Changing Capital Values and the Propensity to Innovate", in Christopher Freeman (ed.), *Long Waves in the World Economy*, Frances Pinter, 1984, p. 31.

Relying on an extensive list of 120 important innovations for the period from the 1850s to the 1960s compiled by K. B. Mahdavi, Alfred Kleinknecht has analyzed these instances of innovation, as well as many others, and classified them as to whether they constitute more or less radical improvements of already existing products, completely new products or materials, or scientific instruments that are primarily of use for research and development. Kleinknecht concludes that there is evidence to support the clustering of basic innovations in both the 1880s and the 1930s. This he suggests is support for the proposition that depressions trigger both radical product innovation as well as improvements in production processes.

> Statistical tests on Mahdavi's data offer weak support for the prosperity-pull hypothesis on important innovations, but they give strong support for the depression-trigger hypothesis: there is a strong clustering of radical product innovations in the period of relatively unstable growth between the two world wars. This appears in sharp contrast to the periods of relative prosperity before the first and after the second world wars, which were obviously poor in initiating (but not in the diffusion of) radical product innovation.[54]

Jacob van Duijn has also made extensive studies of industry innovation over time and argues there is a clear connection between innovation clusters and the occurrence of long waves. He introduces the idea of an innovation life cycle and concludes that there is strong empirical evidence to support a four-phase model. In his model, the first stage occurs with the development of a number of innovations. In the second stage, new products are accepted by customers. This is followed in a third stage in which growth slows for the innovative products as competition increases. Finally, the fourth stage sees the declining sales as saturation of the market occurs.[55]

> Clearly, there is little incentive to embark on risky, innovative ventures during long-wave expansions, when the current crop of growth sectors is still in full bloom. In that respect, the entering of maturity and decline phases of particular industry life cycles can be said to force new product innovations out of necessity. Ultimately, however, innovators need to be convinced that

54 Alfred Kleinknecht, "Observations on the Schumpeterian Swarming of Innovations", in Christopher Freeman (ed.), *Long Waves in the World Economy*, Frances Pinter, 1984, p. 58. Kleinknecht has provided a thorough analysis of all these issues in his book *Innovation Patterns in Crisis and Prosperity: Schumpeter's Long Cycle Reconsidered*, Palgrave Macmillan, 1987, where he concludes: "It is our view that waves of important innovations are an endogenous element of the long wave process. The wave-like occurrence of major innovative breakthroughs is a decisive cause of the fairly simultaneous rise of new branches of industry which foster the long wave upswing." p. 206.

55 Jacob van Duijn, "Fluctuations in Innovation of Time", in Christopher Freeman (ed.), *Long Waves in the World Economy*, Frances Pinter, 1984, p. 20. See also his *The Long Wave in Economic Life*, Allen & Unwin, 1983.

> they are tapping new growth markets. That conviction comes easier during recovery than in the midst of depression.[56]

The issue of whether there is a cyclical pattern of business fluctuations and what the time period of the cycles might be is discussed at length in an informative article by Cleary and Hobbs. In reviewing the data on this question these authors note that, although it is difficult to correlate the existence of long-waves with industrial output measured in physical terms, for most countries studied "variations in the growth of aggregate industrial production can be seen as broadly consistent with the long-wave hypothesis."[57]

> The strongest empirical evidence in favour of the long-wave hypothesis undoubtedly comes from price series. Supporting evidence can also be found in the behaviour of long-term interest rates, world energy production and innovation. . . . The times at which prices and output growth pass their high and low points are taken from the wholesale price and capitalist world industrial production indices.[58]

Their studies indicate that the cycle revolves every 50 to 55 years. Nonetheless, they conclude somewhat equivocally, saying, "It is not easy to reach firm conclusions on the existence, or otherwise, of the long wave from a direct visual examination of the empirical evidence. The ensemble of time series does suggest that there is some validity in the hypothesis, although no single series on its own carries very much conviction."[59]

Schumpeter's theory of business cycles faces similar empirical challenges to Weber's theory of the Protestant ethic. Both theories are highly cogent at the level of pure theory, but various commentators remain unconvinced by the empirical evidence. Both have, however, provided a wealth of empirical materials in support of their theories, which has kept a small army of scholars in business for years in the attempt to confirm or disprove them. As regards Schumpeter's theory of the business cycle, we do not consider it necessary to make a final judgement on whether he has been able to adequately establish the truth of his elaborate schema, which it has to be said is inherently difficult to establish because of the enormous complexity of the matter and the mountain of empirical data that needs to be dealt with. However, we think there is sufficient evidence to establish a less demanding thesis that is consistent with Schumpeter's argument, namely, that capitalist progress involves an evolutionary process that manifests change in the form of waves. Esben Andersen has noted that Schumpeter's propositions about the

56 Ibid., p. 29.

57 M. N. Cleary and G. D. Hobbs, "The Fifty Year Cycles: A Look at the Empirical Evidence", in Christopher Freeman (ed.), *Long Waves in the World Economy*, Frances Pinter, 1984, p. 173.

58 Ibid., p. 180.

59 Ibid., p. 181.

specific phases of business cycles has failed to convince most theorists in the field, but this does not detract from the value of his work because his real contribution concerns waves of economic evolution.

> The type of evolution Schumpeter's capitalist engine produced cannot be covered by terms such as "growth" or "progress" – as these terms ignore the painful transformation of the economic system. . . . Thus, the working of the capitalist engine is either characterized by "revolution" or "absorption of the results of revolution". He considered this to be the essence of "what are known as business cycles". . . . The energy of the propulsive stroke [of Schumpeter's "two-stroke" capitalist engine] is provided by innovations and their finance. The propulsive stroke brings the engine into a maximally dis-equilibrated situation. Then the reaction sets in. The reactive stroke brings the engine back to the idle state of the circular flow.[60]

Capitalism, Socialism and Democracy

In his 1942 preface to *Capitalism, Socialism and Democracy*, Schumpeter says that his book is "the result of an effort to weld into a readable form the bulk of almost forty years' thought, observation and research on the subject of socialism", but there are reasons to believe the book does more than this. In particular, the book contains discussions about contemporary capitalism that appear to entail significant changes to his primary account of the capitalist engine. A number of commentators have argued that in this book Schumpeter effectively advances a modified theory of capitalism based on the fact that the system has now become dominated by big business firms and is oligopolistic,[61] so the original theory based on the dominant role of the individual entrepreneur cannot apply unmodified. The theorist who has taken this proposition furthest is probably Esben Andersen who, while acknowledging that Schumpeter himself did not admit a fundamental change of perspective, thinks there is enough material in *Capitalism, Socialism and Democracy* to construct a coherent account of an alternative theory (Andersen's Mark II theory). In what follows, we shall consider Andersen's reconstruction of Schumpeter's theory of capitalist evolution, which is instructive about aspects of Schumpeter's later thinking on the topic.

60 Esben Andersen, *Joseph A. Schumpeter*, p. 153–4. Andersen has taken up Schumpeter's theories of innovation, adaptation and diffusion and developed his own "post-Schumperterian" model of evolutionary economics. Also see his *Evolutionary Economics: Post-Schumpeterian Contributions*, Pinter, 1994.

61 According to McGraw, the term "oligopoly" was first used in economics by E. H. Chamberlin to refer to a small number of large and powerful firms that compete with one another in the same field. See Thomas K. McGraw, *Prophet of Innovation: Joseph Schumpeter and Creative Destruction*, Harvard University Press, 2007, p. 354.

Andersen first notes that Schumpeter had assumed in his original theory of capitalist development (Andersen's Mark I) that, as existing businesses are basically conservative, the process of evolution is driven by *new* men who generate progress by setting up *new* firms. This may have been largely true as regards the circumstances of the first waves of industrial expansion, but Andersen asks whether it can account for the entire range of economic growth that capitalism manifests today. Andersen believes that Schumpeter came to recognize the partial truth in Marx's claim that in capitalism is there is an intense competitive struggle between the existing capitalist firms. Because of this, their economic strategies for survival cannot be limited to mechanisms of adaptation and the supply of producer goods to emergent new firms. Rather, most pre-existing firms will be engaged in innovation, to some extent, in the effort to secure future streams of profit.

More than this, competition between firms gradually leads to the elimination of the majority of those that originally set out within a given field, and this concentration of the market leads to a system of oligopolistic competition. The remaining firms must continue to compete, and to bring about innovations, they use their own in-house research and development (R&D) departments or purchase embryonic new developments from others. This has a particular advantage over the Mark I situation, where new entrepreneurs must convince bankers with no technical expertise that their projects are worth financing; with in-house R&D, it is the firm itself that makes an assessment of which projects are worth pursuing, and it can do so with the benefit of its own expert knowledge. And the oligopolistic situation has the unique advantage for R&D that the firms in question will have revenues large enough to be able to make significant investments, whereas smaller highly competitive firms cannot afford such semi-speculative outlays. Schumpeter goes further and suggests monopoly is more conducive to innovation than a system in which there is perfect competition. "There are superior methods available to the monopolist which either are not available at all to a crowd of competitors or not available to them so readily: for there are advantages which, though not strictly unattainable on the competitive level of enterprise, are as a matter of fact secured only on the monopoly level, for instance, because monopolization may increase a sphere of influence of the better, and decrease the sphere of influence of the inferior, brains, or because the monopoly enjoys a disproportionately higher financial standing."[62]

Monopoly competition

Given his view of the innovative proficiency of monopoly, Schumpeter consequently took the view that it was not necessarily a good thing for governments to break up monopolies with anti-trust type policies, for industry concentration in the form of monopolies may foster a greater level of innovation than would happen in a perfectly competitive industrial environment. In any event, Schumpeter regarded

62 CSD, p. 101.

perfect competition as something that has probably never occurred and certainly was not present in the capitalism of his own day. Thus he writes,

> If we look more closely at the conditions – not all of them explicitly stated or even clearly seen by Marshall and Wicksell – that must be fulfilled in order to produce perfect competition, we realise immediately that outside of agricultural mass production there cannot be many instances of it. A farmer supplies his cotton or wheat in fact under those conditions: from his standpoint the ruling prices of cotton and wheat are data, though very variable ones, and not being able to influence them by his individual action he simply adapts his output . . . but this is not so even with many agricultural products . . . as regards practically all the finished products and services of industry and trade, it is clear that every grocer, every filling station, every manufacturer of gloves or shaving cream or hand saws has a small and precarious market of his own which he tries – must try – to build up and to keep by price strategy, quality strategy – "product differentiation" – and advertising. . . . in these cases we speak of monopoly competition.[63]

As we have already explained, insofar as there is real competition in the capitalist system, Schumpeter says it lies not so much with lower prices but with competition from new commodities, new technology, new sources of supply and new types of organization. This is the competition that strikes at the margins of profits of existing firms and threatens their very existence – it is the real basis upon which the process of creative destruction works itself out. Schumpeter does not deny that monopoly causes certain losses in efficiency, because a firm enjoying a monopoly position may be under less pressure to keep its prices within limits, but these losses are outweighed by the dynamic gains from innovation. In any event, he says history does not suggest that somehow there was an imaginary golden age of perfect competition in the past and that today we have the phenomenon of monopoly due to a fundamental distortion in the way in which capitalism works. Monopoly has always existed more or less, and yet all through the period of capitalist development there has been constant progress, constant innovation and development. So monopoly can hardly be inimical to progressive trends. An element of monopoly is a direct effect of innovation as such. This is because once the entrepreneur has staked out his new field of endeavour and begun to obtain the rewards of his innovation, he tries to preserve a high level of profit for as long as he can – by further innovation, patents, secrecy, advertising, product differentiation and so on – all of which provides him with a (only temporary) monopoly position.

Schumpeter's key idea is that innovation requires the exploitation of new opportunities, so the fundamental question is to decide which organizations and which firms are best placed to take advantage of such opportunities. The fact that the improvement in the standard of life of the masses has taken place relatively

63 Ibid., pp. 78–9.

uninterruptedly during the period of big business shows that, far from monopoly being the cause of extortionate pricing and restricting innovation, on the contrary, it has generally reduced prices and made many goods that were once luxuries items of mass consumption.

> What we have got to accept is that it [the large-scale establishment] has come to be the most powerful engine of that progress and in particular the long-run expansion of total output not only in spite of, but to a considerable extent through, this strategy [of using excess capacity to deter entry by competing firms] which looks so restrictive when viewed in the individual case and from the individual point of time. In this respect perfect competition is not only impossible but inferior, and has no title to being set up as a model of ideal efficiency. It is hence a mistake to base a theory of government regulation of industry on the principle that big business should be made to work as the respective industry would work in perfect competition.[64]

Schumpeter maintains that over the long-term capitalism has been able to continually increase its industrial output roughly at about the rate of two percent per annum. And he can see no reason why this rate will not continue into the foreseeable future. He is dismissive of theorists, such as the neo-Marxists and Keynesians, who argue capitalism is approaching a crisis point because of what has sometimes been referred to as "the vanishing investment opportunity", and that in order to foster further progress it is necessary for the state to intervene and create new enterprises. This does not mean that Schumpeter rejected deficit financing in every situation. But he does not think that capitalism is in imminent danger of collapsing or of being stuck in stasis because of either the presence of monopoly or due to the absence of potential investment outlets. Indeed, he says the record shows capitalism has over time continually improved the standard of living of the masses, especially when compared with its earlier period. The indictment that capitalism creates unemployment and a class of workers who are chronically poor stands in the past – roughly to the end of the nineteenth century. Provided it keeps up its past performance "the sorry spectres of child labour and sixteen-hour working days and five persons living in one room" are not likely to return.[65]

What links Schumpeter's account of monopoly to his earlier view of competitive capitalism is the idea that economic survival still depends on the creation of new commodities, new technologies, new sources of supply and new forms of organization. The difference is that the individual entrepreneur has been partly eclipsed by the advent of the large-scale corporation. Actually, Schumpeter's propositions about the superiority of monopoly go back some time before *Capitalism, Socialism and Democracy* when he began to note the significance of what he then termed "trustified capitalism". In an essay of 1928, he noted the fact that many

64 Ibid., p. 106.
65 Ibid., p. 70.

large firms have come into being in America and now dominate the economy. The key issue for Schumpeter was: what becomes of the role of the entrepreneur in such circumstances? He answered:

> [Things are] different in "trustifed" capitalism. Innovation is, in this case, not any more embodied *typically* in new firms, but goes on, within the big units now existing, largely independently of individual persons. It meets with much less friction, as failure in any particular case loses its dangers, and tends to be carried out as a matter of course on the advice of specialists. Conscious policy toward demand and taking a long-term view toward investment becomes possible. . . . Progress becomes "automatised," increasingly impersonal and decreasingly a matter of leadership and individual initiative. This amounts to a fundamental change in many respects . . . It means the passing out of existence of a system of selection of leaders which had the unique characteristic that success in rising to a position and success in filling it were essentially the same thing . . .[66]

Thus, it is "permissible to date the *prevalence* of capitalist methods from about the middle of the eighteenth century (for England), and to call the nineteenth century . . . the time of *competitive*, and what has so far followed, the time of increasingly 'trustified', or otherwise 'organised', 'regulated' or 'managed' capitalism."[67]

Surprisingly given the thrust of his work as a whole, these remarks suggest that the entrepreneur may indeed be made obsolete, and if that were the case, much of what Schumpeter says elsewhere about the character of capitalism may be rendered redundant. Of course it is partly with this possibility in mind that Schumpeter became interested in the prospect of a socialist transformation of the capitalist system, because not unlike Marx, he saw the transformation of the private industrial firm into a state-run public enterprise as a not inconceivable development at some time in the future. We shall consider Schumpeter's views in this regard more fully in the next chapter, but for the moment, let us consider further his account of monopoly.

Whether Schumpeter effectively changed the fundamentals of his theory by developing an alternative model along the lines of Andersen's Mark II must remain questionable, because Schumpeter himself does not claim any such a revision and in fact had early in his work referred to "trustification" as one of the ways in which new combinations can be created. Thus the phenomenon of monopolization might

66 "The Instability of Capitalism," EJAS, pp. 70–1.

67 Ibid., p. 48. Perhaps in these remarks Schumpeter overstates the case for "trustified capitalism" and unnecessarily undermines his own thesis. As Arnold Heertje writes, "On the whole, there are traces of a Schumpeterian [trustified] development in our Western economies, but mechanization and routinization of entrepreneurial function is by no means the general picture. . . . In short, it is [as before] the dynamic, ever-changing scene for entrepreneurs who have to be inventive and sensitive to new opportunities". Arnold Heertje, "Schumpeter's Model of the Decay of Capitalism", in Helmut Frisch (ed.), *Schumpeterian Economics*, Praeger, 1981, p. 89.

be regarded as largely consistent with the original Mark I thesis. Nonetheless, it appears that in Schumpeter's later account of trustification the significance of the individual entrepreneur is somewhat reduced and the function of the entrepreneur has been partly bureaucratized.

Of course it is obvious that today the entrepreneur has by no means disappeared from the scene, and in many respects, it could be said such figures remain as prominent as ever. One only has to think of the likes of Steve Jobs, Bill Gates, Jack Ma, Richard Branson, Carlos Slim or Sergey Brin to realize the age of the individual entrepreneur is not finished. But equally it is clear that the large-scale corporation has emerged as a dominant feature of the economic landscape, and these enterprises are able to prosper even though they are directed by figures who, performing in the role of CEOs, are more akin to Schumpeter's professional managers than his entrepreneur. In this regard we can mention cases such as – ExxonMobil, Shell, Samsung, Volkswagen, Toyota, Hewlett Packard, General Electric and Glencore – to name a but few of the largest firms where it would appear that ongoing success no longer depends on individual entrepreneurial initiative.

A final problem that we must consider concerns the impact of monopoly on the state of equilibrium. Schumpeter notes that a monopolist might charge a higher price than would be the case where there are competitors who are prepared to sell at lower prices. But this does not necessarily inhibit the general tendency towards equilibrium. This is because, as long as the monopoly position is surrounded by sufficiently competitive conditions at large, there is no lack of determinateness of prices and quantities and the tendency to equilibrium remains real.[68]

Schumpeter explains that in practice many firms are able produce commodities that are more or less complete substitutes for the products of monopolistic competitors, but awareness of this means that price and quantity adjustments of the monopolistic firm will not in general differ fundamentally from those that would have to made under conditions of perfect competition.

> If we do insist on using the language of the theory of monopolistic competition, the demand curves for the individual firms will, in general and in the long run, display a high elasticity, though not the infinite one of the pure logic

68 As it is a complex topic, we shall refer only to the treatment of the relationship between competition and monopoly in a capitalist system by Piero Sraffa, "The Laws of Returns under Competitive Conditions", *Economic Journal*, 36.144, (1926), pp. 535–50. Sraffa had pointed to the dynamic relationship between monopoly and competition by showing that the monopoly situation is inherently unstable because it calls forth new businesses seeking to better a dominant market player. So whatever monopolies may exist at any one time, they typically do not enjoy their advantage indefinitely. Mention should also be made of the work of Joan Robinson, *The Economics of Imperfect Competition*, Macmillan, 1933 and Schumpeter's review Joseph A. Schumpeter, *Essays on Entrepreneurs, Innovations, Business Cycles, and the Evolution of Capitalism*, Transaction (EEIBC), 1989, pp. 125–33.

> of competition. And this, in turn will enforce approximate realisation of the results of perfect competition that follow from it.[69]

Schumpeter qualifies this by saying that, strictly speaking, his argument only applies to cases that differ from perfect competition in nothing else but product differentiation. The general effect of monopolistic competition, however, will be simply to increase the amount of friction in adjustment.

The rationale of this so-called "product differentiation" is, of course, the creation of a special market for each individual business. Product differentiation comprises not only "real" but also "putative" differences, not just differences in the product as such, but also differences in the services associated with supplying it, as well as every other device that enables a purchaser to associate the product with a particular firm (for example, advertising, branding etc.). Creation of a special market in some ways can be said to increase the friction that prevents buyers from transferring their allegiance from one firm to another. If this friction is sufficiently strong, it may appear to curtail the tendency towards equilibrium. However, Schumpeter says this result does not as a rule occur. "The very essence of monopolistic competition is in the fact that the price at which a quantity can be sold at any time is a function of the behaviour both of the firm itself (not independent of costs of the firm) and of all other firms in the field."[70]

In the next chapter we shall compare and contrast our two thinkers on the key issues raised and finally address the question of how their contributions can be combined to produce the basis of a general theory of modern capitalism.

69 BC, p. 65.
70 Ibid., p. 64.

5 The synthetic combination of Weber with Schumpeter

In what follows, I wish to set out lines of intersection and points of complementarity between the respective contributions of Weber and Schumpeter with a view to providing a synthetic combination of their respective theories as the basis of a general theory of modern capitalism. At the outset, however, we must confront a problem arising from possible incompatibilities between the approaches of the two writers. I refer in particular to Schumpeter's rejection of Weber's position on certain methodological issues, especially as these concern religious factors in the rise of capitalism and as to the rationalization of conduct generally. We have discussed aspects of these issues in earlier chapters, but the question remains whether given certain divergences of perspective it remains possible to combine the two approaches. More specifically, can Schumpeter's theory about the functioning of the capitalist engine be combined with Weber's account of the modern vocational ethos and the rationalization of economic activity?

The definition of modern capitalism

An inquiry into the relationship of Schumpeter and Weber must first consider the compatibility of their respective definitions of capitalism. As we have seen, for Weber, modern capitalism is defined primarily *sociologically*, in terms of the orientation of the actor to profit opportunities in the market and utilizing the formally rational means of double-entry bookkeeping. Weber's capitalist entrepreneur calculates each step of his activity in consideration of the chances of profit estimated in accordance with the known costs of production and the expected sales returns of the goods to be produced. Insofar as his activity achieves a high level of rationality, these calculations are performed rigorously and systematically. Calculations ideally occur in the situation of the free market with free labour and the absence of monopoly or excessive state interference.

Schumpeter's approach to modern capitalism is also focused on the role of the entrepreneur, but he wants to deal more explicitly with the workings of the mechanism market exchange as conceived by pure economics (Walras). As we have shown, he too sees capitalism as a system oriented peacefully to profit making, but his theory describes capitalism as a dynamic system of evolutionary change. This aspect is dependent on the phenomenon of innovation that takes place through the creation of credit for the funding of new enterprises. It is noteworthy that Schumpeter does not emphasize capital accounting, as does Weber, though he counts it as an innovation that enabled capitalism to become more efficient. Also of importance is the fact that Schumpeter does not consider perfect competition and the absence of monopoly crucial for capitalist progress; indeed, contrary to the implications of Weber's view, he suggests that a certain level of oligopoly is actually more favourable for capitalist progress than perfect competition. Otherwise, Schumpeter generally accepts the achievements of classical economics, especially those of Walras and the marginalist school. Where he differs from Weber, in the broad, is in his emphasis on the dynamic, discontinuous character of capitalist progress.

Weber, by contrast, did not dwell on the instability of capitalism, its inherent tendency to revolutionize its own achievements and to bring on crises that might even cause its collapse. Weber's emphasis on rationality, routine and calculation suggests he considered capitalism more stable and predictable than Schumpeter. Yet Weber was not unaware of the volatility of capitalism. As we have seen, he wrote extensively on the stock exchange and futures trading early in his career. We also note that he provided a detailed discussion of speculative crises in his *General Economic History*. In that work he specifically refers to the cyclical character of speculative crises arising in England in the early nineteenth century.

> They have recurred almost regularly at intervals of about 10 years – 1815, 1825, 1835, 1847 etc.... The first of these crises and their periodic recurrence were based on the possibility of speculation and the resultant participation of outside interests in large business undertakings. . . . In 1815 the prospect of lifting the continental blockade had led to a regular rage for founding factories; but the war had destroyed the buying power of the continent and it could no longer take the English products. This crisis was barely overcome, and the continent had begun to develop buying power, when in 1825 a new crisis set in because means of production, though not goods, had been produced on a scale never known before and out of correspondence with the needs.[1]

These remarks are partly consistent with Schumpeter's views and even imply the existence of cycles generated by the internal machinations of the capitalist engine as such.

A further area in which the views of Weber and Schumpeter intersect in fruitful ways concerns the phenomenon of credit. We have seen that Schumpeter defines capitalism as enterprise conducted with borrowed money or credit, a feature that accounts for the ability of the system to continually generate new combinations and so forth. Weber also regards credit as critical because he regards one of the factors that gave rise to the advent of monetary accounting; the separation of the accounts of the household from those of the enterprise was in large measure induced by the interest of obtaining credit. Thus, around the time in which both

1 GEH, p. 290.

Weber and Schumpeter accept that modern capitalism took off, that is, in the early seventeenth century, they agree the large-scale provision of credit by banks was an essential catalyst. Weber's account focuses on the causal significance of the factors facilitating this development, whereas Schumpeter's focus is on the functional role of credit in driving the capitalist engine.

A final issue that warrants comment concerns the question of whether the entrepreneur, under capitalist modernity, exhibits the qualities of a charismatic leader. Certainly in Weber's view entrepreneurs are not well suited to political leadership because their need to constantly attend the market conditions militates against involvement in the equally demanding domain of party politics, and in any event, the politician requires quite different inner qualities. But though the entrepreneur may sit in an office, he is much more than a bureaucratic official, because he actually *leads* his enterprise in the battle for economic survival. To an extent, therefore, the entrepreneur may possess aspects of charisma and is thus a counter to the thoroughgoing bureaucratization of the economy that was Weber's abiding concern. We note that the disciplinary power the entrepreneur exercises over his employees, in the strict sense, does not derive from a charismatic source, as they are generally paid workers. But some close confidants of the entrepreneur may be devoted to their leader so as to perform work services beyond the call of duty and others may provide financial support from faith in the leader's vision.

Schumpeter's critique of Weber's methodology

Before we explore the issue of methodological compatibility, it should be born in mind that, despite some criticisms, in general terms, Schumpeter was an admirer of Weber and on several occasions wrote very highly of him. We note Schumpeter's extremely generous praise of Weber, both as a scholar and a man, contained in an essay he wrote following Weber's death in 1920. But even in this essay, Schumpeter expresses reservations about Weber's command of economics and his adequacy on purely economic questions. At one point we read, "Thus, Weber was a sociologist above all. Even though he was a sociologist with a penchant for things that are primarily concerned with economics, he was an economist only indirectly and secondarily. His interest in economics does not focus on the mechanism of economic life as described by economic theory, nor on the real historical phenomenon for its own sake, but rather on the sequence of historical types and their socio-psychological profusion."[2] While this assessment is not altogether unjustified, one senses these comments are somewhat patronizing.

Undoubtedly, both Weber and Schumpeter made significant contributions to methodological questions and the related debates that raged in their day. We shall first consider Weber's methodological contributions. As we have seen, Weber began his scholarly career, to a certain extent, in the camp of the German Historical

2 Joseph Schumpeter, "Max Weber's Work", in Richard Swedberg (ed.), *Joseph Schumpeter: The Economics and Sociology of Capitalism*, Princeton University Press, 1991 (ESC), p. 225.

School led by Gustav Schmoller. Schmoller's position has been commonly understood as being totally opposed to theory, but this is not strictly correct. He did not believe research should be restricted merely to the collection and description of historical materials and never completely rejected the methods of the natural sciences, general concepts or law-like theorems as developed by economics. However, his basic position was that the social sciences must begin with the collection and summarization of empirical data, and he believed this task had not been developed sufficiently to allow the extensive use of deductive abstract methods and the related formulation of laws. Schmoller summarized his view in the following statement: "We do not think that we must have laws at once at any price: we do not believe that we can pick them like blackberries, because we look first of all for true knowledge, i.e., necessarily and universally valid judgement. Where no law exists, we must be content with (1) the extensive observation of reality, (2) the classification of these materials and (3) the enquiry of causes".[3] Though influenced by Schmoller, as suggested above, Weber developed his own unique methodological approach which was much more sympathetic to theory.

It would appear that Weber's view of theory was influenced by a number of figures including Rickert, Simmel and Menger.[4] Thus in 1904, Weber set out his methodological position, and his distance from Schmoller in particular, as follows:

> If one perceives the implications of the fundamental ideas of modern epistemology that ultimately derives from Kant; namely, that concepts are primarily analytical instruments for the intellectual mastery of empirical data and can be only that, the fact that precise genetic concepts are necessarily ideal types will not cause him to desist from constructing them. The relationship between concept and historical research is reversed for those who appreciate this; the goal of the Historical School then appears as logically impossible, the concepts are not ends but are means to the end of understanding phenomena which are significant from individual viewpoints. Indeed it is just *because* the content of historical concepts is necessarily subject to change that they must be formulated precisely and clearly on all occasions. In their application their character as ideal analytical constructs should be carefully kept in mind and the ideal type and the historical reality should not be confused with each other.[5]

Weber also accepted the method of "understanding" (*Verstehen*) as necessary for conceptualization of the motives of individuals that are assumed to be causes of

3 Quoted in Yuichi Shionoya, *Schumpeter and the Idea of Social Science: A Metatheoretical Study*, Cambridge University Press, 1997, p. 201.

4 See the useful discussion of the intellectual milieu in which Weber developed his methodological perspectives in Fritz K. Ringer, *Max Weber's Methodology: The Unification of the Cultural and Social Sciences*, Harvard University Press, 1997, pp. 7–35.

5 Max Weber, *The Methodology of the Social Sciences*, Free Press, 1949 (MSS), pp. 106–7.

human actions.[6] This involves the approach called "methodological individualism", because historical and social phenomena are ultimately interpreted in terms of the actions of individuals.[7] The method of *Verstehen* indicates the scientific procedure by which the observer grasps the conduct of an individual by interpreting the subjective meaning of their actions.[8] The theory of the ideal type has the role of clarifying the logical status of socio-historical concepts. Ideal types do not describe the elements that a class of phenomena have in common in the real world but rather those they have in common with a theoretically constructed model. The world described by ideal types is an imaginary world or utopia, and the theory constructed by the means of these concepts is not a copy of reality but a heuristic device to aid in the comprehension of reality.

Despite Weber's evident sympathy for theory, Schumpeter is highly critical of Weber's use of ideal types. At one point in a footnote, he says that Weber in effect created a spurious problem in trying to contrast an ideal feudal man with an ideal capitalist man and then seeking to explain the transition from one to the other. "Unfortunately, Max Weber leant the weight of his great authority to a way of thinking that has no basis than a misuse of the method of ideal types. Accordingly he set out to find an explanation for a process which sufficient attention to historical detail renders self-explanatory. He found it in the New Spirit – i.e. a different attitude to life and its values – engendered by the Reformation."[9] He goes on to say, "The historical objections to this construction are too obvious to detain us. Much more important is it to see the fundamental methodological error involved."[10] Clearly Schumpeter shows little appreciation of the methodological intricacies of the ideal type and its role in causal analysis as advanced by Weber.[11] As to whether Weber committed any "methodological errors", as far as the present writer is concerned, Schumpeter does not demonstrate any obvious ones in the remarks quoted or anywhere else. In any event, we have suggested that, despite his apparent rejection of Weber's methodology, Schumpeter in fact routinely employs ideal type constructions himself.

Further evidence of Schumpeter's lack of sympathy for Weber on methodology can be gleaned from a footnote in *The History of Economic Analysis* in a section that refers to the philosophical background of the period of the late 1800s in Germany. Schumpeter makes reference to the influence of the philosophers

6 Weber's appreciation to the idea of "understanding" was less a result of the direct influence of the work of Wilhelm Dilthey than it was a consequence of his close association with Simmel.

7 The concept of "methodological individualism" was possibly first elaborated by Schumpeter, on the basis of Menger's use of the term, in his early work *The Nature and Essence of Economic Theory*, especially Part 1, Chapter 6: " . . . we are not interested in the individual process but they help us to describe the mass phenomena in our field" (p. 62).

8 Weber did not endorse Dilthey's idea that "understanding" is acquired by an "empathetic re-experiencing" of the actor's thoughts and feelings.

9 HEA, p. 80.

10 Ibid., pp. 80–1.

11 Importantly, Schumpeter makes little, if any, direct reference to Weber's methodological essays and seems to have based his view solely on an interpretation of *The Protestant Ethic*.

Wilhelm Windelband and Wilhelm Dilthey. Windelband had advanced the idea of a fundamental a dichotomy between the historical/cultural sciences (*Ereigniswissenschaften*) and the natural sciences (*Gesetzeswissenschaften*), arguing that sciences of cultural life produce knowledge of singular individual events ("idiographic knowledge"), whereas the sciences of nature aim to formulate invariant laws ("nomothetic knowledge"). And Dilthey had been responsible for a related, though not identical, distinction between the intellectual processes of "explanation" (*Erklären*) in terms of causes and those involving the "understanding" (*Verstehen*) of the inner mental states of individuals. Schumpeter argues that these thinkers made a fundamental mistake when they attempted to use their analytic distinctions to characterize the social sciences as belonging completely to the field of understanding and the idiographic because "great parts of the social sciences ride astride this dividing line, which fact seriously impairs its usefulness."[12] He goes on to refer to Weber as having been an unfortunate victim in all this. Weber failed to see that the distinction between the ideographic and the nomothetic sciences had serious negative consequences: "That this was apt to mislead the many economists who listened to them – Max Weber, e.g., was strongly influenced by Rickert – was as inevitable as it was regrettable. But let us note the striking saying of Dilthey that reads like a motto of Max Weber's methodology; "we *explain* the phenomenon of nature, we *understand* the phenomenon of mind (or of culture)."[13]

Schumpeter's objections to Weber's Protestant ethic thesis largely stem from his view that the emergence of capitalism must have arisen from an evolutionary process wherein a small innovative sector within a largely feudal economy was able to introduce novel productive arrangements that, once in place, could not be abandoned. With the introduction of banking credit, entrepreneurial innovation turbocharged the nascent capitalist engine, which has continued to evolve ever since. We believe Schumpeter's critique of Weber is, however, misconceived and wrongly places Weber in the camp of Dilthey. First, Weber did not endorse Dilthey's idea that psychic reality is more immediately given to the observer than physical reality, because Weber maintains, "we can only ever uncover the thoughts of others by means of an interpretation amongst the motives underlying a course of events . . ."[14] But second, Weber believed the processes of "understanding" and "explanation" are often linked and cannot be permanently separated into the two distinct types of science. As Hans Bruun puts it quoting a comment of Weber, "[Weber] says that true 'nomothetic' and 'idiographic' statements may, in spite of their logically different character, be part not only of the same scholarly work, but even of *one and the same* sentence."[15]

12 Ibid., p. 777.

13 Ibid.

14 Weber's "Handwritten Note" reproduced in Max Weber's, *Collected Methodological Writings*, Routledge, 2012, pp. 415–6.

15 Hans Bruun, *Science, Values and Politics in Max Weber's Methodology*, Ashgate, 2007, p. 38.

Clearly the remarks of Schumpeter critical of Weber express a distinct ambivalence about and even hostility to his methodological and epistemological positions. Unfortunately, it is necessary to conclude that some of the statements made by Schumpeter reflect poorly on the quality of his thinking with regard to methodological issues. In *The History of Economic Analysis*, he attempts to provide something of an intellectual history of the period of the early twentieth century and clearly demonstrates wide reading of and familiarity with the major thinkers of the day, but he never truly comes to grips with the sophisticated methodological analyses of Weber. It is simply not true to say that Weber's methodology would be encompassed by the statement of Dilthey just quoted. And contrary to Schumpeter's suppositions, Weber is quite prepared to admit that law-like relationships are to be found in the social domain and these may well share features with causal analysis in the natural sciences. Of course, what he did not accept was that there were "laws" of history or of historical development such as those advanced by figures like Roscher, Hegel or Marx.[16]

When Weber talks about the methods of sociology, he sometimes speaks of "explanatory understanding" or of "understanding explanation", and he saw the need to combine aspects of both understanding and explanation in order to produce adequate scientific results. And of course all this was brought to the fore in the creation of a completely new approach to social analysis, namely with the advent of "sociology" of which he is a founding father.[17] From what we have said above, it is clear Weber fully appreciated the role of theory in economics and developed theories of his own in socio-historical analysis to a high level. As Yuichi Shionoya, otherwise an admirer of Schumpeter, says,

> Weber's notion of the ideal type was essentially intended to reveal the structure of linkage between theory and history, not to exaggerate the distinction or dichotomy between the two. Specifically it was a solution to the question of how historical concepts can be general and yet not lose their individuality. With regard to this question, Schumpeter had dismissed the importance of the neo-Kantian distinction between the abstract and the concrete, between the general and the individual because the one requires the other in a continual process of concept formation.[18]

16 Shionoya seems to concede as much in his otherwise sympathetic reading of Schumpeter's methodology when he writes of "Schumpeter's harsh criticism and partial misunderstanding of Weber's methodology", Shionoya, *Schumpeter and the Idea of Social Science*, p. 216.

17 A useful clarification of Weber's views in this regard is to found in Fritz Ringer's, *Max Weber: An Intellectual Biography*, University of Chicago Press, 2004, pp. 89–104.

18 Shionoya, *Schumpeter and the Idea of Social Science*, p. 213. On another occasion in his *History of Economic Analysis*, Schumpeter's expresses his view of Weber's understanding of economics in most unflattering terms. He writes, "As a matter of fact, in the epoch of his ripest thought, M. Weber was not unwilling to declare that, so far as his almost complete ignorance of it enabled him to judge, he saw no objection of principal to what economic theorists actually did, though he disagreed with them on what they thought they were doing, that is, on the epistemological interpretation of their procedure" (HEA, p. 819). There is a footnote to this passage in which Schumpeter adds, "It was

From the above, we can only conclude that Schumpeter misconstrued the notion of *Verstehen* as employed by Weber. As we have already claimed, Weber's methodology is much sounder than Schumpeter allows, and to this day, in our view, it remains the most comprehensive and adequate account of the methods of the social sciences that we have. I am therefore in agreement with Fritz Ringer, whose recent study of *Max Weber's Methodology* sees it as the most coherent statement of the principles that must govern any serious social scientific research for the time being and into the foreseeable future.[19] Accordingly, we shall maintain that Schumpeter's work in epistemology remains questionable, but this does not necessarily invalidate his contributions to economic theory.[20]

Perhaps the impasse between Weber and Schumpeter as to methodology is not so deep and intractable as the above would suggest. In his book on Schumpeter, Shionoya has provided, by far, the most detailed and thorough analysis of Schumpeter's methodology to date, and he addresses the relationship of Schumpeter to Weber at some length. Despite the apparent divergence of the two methodologies, Shionoya concludes that they are not necessarily incommensurable. He interprets Schumpeter's methodology as basically a version of "instrumentalism" by which he means a pragmatic approach similar to that advanced by philosophers like Mach and Poincaré, who were important in the natural sciences. He quotes the following statement on the role of theory from Schumpeter's early work on methodology *Das Wesen und der Hauptinhalt der theoretischen Nationalökonomie*:

> The crucial point, upon which everything depends, lies in the distinction between two different aspects of the matter: on the one hand, we have fundamental arbitrariness of theories, on which their system, rigor, and exactness are based; on the other hand we have the conformity of theories to, and their dependence on, phenomena, and this alone gives content and significance to theories. If one distinguishes between these concerns and places them in a

with this motivation that he invited two strong partisans of economic theory, in the Marshallian sense, to write the 'theory' and the sketch of the history of doctrine and methods for his *Grundriss der Sozialokönomik*". In a further note, the editor points out the two theorists Schumpeter is referring to were of course himself and Friedrick Wieser. Schumpeter seems to be saying that Weber's inviting of himself and Wieser to make the *Grundriss* contributions shows that he was in some way amenable and perhaps sympathetic to economic theory though he did not really understand it. On the contrary, we say Schumpeter was not aware of the depth of Weber's appreciation of economic theory and of the latter's acceptance of much if not most of the major theoretical approaches of the Austrian Marginalist School.

19 Fritz Ringer, *Max Weber's Methodology: The Unification of the Cultural and Social Sciences*, Harvard University Press, 1997, pp. 168–74. I note here several other important contributions to the appreciation of Weber's methodology including Sven Eliason, *Max Weber's Methodologies*, Polity, 2002 and Toby Huff, *Max Weber and the Methodology of the Social Sciences*, Transaction Books, 1984, and a new edition of Hans Bruun, *Science, Values and Politics in Max Weber's Methodology*, Ashgate, 2007.

20 I say this despite the efforts of Shionoya in his otherwise commendable book *Schumpeter and the Idea of Social Science* to sympathetically explicate Schumpeter's methodology.

> proper relationship with each other, a clear interpretation will follow, and thus the difficulties and doubts that we come across in the usual discussion of these questions will be effectively overcome.[21]

Shionoya argues that Weber too was a kind of instrumentalist from a methodological point of view, and he interprets his use of ideal types as indicative of the same basic position on the relation of idea to reality as that held by Schumpeter. Thus he suggests that Weber and Schumpeter reached the same conclusions regarding concept formation but arrived there by different routes: positivism in Schumpeter's case and neo-Kantianism in Weber's. The methodologies of Weber and Schumpeter parallel one another and were essentially rooted in instrumentalism."[22] Further, Shionoya adds support to the thesis of the present writer by implying that the apparent methodological differences between the two thinkers should not prevent their substantive work being seen as basically compatible. He concludes saying, "Weber's sociology was much more concerned with comparative static social systems than the dynamic process of evolution. This may explain why evolution-minded Schumpeter felt closer to Marx and Schmoller."[23] While I do not share Shionoya's view that characterizes Weber as an instrumentalist akin to Schumpeter, I agree that the substantive work of the two can be brought together despite apparent methodological differences.

The compatibility of Weber's approach with that of Schumpeter

Schumpeter's lack of sympathy for the *Verstehen* approach in sociology is all the more remarkable because he places enormous store on his account of the mentality of the entrepreneur. It does not seem to have occurred to him that the origin of the particular aptitude for enterprise, which he so graphically, and shall we say, sympathetically, describes, requires explaining as such. Despite his depiction of the entrepreneur as eschewing hedonistic indulgence so as to ensure funds are reserved for new and expanded investments and despite his acknowledgement of the rationality underlying the entrepreneur's introduction of novel methods of production, Schumpeter does not acknowledge the relevance of Weber's analysis of the work ethic and the problem of its origins in Protestant inner-worldly asceticism. Schumpeter is adamant that the aptitude of the entrepreneur is not found universally and indeed is sufficiently rare for those suited to entrepreneurship to require being "selected," in the Darwinian sense as it were. But if selection takes place, the aptitude in question must surely be produced somehow, or be supported by particular cultural conditions and discouraged by others. Once this is admitted, of course, Schumpeter must find himself on Weber's methodological turf, and so

21 Quoted in Shionoya, *Schumpeter and the Idea of Social Science*, p. 105.
22 Ibid., p. 220.
23 Ibid.

the latter's analysis of the peculiar rationalism of the modern bourgeoisie, with its vocational orientation, as well as the diffusion of the work ethic across other strata, comes into play. Schumpeter's entrepreneur, with his orientation solely to the market situation and the price mechanism in concert with the rationality of business management and a calculating mentality, are eminently suited to treatment by the Weberian approach. It is worth recalling Weber's description of those that harboured the spirit of capitalism in the *Protestant Ethic*: "they were men who had grown up in the hard school of life, calculating and daring at the same time, above all temperate and reliable, shrewd and completely devoted to their business, with strictly bourgeois opinions and principles."[24] These dispositions, we submit, are not a mere reflex of Schumpeter's capitalist mechanism. We are with Weber in saying that such a mechanism by itself could not conjure up individuals with precisely those qualities that would make them successful entrepreneurs and captains of industry; many other factors of a non-economic character were also needed.

But just as Weber's work can complement Schumpeter's approach in the fashion just indicated, I believe Schumpeter adds valuable insights to Weber's account of capitalism. This is the case, in part, because Schumpeter is able to demonstrate the precise economic function of the entrepreneur – as the figure who, by setting up new combinations, inaugurates improvements in the production function that generate capitalist progress. It is notable that Weber does not have an account of capitalist economic progress as such; that is, he does not directly address why the capitalist system institutionalizes constant improvements in industrial technology and productivity thereby ensuring ever-increasing standards of living. Both Weber and Schumpeter regard entrepreneurs as crucial to their respective accounts of capitalism but have different perspectives as to their role. Weber constructs the origin of modern entrepreneurship in the religious cultural context of the seventeenth century and sees the occidental bourgeoisie as the carrier of a highly acquisitive but ascetic disposition that is unique to the modern West. Schumpeter, by contrast, disregards Weber's cultural determinism and believes entrepreneurs can arise at any time, and did so as early as the Middle Ages. But he seems unaware of Weber's elaborate criticisms of the suggestion that figures like the Fuggers or Medici were truly modern entrepreneurs.

This divergence of view raises a fundamental question as to whether Weber's account of the origins of capitalism as we have explicated it in the previous chapters is compatible with Schumpeter's account of capitalism as arising from his evolutionary schema. Our response to this is to suggest that the obvious incompatibility can be overcome if we treat Schumpeter's evolutionary paradigm as an ideal type in the fashion that Weber adopted with marginal utility. Thus, we believe Weber's insistence on the historical individuality of modern capitalism can be made consistent with the idea that capitalist progress involves processes of selection and adaptation, as long as this is not assumed the equivalent of a law of history. Schumpeter himself seems to envisage just this when he acknowledges

24 PE, p. 69.

that his account of business cycles only applies strictly if non-economic elements are excluded from the analysis, which he admits is an unrealistic assumption. And in his later years, Schumpeter seems to have acknowledged that economics could never become an exact science on the model of the natural sciences. On one occasion he even comes close to stating a view close to Weber as to the historically unique role of charismatic individuals: "Without committing ourselves to hero worship or to its hardly less absurd opposite, we have got to realize that, since the emergence of exceptional individuals does not lend itself to scientific generalization, there is here an element that, together with the element of random occurrences with which it may be amalgamated, seriously limits our ability to forecast the future."[25] However, all this goes against Schumpeter's insistence that the capitalist system generally follows the course determined by his "mechanism" and weakens his claim to have provided a complete account of the evolution of the modern capitalism.

Weber's and Schumpeter's evaluation of modern capitalism

Both Weber and Schumpeter considered capitalism questionable from both moral and other value points of view. Schumpeter famously describes capitalism as a system based on a "process of creative destruction." In his *Capitalism, Socialism and Democracy* he explains what he means by this dramatic phrase as follows:

> The fundamental impulse that sets and keeps the capitalist engine in motion comes from new consumers' goods, the new methods of production or transportation, the new markets, the new forms of industrial organizations that capitalist enterprise creates. . . . [However,] the opening up of new markets, foreign or domestic, and the organizational development from the craft shop and factory to such concerns as U.S. Steel illustrate the same process of industrial mutation – if I may use that biological term – that incessantly revolutionizes the economic structure *from within*, incessantly destroying the old one, incessantly creating a new one. This process of Creative Destruction is the essential fact about capitalism. It is what capitalism consists in and what every capitalist concern has got to live in.[26]

These remarks about "creative destruction" warrant comparison with Weber's notion of the ineluctable conflict between formal and substantive rationality.[27] Both

25 Thomas K. McCraw, *Prophet of Innovation: Joseph Schumpeter and Creative Destruction*, Harvard University Press, 2007, pp. 475–6.

26 CSD, p. 83.

27 Weber's idea of the conflict between formal and substantive rationality is only one dimension of his account of the role of conflict in social relations. In broad terms, it is probably accurate to describe Weber's approach generally as "conflict sociology", as he sees struggle between individuals and groups as ineluctable. This partly accounts for his rejection of all utopian solutions to the human predicament.

Schumpeter and Weber are aware of the obvious negative impacts of business failure on those directly affected, including the workers who become unemployed and the shareholders who lose their investment. But there are differences of emphasis. The negative side of Schumpeter's creative destruction seems to refer primarily to the effects of the competition between businesses, and perhaps also between different local and national economies, where new combinations have arisen and driven existing firms and sometimes whole industries into oblivion. But he implies this is partly compensated by the creative impact of more efficient industrial techniques and the benefits of better and cheaper commodities; though resentment at the destructive consequences of capitalist progress also gives rise to opposition to capitalism as such in the form of calls for socialism. But importantly, Schumpeter does not register any negative effects for those operating of the businesses that are ultimately successful in the competitive market struggle.

For Weber, by contrast, even for those who found, work in and manage firms that are "winners" in the market struggle there are decisive negative consequences. This is because to become successful these firms must adopt a formally rational orientation of economic conduct and this entails the sacrifice of substantive values – the pursuit of profit for its own sake, and for ever-renewed sums of profit, is irrational from a "natural" point of view. Weber's insistence of conflict between formal and substantive rationality highlights, in particular, the unbrotherly effects of capitalist progress. The further implication of life adapted to the capitalist order is that it imposes a specific fate on the individual, whether an entrepreneur or an employee/worker. He must fashion for himself a work-a-day attitude and adopt a methodical and disciplined life orientation, as these are requirements of economic survival. In referring to the unavoidable aspects of compulsion, standardization and constraint suffered by the individual forced to live under the competitive conditions of the market system, Weber employs the now famous metaphor of the "iron cage".

> The Puritan wanted to work in a vocation [*wolte Berufsmench sein*]; we must do so. For when asceticism was carried out of monastic cells into vocational life and began to dominate inner-worldly morality, it helped to build the tremendous cosmos of the modern economic order. This order is now bound to the technical and economic presuppositions of mechanical, machinelike production, which today determines with irresistible force the life style [*Lebensstil*] of all individuals born into this mechanism, not only those directly engaged in economic enterprise, and perhaps will determine it until the last ton of fossil coal is burned. In Baxter's view the care for external goods should only lie on the shoulders of the saint like "a light cloak, which can be thrown aside at any moment". But fate [*Verhängnis*] decreed that the cloak should become an iron cage.[28]

28 From *The Protestant Ethic* as quoted in Lawrence A. Scaff, *Fleeing the Iron Cage: Culture, Politics, and Modernity in the Thought of Max Weber*, University of California Press, 1989, p. 88.

Weber does not say that the ascetic legacy of the Puritans has ceased to be of consequence, nor that a vocational ethos no longer has a bearing on the present manner of economic life. Both these elements continue to resonate, but now that the economic system of capitalism has come fully into its own, these initial dispositions of action have been modified and detached from their religious origins: capitalism now rests on "mechanical foundations" and no longer needs the support of religious asceticism. At one point Weber characterizes the modern economic system as a "masterless slavery" because "the need for competitive survival and the conditions of the labour, money and commodity markets" imposes an impersonal order on individuals to which they must submit.[29] With this term Weber highlights the intense pressure and regimentation forced by the modern economic predicament but, at the same time, the expression eschews any suggestion of Marxian class domination – because *both* capitalists and workers are subject to this pressure, albeit in differing ways.[30]

Weber's general attitude towards modern capitalism

Contrary to Marx, Weber took the view that capitalism as a socio-economic system might persist indefinitely into the future – "until the last ton of fossilized coal is burnt"[31] – and thus he rejected the view that inherent contradictions of capitalism would cause a final collapse at some point in the not too distant future. This is an issue upon which Weber's position possibly diverges from that of Schumpeter, who to a certain extent is open to the Marxian conclusion that the capitalist era has a limited life-span – though he thinks this for different reasons. Further, Weber was highly sceptical about Marxist theories concerning the desirability of socialism due to the superiority of a "planned economy" over chaotic, crisis-prone capitalism.[32] Marx's predictions were based on his so-called "pauperisation thesis" in combination with his theory about the inevitable concentration and centralization

29 ES, p. 1186.

30 Weber rejects Marx's theory of the political rule of the dominant economic class in part because in many cases the politically dominant groups and the economically dominant classes are at odds, as for example in the Germany of his day. Weber was particularly concerned at the political "backwardness" of the German bourgeoisie despite the fact that Germany had developed an advanced modern economy. Partly because the German bourgeoisie had not "gone through 'the school of hard asceticism'" as had England, it remained infatuated with Bismarckian Caesarism. See Peter Ghosh, *Max Weber and the Protestant Ethic: Twin Histories*, Oxford University Press, p. 381.

31 PE, p. 181.

32 At this point it is worth mentioning an anecdote that indicates the respective attitudes of Weber and Schumpeter as regards the prospect of socialism. Karl Jaspers relates how Weber and Schumpeter met in a Vienna coffeehouse after the Russian Revolution, during which Schumpeter expressed his pleasure that now the viability of socialism would no longer be an academic issue. Weber apparently exploded saying that the Russian development was a crime that would lead to unparalleled misery. "'Quite likely,' answered Schumpeter, 'but what a fine laboratory.' 'A laboratory filled with mounds of corpses,' Weber answered." After further argument, Weber apparently stormed out. Cited in Swedberg, Introduction to Richard Swedberg (ed.), *Joseph A. Schumpeter: The Economics and Sociology of Capitalism*, Princeton University Press, p. 90.

of capitalist economic power, all of which he thought would lead to increasingly intense system-wide economic crises that would culminate in a political transformation. Against this, in an essay on socialism delivered in 1918, Weber referred to the increasing self-regulation of capitalism through cartels and syndicates, and these would reduce the impact of economic crises.[33] He also differed significantly from Marx with his recognition of the significance of the middle classes, persons who do not occupy the same property-less situation as the working class and who are beneficiaries of capitalist prosperity. Such bourgeois groups would not be easily radicalized along socialist lines and had much to lose in any revolutionary overturning of the existing order.

Even so, Weber was not unsympathetic to the desire of workers for greater economic and political opportunities, and he criticized his own bourgeois compatriots for their authoritarianism and unfounded fear of working class emancipation.

> We reject, partly in principle and partly as inadequate, the point of view of master rule or patriarchalism, the bonds of the welfare institutions and those who would treat the worker as an object for bureaucratic regulation, and insurance legislation that merely creates dependency. We affirm the equal participation of the workers in the collective determination of working conditions, and to this end, we also affirm the strengthening of their organizations, which spearhead this effort; we see the comradeliness and class dignity that develops in this way as a positive value . . . we want to live in a land of citizens, not of subjects.[34]

Even if a socialist economy were feasible, Weber remained resolutely opposed the idea that socialism would improve the lot of the masses. As to the much-derided separation of the worker from the means of production, which was a focal point of the Marxian critique of capitalism, Weber insisted the alienation of the worker would not be overcome by a socialist transformation of the economy. "It is a serious mistake to think that this separation of the worker from the means of operation is something peculiar to industry and, moreover, to *private* industry. The basic state of affairs remains the same when a different person becomes lord and master of this apparatus, when, say, a state president or minister controls it instead of a private manufacturer."[35] Thus Weber argued that a future elimination of private ownership of the means of production would not eliminate the fundamental problems of industrial society, for those in managerial positions would continue to dominate the workers, and there would be other undesirable effects as well. Insofar as he accepts the Marxian idea of the "alienation of the

33 Max Weber, "Socialism", in Peter Lassman and Ronald Spiers (eds.), *Max Weber's Political Writings*, Cambridge University Press, 1994, pp. 272–303.

34 Quoted in Wolfgang Mommsen, *Max Weber and German Politics*, University of Chicago Press, 1984, p. 120.

35 Weber, "Socialism," p. 281.

worker", Weber attributes the problem as much to the effects of large-scale bureaucratic structures and the centralization of power in the hands of the all-powerful state. Any socialist economy would simply perpetuate these problems and, if anything, make them worse. "This [problem of alienation] would also be true particularly of any *rationally* organized socialist economy, which would retain the expropriation of all workers and merely bring it to completion by expropriating the private owners."[36]

Weber did not deny that a capitalistic political order could be overthrown and, in fact, he lived to see not only the Russian revolution but also the revolutionary upheaval in Germany in 1918–19. In Germany during the latter period of the war and just after, there was intensive debate about possible socialization of the economic system and there were moves towards the nationalization of industry and banking. Weber was passionately engaged in these debates and in his writings made significant contributions to the theory of a socialist economy.[37] He did not share the view, which other liberal commentators held at the time, that a socialist economic system could not be viable.

> A progressive elimination of private capitalism is theoretically conceivable, although it is surely not so easy as imagined in the dreams of some literati who do not know what it is all about; its elimination will certainly not be a consequence of this war. But let us assume that sometime in the future it will be done away with. What would be the practical result? The destruction of the iron cage of modern industrial labour? No! The abolition of private capitalism would simply mean that the top management of the nationalised or socialised enterprises would become bureaucratic as well.[38]

Ultimately, Weber rejects socialism because it cannot effectively resolve the fundamental problem of how, given the tendency towards bureaucratization of all aspects of social life, "some remnants of 'individualistic' freedom of movement" can be retained.

A final argument against socialism is contained in a passage in *Economy and Society* in which Weber discusses "The Mainspring of Economic Activity". He raises the possibility of a socialistic planned economy in which decision-making would be in the hands of a central authority and then invites the reader to consider the ideal state in which some right of "co-determination" is given to the population at large. But immediately this were instituted, Weber insists, it would result in "the fighting out of interest conflicts centring on the manner of decision-making and, above all, on the question of how much should be saved . . ." But, he goes on, "What is decisive is that in socialism, too, the individual will under these

36 ES, p. 139.

37 See for example section 14 of Chapter 2 of *Economy and Society* that deals with the concept of planned economy.

38 ES, pp. 1401–2.

conditions ask first whether to him, personally, the rations allotted and the work assigned, as compared with other possibilities, appear to conform with his own interests. . . . violent power struggles would be the normal result . . ." These would be disputes over ration allocations, extra rewards for heavy labour, work conditions, unpopular supervisors and many other issues, and they would soon give rise to organized interest groups. Just as under capitalism, individual interests would underlie the motivation of the majority, even where the ideological commitment to socialist values was vigorously promoted. This pessimism/realism about human nature is justified in Weber's view, because the mass of men do not act from self-sacrificing motives, "and it is an induction from experience that they cannot do so and never will."[39]

Weber also differed from Marxism in regard to the nature of classes and class struggle. He did not deny altogether the significance of class conflict and recognized that in certain circumstances naked class interest could lead to mass action and even be decisive for political outcomes, but generally speaking, this was not the case. Weber did not think that the distinctions between classes were as straightforward and that class interests were as polarized as Marx believed. So, for example, Weber distinguished between property and commercial classes and pointed out that property classes tend to cause the economic system to stagnate because they have less interest in change, whereas commercial classes, on the other hand, are more prone to contribute to progressive outcomes. The key positively privileged classes are made up of entrepreneurs, managers and those in the professions whose skills and expertise based on education are crucial for the development of the modern industrial system.

Overall, Weber took the view that, rather than abolishing capitalism, the better option is to modify and humanize it. Thus, he defended the market system in a qualified way by arguing that, in spite of its problems, for the foreseeable future it remains the most practical way of maintaining a measure of both freedom and prosperity. He therefore sought to reinforce the same dynamic features of the capitalist system that Schumpeter celebrated, and he promoted measures designed to limit the bureaucratization accompanying the growth of the modern state. At the same time, he supported the emancipation of the working class both in political and in social terms, seeking, in particular, reforms that would allow socialist political parties full participatory rights in a parliamentary system; ideally this would be based on the English model. At the same time, he encouraged the "bourgeoisification" of the socialist parties and welcomed their preparedness to forego revolution and engage with the electoral process. He not only advocated measures to extend working class political rights, he was also sympathetic to the working class movement and unions in the struggle with entrepreneurs over better wages and conditions. He supported progressive social legislation in order to improve

39 ES, p. 203. Schumpeter expresses a similar view in *Capitalism, Socialism and Democracy*, at p. 210.

health and safety standards and protection of the weak, in part for ethical reasons, in part because it would increase the power position of the weaker classes.[40]

Wolfgang Mommsen has suggested that Weber's attitude to cartels and monopolies represents something of a contradiction within his position on capitalism because in some ways these are the natural outgrowth of a competitive situation in which sooner or later the strong come to dominate. So the question arises whether Weber favoured a radical laissez-faire economy, as later advocated by Mises, Hayek and others, or whether in seeking to curb the excesses of capitalism he was advocating a kind of regulated capitalism and was thus closer to social democracy than to classical liberalism. Mommsen suggests Weber never systematically discussed this contradiction. He argues it is difficult to know whether Weber would have favoured a liberal or an interventionist policy in the present – to put it bluntly, "would he have given preference to Keynes or Friedman?"[41] Mommsen says that Weber's general goal was to ensure dynamic economic growth so as to avoid a situation in which a dominant class can perpetuate itself by holding society in a state of petrification. He feared equally the prospect of political and economic stultification. To overcome the decadence of the Wilhelminian system, he urged the bourgeoisie to take political responsibility and assume the leadership of Germany into the future. Here we cannot discuss further the many complexities of Weber's political views, especially as regards the role of charismatic leadership and his conception of "plebiscitary leadership democracy", as these issues take us beyond our present tasks.

Weber's position was not that capitalism should be defended at all costs on quasi-ideological grounds – that it could be justified as an ideal system as, say, in Manchester liberalism. In any event, a pure form of laissez-faire capitalism did not exist in Weber's day, had never existed previously and was unlikely in the future. But major elements of the ideal type of competitive capitalism were present in many societies and, to a degree, have underpinned the ongoing efficiency and productivity of the modern economic system. The challenge for Weber was to retain the liberal values and human rights that have come down to us from the era of the rise of the modern bourgeoisie along with the benefits of the dynamic economy. Unfortunately, the reality is that some substantive values can only be achieved at the cost of curtailing and undermining the formal rationality of the capitalist system. Hence, Weber's insistence that formal and substantive rationality are in eternal conflict and that an ultimate resolution of this antinomy is not possible.

Finally, Weber's attitude towards capitalism must be understood in the context of his general view of the nation state and his support for Germany's emergence as a leading world power. His politics was tempered by his appreciation of the

40 See Dieter Krüger's discussion of Weber's involvement with the *Verein für Sozialpolitik* in his essay "Max Weber and the Younger Generation in the Verein für Sozialpolitik".

41 Wolfgang Mommsen, *The Political and Social Theory of Max Weber: Collected Essays*, Polity, 1989, p. 67.

ultra-realism and anti-utopianism of figures like Machiavelli and Nietzsche. According to Lawrence Scaff,

> political economy (*Nationalökonomie*) had a strong national component for Weber, much as it had had earlier for List. In contrast to the classical theory of value and exchange, Lists's theory of the "national system" stressed the development of "productive forces" and acceptance in principle of protectionism and state intervention. . . . Weber placed political economy in the service of "the permanent economic and political *power* interests of the nation," insisting that the popular "economic point of view" contained no standards of practical judgement.[42]

These ideas were notably set out in Weber's Inaugural Lecture of 1895 "The National State and Economic Policy". His general perspective on the role of the economy can be gleaned from the following passage:

> The economic policy of a German state, and the standard of value adopted by a German economic theorist can therefore be nothing other than a German policy and a German standard. . . . we should not abandon ourselves to the optimistic expectation that we have done what is necessary once we have developed economic progress to the highest possible level . . . Processes of economic development are in the final analysis also *power struggles*, and the ultimate and decisive interests at whose service economic policy must place itself are the interests of national *power* . . .[43]

Whether Weber held completely to these attitudes expressed so forcefully in his early career until after the war is questionable, as later works such as "Politics as a Vocation"[44] and "Parliament and Government in a Reconstructed Germany"[45] are decidedly more nuanced and have a very different tone and quite other emphases. Weber's political position, especially in the light of the fate of Germany subsequent to the two world wars, has been subject to significant criticism,[46] but we cannot explore these questions further here. Suffice it to say that we do not consider Weber's broad contributions to the theory of capitalism to be seriously flawed as a consequence of his nationalist predilections.

42 Lawrence Scaff, "From Political Economy to Political Sociology: Max Weber's Early Writings", in Ronald Glassman and Vatro Murvar (eds.), *Max Weber's Political Sociology: A Pessimistic Vision of a Rationalized World*, Greenwood, 1984, pp. 88–9.

43 Max Weber, "The Nation State and Economic Policy", in Keith Tribe (ed.), *Reading Weber*, Routledge, 1989, p. 198.

44 FMW, pp. 77–128.

45 ES, pp. 1381–469.

46 The most detailed and nuanced critique of Weber's politics is Mommsen, *Max Weber and German Politics*.

Schumpeter's view of the prospect of socialism

In apparent contrast to Weber, Schumpeter appears to see socialism, somewhat like Marx, as the ultimate destiny of a capitalist society. Furthermore, again like Marx, he at times suggests a transition to socialism would not necessarily undermine the progressive achievements of the capitalist era.[47] But this straightforward interpretation of his position is misleading, as the remarks giving rise to such an understanding must be seen in the context of his broad perspective on the capitalism versus socialism issue. In this regard, it is clear that he always remained a vigorous supporter of capitalism and a trenchant critic of socialism. Thus, as Thomas McGraw points out,

> the organization of Schumpeter's discussion of socialism [in *Capitalism, Socialism and Democracy*] has elements of a shell game. At first his argument seems designed to establish the viability of socialism and its likely replacement of capitalism. But there follows such a lengthy series of convoluted qualifications and assumptions as to raise doubts about his candour. Although he has adopted the outward form of an inquiry rather than a polemic, a careful reading leaves little question that his purpose has been to praise capitalism and condemn socialism.[48]

Let us nonetheless review his arguments for the viability, and indeed likely eventuality, of socialism.

Somewhat paradoxically, Schumpeter considers socialism a real possibility in the future because he thinks a central bureaucracy could, at least in theory, continue the innovative role that has hitherto been borne by the entrepreneur. I say paradoxically because Schumpeter had hitherto emphasized the unique and ostensibly irreplaceable role of the individual entrepreneur; only such an individual

47 Some commentators have thought that Schumpeter's involvement with Austrian socialization efforts, his role as a minister and his predictions about the demise of capitalism meant that he had become a committed socialist, but this is not so. This is made clear in the pamphlet he wrote in 1918 entitled, in English, "The Crisis of the Tax State" that contained an outline of his policy recommendations just prior to his becoming Finance Minister. On the issue of how best to transition from war to peacetime production, Schumpeter advocated that the best thing the government could do was to refrain from interfering so as to "release the tremendous reserves of energy, which in Austria are wasted by the incessant battle against the shackles by which foolish legislation, administration and politics restrain every economic move, and which deflect the entrepreneur from his organization, technical and commercial tasks, leaving him as the only way to success the backstairs to political and administrative bureaus. . . . I do not want to extol the free enterprise economy as the last word or wisdom. Nor am I an uncritical admirer of the bourgeoisie. But what needs to be done now, is exactly what it can do best . . . The hour of socialism will come, but it has not arrived as yet. . . . The hour that is, belongs to free enterprise. Only at the price of heavy sacrifice even for the working classes could the free enterprise system be given up at this time." Quoted in Gotttfried Haberler, "Joseph Alois Schumpeter: 1883–1950", *The Quarterly Journal of Economics*, 64.3, (1950), pp. 348–9.

48 McGraw, *Prophet of Innovation*, pp. 366–7.

can rupture the traditionalistic and stagnating reproduction of the "circular flow". In an essay entitled "Can Capitalism Survive?" based on a talk given in 1936, Schumpeter discussed the long-term prospects for the capitalist economic system at some length. He first posits the view that, despite the phenomenon of business cycles and the tendency for periodic crises, the underlying progressiveness of capitalist development is something that will continue into the foreseeable future. On the basis of tendencies operating in the 1930s, he projected what the likely performance of the economy might be in fifty years hence. "Now I hold that there is no reason to assume that if the system is left to itself distribution will change very much, and if we apply the distribution and functioning which we get now to 1978, we should stand to get an income a head which would do away with the phenomenon of poverty, in whatever sense it is useful to speak of poverty. This does not mean that there will be no people suffering from poverty."[49] But despite the prospect of capitalism enjoying ongoing development and prosperity, Schumpeter comes to the surprising conclusion that capitalism is unlikely to survive in the long term.

> Capitalism so transforms our requirements, our cultural scheme and values, as to make those economic adjustments which economic machineries demand unbearable, as to draw away the beliefs, the social psychological basis from under the institutions of property and so on for good or for ill. And as soon as that happens, we make another discovery . . . capitalism is an organization which can't stand on its own feet. It did well for a time in Europe as long as it was protected by an aristocracy and a monarchy which had free capitalistic rules, [but it] tumbled down at once when these things were removed. If it came to stay for a time here [in the United States] it was only because the fascinating sound of the opportunities for new millions drew the minds of people from other things but it probably can't stand by itself yet. And so I come to the diagnosis that the system will not survive, if by an entirely different line of reasoning [than Marx]. But the result as far as prediction goes, is very much the [Marxian] one, although I am not a Marxist and although I have no tendency for socialist systems at all. It is of course that . . . such a process of dying off takes time, and that in the process of dying off many intermediate points and intermediate forms of organization are likely to occur. It is futile to think that regulated capitalism can stand any more than unregulated capitalism. Political support would not be forthcoming for either.[50]

He goes on to speculate that the building of an efficient well-trained civil service and the creation of a form of socialism managed by such a body is the likely outcome.

49 Joseph Schumpeter, "Can Capitalism Survive?", in *ESC*, p. 304.
50 Ibid., pp. 305–6.

In *Capitalism, Socialism and Democracy*, Schumpeter explores these themes of the transformation of advanced capitalism at some length. There he writes:

> Progress itself may be mechanized as well as the management of the stationary economy, and this mechanization of progress may effect entrepreneurship and capitalist society as much as the cessation of economic progress would. . . . Thus economic progress tends to become depersonalised and automatized. Bureau and committee work tends to replace individual action. . . . Since capitalist enterprise, by its very achievements tends to automatize progress, we conclude that it tends to make itself superfluous – to break to pieces under the pressure of its own success.[51]

There are further features that will lead eventually to the demise of capitalism. Most significant amongst these is the impact of monopolistic, large-scale business organization. Many things that were once visualized by the genius of the entrepreneur can now be strictly calculated. There are processes of rationalization and specialization at work. The entrepreneur is displaced and the bourgeoisie are reduced to mere stockholders without any unique creative role. This effectively transforms the economy into a form of socialism.

Schumpeter defines socialism as "an institutional pattern in which the control over the means of production and over production itself is vested with a central authority."[52] Schumpeter seems to accept that socialism is a perfectly feasible way of coordinating an industrial economy: there is nothing "wrong with the pure logic of the socialist economy."[53] He refers to Vilfredo Pareto, who in his *Cours d'Economie Politique* had followed the original contributions on the theory of the socialist economy of Enrico Barone. These thinkers had shown that under the conditions of a feasible socialist system it is possible "to derive, from its data and from the rules of rational behaviour, uniquely determined decisions as to what and how to produce . . . [that] those data and rules, under the circumstances of a socialist economy, yield equations which are independent and compatible . . . and sufficient in number to determine uniquely the unknowns of the problem before the control board or ministry of production."[54] Barone's position, according to Schumpeter, was in effect nothing but the Walrasian system applied to a centrally planned economy. The idea that a central bureaucracy could set prices sufficiently rational to be capable of generating an efficient allocation of resources, as is known, was later refined by figures like Oscar Lange and A. P. Lerner. Indeed, Schumpeter goes further than simply saying that a socialist economy is perfectly feasible and suggests it may even be capable of quite high levels of rationality. Somewhat contradictorily given the thrust of his analysis of capitalism, he suggests that socialism may actually be an

51 CSD, pp. 131–4.
52 Ibid., p. 167.
53 Ibid., p. 172.
54 Ibid.

improvement on the efficiency of the capitalist economic system because central direction will avoid "the uncertainty about the reaction of one's actual and potential competitors and about how the general business situations are going to shape."[55] Further, a socialist economy could potentially eliminate economic cycles and the associated problems of unemployment and inflation. Indeed, "socialist management may conceivably prove to be as superior to big business capitalism as big business capitalism has proved to be to the kind of competitive capitalism of which English industry of 100 years ago was the prototype."[56]

But this speculation must be qualified by the ironical subtext of Schumpeter's discussion in *Capitalism, Socialism and Democracy*. It has to be remembered that he was writing in the 1930s and 1940s, when the brutal experience of socialism in the Soviet Union had become known. Schumpeter had no illusions that ruthless enforcement of the dictates of the central authority was an almost certain outcome of any future experiment with socialistic planning in the West, an outcome that would hardly be compatible with democracy. Thus he noted that under socialism, the industrial managers would use all means of totalitarian discipline to ensure compliance with the system's requirements; for to oppose the central authority would amount to attacking the government itself and would be regarded as "a semi-criminal practice. A strike would be mutiny."[57] Schumpeter refers on a number of occasions to events in the Soviet Union and says, contrary to the ideal of freedom that Marx had held, in the Soviet Union after 1932, "the industrial proletariat was more in hand than it had been under the last Tsar."[58] He notes that there is no opposition to government dictates, no intellectuals to challenge policy and no public opinion to express dissatisfaction. "Dismissal [from employment] spelling privation, shifts amounting to deportation, 'visits' by shock brigades and occasionally by comrades of the Red Army are . . . independent means in the hands of the government by which to safeguard performance."[59] Schumpeter's subsequent discussion, in which he pretends to suggest such things can be overlooked because they are unfortunate results of the "unripeness" of the situation in which Russia became socialist, leaves one no doubt that from his point of view the Soviet socialist experiment has been a catastrophic failure and such outcomes are likely elsewhere.

Schumpeter was most concerned that the intellectual classes of his day – Weber's *literati* – in their constant criticism of capitalism are naïvely facilitating a transformation to dictatorial socialism blissfully ignorant of the nightmare that will follow. It was in this context that he felt obliged to defend capitalism against its detractors, and this was real purpose of *Capitalism, Socialism and Democracy*.

55 Ibid., p. 186.
56 Ibid., p. 196.
57 Ibid., p. 215.
58 Ibid., p. 216.
59 Ibid., p. 217.

Schumpeter on the culture of capitalist society

In his discussions of the possible future transformation of capitalism, Schumpeter developed an avowedly sociological approach, which in some sense is at odds with his usual focus on the purely economic. He makes an important distinction between capitalism understood as the economic system proper and the "capitalist order", by which he means the political and social conditions that underpin the economic system. And increasingly as he develops his argument about the future of capitalism, the analysis focuses on the socio-political order. In the case of England, Schumpeter argues that the support of the aristocracy was crucial for the capitalist order in its infancy; for it "made itself the representative of bourgeois interests and fought the battles of the bourgeoisie."[60] He claims even mature capitalism requires a society that has a protecting social stratum. He points out that it emerged in the "steel frame" of feudalist society: "with the utmost ease and grace the lords and knights metamorphose themselves into courtiers, administrators, diplomats, politicians and into military officers of a type that had nothing to do with that of the medieval knight."[61] The symbiosis of the two strata, the mediaeval knights and the capitalist bourgeoisie, created the conditions under which capitalism could flourish because the capitalist class needed a master and it could not provide this itself. But this lack is fatal for the future of capitalism, because capitalist progress tends to destroy the stratum that it depends on.

Today, aristocratic support no longer exists and instead there are significant social forces aligned against the capitalist system. In particular, Schumpeter complains that the intellectuals have become increasingly hostile towards capitalism and are undermining belief in the system. His reasoning on this involves a number of steps: "One of the most important features of the later stages of capitalist civilization is the vigorous expansion of the educational apparatus and particularly facilities of higher education." This creates an oversupply of services in professional, quasi-professional and in the end in all white-collar positions, causing unemployment or "unsatisfactory" employment – that is, low paid work or work in substandard conditions. These individuals swell the ranks of the intellectuals who become increasingly disaffected and resentful at a society that disappoints their career expectations. The intellectuals' role is particularly important in the trade unions, for "they verbalized the movement, supplied theories and slogans for it – class warfare is an excellent example – made it conscious of itself and in doing so changed its meaning . . . and radicalised it, eventually imparting a revolutionary bias to the most bourgeois trade-union practices, a bias which most non-intellectual leaders at first resented."[62]

60 Ibid., p. 136.
61 Ibid., p. 137.
62 Ibid., pp. 153–4.

> Capitalism, whilst economically stable, and even gaining in stability, creates, by rationalising the human mind, a mentality and a style of life incompatible with its own fundamental conditions, motives and social institutions, and will be changed, although not by economic necessity and probably even at some sacrifice of economic welfare, into an order of things which will be merely a matter of taste in terminology to call Socialism or not.[63]

According to Schumpeter, a sympathetic appreciation of socialism is fostered by the very rationalism of the bourgeoisie itself. It is the peculiar role of bourgeois intellectuals to engage in a kind of imminent critique of a capitalist order. "The bourgeois finds to his amazement that the rationalist attitude does not stop at the credentials of kings and popes but goes on to attack private property and the whole scheme of bourgeois values. The bourgeois fortress thus becomes politically defenceless."[64] There is no longer any passion to defend the capitalist order. Schumpeter obviously has in mind here the role of intellectuals such as those he must have encountered on a regular basis in his academic career. Bureaucrats are open to conversion to the thinking of these intellectuals with whom, through similar education, they have much in common.[65] All this leads to a kind of despair in which the bourgeois is simply unable to defend his world. "The only explanation for the meekness [of the bourgeoisie] we observe is that the bourgeois order no longer makes sense to the bourgeois himself and that, when all is said and nothing is done, it does not really care."[66] In the absence of an effective stratum to protect it, the capitalist system is left without the conditions of its ongoing existence.

Schumpeter further suggests that the demise of small-scale business fosters resentment amongst sections of the population. "The political structure of the nation is profoundly affected by the elimination of a host of small and medium-sized firms the owner-managers of which, together with their dependents, henchmen and connections, count quantitatively at the polls and have a hold on what we may term the foreman class that no management of a large unit can ever have; the very foundation of private property and free contracting wears away in a nation in which its most vital, most concrete and most meaningful types disappear from the moral horizon of the people."[67] Admittedly, Schumpeter says that for the immediate future "enterprise is still active, the leadership of the bourgeois group is still the prime mover of the economic process." However, the tendency towards another entirely different structure of civilization, namely socialism, "slowly works deep

63 Joseph Schumpeter, "The Instability of Capitalism", in *EJAS*, pp. 71–2.

64 CSD, p. 143. Schumpeter's views were quite prophetic given the rise of the counterculture in the sixties and the related social movement based on rejection of capitalist values that arose in Western societies at that time. Nonetheless, capitalism did not collapse, the socialist movement was not able to sustain the momentum it gained through that explosion of sentiment and has atrophied.

65 Ibid., p. 155.

66 Ibid., p. 161.

67 Ibid., p. 140–1.

down below" so that in the long run, perhaps in a hundred years or more, such forces will triumph.[68]

But still Schumpeter does not believe socialism is inevitable and much of his brooding over its prospect is designed to warn his readers that they ought not to be seduced by the superficial appeal of such a system. He particularly emphasizes the link of capitalism with democracy: "Modern democracy rose along with capitalism, and in causal connection with it."[69] Socialism will not readily be made consistent with a democratic and free polity. As to Schumpeter's view that even though capitalism as an economic system has been remarkably successful it is at considerable risk as a political system, we agree with the assessment of his famous pupil Paul Samuelson on this matter: Samuelson argues convincingly that it is most unlikely that ongoing capitalist progress would lead to political moves to change the system to something totally different.[70]

The problem of the mixed economy

After the end of World War Two, Schumpeter began to consider the impact of the increasing involvement of government regulation of and intervention in the economy and in the provision of welfare short of full socialism. These features had become so evident that amongst the issues they raised was the question as to whether a pure capitalist system still existed and whether these developments harboured the beginning of the end of the market system. Referring to the position in America, Schumpeter thought that because of its prodigious wealth capitalism there seemed perfectly compatible with a generous system of social welfare. A tax burden of as much as 20 percent he surmised would not be likely to harm the capitalist engine. "In the United States alone there need not lurk behind modern programs of social betterment, that fundamental dilemma . . . between economic progress and immediate increase of the real income of the masses." Indeed, so much was it the case that America could indulge high wage levels that to an extent it "may annihilate the whole case for socialism."

But the advent of extensive government intervention in the economy raises the issue of whether a capitalist economic system as such continues to exist. By 1948, Schumpeter thought that a kind of capitalist-socialist compromise had been reached. "We have neither laissez-faire liberalism nor socialism but a combination of the two that is perhaps inevitable but nevertheless illogical." To characterize this halfway house, with post-war Britain and America's New Deal-based welfare policies in mind, Schumpeter coined the term "laborism", which he argued, contrary to Marx, "is the last stage of capitalism. Laborism signifies here . . . capitalist

68 Ibid., p. 163. For a detailed critique of Schumpeter's ideas on the demise of capitalism, see Richard Coe and Charles Wilbur, *Capitalism and Democracy; Schumpeter Revisited*, University of Notre Dame, 1985.

69 CSD, p. 296.

70 See Paul Samuelson, "Schumpeter as an Economic Theorist", in Helmut Frisch (ed.), *Schumpeterian Economics*, Praeger, 1981, pp. 14–17.

society at a stage in which the labour interest is predominant. Marx would have thought this impossible." And then in 1950 in the essay "The March into Socialism", published as the final chapter to the third edition of *Capitalism Socialism and Democracy*, Schumpeter writes: "All I wish to emphasize is the fact that we have travelled far indeed from the principles of laissez-faire capitalism and the further fact that it is possible so to develop and regulate capitalist institutions as to condition the working of private enterprise in a manner that differs but little from genuine socialist planning."[71]

But in these late remarks Schumpeter did not think a final victory of socialism was nigh. He noted that many economists take the view that a balance between interests of capital and labour ("labourist capitalism") was possible to endure indefinitely into the future:

> On the one hand, the vast productive possibilities of the capitalist engine that promise indefinitely higher standards of life, supplemented by gratis services *without* complete "expropriation of the expropriators"; on the other hand, the extent to which capitalist interest can in fact be expropriated without bringing the economic engine to a standstill and the extent to which this engine may be made to run in the labour interest.

Against this optimistic view Schumpeter retained a sceptical, pessimistic tone,

> We need not accept the stagnation thesis as it stands in order to be disturbed by the possibility that this thesis may come true after all if private-enterprise system is permanently burdened and "regulated" beyond its powers of endurance. In this case, an outright socialist solution may impose itself even on the enemies of socialism as the lesser evil.[72]

Schumpeter also notes how economic theory has moved on from the early enthusiasm of perfect competition. In his *History of Economic Analysis*, Schumpeter explains how the ideal type of competitive capitalism nonetheless remains of heuristic value for research:

> Modern theory no longer undertakes to show that free trade is the right policy for all times and places. But it shows much better than could have been shown by Smith or Mill what will be the effects of a particular measure of protection on the interests of all classes of society. Modern theory no longer undertakes to prove that perfect competition is an ideal. But it can show what the effects of given deviations from competition will be.[73]

71 CSD, pp. 418–9.
72 Ibid., p. 419.
73 HEA, p. 1145.

Of course Weber was not unaware of the increasing role of state regulation and social welfare. In Germany there had been important early welfare reforms going back to the nineteenth century with Bismarck and under Lloyd George and Beveridge in England. Furthermore, theoretical reflection on this had begun at least as early as Marshall's *Class, Citizenship and Social Development.*[74] Weber did not provide detailed discussion of the idea of the welfare state as such, but he did briefly consider the role of such a state in regulating a capitalist economy in certain sections of *Economy and Society*. His discussion is in very broad historical terms, but at one point, he notes the following: "What is important for profit-making enterprises with fixed capital and careful capital accounting is, in formal terms, above all, the calculability of the tax load. Substantively, it is important that there shall not be unduly heavy burdens placed on the capitalistic employment of resources, which means, above all, on market turnover."[75] This statement would appear to set an upper limit as to how far a state might interfere in the regulation of a capitalist economy and to what extent it could satisfy its needs through taxation without paralyzing the economy. As noted above, Schumpeter has the same concern. On the other hand, as we have already stated, Weber was a strong supporter of welfare reforms in the Germany of his day, and he clearly believed that, provided the state did not haphazardly make excessive requisitions at the expense of business, it could afford to finance its programs without undermining the formal rationality of the economy. He does not appear to have addressed the issue of how far the state should directly regulate the market economy by, for example, providing counter-cyclical stimulus spending or other interventions that would alter the free play of market forces. Again these are problems that only came to the fore in the period after Weber's death, especially with the experience of the Great Depression and later with phenomena like "stagflation" and the so-called Global Financial Crisis.

Schumpeter's critique of Keynes

Leaving to one side Schumpeter's speculations regarding the possibility of a transition to socialism, his writings otherwise seem to presuppose the continuation of capitalism for the foreseeable future, and his analyses are generally supportive of a largely unregulated market system. In this regard, it is worth considering further his views on the emerging role for the interventionist/welfare state, views that are closely bound up with his response to Keynes's celebrated book *The General Theory of Employment, Money and Interest*. It is apparent that Schumpeter had a competitive and somewhat combative relationship with Keynes. As already

74 On the history of the welfare state, see generally the works of Stein Rokkan and Peter Flora. A good introduction is Peter Flora and Jens Alber, "Modernization, Democratization, and the Development of the Welfare States in Western Europe", in Peter Flora and Arnold J. Heidenheimer (eds.), *The Development of Welfare States in Europe and America*, Transaction Books, 1981, pp. 37–80.

75 ES, p. 200.

pointed out, the publication of Keynes's book to some extent appears to have gazumped Schumpeter insofar as its "success" caused Keynes to steal the limelight and overshadow his own achievements.[76] The enthusiasm for the Keynesian perspective and the adoption of its policy implications by successive Western governments in the post-war period considerably irritated Schumpeter who believed the argument of *The General Theory* was seriously flawed. Not surprisingly given his attitude, he does not address Keynes at length in any of his works, though there are several short pieces that discuss his writings. There is no doubt that Schumpeter acknowledged, the importance, even greatness, of Keynes who he acknowledged was a person of brilliance and originality, but he remained a staunch critic.

Schumpeter gives a brief summary of Keynes' *The General Theory* in a review essay of 1936 and considers Keynes the man in a longer, more biographical piece first published in 1946.[77] He also referred to Keynes' work on numerous occasions in his *History of Economic Analysis*, but did not treat his theory at the length and detail that might be expected of such a figure. He argued that Keynes employed a highly simplified model of the economic system that enabled him to portray his vision more acutely.[78] Expressing his basic difference from Keynes and to some extent indicating the line of criticism that he was to adopt, Schumpeter claimed Keynes's simplified structure had the disadvantage of avoiding all the complications arising from process analysis. Keynes's approach was basically one of macro-statics as against macro-dynamics. Although there are some dynamic elements, such as the role of expectations, generally speaking, the concern is with static equilibrium. Related to this is a focus on the range of short-run phenomena. As against Schumpeter's long-term, historical view of the development of the entire capitalist era, the Keynesian approach is very much preoccupied with the immediate period of the present and a few years either side. Schumpeter claims, this

> limits the applicability of his analysis to a few years at most – perhaps the duration of the "40 months cycle" – and, in terms of phenomena, to the factors that *would* govern the greater or smaller utilisation of industrial apparatus *if* the latter remains unchanged. *All the phenomena incident to the creation and change of this apparatus, that is to say, the phenomena that dominate the capitalist processes, are thus excluded from consideration.*[79]

76 On the reception of *Business Cycles* and Schumpeter's disappointment at the "success" of Keynes's *General Theory* see McGraw, *Prophet of Innovation*, pp. 270–8.

77 See his "Review of Keynes's General Theory", in EJAS, pp. 153–7, and "Keynes, the Economist", in *Three Views of Keynes the Economist*, Kessinger, pp. 73–101 (the same text under the title "John Maynard Keynes (1883–1946)" is also in TGE, pp. 260–94).

78 Keynes adopted the use of three schedule concepts – the consumption function, the efficiency of capital function and the liquidity preference function – from which he developed a fully-fledged aggregative schema.

79 "Keynes, the Economist," p. 99-100.

Though Keynes claimed his approach was "general", indicating he had sought to establish a theory of wide application dealing with the long-term course of the capitalist economy, he basically operated with a short-run model and did so by reasoning largely about a stationary process that oscillates about the level at which full employment is the limit. As against Marx who saw the evolution of capitalism leading to its breakdown and collapse, Keynes took the view that in its worst stages the capitalist economy leads to a stationary state that threatens to break down but does not necessarily do so. Nonetheless, as with Marx, the capitalist breakdown arises from causes inherent to the working of the economic system itself and not by the action of external factors.

Schumpeter argues that Keynes' picture of reality comes closest to being accurate for the case of depression and thus he has rightly been described as an economist of depressions. But the other area in which Keynes's theory has become significant and in which it seeks to make a decisive contribution is in relation to the so-called "secular stagnation thesis". This theory concerns itself with the predicament of economies that appear to be stuck in a stage of little or no growth, in which there is underutilization of available resources, in particular of labour, and there appears to be no foreseeable likelihood of the economy returning to a state of equilibrium.[80] But the fundamental criticism from Schumpeter's point of view remained that the Keynesian system cannot truly describe itself as a "general theory". No doubt in some of the analyses of particular situations of the economy that Keynes examines, there are genuine insights, but they cannot hold for more than that. Keynes' analyses do not amount to a theory that would account for the operation of the capitalist system over the long term, by which Schumpeter means a period extending over centuries.

Schumpeter notes with a certain sense of annoyance that *The General Theory* became an instantaneous success and developed a school of followers who loyally defended and even propagandized it. He suggests that there are only two other analogous cases where an economic theory has become the basis of a kind of movement or school, namely, with the Physiocrats and the Marxists. The implication of this is to suggest that Keynes' "success" owed more to its appeal as an ideology than to its scientific soundness.

> Before the appearance of the *General Theory*, economics had been growing increasingly complex and increasingly incapable of giving straightforward answers to straightforward questions. The *General Theory* seemed to reduce it once more to simplicity, and to enable the economist once more to give simple advice that everybody could understand. But, exactly as in the case of Ricardian economics, there was enough to attract, to inspire even, the sophisticated. The same system that linked up so well with notions of the untutored mind

80 For a critical analysis of the role of Keynesianism in the context of modern politics from a neo-Marxist point of view, see Claus Offe, "Competitive Party Democracy and the Keynesian Welfare State: Factors of Stability and Disorganization", *Policy Sciences*, 15.3, (1983), pp. 225–46.

> proved satisfactory to the best brains of the rising generations of theorists. Some of them felt – still feel for all I know – that all other work in "theory" should be scrapped. All of them paid homage to the man who had given them a well-defined model to handle, to criticise, and to improve – to the man whose work symbolises at least, even though it may not embody, what they wanted to see done.[81]

In general Schumpeter took the view that, as with his view of Marx, it was possible to admire Keynes, even though his social vision was mistaken and many of his propositions were downright misleading.

Schumpeter's more specific criticism of the Keynesian approach concerns its reliance on aggregative concepts. He points out that the major variables Keynes chooses, with the exception of employment, are monetary quantities or expressions and, as national income is the central variable, income analysis. He claims that Quesnay's *tableau économique* was Keynes' true predecessor.[82] He is adamant that aggregative analysis, if not backed by deeper theoretical and empirical work, is an extremely questionable basis for economic theorizing. Hence, in regard to the emphasis on expectations he says,

> But expectations are not linked by Mr. Keynes to the cyclical situations that give rise to them and hence become independent variables and ultimate determinates of economic action. Such analysis can at best yield purely formal results and never go below the surface. An expectation acquires explanatory value only if we are made to understand *why* people expect *what* they expect. Otherwise expectation is a mere *deus ex machina* that conceals problems instead of solving them.[83]

A further point of criticism concerns Keynes' claims that the economy stagnates due to excessive saving. Far from saving being excessive so as to affect the propensity to invest, Schumpeter argues that, because the real impetus for investment is the drive to finance changes in the production function, this drive as a motive force precedes decisions about saving. Thus the propensity to consume and the inducement to invest are not as Keynes argues independent of one another; for there are always opportunities for further investment, in part because there are always unsatisfied wants but also because new needs are always capable of being generated. Hence, Schumpeter was strongly critical of the Keynesian solution to economic stagnation that suggested even wasteful spending was worthwhile, as long as it created new demand.

But perhaps the most basic criticism of the Keynesian policy prescriptions concerns the fact that he was fundamentally recommending that problems in the

81 "Keynes, the Economist," p. 99–100.

82 Ibid., p. 92.

83 "Review of Keynes's General Theory," p. 154, n. 3.

economic sphere should be dealt with by actions in the political sphere. As Schumpeter puts it in *Capitalism, Socialism and Democracy*, "Nothing should be more obvious than that the business mechanism cannot function according to design when its most important 'parameters of action' – wages, prices, interest – are transferred to the political sphere and there dealt with according to the requirements of the political game or . . . according to the ideas of some planners."[84] In other words, if politicians interfere with the self-adjusting mechanisms of the capitalist system, we should hardly be surprised that the results do not produce a state of employment at the equilibrium level. If anything, interference by the political authorities is prone to cause more problems than it solves, with the likelihood that price regulation, irrational taxation and questionable administrative actions will give rise to disruptive effects in their own right. This is not to say that Schumpeter refused to accept that there may be situations in which something akin to a Keynesian policy prescription would be justified, but this is more the exception than the rule. Thus he did not reject deficit financing in every case and accepted that it may be a justified where there is a danger of what he called a downward cumulative process.[85] The underlying problem with the Keynesian approach to policy, however, is that it leads to continual manipulation of the market by so-called "demand management". Thus, if the rate of interest increases, this means that investment will fall because individuals will choose to hold their money as savings rather than invest. Keynes believed that the employment situation was more likely to be exacerbated the wealthier a society becomes, because in such a society, the rate of saving will increase as incomes increase and opportunities to invest gradually diminish. Thus the key problem to be solved is that of finding outlets or opportunities for new investment with the savings that are held. For Keynes the underlying dilemma confronting a modern capitalist economy is that the rate of interest cannot be reduced sufficiently low to give rise to enough investment to create full employment.

Finally, Schumpeter concludes that the assumptions Keynes relies on are questionable because he assumes, in effect, that technology is a given and not subject to progress, so that as the ordinary business activity proceeds it leads to decreasing returns to scale. Thus, the only solution Keynes could recommend was governmental intervention in the economy, both by central regulation of investment and by direct government spending financed through loans. This will artificially stimulate demand and thereby raise economic activity to a level that would reinstate full employment. Of course, Keynes's supposed success in part depended on the circumstances in which his prescriptions were made, coming as they were at the time of the Great Depression with the massive unemployment that persisted year after year. His policy program offered a set of proposals that addressed the despair of many and on the face of it, appeared to be a solution to the crisis of the times. But it did not, according to Schumpeter, really solve any economic problems, and the theory failed to grasp the character of capitalism considered as a general system.

84 CSD, p. 386.
85 Ibid., p. 397.

The Schumpeterian concept of evolution

The term "evolution" is not only commonly employed by Schumpeter to describe the overall process of development of the capitalist system, it is pivotal to his whole schema. Obviously, there is a parallel between his use of the term and the Darwinian notion, and perhaps there is a more direct connection as well. Darwin's notion, as is well known, was oriented to explaining the long-term course of development of life forms on earth. The process of "natural selection" is presented as the key to explaining of how distinct species arise, then persist or die out, and the schema is deemed sufficient by itself for this purpose, as supernatural causes are not required. If we turn to the use of the term evolution in the Schumpeterian system, there are some obvious analogous features, but things are also somewhat different.

Before we explore Schumpeter's use of the term evolution further, it is well to consider his own remarks on Darwin and the influence, if any, of evolutionary biology in economics. In general terms, Schumpeter seems to deny any direct connection between evolution in biology and in economics. In his *History of Economic Analysis* he at one point discusses Darwin and specifically considers the possibility of a relation to his own ideas but is quite wary of embracing a close association.

> We notice the attempts that were made to apply the Darwinian concepts of Struggle for Existence and Survival of the Fittest to the facts of industrial and professional life in capitalist society. . . . it may be – we cannot argue the case here – that certain aspects of the individual-enterprise system are correctly described as a struggle for existence, and that a concept of survival of the fittest in this struggle can be defined in a non-tautological manner. But if this be so, then these facts would have to be analysed with reference to economic facts alone and no appeal to biology would be of the slightest use . . .[86]

Schumpeter could perhaps be said to be following Darwinian notions because of his account of how over the course of time various companies, industries, products and even whole national economies have come into being, grown and prospered and then in some cases declined and disappeared altogether. It is not difficult to see the obvious correspondence between the two theories in this respect. For example, just as one would say that for a time certain animal species arose and were successful, so Schumpeter can point to the rise of particular businesses as likewise having "evolved" and, for a time at least, having prospered. Changes in both the biological and economic domains have numerous other features in common. In each case, there is no necessary or inevitable rationale why a phenomenon appears at a given time; success or failure is always somewhat fortuitous, "timing" makes all the difference. The advent of new businesses occurs in an uneven fashion, while incremental adaptation to the surrounding environment occurs

86 HEA, p. 789.

continually. Later developments are in part built on the achievements of earlier ones. In the case of both economic and biological evolution there are powerful elements of competition at work that influence how successful an emerging entity will be and how long it may survive. Finally, there are many instances where, like species, a type of industry fails to adapt to the changing environment, begins to struggle and finally goes out of business.

We know from surveying recent examples that many commercial products have appeared on the scene but have had a relatively short span during when they were successful and remained profitable. For example, the production of jute, crucial for production of hessian bags, was a very important industry for a period in the early twentieth century because it was the only effective means by which certain bulk commodities like wheat, barley, cotton and wool could be handled in long distance trade. Now, of course, with advances in bulk handling, the production and use of jute is of much less significance. The material Bakelite was initially important owing to its use in electrical fittings, but today plastics have largely replaced it. The steam engine, once so crucial in mining, transport and agriculture, has totally disappeared from the landscape of the modern economy. There are countless other examples of this type of change, such as the videocassette, the typewriter and film cameras. And we know that whole regions previously central for the production of particular goods have subsequently gone into decline. One can point to cities such as Belfast or Newcastle where ships were once manufactured in large numbers, or Pittsburgh and Cleveland in America where steel was once king, or Detroit where automobile production was huge. Whole economies have been subject to this logic of decline. British and American manufacturing industries have declined markedly in the past two decades, whereas the economies like those of China, India, Brazil and South Korea are expanding rapidly and, to a degree, taking the place of the older players.

It is worth noting some other examples whereby new technologies and new products have emerged and to some degree revolutionized economic circumstances. Consider the development of the transistor that, although an American invention, was cleverly taken up by Japanese manufacturers. To a large degree its productive use, together with the later development of microprocessors, was responsible for the huge increase in exports by companies such as Sony, Hitachi, Sharp, National-Panasonic, Toshiba, Canon and others. Later, companies from South Korea such as Samsung and LG also began to achieve huge export volumes in electronics and household goods. At the same time as these businesses were taking off, there was a corresponding decline in what were previously highly successful companies in America, such as Eastman Kodak, Bell & Howell, and Xerox. The ability of the Japanese and South Koreans to take up new inventions, to innovate and create cheaper and better products than the corresponding American companies is a classic recent illustration of Schumpeter's creative destruction at work on a global scale.[87] Schumpeter wants to say these occurrences are perfectly

87 One graphic statistic is that of ninety TV manufacturers that previously operated in America none remain today. Of course, there are many new American companies that have come into being in

"normal" for the capitalist system, even though they cause dramatic and sometimes highly negative consequences for the losers.

Schumpeter's main purpose in using the concept of evolution is to say that relentless contest and competition is unavoidable in the struggle for economic survival. The apparent success of a given business will not guarantee its longevity. The high profitability of a particular company fosters the will and the drive of other entrepreneurs to outdo an existing market leader, to develop new products or find better, cheaper ways of doing things. No company or industry is immune from this contest, just as no animal species can consider that its niche is secure. We see that even the most "successful" economies of the very recent past now face real difficulties of maintaining their position. The Japanese economy, which was powering ahead in the 1970s and 1980s, has in the last ten years slowed considerably and is all but stagnant. Newer economic developments in Asia, South America and elsewhere are beginning to have a major impact on world trade. The older established economies are attempting to maintain their dominance by focusing their energies on services and high technology products because they cannot compete in the production of labour-intensive goods.

But having explored the parallels between biological and economic evolution, care must be taken to avoid any suggestion that Schumpeter was endorsing competitive struggle from an ethical point of view or adopting a social-biological perspective, for there are important differences. For one has to recognize that the events that occur in history are not a process of nature and that, however easy it may be to draw analogies between the struggle for existence between animal species and that between economic players, the fact that the latter struggle takes place within a social, cultural and political environment means that purely economic factors of competitive advantage are by no means decisive for outcomes. This use of the concept of evolution also raises the question as to whether one can speak of "progress" occurring as a result of an evolutionary process. Schumpeter does not to my knowledge expressly deal with this issue, but it is likely he would not have regarded evolutionary advance as inherently progressive. Clearly any assumption of "progress" depends upon certain presuppositions, such as that economic growth, profitability or material wellbeing are the decisive criteria.[88] Weber, on the other hand, discussed the issue of progress at some length and it to this we now turn.

---

recent times and achieved success, such notable cases as Apple, Intel, Dell, Google, and Amazon, and still others have remained prosperous throughout, such as Ford, General Electric, Coca Cola and Boeing.

88 For a discussion of the issues involved in employing the concept of evolution in economics, see Richard Nelson, "Evolutionary Theorizing about Economic Change", in Neil J. Smelser and Richard Swedberg (eds.), *The Handbook of Economic Sociology*, Princeton University Press, 1994, pp. 108–36.

Weber's analysis of "progress"

For comparative purposes, we shall briefly consider Weber's discussion of the concept of "progress", as this is an interesting contrast to Schumpeter's evolution. In Weber's writings he periodically raised the issue of the meaning of the long-term course of historical development. He touches on this topic at numerous points in his methodological writings and in his essays "Science as a Vocation" and "Religious Rejections of the World and Their Directions".

As we have noted above, Weber was especially concerned in his methodological writings to criticize the idea that there is a logic of inevitable progress at work in history owing to "laws of development".[89] And yet he wants to account for the phenomena of rationalization and modernization and the appearance of "progress", especially in economic affairs. For in the modern West, scientific/technical and industrial progress is palpable and cannot be denied. Weber explains that

> One can naturally use the term "progress" in an absolutely non-evaluative way if one identifies it with the "continuation" of some concrete process of change viewed in isolation. But in most cases, the situation is more complicated. . . . There is a recurrence . . . of the widespread confusion of the three following meanings of the term "progress": (1) merely "progressive differentiation", (2) progress of *technical* rationality in the utilization of means and, finally (3) increase in value.

Weber goes on to point to the fact that progress in one sense is not necessarily progress in another.

> Thus a progressive subjective rationalization of conduct is not necessarily the same as progress in the direction of rationally or technically "correct" behaviour. . . . Given a specified end, then it is possible to use the terms "technical correctness" and "technical progress" in the application of means, without any insuperable dangers of ambiguity. . . . [But] only when a specified condition is taken as a standard can we speak of progress in a given sphere of technique, for example, commercial technique or legal technique. We should make explicit that the term "progress" even in this sense is usually only approximately precise because the various technically rational principles conflict with one another . . . We may also speak of "economic" progress towards a relative optimum of want-satisfaction under conditions of given resources, if it is assumed there are given wants and their rank order is accepted . . ."[90]

Thus for Weber there is no generalized "progress" arising from the economic development of capitalism. Even though he also largely accepts Simmel's

89 See the analysis in the essay "'Objectivity' in Social Science and Social Policy", MSS, pp. 102–3.
90 "The Meaning of 'Ethical Neutrality' in Sociology and Economics", MSS, pp. 27–34.

arguments about the "progressive differentiation" of modern culture brought about by the effects of the widespread use of money, he denies this is unambiguously progress. "Whoever wishes to state a value-judgement regarding the fact of differentiation as such . . . will come upon the question of the price which is 'paid' for this process . . . 'progressive differentiation' is to be identified with an increase in 'value' only in the intellectualistic sense of an increase in self-awareness or of an increasing capacity for expression and communication."[91] Further, as he argues in his seminal essay "Religious Rejections of the World and Their Directions", the differentiation of culture under modern conditions has led to the fragmentation of lived experience and the separation of the life-world into different value spheres ("the economic", "the political", "the aesthetic", "the erotic", "the intellectual"). And the demands of these unavoidably come into conflict with each other. Thus the individual living in modern society is confronted with the "warring gods".

> For the rationalization and the conscious sublimation of man's relations to the various spheres of values, external and internal, as well as religious and secular, have then pressed toward making conscious the *internal and lawful autonomy* of the individual spheres; thereby letting them drift into those tensions which remain hidden to the originally naïve relation with the external world.[92]

Weber's "existential" answer to this dilemma is partly suggested in the essay "Science as a Vocation" when he says "speaking directly, the ultimate possible attitudes towards life are irreconcilable, and hence the struggle can never be brought to a final conclusion. Thus it is necessary to make a decisive choice."[93]

Generally speaking, Schumpeter was not as disposed towards philosophical reflection as Weber. Weber can even be said to have developed, and even embodied, a unique philosophical outlook – this led figures such as Karl Jaspers to credit Weber, both in his person and in his writings, with advancing a form of "existentialism".[94] Schumpeter was more influenced by positivist notions of philosophy of science – figures such as Ernst Mach were prominent in Schumpeter's Vienna – which led him to focus almost exclusively on what he believed the sciences could establish by rigorous analysis while excluding metaphysical and religious speculation.

Towards a synthesis of Weber and Schumpeter

Having pointed to the differences between Weber and Schumpeter on the nature of capitalism, it should nonetheless be recognized that there are clearly

91 Ibid., p. 28.

92 See "Religious Rejections of the World and Their Directions", FMW, p. 328.

93 "Science as a Vocation", FMW, p. 152.

94 See Karl Jaspers, *Karl Jaspers on Max Weber*, Paragon, 1989, passim.

a great many commonalities and points of agreement. First and foremost, both thinkers see capitalism as the most fateful force of modern society and the key institution requiring our understanding. Second, both thinkers accepted that capitalism as an economic system had achieved a high level of prosperity for the mass of the population and that any socialist transformation in the short term was unlikely to be an improvement in this respect. But third, though they rejected socialism, they both saw socialism as an understandable reaction to the volatility of capitalism, and as a predictable response to the inequality and relative deprivation a consequence of the competitive market. Fourth, despite such negatives, as we have seen, both Weber and Schumpeter provide (qualified) justifications for the capitalist system as a whole. For they both believed that the free market system, though by no means ideal, ought be supported, at least for the time being.

As we have seen, the role of the entrepreneur is central for both Schumpeter and Weber. Weber gives an elaborate account of the development of this type of individual, but he also provides analyses of the rational social structures that have facilitated the emergence of the capitalist economic system as a whole, particularly those of the state and law. To a certain degree Weber's work is a corrective of Schumpeter's overestimation of the explanatory power of his "mechanism" as an account of the course of European economic development down to the present.[95] Weber, in our view, convincingly describes the way in which various institutional developments occurring in the Middle Ages and the Reformation were crucial to the advent of the modern world generally and the capitalist system in particular. Some of these phenomena, it has to be said, are not adequately addressed in the work of Schumpeter. On the other hand, Weber did not embark on a detailed examination of the *functioning* of capitalism conceived as a dynamic economic system with its own inherent logic of development. Nor does he focus on the fact that capitalism is subject to regular and far-reaching fluctuations of the kind that Schumpeter shows are integral. Furthermore, Weber did not address some of the issues to do with the regulation of the capitalist system and the expansion of welfare services that Schumpeter began to address following World War Two.

Both Schumpeter and Weber conceived of modern capitalism as a system in which economic regulation and state ownership were of relatively minor significance. But both were aware of the expanding role of the state, and in particular, they recognized its increasing interference in economic affairs and the related growth in bureaucratic administration. But neither built into their theory a detailed account of what is now understood by concepts such as "organized

95 A similar error, in our view, of overestimating the role of a supposed "mechanism" in explaining long-term historical developments is made by Norbert Elias with his notions of the "civilizing process", and the growth of the state.

capitalism",[96] the "managed economy",[97] the "mixed economy"[98] or the "welfare state."[99] And neither considered at length the role of the state in directly fostering economic activity or in operating economic enterprises short of full socialization. But as the developments referred to were only in their infancy in the 1920s and 1930s, it is understandable that neither addressed them at any length.

The problem of rationalization

One final area in which there appear to be points of intersection between Weber and Schumpeter concerns the phenomenon of economic and societal rationalization. This is the case even though, unlike Weber, Schumpeter does not generally use the concept rationality to describe the outlook of the entrepreneur. In what follows, I shall argue that Weber's concepts of rationality and rationalization are nonetheless applicable to the way in which Schumpeter describes the functioning of the capitalist system. First, in regard to calculation generally, Schumpeter recognizes that the manager of a business must apply himself systematically, attending to the factors of production, adjusting them, buying and selling inputs in accordance with the market prices, and so on – in effect conducting the enterprise in a fashion similar to that implied in Weber's analysis of the use of capital accounting. Indeed, in the circumstances of competitive capitalism Schumpeter thinks the entrepreneur's innovation requires an even *higher* level of rational calculation than that of the ordinary business manager. But for Schumpeter, there is also perhaps a degree of irrationality associated with the factor of "vision". For the entrepreneur developing a new combination is operating in an uncertain field with imperfect knowledge. No doubt at times he faces extreme difficulties that threaten the viability of the whole project, but to succeed, he must persist regardless of the immediate prospects. He needs to inspire those around him that he has what it takes to bring the new enterprise to fruition, to keep their loyalty and induce them to invest needed funds. The corresponding feature from a Weberian perspective is that the entrepreneur possesses the element of charisma.

Schumpeter's entrepreneur must have the capacity to envisage market possibilities in accordance with his imagined venture, which leads to plans through which a novel project is to be realized. The entrepreneur who develops such new approaches must do so partly in accordance with Weber's notion of "ends-rational" or "instrumentally rational" (*zweckrational*) action. Weber's detailed explication of this concept is defined in *Economy and Society* as the circumstance where: "the end, the means, and the secondary results are all taken into account and weighed. This involves rational consideration of the alternative means to the end, of the

96 See Scott Lasch and John Urry, *The End of Organized Capitalism*, Polity, 1987.
97 See Alec Cairncross, *The Managed Economy*, Blackwell, 1970.
98 See Andrew Shonfield, *In Defence of the Mixed Economy*, Oxford University Press, 1965.
99 See Wolfgang Mommsen, *The Emergence of the Welfare State in Britain and Germany*, Croom Helm, 1981 and Derek Fraser, *The Evolution of the British Welfare State*, Macmillan, 1973.

relations of the end to the secondary consequences, and finally of the relative importance of different possible ends."[100] It is important to recognize that this definition does not focus solely on the rational choice of means to an end, which for Weber is a merely "technical" question. In economics, equally important is rational choice between ends, so that for action to be truly rational in this sense the means, the ends themselves and the possible consequences must all be weighed. And "weighing" entails some process of reasoning or control by the intellect – throwing dice, resorting to intuition or seeking a magical solution will not do. Weber clarifies what he means by instrumentally rational action by radically distinguishing it from another type of rational action, namely, value-rational (*wertrational*) action, which involves making a choice of ends based on consistency with ultimate values: "In this case, action is instrumentally rational only in respect to the choice of means."[101] The entrepreneur does not seek merely to pursue a particular end solely with the best technical means; for he is equally concerned to decide *between* ends given the available means to achieve them in the light of the secondary consequences that include both actual costs and opportunity costs. The rationality of decision-making can be enhanced by the use of rational techniques of various kinds, such as capital accounting, technical manuals, scientific reports, expert advice, strategic thinking, budgeting and so on. Weber's general view is that these types of action are becoming more and more significant in the modern world, especially in the sphere of economic life, and this is partly what he means by the progressive rationalization of society.

In our final chapter we shall summarize our argument and indicate how a general theory of modern capitalism can be of use in analysing contemporary developments.

100 ES, p. 26.
101 Ibid.

6 Towards a general theory of modern capitalism

We have argued that in the writings of Weber and Schumpeter are contained the elements of a comprehensive theory of the origins, foundations and operation of modern capitalism. We have attempted to establish that their contributions are not only largely compatible but complement each other and can be synthesized to produce a coherent theory of the totality of modern capitalism. We have sought to show that Weber's account of the institutional framework of capitalism is largely adequate in relation to Schumpeter's account for the operation of the market system. In other words, Weber provides the sociological complement to Schumpeter's economic theory, whereas Schumpeter provides an economic theory that accounts for the ongoing operation of the system that had first arisen in the modern era.

But more than this, we maintain that the key elements of a general theory of modern capitalism are contained in the combination of Weber's ideal type of rational capitalist enterprise with Schumpeter's account of the process of capitalist evolution. We believe these two sets of ideal types *in combination* provide a complex model of a type of economic system that approximates to a high degree the form of economy that arose first in the West in the nineteenth century and has spread more widely through the twentieth. Again it must be emphasized that the model in question is merely an ideal type, and this means that it is not a precise description of reality but merely a means for possible empirical investigation of actually existing economies. Clearly, some instances will approximate the model more than others; some may not fit the parameters at all. But the model has the prime purpose of clarifying what is meant by "capitalism", thus avoiding the all too vague and indeterminate usage of many commentators that readily see "modern capitalism" wherever they find money-making of any kind.

We wish to know whether socio-economic arrangements such as those we observe today in the diverse range of countries – such as Russia, China, India, Brazil, South Korea and Indonesia, for instance – are truly capitalist in the sense of the economies of the West and, if so, to what extent and with what significance. Of course, in seeking answers to such an inquiry, we do not presume that the Western case, as exemplified by Europe and America, is normatively ideal; nor do we think that the rest of the world is destined to follow that lead. Indeed, insofar as we have regard for Weber's account of the origins of the occidental bourgeoisie and its role in the inauguration of modern capitalism, we must doubt whether many non-Western societies can develop such an economic formation at all.

Some commentators will no doubt object to our use of Weber in the way proposed, for it can be argued that he conceptualized modern capitalism solely as an historical individual and that this precludes the adoption of his theory as a general type that can be used to analyze, say, non-Western economies. We disagree, because the concept we have outlined as the ideal type that fits best with modern capitalism is Weber's own type: "rational capitalism", constructed in terms of the maximum level of formal rationality. And it might also be put against our view that Schumpeter's evolutionary mechanism is incompatible with Weber's account of the origins of capitalism. In other words, it could be argued that we are misguided in attempting to combine theories that are incommensurable. In response to this we say first that we are not claiming Weber and Schumpeter agreed on all these methodological and substantive issues; indeed we have discussed their differences at length. But we do claim that the gravamen of their theories can be extracted from the body of their work and, with some modifications, combined as outline above.

In the case of Schumpeter, a major criticism we have made is that he overestimates the universality of his "capitalist mechanism". He says that the capitalist mechanism, in the requisite sense, was operative even as far back as mediaeval times, but this fails to adequately account for the changes that were brought by the Reformation, which we say with Weber was a watershed that ushered in more rationalized forms of economic life that would not have arisen otherwise. The way Schumpeter deploys his notion of the capitalist mechanism risks making progress appear to be an inevitable outcome driven by the propensity of human beings to invent and innovate, whereby sooner or later the market system in its fully modern form was destined to emerge.[1] Weber's writings, especially his comparative works dealing with the economic ethics engendered by the civilizations of India and China, indicate that there was nothing inevitable about the outcome that we now accept as "Western modernity". In our view, by this counterfactual argument Weber has conclusively established there were profound cultural barriers to the endogenous development of a modern-type economic system in those civilizations – and by extension elsewhere, for example, in the Islamic world. So we maintain that Schumpeter's account of the capitalist mechanism and his conception of the process of progressive evolution is only valid for the modern era and should not be pressed to account for developments occurring in premodern times or non-Western societies today. Schumpeter makes a basic methodological error when he implies the advent of such institutions as double-entry accounting or the corporate form of business arose because their potential for competitive advantage

1 A recent attempt to locate the presence of significant market forces as far back as Roman times which lends some support to a Schumpeterian perspective in this regard is Peter Temin, *The Roman Market Economy*, Princeton University Press, 2013. This work, however, in my view, exaggerates the role of market forces in antiquity and does not deal with the problems of oikos economy and political capitalism, questions dealt with extensively in my *Antiquity and Capitalism*.

was recognized and seized by innovative entrepreneurs. Rather than this, as Weber showed, such institutions have complex histories of their own, however connected those histories may be to the economic developments of the day.

There are other issues for our thesis that arise from the fact that, to some degree, the works of Weber and Schumpeter have inevitably become dated by the passing of the years. There have, of course, been many developments in the economy and in economic theory since their time. We have referred, for example, to the development of the welfare state and the related phenomenon of the "mixed economy" in the socio-economic systems of modern Europe, North America and elsewhere. Nonetheless, we maintain that these are cases of economic systems that still remain capitalistic in all relevant respects. Whereas Weber did not anticipate the extent to which the state was to become involved in regulating and managing the capitalist economy, as we have seen, Schumpeter was well aware of this tendency and addressed it at some length. But Schumpeter did not think capitalism was incompatible with the welfare state, nor that counter-cyclical intervention would overcome the phenomenon of the business cycle. However, it has to be admitted that neither fully realized the extent to which modern governments would come to develop the range of bureaucratic agencies and policy instruments with the purpose of "managing" the market economy – with the goal of maintaining steady growth, full employment, low inflation, currency stability, etc. Here we confront the advent of so-called "organized capitalism", a state of affairs that is typical of many modern societies today.

It is worth noting that neither Weber nor Schumpeter were able to anticipate many of the economically relevant developments that have occurred in the post-war era – such as "wage-earner funds", "sovereign wealth funds", compulsory superannuation, worker-participation, "just-in-time", "quality circles", workplace insurance, "corporatization" and "privatization" – to name but a few. Nor did they fully appreciate the significance of a development of widespread share ownership and the separation of ownership and control, classically analyzed by Berle and Means in *The Modern Corporation.* There are still other changes that were only partially foreseen by Weber and Schumpeter in their various writings, for example, the extensive development of the service economy or the large-scale investment by the state in education, training and research institutions.

It is probably fair to say that both Weber and Schumpeter overestimated the prospects of socialism insofar as they both thought that a socialist organization economy could be viable and, even in the case of Schumpeter, to a degree progressive. By "socialism" both Weber and Schumpeter assumed that, as a minimum, central control of the commanding heights of the economy and the elimination of private enterprise was entailed. Weber did not oppose socialism because it would necessarily lead to economic collapse and mass poverty but because of its likely negative impact on freedom and individualism. Although he had numerous forebodings about the prospects for human freedom in the case of the socialist experiment then unfolding in Russia, he could not foresee that the Soviet system would be as formidable as it turned out to be. Schumpeter had the benefit of living through the period when the horrors of the Stalinist terror were becoming known but still believed that socialism might eventually supplant capitalism. Of course, with the hindsight provided by the demise of the Soviet Union, we can now say that the appeal of socialism, while not completely moribund, no longer has the force it had during the twentieth century; thus, today a socialist transformation of any advanced capitalist economy seems an extremely unlikely prospect anywhere – that is, provided we do not regard welfare capitalism as a form of socialism. This is not to suggest that radical critiques of capitalism are no longer possible; these will no doubt continue as long as democratic freedoms survive. Nor do we wish to rule out that a renaissance of socialist thought and a revamped movement seeking fundamental social change in some form is just around the corner.[2]

But despite the novel developments mentioned above, we maintain that the basic mechanism of the capitalist system, operating on the basis of the private profit-making firm and oriented to market opportunities, remains essentially the dominant economic structure in the West and elsewhere. We say that the list of developments alluded to, some of which post-date the era of Weber and Schumpeter, do not alter the fundamentals as we have described them. For today, most progressive economic activity, not just in the West but also increasingly in the East Asian economies and elsewhere, is substantially oriented in a capitalist fashion in the sense conceptualized by Weber and Schumpeter. And further, such capitalism is not only already present or emergent in the developing world under the impact of globalization, but it is being actively encouraged and facilitated by all manner of policies and interests. For several decades now, the promotion of capitalism has been a key feature in a range of underdeveloped nations eager to grow and prosper, and these policies are strongly supported by international organizations such as the Organization for Economic Cooperation and Development, The European Economic Community, the World Bank, the International Monetary Fund and the World Trade Organization. The more influential leaders of developing countries and many of their intellectual elites seem to assume that, in one way or another, progress depends on the advance of a capitalistic business engine. It would appear that the socialist model of rapid economic development has now been largely abandoned in all but a few instances – contemporary China is a fascinating hybrid case that raises complicated questions of analysis and interpretation in this regard, but we cannot explore these for the moment. Of course, there are particular national characteristics and unique cultural factors that can be discerned in the various developing economies undergoing capitalist modernization that will determine more exactly how a particular society will foster business enterprise and organize its economy.

2 It is worth noting that trenchant critics of capitalism, such as Richard Westra, continue to believe Marx's analysis as set out in *Capital* remains the seminal text for the socialist critique of capitalism. This line of socialist thought regards the Soviet and Chinese experiments in central planning and socialist reconstruction to have been a fundamental misconception of what is required for the socialist transcendence of capitalism. See his analysis in his "Introduction" to Richard Westra, *Confronting Global Neoliberalism: Third World Resistance and Development Strategies*, Clarity, 2010.

The preconditions of capitalist development

Having suggested that there is a trend towards capitalism in third world nations, we must, however, qualify that claim, for there are important caveats that follow from Weber's theory. Given the historical analyses in *The Protestant Ethic, General Economic History* and *Economy and Society*, in particular, the argument that the genesis of modern capitalism was dependent on a unique set of preconditions, the question arises about the prospects for rational capitalism in societies that have not passed through an equivalent historical experience. That is, can societies that have not developed institutions similar to those of the premodern West expect to become capitalist in the same sense? Is it feasible that societies lacking a rational state apparatus and that have not instituted enforceable contract law can develop a rational capitalist system? Such societies, even if they have been touched by the forces of modernity to some degree and are linked into world trade and the international division of labour, may nonetheless remain stuck in a "half-way house" that is neither free market capitalism nor a premodern traditional economy. In many countries in Africa, South America and the Middle East one can only speak of a capitalist system in a limited sense, for with dictatorship, oppressive social conditions and a lack of political and civil rights, generally it is likely that the predominant form of capitalism will be based on the exploitation of political power (Weber's type of "political capitalism"). These societies may have segments of modern-type enterprise oriented to market opportunities – where for example Western-based companies pursue business along conventional lines, such as happens commonly with mining enterprises or plantations operating in the third world – but such societies are also likely to suffer the dominance of magnates who are essentially rent seekers.

In the case of Russia, we note that the economy has modernized to a degree without embracing a completely free market, largely through reliance on the export of its vast natural resources. The recent Russian experience is remarkable in a number of ways. It is apparent that the goal of setting up a private enterprise economy throughout the entire country was not only the first case in history of an attempt to bring about a capitalist market system after a period of socialism, it was also the first case of an attempt to introduce capitalism through a state orchestrated process of deliberate policymaking (Yeltsin).[3] Hitherto, all cases of society-wide market capitalism have emerged without a conscious program to achieve this outcome and have involved a long period of historical development. In the case of Russia, a capitalist economy was instituted in the immediate years after 1989 by government fiat, and as a first step, state assets were sold off on a massive scale. But the process has hardly achieved the goals its proponents set, and the rise of Putin and

3 On the institution of capitalism in Russia, see Anders Åslund, *How Russia became a Market Economy*, Brookings Institution, 1995, *Russia's Capitalist Revolution: Why Market Reform Succeeded and Democracy Failed*, Peterson Institute for International Economics, 2007 and Joseph R. Blasi, Kroumova Maya and Kruse Douglas, *Kremlin Capitalism: The Privatization of the Russian Economy*, ILR Press, 1997.

the so-called "oligarchs" has turned the course of economic development in a different direction. So will the Putin's quasi-dictatorial control and the domination of the "oligarchs" prevent the emergence of a private entrepreneurial economy in the same mould as the West? The present dismal performance of the Russian economy suggests that Russia will not achieve a vibrant capitalist economy for the foreseeable future.

Similar ambiguity to that referred to in relation to Russia attends the case of China; though in this instance, very high rates of economic growth have propelled it to a position that even rivals America and Japan. Since Deng Xiaoping's ascendency around 1978, the authorities have gradually fostered profit-oriented enterprise through various reforms. Turning away from the policy of autarky inspired by Mao, the authorities began to copy the approach of various newly industrialized economies such as South Korea, Taiwan, Hong Kong and Singapore, where high growth rates had become a regular feature. In 1979, China enacted the "Law of the Peoples' Republic of China Concerning Joint Ventures with Chinese and Foreign Investment" and also in order to attract foreign investment declared Guandong and Fujian provinces with "special policies and flexible measures".[4] Following this, Shenzhen next to Hong Kong, Zhuhai next to Macau and Santou were designated Special Export Zones (SEZ) with the charter that they experiment with a market-oriented economy ("with Chinese characteristics"). Other areas were subsequently designated SEZs, such as Xiamen near Taiwan, Hainan Island and Guangdong Province. Then in 1984, fourteen coastal cities, including Tianjin and Shanghai, were designated "open cities", and thereafter, numerous other areas received special designations designed to open the economies of these areas to foreign investment and market enterprise. From the inception of the SEZs, capital inflows became substantial and in the 1990s, they took off, with China becoming the second largest recipient of foreign investment capital in the world. At first, foreign investment was directed to labour-intensive light industry, but it has gradually shifted to capital- and technology-intensive sectors. In the second half of the 1990s, IT became the focus of investment. The modes of foreign investment have changed with time, beginning at first as contractual joint ventures, but now there are equity joint ventures and wholly owned foreign owned enterprises.[5] Undoubtedly China will continue to grow at a high rate for some time – because of its vast supply of cheap labour, its preparedness to ruthlessly exploit the natural environment, and its clever use of often pirated foreign technology – but without becoming a truly modern capitalist system. So can China develop an indigenous market economy that is not parasitic on the demand provided by American and European consumers? China seems poised between two possible courses of development: the

4 For an analysis of the legal basis of the reform, see William Jones (ed.), *Basic Principles of Civil Law in China*, Chapter Six.

5 On the development of capitalistic institutions in China see David Faure, *China and Capitalism: A History of Business Enterprise in Modern China*, Hong Kong University Press, 2006 and Rongxing Guo, *How the Chinese Economy Works*, Palgrave Macmillan, 2009.

rapid growth in exports in recent years would suggest it may eventually overtake the West as the largest economic system in the world, yet the extraordinary levels of corruption, the domination of the party apparatus, and the rise of the so-called "princelings" suggest that the system will not easily morph into a form of free market capitalism of the modern type. Crucially, the Chinese Communist Party remains very much in control.

The collapse of the Soviet Union and its socialist empire in 1989 was an event of epochal significance, because it appears to mark the end of an era in which many commentators, theorists and political movements took it for granted that sooner or later capitalism was doomed and the inevitable outcome of its demise would be socialism. The Soviet Union had been for many the vanguard of the world socialist movement, and it had fostered and sponsored socialist movements around the world. During the post-war era the so-called "transition to socialism" was an oft-discussed issue amongst the Left, and the goal of socialism was the expressed end of many social-democratic political parties. But post-1989, not only has the worldwide socialist movement significantly declined and socialism/communism all but disappeared from the political landscape, support for capitalism both in the former communist countries, in the democratic West and in many developing countries has grown beyond all expectations. This is not to say that capitalism is utterly ascendant in its pure free market form, for there are still many critics of the excesses of rampant capitalism who seek to limit the power of the dominant market players. But importantly, such criticisms, whether from either the left or the right of the political spectrum, now take it for granted that some version of a capitalist market system must remain as the basic economic structure of society. Thus it is today generally accepted that the material progress generated by the capitalist engine is socially desirable, despite the presence of negatives of various kinds such as inequality, consumerism, pollution, global warming, environmental degradation, exhaustion of resources, etc.[6] There are numerous other negative consequences of capitalist economic progress that might be cited – such as the obesity epidemic, the drug trade, the destruction of ethic identities, the homogenization of culture or the destruction of traditional cultures – features which might be said to have arisen directly from *too much* progress, too much disposable income and excessive consumption. But, on the other hand, the developing world is pleading for greater material progress and especially for improvements in welfare measures relating to health, education and housing that it is hardly possible to argue should not be met. Thus it has been universally recognized that enormous economic progress shown by China, especially since the late 1990s in bringing many millions of people out of poverty, is an achievement to be applauded. Clearly, balancing economic progress with its human costs remains an ongoing task for social and economic policy now and into the foreseeable future.

6 Of course, we note that some critics have argued that the world is heading for some kind of apocalypse collapse or even end because the unrestrained development of capitalism threatens the survival of human kind in various ways.

The continuing relevance of Schumpeter's theory of business cycles

As we have seen, a key claim of Schumpeter is that innovations occur in clusters and these produce spurts of economic development. He describes the overall outcome as manifesting wave-like patterns that can be discerned by statistical analysis of time series. In his historical analyses he highlighted the advent of steam power/railroadization and electrification as paradigmatic cases where initial inventions coupled with further innovations had far-reaching economic effects. Since Schumpeter's day, we can point to numerous other examples of this kind of clustering, and these are surely amenable to analysis in terms of wave-type patterns. Thus, for example, beginning with the development of the transistor in the 1950s, a whole host of novel products, processes and further innovations came rapidly into existence. Associated with the advent of the transistor were new consumer products, such as the transistor radio and other audio and communication equipment, and these were soon followed by the use of integrated circuits and lasers in electrical appliances such as televisions, stereos, telephones and then the personal computer. The advance of the computer found many applications in industry, such as robotics and computer numerical control machines. Further advances have been occasioned by intensive miniaturization and complexification. The mobile telephone, CD player, iPod, laptop, tablet computer and iPhone are the most well-known product innovations of this type, but the technology of using microprocessors is now ubiquitous and is utilized in almost every household, automotive or industrial application. Yet another advance is associated with the further development of the computer that followed approximately 20 years after its initial launch.

The full potential of the computer and perhaps the high point of its economic significance should probably be dated around 1995 when the internet became fully functional in its current form. This last innovation gave rise to many avenues of further enhancement, all dependent on exploiting the advantages this hyper-communication facilitates. These last include such things as ecommerce, email, advanced telephonics, video streaming, remote conferencing, information storage, word processing, document transfer, GPS, and "apps", to name but a few. And there are many related socio-economic impacts that are made possible from such advances, such as globalization of economic relations, language translation, internationalization of institutions, increased computing power for research purposes, not to mention benefits for business management, share trading, record keeping and accounting. There are obvious possibilities for new clusterings of innovation around the biotechnical advances associated with unravelling the mysteries of DNA and the discovery of the genetic code of living beings and organisms. Such innovations have many potential applications in novel areas, such as the production of new foods, new ways of growing foods, improving crop yields, new ways of producing fuels, and new forms of energy. There has been steady expansion of service industries with the rise of the middle classes and increased access to education and leisure opportunities. A notable field in which service industries have flourished is tourism. In some countries, tourism has become the single most important national income earner; related to the tourist industry are a whole series of related service industries such as the restaurant trade, resorts, eco-tourism, international transportation, trekking, education and sporting-related travel. As some economies have begun to decline significantly in terms of their manufacturing capacity, most noticeably in the first industrial nations such as England and now America and Australia, these countries are expanding their service industries. We see educational institutions in particular becoming a major source of national income, and in America, the entertainment industry in the form of television, film production and music are important industries.

Despite the prima facie success of the Schumpeterian system in explaining the phenomenon of economic growth, the question must nonetheless be put as to whether the advances of the type mentioned above are amenable to analysis in terms of the regular wave periods (Kondratieffs, Kitchins, Juglars) that Schumpeter believed are a regular feature of capitalism. The constant stream of advances associated with transistorization, miniaturization, integrated circuits and computerization, as well as so-called recent applications of nano- and biotechnology, might suggest that, rather than the clustering of innovations, there is a process of regular and continuous progress. In defence of Schumpeter, however, one can point to economic fluctuations and recent crises that appear to be correlated with the innovations of the type Schumpeter emphasized. Thus, we have seen major downturns in the economic performance of many companies and even whole economies following changes in technology – the dot.com bubble, the NASDAQ crash, the Asian Financial Crisis and the Global Financial Crisis. Of course, a thorough analysis of all these developments would require an exhaustive consideration of the empirical data and takes us beyond our brief for the moment.

The continuing relevance of Weber's work ethic

We believe that Weber's contribution to the understanding of the institutional basis of capitalism is not merely of consequence for historical understanding but remains relevant for understanding contemporary issues, especially regarding the role of work ethic. It is of more than passing interest that the term "work ethic" has become part of the vernacular of modern industrial society. We even find it used by sporting commentators and team coaches when they refer to the diligence with which players carry out their tasks on the field. Weber did not consider that the Protestant work ethic had ceased to be a factor in modern culture, though "the idea of duty in one's calling prowls about in our lives like the ghost of dead religious beliefs."[7] Weber's work ethic entailed more than the idea that capitalism requires devotion to hard work. Rather, Weber emphasized that what Protestantism encouraged was "rational labour in a calling", and this was

7 PE, p. 182.

to be understood as part of the rationalization of the conduct of life generally. Although he was primarily concerned with the origins of the modern work ethic, it is worth considering whether a given culture and its institutional structures inculcate and foster a work ethic of sufficient intensity to have an impact on capitalist life forms today. It has often been noted that depressed social groups, certain ethnic or religious groups, sometimes the work force of whole nations, fail to engender the cultural orientation and work discipline required by competitive market-oriented business. This is particularly apparent in the case of some non-Western societies, where cultural practices are conditioned by religious or traditional values that do not value methodical work and have no concept of the professional vocation.

In the case of an economy like that of modern China, its high economic growth and the evident industriousness of its working population are indications that a work ethic of some form is operative. Whether this can be described as a work ethic in the sense of a sense of duty to a calling is, however, doubtful. Perhaps the disposition of the Chinese for hard work is partly reactive and can be attributed to a more basic concern with economic survival. In an environment still influenced by the legacy of the Maoist-inspired stringencies people know that extreme poverty and even starvation may not be far off; once a market system was partially introduced in the 1990s after the reforms of Deng Xiaoping, the forces suddenly unleashed seem to have promoted a highly competitive and materialistic ethos, in which the pursuit of economic success, ostentatious consumption and, amongst the elite, the cultivation of luxury have become common features. A different outcome is perhaps illustrated by the case of Russia, whose communist regime engendered a kind of survival ethic wherein intense work effort was only capable of being exacted from the population by more or less brutal means. Now that this system has collapsed and a kind of quasi-capitalism has come into being, the motivation to work lacks any intensity, because under the extremely corrupt circumstances prevailing, it is uncertain whether the financial rewards an individual can expect from work will bear any relation to the effort put in. This is a consequence of the fact that workers are often not paid their nominal wages, or they have their earnings frittered away by inflation or various forms of criminal extortion and so on.

In the advanced West, Weber's work ethic has perhaps found a new lease on life in the movement to reform business management in accord with ethical principles. This has arisen in part in reaction to various forms of corporate malfeasance – such as tax evasion, false advertising, planned obsolescence, bribery and exorbitant executive salary payments, not to mention the outright fraudulent conduct of those financial brokers that triggered to the so-called Global Financial Crisis. Related to this is the growth of business studies as an academic discipline and the teaching of "business ethics", both of which seek to infuse the acquisitive orientation with a vocational ethos grounded in part on ethical norms. However, these movements are to a degree at variance with the imperatives of impersonal competition enjoined by the logic of market struggle under capitalist conditions.

Financial capitalism

In September 2008, the failure of the investment bank Lehman Brothers was the trigger for the collapse of many other large financial institutions in America and elsewhere, a cascading series of events that has been dubbed the Global Financial Crisis.[8] This threatened a worldwide recession that, for a time, was feared might become a depression of cataclysmic proportions. The fact that such an event as the Global Financial Crisis occurred does not surprise the student of Schumpeter for whom economic crises are all but inevitable and, in one way or another, are merely a manifestation of the business cycle phenomenon. Nonetheless, a number of commentators believe there are novel features of the recent crisis that require a more critical analysis of the role of finance and banking.

Numerous commentators have analyzed the enormous expansion of the financial sector in modern economies and the related growth of credit. Richard Duncan, for example argues that abandoning the gold backing of the dollar around 1964 ushered in an era of extraordinary credit growth in America. From 1964 to 2007, he says credit underwent a 50-fold increase, and this is what largely fuelled the profitability and prosperity of the intervening years. Duncan charts the historical course of this explosion in credit, a phenomenon he cryptically encapsulates with the term "creditopia". He points out that in 1945 the largest debtor in the United States by far was the government, which held 71%, whereas the corporate sector had 13%, the household sector 8% and the financial sector (defined as including government-secured enterprises like Fannie Mae and Freddie Mac, commercial banks, issuers of asset-backed securities, finance companies, funding corporations and savings institutions) a mere 1% of all debt. By 2007, these proportions had radically changed: government debt had declined to merely 10% of total credit market debt, while the household sector had increased to 28%, and the financial sector had surged to 32%. The increase in government-backed mortgage pools accounted for a very large part of these increases. According to Duncan, "relative to the overall size of the economy, the financial sector's debt rose from 21 percent of GDP in 1980 to 116 percent in 2007. The household sector's debt rose from 50 percent to 98 percent of GDP over the same period."[9] Duncan tells us that related to this is the fact that, "more than two million manufacturing jobs (or 15% percent of the total) have been lost since the end of 2007. Nearly a third of all U.S. manufacturing jobs have disappeared over the last ten years."[10] So the United States continues to operate by increasing its imports of goods from overseas, especially from China, and to purchase these and to maintain current living standards, the government and consumers increasingly borrow the required funds with a serious question over whether the debt can ever be repaid.

8 For an account of the crisis see Geoffrey Ingram, *Capitalism*, Polity, 2008, pp. 227–64.

9 Richard Duncan, *The New Depression: The Breakdown of the Paper Money Economy*, Wiley, 2012, pp. 36–7.

10 Ibid., p. 104.

A complementary account of the growth of the financial sector in the United States' economy is that of Greta Krippner, who describes the process as one of "financialization". She notes that there are two senses in which financialization (in which she includes insurance and real estate) is occurring: there has been a significant growth in the profits of the financial sector as such; and non-financial firms increasing rely on financial activities to augment their profits. She notes that the massive expansion of credit in the United Sates has "contributed to increased interest rate volatility, further engorging the financial sector institutions that peddled interest rate swaps, derivatives and securitized transactions. In short, under financialization, the endless expansion of credit, increased volatility in the economy, and the growth of financial activities became locked in a tight embrace."[11]

There are many critiques of the economic turn described by Duncan, Krippner and others, a development associated with other changes that leftist authors now typically describe as the era of "neo-liberalism". These critical analyses usually date the rise of neo-liberalism in the 1970s with the oil crisis; after which came a spate of neo-conservative leaders, such as Reagan, Kohl and Thatcher, who partially reversed the movement towards increasing Keynesian-style state intervention and expanding welfare.[12] Though in the period in question capitalism in the West has broadly managed to achieve steady growth, neo-Marxists such as Richard Westra, Robert Albritton and Moishe Postone continue to rail against the evils of the market economy now operating on a global stage, arguing variously that the greater the "success" the worse it really is.[13] Westra has gone further than most in his condemnation of what he terms the "evil axis of finance", by which he means the financial entanglement of the United States, Japan and China that has emerged under the manipulating control of Wall Street. He writes, "The rise of the evil axis of finance is . . . the condition of possibility for the transubstantiation of the US into a global economy. Without the evil axis of finance and impelling of the world's idle dollars to the US T-bill IOU's and other dollar denominated savings, to then be reincarnated by Wall Street for its sinister purposes, the US will have to seek out a wholly new economic orientation."[14] Westra explores the nature of the three-way trade connections between the US, Japan and China at length and points to the root cause of this being the exhaustion of the old form of capitalism that was based on the mass production of material goods. According to Westra, capitalism is no longer self-supporting and increasingly relies on the state to prevent its

11 Greta Krippner, *Capitalizing on Crisis: The Political Origins of the Rise of Finance*, Harvard University Press, 2011, p. 56. For an interesting account of the emergence of a culture of finance, which explores the relation of stock trading to gambling, see Marieke de Goede, *Virtue, Fortune, and Faith: A Genealogy of Finance*, University of Minnesota, 2005.

12 See for example Monica Prasad, *The Politics of Free Markets: The Rise of Neoliberal Economic Policies in Britain, France, Germany and the United States*, University of Chicago, 2007.

13 See the collection edited by Robert Albritton, Bob Jessop and Richard Westra, *Political Economy of Global Capitalism: The 21st Century, Present and Future*, Anthem, 2010.

14 Richard Westra, *The Evil Axis of Finance: The US-Japan-China Stranglehold on the Global Future*, Clarity, 2012, p. 209.

collapse. But further, the exhaustion of capitalism is evidenced by "the demise of the production-centred society itself",[15] with fewer and fewer people engaged in civilian manufacturing employment.

Here we cannot pursue the many issues raised by the decline in manufacturing, the rise of finance, the global financial crisis and so forth for the moment, but a few comments in relation to our thesis are needed. First, it is apparent from the analyses of Duncan and others that much of the prosperity of the Unites States since World War II has been driven directly by the expansion of credit and the financial sector. It is worth noting that such a connection is what we might expect from Schumpeter's emphasis on the role of credit creation in the genesis of capitalist prosperity. Further, the genesis of crises as a result of excessive confidence in the continuing expansion of profit opportunities is also a feature that a Schumpeterian perspective would see as "typical". But what is not anticipated in Schumpeter's theory is that the excessive creation of credit by financial institutions and new types of financial dealing and market manipulation would be the determinant of the system crisis; for Schumpeter presupposes that the expansionary phase that eventually busts is driven by production enterprises in the real economy. But in the present situation of the United States and to a degree elsewhere, it appears that the financial sector has taken the lead in developing new strategies of investment – with devices like forwards, derivatives, options, swaps, leveraged buyouts, arbitrage, margin calls and hedging – to pursue profits in fields quite removed from direct industrial production.

Some commentators suggest that the present forms of financial dealing are unprecedented in the extent to which stock market transactions, in particular, have been uncoupled from the exchange of goods in the real economy. Joseph Vogl has explored this idea at some length. He quotes a passage from Weber's early essay on the stock exchange, which describes the way in which futures trading "circumvents both the physical conditions of production and the material conditions of transfer and transportation":

> A deal is struck over a set of goods that are not present, and are often "in transit" somewhere, or yet-to-be produced; and it takes place between a buyer who usually does not himself wish to "own" these goods (in any regular fashion) but who wishes – if possible before he receives them and pays for them – to pass them along for profit, and a seller, who usually does not yet have those goods, usually has not produced them, but wishes to furnish them for some earnings of his own.

Vogl comments on this ephemeral character of the futures trade as follows:

> The dynamics of futures trading – the driving force and the crux of the capitalist economy – thus depends on two central functional elements. The first

15 Ibid., p. 177.

> of these is the self-referential communication: prices refer not to goods and products but to prices themselves; prices for things that are not currently to hand are calculated on the basis of price forecasts for things that will not be to hand in the future. Prices are paid with prices. Prices are themselves commodities, freed from the burden of inconveniences that encumber material possession, and they might rightly be classified as self-referential market events. . . . Where the criterion for distinguishing between real and imaginary value no longer applies, and where hedging (or trade with financial derivatives), not only requires investment in risk (and thus more trade with financial derivatives), not only does investment become indistinguishable from speculation but both gain a new lease of life . . . speculation now no longer differs from its former antitheses, whether trade on the one hand or gambling and bettering on the other.[16]

The most articulate account of the rationality of derivatives and futures trading is probably that provided by Merton Miller, famous not only for receiving with Myron Scholes the 1997 Nobel Prize for economics but equally notorious for his role in the development of the hedge fund called Long-Term Capital Management (LTCM).[17] In 1994, Miller and Scholes, in cooperation with Salomon Brothers, set up LTCM and commenced to trade with a global focus in the area of arbitrage. They began with a starting capital of US$3 billion, and by 1995 LTCM was returning to investors profits in the order of 40%. However, owing to Russia's default in 1998, LTCM suffered a catastrophic reversal, losing US$500 million in a single day. Despite the glowing endorsement accompanying their award of the Nobel Prize, that by using their technique of dynamic hedging in futures trading traders could effectively eliminate risks, LTCM eventually collapsed and became bankrupt in 2000. This collapse, however, was not an exceptional event, as many other financial institutions copied the model of LTCM and its approach was arguably responsible for the later collapse of Enron and others.

But regardless of the LTCM debacle, Miller is also a prolific writer and cogent analyst of the financial scene.[18] Despite the salutary saga of LTCM, Miller argues that the new forms of trading using derivatives and hedging are, in principle, perfectly valid as instruments of financial management. He explains that once the potential for risk management was seen, "Option-like structures were soon seen to be lurking everywhere. . . . The future is uncertain . . . and in an uncertain environment, having the flexibility to decide what to do after some of that uncertainty is resolved definitely has value. Option-pricing theory provides the means for assessing that value."[19]

16 Joseph Vogl, *The Spectre of Capital: Cultural Memory in the Present*, Stanford University, 2010, pp. 66–7.

17 I rely on de Goede, *Virtue, Fortune, and Faith* for the following account: pp. 125–43.

18 See the collection Merton Miller, *Merton Miller on Derivatives*, Wiley, 1997.

19 Cited in de Goede, *Virtue, Fortune, and Faith*, p. 140.

Here we cannot resolve the truth of the conflicting claims of Vogl and Merton as to whether modern finance has taken capitalism to a new stage altogether beyond the models developed by Weber and Schumpeter. Clearly the issue of finance is central to the story of capitalism and no doubt there are important elements of continuity however much there are novel developments.

Bibliography

Adorno, Theodor, and Max Horheimer, *The Dialectics of Enlightenment*, Stanford University Press, 2002.

Albritton, Robert, Bob Jessop, and Richard Westra, *Political Economy and Global Capitalism: The 21st Century, Present and Future*, Anthem, 2010.

Andersen, Esben Sloth, *Evolutionary Economics: Post-Schumpeterian Contributions*, Pinter, 1994.

Andersen, Esben Sloth, Joseph A. Schumpeter: *A Theory of Social and Economic Evolution*, Palgrave, 2011.

Antonio, Robert J., and Ronald M. Glassman, *A Weber-Marx Dialogue*, University Press of Kansas, 1985.

Åslund, Anders, *How Russia Became a Market Economy*, Brookings Institution, 1995.

Åslund, Anders, *Russia's Capitalist Revolution: Why Market Reform Succeeded and Democracy Failed*, Peterson Institute for International Economics, 2007.

Backhaus, Jürgen, Joseph Alois Schumpeter: *Entrepreneurship, Style and Vision*, Kluwer, 2003.

Barbalet, Jack, We*ber, Passion and Profits: "The Protestant Ethic and the Spirit of Capitalism" in Context*, Cambridge University Press, 2008.

Bell, Daniel, *The Cultural Contradictions of Capitalism*, Basic Books, 1976.

Bellofiore, Riccardo, "Money and Development in Schumpeter", *Review of Radical Political Economics* 17 (1985), pp. 21–40.

Bendix, Rheinhard, *Max Weber: An Intellectual Portait*, Methuen and Co., 1966.

Bergloìf, Erik, Andrei Kunov, Julia Shvets, and Ksenia Yudaeva, *The New Political Economy of Russia*, The MIT Press, 2003.

Bittman, Michael, "A Bourgeois Marx? Max Weber's Theory of Capitalist Society: Reflections on Utility, Rationality and Class Formation", *Thesis Eleven* 15 (1986), pp. 81–91.

Blasi, Joseph R., Kroumova Maya, and Kruse Douglas, *Kremlin Capitalism: The Privatization of the Russian Economy*, ILR Press, 1997.

Blaug, Mark, *Economic Theory in Retrospect*, Cambridge University Press, 1985.

Bloch, Henri-Simon, "Carl Menger: The Founder of the Austrian School", *Journal of Political Economy* 40, June (1940), pp. 428–33.

Böhm Bawerk, Eugen, *Capital and Interest: A Critical History of Economical Theory*, Kelley & Millman, 1957.

Bottomore, Tom, "The Decline of Capitalism, Sociologically Considered", in Arnold Heerjie (ed.), *Schumpeter's Vision*, Praeger, 1981, pp. 22–44.

Bottomore, Tom, *Between Marginalism and Marxism: The Economic Sociology of J.A. Schumpeter*, Harvester Wheatsheaf, 1992.

Boycko, Maxim, Andrei Shleifer, and Robert Vishny, *Privatizing Russia*, MIT Press, 1995.
Boyle, Elizabeth, and Stephen J. Mezias, *Organizational Dynamics of Creative Destruction: Entrepreneurship and the Emergence of Industries*, Palgrave Macmillan, 2002.
Braverman, Harry, *Labor and Monopoly Capital: The Degradation of Work in the Twentieth Century*, Monthly Review Press, 1974.
Brouwer, Maria, *Schumpeterian Puzzles: Technological Competition and Economic Evolution*, Harvester Wheatsheaf, 1991.
Bruun, Hans Henrik, *Science, Values and Politics in Max Weber's Methodology*, Ashgate, 2007.
Burger, Thomas, *Max Weber's Theory of Concept Formation; History, Laws and Ideal Types*, Duke, 1976.
Busch, Ulrich, "Joseph A. Schumpeter's 'Soziologie des Geldes'", in Jürgen Backhaus (ed.), *Joseph Alois Schumpeter: Entrepreneurship, Style and Vision*, Kluwer, 2003, pp. 191–202.
Cairncross, Alec, *The Managed Economy*, Blackwell, 1970.
Caldwell, Bruce J., Carl Menger, and Mason Barnett, *Carl Menger and His Legacy in Economics*, Duke University Press, 1990.
Camic, Charles, Philip S. Gorski, and David M. Trubeck, *Max Weber's Economy and Society: A Critical Companion*, Stanford University Press, 2005.
Carlin, Edward, "Schumpeter's Constructed Type: The Entrepreneur", *Kyklos* 9.1 (1956), pp. 27–43.
Chalcraft, David, and Austin Harrington, *The Protestant Ethic Debate: Weber's Replies to His Critics, 1907–1910*, Liverpool University Press, 2001.
Chamberlin, Edward H., "The Origin and Early Development of Monopolistic Competition Theory", *The Quarterly Journal of Economics* 75.4 (1961), pp. 515–43.
Chamberlin, Edward H., "The Impact of Recent Monopoly Theory on the Schumpeterian System", in Seymour Edwin Harris (ed.), *Schumpeter, Social Scientist*. Harvard University Press, 1951, pp. 83–88.
Clarke, Simon, *Marx, Marginalism and Modern Society from Adam Smith to Max Weber*, Macmillan, 1991.
Cleary, M. N., and G. D. Hobbs, "The Fifty Year Cycles: A Look at the Empirical Evidence", in Christopher Freeman (ed.), *Long Waves in the World Economy*, Frances Pinter, 1984.
Clemence, Richard V., and Francis S. Doody, *The Schumpeterian System*, Addison-Wesley Press, 1950.
Clemence, Richard V., *Essays of J.A. Schumpeter*, Addison-Wesley, 1951.
Coe, Richard, and Charles Wilbur, *Capitalism and Democracy: Schumpeter Revisited*, University of Notre Dame, 1985.
Cohen, Jere, Lawrence. Hazelrigg, and William. Pope, "De-Parsonizing Weber: A Critique of Parsons' Interpretation of Weber's Sociology", *American Sociological Review* 40.2 (1975), pp. 229–41.
Collins, Randall, "Weber's Last Theory of Capitalism: A Systematization", *American Sociological Review* 45, December (1980), pp. 925–42.
Collins, Randall, *Weberian Sociological Theory*, Cambridge University Press, 1986.
Cooper, George, *The Origin of Financial Crises: Central Banks, Credit Bubbles and the Efficient Market Fallacy*, Harriman House, 2008.
Crafts, Nicolas, and Gianni Toniolo, *Economic Growth in Europe since 1945*, Cambridge University Press, 1996.
Crone, Patricia, *Slaves on Horses: The Evolution of the Islamic*, Polity Cambridge University Press, 1980.

Davis, H. B., "Schumpeter as Sociologist", *Science and Society* 24.1 (1960), pp. 13–35.

de Goede, Marieke, *Virtue, Fortune, and Faith: A Genealogy of Finance*, University of Minnesota, 2005.

De Vries, Jan, *The Economy of Europe in an Age of Crisis, 1600–1750*, Cambridge University Press, 1976.

Diggins, John P., *Max Weber: Politics and the Spirit of Tragedy*, Basic Books, 1996.

Duiji, Jacob van, *The Long Wave in Economic Life*, Allen & Unwin, 1983.

Duijn, Jacob van, "Fluctuations in Innovation over Time", in Christopher Freeman (ed.), *Long Waves in the World Economy*, Frances Pinter, 1984, pp. 19–30.

Duncan, Richard, *The Corruption of Capitalism*, CLSA Books, 2009.

Duncan, Richard, *The New Depression: The Breakdown of the Paper Money Economy*, Wiley, 2012.

Eliaeson, Sven, *Max Weber's Methodologies: Interpretation and Critique*, Polity, 2002.

Elias, Norbert, *The Civilizing Process*, Blackwell, 1978.

Elliott, John, "Marx and Schumpeter on Capitalism's Creative Destruction", *The Quarterly Journal of Economics*, August (1980), 95(1), pp. 45–68.

Ellman, Michael, and Vladimir Kontorovich, *The Disintegration of the Soviet Economic System*, Routledge, 1992.

Endres, Anthony, *Neoclassical Microeconomic Theory: The Founding Austrian Version*, Routledge, 1997.

Engels, Friedrich, "On Authority", in *Marx and Engels: Collected Works*, Vol. 1, Moscow, 1950, pp. 575–78.

Faure, David, *China and Capitalism: A History of Business Enterprise in Modern China*, Hong Kong University Press, 2006.

Flora, Peter, and Arnold J. Heidenheimer, *The Development of Welfare States in Europe and America*, Transaction Books, 1981.

Fraser, Derek, *The Evolution of the British Welfare State*, Macmillan, 1973.

Freeman, Christopher (ed.), *Long Waves in the World Economy*, Frances, Pinter, 1984.

Frieden, Jeffrey, *Global Capitalism: Its Fall and Rise in the Twentieth Century*, Norton, 2006.

Frisch, Helmut, *Schumpeterian Economics*, Praeger, 1981.

Galbraith, John Kenneth, *The New Industrial State*, Houghton Mifflin, 1967.

Garrison, Roger, "Austrian Capital Theory: The Early Controversies", *History of Political Economy* 22 (1990), pp. 133–154.

Gerth, Hans, and C. Wright Mills, *From Max Weber: Essays in Sociology*, Routledge & Kegan Paul, 1948 (FMW).

Ghosh, Peter, "Capitalism and *Herrschaft*: Max Weber in St. Louis", in Peter Ghosh (ed.), *A Historian Reads Max Weber*, Harrassowitz Verlag, 2008, pp. 119–70.

Ghosh, Peter, "'Robinson Crusoe', the *Isolated Economic Man*: Marginal Utility Theory and the 'Spirit' of Capitalism", in Peter Ghosh (ed.), *A Historian Reads Max Weber*, Harrassowitz Verlag, 2008, pp. 269–97.

Ghosh, Peter, *Max Weber and the Protestant Ethic: Twin Histories*, Oxford University Press, 2014.

Ghosh, Peter, "A Situation Report *c.* 1897", in Peter Ghosh (ed.), *Max Weber and the Protestant Ethic: Twin Histories*, Oxford University Press, 2014, pp. 12–30.

Giddens, Anthony, *Capitalism and Social Theory*, Cambridge University Press, 1975.

Gilpin, Robert, *The Challenge of Global Capitalism: The World Economy in the 21st. Century*, Princeton University Press, 2000.

Glassman, Ronald, and Vatro Murvar, *Max Weber's Political Philosophy: A Pessimistic Vision of a Rationalized World*, Greenwood, 1984.
Gordon, Barry, *Economic Analysis before Adam Smith: Hesiod to Lessius*, Barnes & Noble Books, 1975.
Gordon, Robert, "Current Research in Business Cycles", *American Economic Review*, May XXXIX, (1949), pp. 47–63.
Gough, J. W., *The Rise of the Entrepreneur*, Schocken Books, 1970.
Graham, Cosmo, "The Bank of England, the City and the Reform of the Stock Exchange: Continuing the Self-Regulatory Community?", *Northern Ireland Legal Quarterly* 36.2 (1985), pp. 122–44.
Guo, Rongxing, *How the Chinese Economy Works*, Palgrave Macmillan, 2009.
Haberler, Gotttfried, "Joseph Alois Schumpeter", *The Quarterly Journal of Economics* 64.3 (1950), pp. 333–72.
Haberler, Gotttfried, "Schumpeter's *Capitalism, Socialism and Democracy* after Forty Years", in Arnold Heerjie (ed.), *Schumpeter's Vision*, Praeger, 1981, pp. 69–94.
Habermas, Jürgen, *Knowledge and Human Interests*, Beacon, 1971.
Habermas, Jürgen, *The Theory of Communicative Action: Reason and the Rationalization of Society*, Beacon, 1984.
Hammond, Peter, "Must Monopoly Power Accompany Innovation?", in Christian Seidl (ed.), *Lectures on Schumpeterian Economics: Schumpeter Centenary Memorial Lectures*, Springer-Verlag, 1984.
Hansen, Alvin, "Schumpeter's Contribution to Business Cycle Theory", in Seymour Edwin (ed.), Harris. *Schumpeter, Social Scientist*, Harvard University Press, 1951.
Hanusch, Horst, *Evolutionary Economics: Applications of Schumpeter's Ideas*, Cambridge University Press, 1988.
Harris, Ron, "Spread of Legal Innovations Defining Private and Public Domains", in Charles Camic, Philip S. Gorski, and David M. Trubeck (eds.), *Max Weber's Economy and Society: A Critical Companion*, Stanford University Press, 2005, pp. 127–68.
Harris, Seymour Edwin, *Schumpeter, Social Scientist*, Harvard University Press, 1951.
Hayek, Friedrich A. von, *The Road to Serfdom*, University of Chicago Press, 1944.
Hayek, Friedrich A. von, *Individualism and Economic Order*, University of Chicago Press, 1996.
Heertje, Arnold, "Schumpeter's Model of the Decay of Capitalism", in Helmut Frisch (ed.), *Schumpeterian Economics*, Praeger, 1981, pp. 84–94.
Heertje, Arnold (ed.), *Schumpeter's Vision*, Praeger, 1981.
Heertje, Arnold, and Mark Perlman, *Evolving Technology and Market Structure: Studies in Schumpeterian Economics*, University of Michigan Press, 1990.
Hennis, Wilhelm, *Max Weber: Essays in Reconstruction*, Allen & Unwin, 1988.
Hennis, Wilhelm, and Keith Tribe, *Max Weber's Central Question*, Threshold, 2000.
Hicks, John, *Capital and Growth*, Oxford University Press, 1965.
Hicks, John, and Wilhelm Weber, *Carl Menger and the Austrian School of Economics*, Clarendon Press, 1973.
Hicks, John, *The Crisis in Keynesian Economics*, Basic Books, 1974.
Hindess, Barry (ed.), *Sociological Theories of the Economy*, Macmillan, 1977.
Holton, Robert, *Cities, Capitalism, and Civilization*, Allen & Unwin, 1986.
Holton, Robert, and Bryan S. Turner, *Max Weber on Economy and Society*, Routledge, 1989.
Holton, Robert, *Economy and Society*, Routledge, 1992.

Horwitz, Morton, "The Historical Foundations of Modern Contract Law", *Harvard Law Review* 87.5 (1974), pp. 917–56.
Huff, Toby E., *Max Weber and the Methodology of the Social Sciences*, Transaction Books, 1984.
Huff, Toby E., *Max Weber and Islam: Interpretations and Critiques*, Transaction, 1999.
Hughes, Jonathan R. T., *The Vital Few: American Economic Progress and Its Protagonists*, Houghton Mifflin, 1965.
Hunt, Bishop, *The Development of the Business Corporation in England: 1800–1867*, Harvard University Press, 1936.
Huxley, Julian, *Evolution: The Modern Synthesis*, Allen & Unwin, 1944.
Ingham, Geoffrey, *The Nature if Money*, Polity, 2004.
Ingham, Geoffrey, *Capitalism*, Polity, 2008.
Jaffé, William, "Walras's Theory of *Tâtonnement*: A Critique of Recent Interpretations", *Journal of Political Economy* 75 February (1967), pp. 1–19.
Jaffé, William, and Donald Walker (ed.), *William Jaffé's Essays on Walras*, Cambridge University Press, 1983.
Jaspers, Karl, *Karl Jaspers on Max Weber*, Paragon, 1989.
Jones, Bryn, "Economic Action and Rational Organization in the Sociology of Weber", in Barry Hindess (ed.), *Sociological Theories of the Economy*, Macmillan, 1977, pp. 28–65.
Jones, Eric, *The European Miracle: Environments, Economies, and Geopolitics in the History of Europe and Asia*, Cambridge University Press, 1981.
Jones, William (ed.), *Basic Principles of Civil Law in China*, Sharpe, 1989.
Kaebler, Lutz, "Introduction" to Max Weber (ed.), *The History of Commercial Partnerships in the Middle Ages*, Rowman & Littlefileld, 2003, pp. 1–48.
Kagarlitsky, Boris, *Russia under Yeltsin and Putin: Neo-Liberal Autocracy*, Pluto Press, 2002.
Kalberg, Stephen, *Max Weber's Comparative-Historical Sociology*, University of Chicago Press, 1994.
Kalberg, Steven, "The Search for Thematic Orientations in a Fragmented Oeuvre: The Discussion of Max Weber's Recent Sociological Literature", *Sociology* 13.1 (1979), pp. 127–39.
Kalberg, Steven, "Max Weber's Types of Rationality: Cornerstones for the Analysis of Rationalization Processes in History", *American Journal of Sociology* 85.3 (1980), pp. 1145–79.
Kamien, Morton I., and Nancy Lou Schwartz, *Market Structure and Innovation*, Cambridge University Press, 1982.
Käsler, Dirk, *Max Weber: An Introduction to His Life and Work*, Polity, 1998.
Keynes, John Maynard, *A Treatise on Money*, Harcourt, Brace and Company, 1930.
Keynes, John Maynard, *The General Theory of Employment, Interest, and Money*, Palgrave Macmillan, 2007.
Klebnikov, Paul, *Godfather of the Kremlin: Boris Berezovsky and the Looting of Russia*, Harcourt, 2000.
Kleinknecht, Alfred, "Observations on the Schumpeterian Swarming of Innovations", in Christopher Freeman (ed.), *Long Waves in the World Economy*, Frances Pinter, 1984.
Kleinknecht, Alfred, *Innovation Patterns in Crisis and Prosperity: Schumpeter's Long Cycle Reconsidered*, Palgrave Macmillan, 1987.
Kondratieff, Nikolai., "Die Langen Wellen der Konjunktur", *Archiv für Sozialwissenschaft und Sozialpolitik* 56 (1926), pp. 573–609.

Koppl, Roger, Jack Birner, and Peter Klitgaard, *Austrian Economics and Entrepreneurial Studies*, JAI, 2003.
Krippner, Greta, *Capitalizing on Crisis: The Political Origins of the Rise of Finance*, Harvard University Press, 2011.
Krüger, Dieter, "Max Weber and the Younger Generation in the Verein für Sozialpolitik", in Wolfgang J. Mommsen, and Jürgen Osterhammel (eds.), *Max Weber and His Contemporaries*, Allen & Unwin, 1987, pp. 71–87.
Kuznets, Simon, "Schumpeter's Business Cycles", *American Economic Review* 30.2 (1940), pp. 257–71.
Langlois, Richard N., Th*e Dynamics of Industrial Capitalism: Schumpeter, Chandler, and the New Economy*, Routledge, 2007.
Lardy, Nicholas R., *China in the World Economy*, Institute for International Economics, 1994.
Lardy, Nicholas R., *China's Unfinished Economic Revolution*, Brookings Institution, 1998.
Lasch, Scott, and John Urry, *The End of Organized Capitalism*, Polity, 1987.
Lassman, Peter, and Ronald Spiers (eds.), *Max Weber's Political Writings*, Cambridge University Press, 1994.
Lehmann, Hartmut, and Guenther Roth, *Weber's Protestant Ethic: Origins, Evidence, Contexts*, German Historical Institute, 1993.
Leontief, Wassily, "Joseph A. Schumpeter (1883–1950)", *Econometrica* 18.2 (1950), pp. 103–10.
Lindberg, Léon N., *Stress and Contradiction in Modern Capitalism: Public Policy and Theory of the State*, Lexington Books, 1975.
Lipsom, Ephraim, *The Economic History of England*, Adam & Charles Black, 1971.
Listition, Steven, "Historical Preface to Max Weber', 'Stock and Commodity Exchanges'", *Theory and Society* 29 (2000), pp. 289–304.
Love, John, "Max Weber's and the Theory of Ancient Capitalism", *History and Theory* 25.2 (1986), pp. 153–72.
Love, John, *Antiquity and Capitalism: Max Weber and the Sociological Origins of Roman Civilization*, Routledge, 1991.
Love, John, "Developmentalism in Max Weber's Sociology of Religion: A Critique of F. H. Tenbruck", *European Journal of Sociology* 34 (1993), pp. 339–69.
Love, John. "Max Weber's Ancient Judaism", in Stephen P. Turner (ed.), *The Cambridge Companion to Weber*, Cambridge University Press, 2000, pp. 172–99.
Love, John, "Max Weber's Orient", in Stephen P. Turner (ed.), *The Cambridge Companion to Weber*, Cambridge University Press, 2000, pp. 200–22.
Löwith, Karl, *Max Weber and Karl Marx*, Allen & Unwin, 1982.
Maddison, Angus, *Phases of Capitalist Development*, Oxford University Press, 1982.
Maddison, Angus, *Dynamic Forces in Capitalist Development: A Long-Run Comparative View*, Oxford University Press, 1991.
Maier, Charles S., *Dissolution: The Crisis of Communism and the End of East Germany*, Princeton University Press, 1997.
Marcuse, Herbert, *One-Dimensional Man*, Beacon, 1964.
Marcuse, Herbert, *Negations: Essays in Critical Theory*, Beacon Press, 1968.
Marget, Arthur, "The Monetary Aspects of the Schumpeterian System", in Seymour Edwin Harris (ed.), *Schumpeter, Social Scientist*, Harvard University Press, 1951, pp. 62–71.
Marshall, Alfred, *Principles of Economics*, Macmillan, 1961.
Marshall, Gordon, *In Search of the Spirit of Capitalism*, Hutchinson, 1981.

Mayr, Ernst, *The Growth of Biological Thought: Diversity Evolution and Inheritance*, Belknap, 1982.

McCraw, Thomas K., *Prophet of Innovation: Joseph Schumpeter and Creative Destruction*, Harvard University Press, 2007.

McGregor, Richard, *The Party: The Secret World of China's Communist Rulers*, Harper, 2012.

Mensche, Gerard, Charles Coutinho, and Klaus Kaasch, "Changing Capital Values and the Propensity to Innovate", in Christopher Freeman (ed.), *Long Waves in the World Economy*, Frances Pinter, 1984, pp. 31–47.

Miller, Merton, *Merton Miller on Derivatives*, Wiley, 1997.

Mitchell, Wesley C., *Business Cycles: The Problem and Its Setting*, National Bureau of Economic Research, 1927.

Mitzman, Arthur, *Sociology and Estrangement: Three Sociologists of Imperial Germany*, Knopf, 1973.

Mokyr, Joel, *The Enlightened Economy: Britain and the Industrial Revolution: 1700–1850*, Penguin, 2009.

Mommsen, Wolfgang J., *The Emergence of the Welfare State in Britain and Germany*, Croom Helm, 1981.

Mommsen, Wolfgang J., *Max Weber and German Politics*, University of Chicago Press, 1984.

Mommsen, Wolfgang J., and Jürgen Osterhammel (eds.), *Max Weber and His Contemporaries*, Allen & Unwin, 1987.

Mommsen, Wolfgang J., *The Political and Social Theory of Max Weber: Collected Essays*, Polity, 1989.

Mulgan, Geoff, T*he Locust and the Bee: Predators and Creators in Capitalism's Future*, Princeton University Press, 2013.

Musgrave, Richard, "Schumpeter's Crisis of the Tax State: An Essay in Fiscal Sociology", *Journal of Evolutionary Economics* 2.2 (1992), pp. 89–113.

Myint, Hla, *Theories of Welfare Economics*, Kelley, 1965.

Nathan, Andrew J., Tianjian Shi, and Helena V. S. Ho, *China's Transition*, Columbia University Press, 1997.

Neal, Larry, *The Rise of Financial Capitalism: International Capital Markets in the Age of Reason*, Cambridge University Press, 1990.

Neal, Larry, and Jeffrey Williamson (eds.), *The Cambridge History of Capitalism*, 2 Vols, Cambridge University Press, 2014.

Nelson, Benjamin, *The Idea of Usury: From Tribal Brotherhood to Universal Otherhood*, Princeton University Press, 1949.

Nelson, Richard R., and Sidney G. Winter, *An Evolutionary Theory of Economic Change*, Harvard University Press, 1982.

Nelson, Richard R., "Evolutionary Theorizing about Economic Change", in Neil J. Smelser, and Richard Swedberg (eds.), *The Handbook of Economic Sociology*, Princeton University Press, 1994, pp. 108–36.

Oakes, Guy, "Introduction" to Heinrich Rickert (ed.), *The Limits of Concept Formation in Natural Science: A Logical Introduction to the Historical Sciences*, Cambridge University Press, 1986, pp. vii–xxviii.

Oakes, Guy, Weber and Rickert: *Concept Formation in the Cultural Sciences*, MIT Press, 1988.

Oakley, Allen, *Schumpeter's Theory of Capitalist Motion: A Critical Exposition and Reassessment*, Elgar, 1990.

Offe, Claus, "Advanced Capitalism and the Welfare State", *Politics and Society*, Summer (1972), pp. 479–88.

Offe, Claus, "Competitive Party Democracy and the Keynesian Welfare State: Factors of Stability and Disorganization", *Policy Sciences* 15.3 (1983), pp. 225–46.

Offe, Claus, and John Keane, *Contradictions of the Welfare State*, MIT Press, 1984.

Offe, Claus, *Reflections on America: Tocqueville, Weber and Adorno in the United States*, Polity, 2005.

Orati, Vittorangelo, Shri Bhagwan Dahiya, and Joseph Alois Schumpeter, *Economic Theory in the Light of Schumpeter's Scientific Heritage*, Spellbound Pub., 2001.

Osterhammel, Jürgen, "Varieties of Social Economics: Joseph Schumpeter and Max Weber", in Wolfgang J. Mommsen, and Jürgen Osterhammel (eds.), *Max Weber and His Contemporaries*, Allen & Unwin, 1987, pp. 106–20.

Parsons, Stephen D., *Money, Time and Rationality in Max Weber: Austrian Connections*, Routledge, 2003.

Parsons, Talcott, "Introduction", in Talcott Parsons (d.) *Max Weber, the Theory of Social and Economic Action*, The Free Press, 1947.

Poggi, Gianfranco, *The Development of the Modern State: A Sociological Introduction*, Stanford University Press, 1978.

Poggi, Gianfranco, *Calvinism and the Capitalist Spirit: Max Weber's Protestant Ethic*, University of Massachusetts Press, 1983.

Pomeranz, Kenneth, *The Great Divergence: China, Europe, and the Making of the Modern World Economy*, Princeton University Press, 2000.

Pounds, Norman John Greville, *An Economic History of Medieval Europe*, Longman, 1974.

Prasad, Monica, *The Politics of Free Markets: The Rise of Neoliberal Economic Policies in Britain, France, Germany and the United States*, University of Chicago, 2007.

Radkau, Joachim, *Max Weber: A Biography*, Polity, 2009.

Redner, Harry, *Totalitarianism, Globalization, Colonialism: The Destruction of Civilization since 1914*, Transaction, 2014.

Rickert, Heinrich, *The Limits of Concept Formation in Natural Science: A Logical Introduction to the Historical Sciences*, Cambridge University Press, 1986.

Ringer, Fritz K., *Max Weber's Methodology: The Unification of the Cultural and Social Sciences*, Harvard University Press, 1997.

Ringer, Fritz K., *Max Weber: An Intellectual Biography*, University of Chicago Press, 2004.

Robbins, Lionel, "On a Certain Ambiguity in the Conception of Stationary Equilibrium", *Economic Journal* 40.158 (1930), pp. 194–214.

Robbins, Lionel, "Schumpeter's History of Economic Analysis", *Quarterly Journal of Economics* 69.1 (1955), pp. 1–22.

Robinson, Joan, *The Economics of Imperfect Competition*, Macmillan, 1933.

Roth, Guenther, and Wolfgang Schluchter, *Max Weber's Vision of History: Ethics and Methods*, University of California Press, 1979.

Rothchild, Kurt, "Schumpeter and Socialism", in Arnold Heerjie (ed.), *Schumpeterian Economics,* Praeger, 1981, pp. 113–25.

Sakakibara, Eisuke, *Beyond Capitalism: The Japanese Model of Market Economics*, University Press of America, 1993.

Samuelson, Paul, "Dynamics, Statics and the Stationary State", *Review of Economic Statistics* 25.1 (1943), 58–68.

Samuelson, Paul, "Schumpeter as an Economic Theorist", in Helmut Frisch (ed.), *Schumpeterian Economics*, Praeger, 1981, pp. 1–27.

Samuelson, Paul, "Schumpeter's Capitalism, Socialism and Democracy", in Arnold Heerjie (ed.), *Schumpeter's Vision*, Praeger, 1981, pp. 1–21.

Sapori, Armando, *The Italian Merchant in the Middle Ages*, Norton, 1970.

Scaff, Lawrence A., "From Political Economy to Political Sociology: Max Weber's Early Writings", in Ronald Glassman and Vatro Murvar (eds.), *Max Weber's Political Sociology: A Pessimistic Vision of a Rationalized World*, Greenwood, 1984, pp. 83–108.

Scaff, Lawrence A., *Fleeing the Iron Cage: Culture, Politics, and Modernity in the Thought of Max Weber*, University of California Press, 1989.

Scaff, Lawrence A., "Weber before Weberian Sociology", in Keith Tribe (ed.), *Reading Weber*, Routledge, 1989, pp. 15–41.

Scaff, Lawrence A., *Max Weber in America*, Princeton University Press, 2011.

Scherer, F. M., "Schumpeter and Plausible Capitalism", *Journal of Economic Literature* 30.3 (1992), pp. 1416–33.

Schluchter, Wolfgang, *The Rise of Western Rationalism: Max Weber's Developmental History*, University of California, 1981.

Schluchter, Wolfgang, *Paradoxes of Modernity: Culture and Conduct in the Theory of Max Weber*, Stanford University Press, 1996.

Schön, Manfred, "Gustav Schmoller and Max Weber", in Wolfgang J. Mommsen and Jürgen Osterhammel (eds.), *Max Weber and His Contemporaries*, Allen & Unwin, 1987, pp. 71–87.

Schumpeter, Joseph, *The Theory of Economic Development: An Inquiry into Profits, Capital, Credit, Interest, and the Business Cycle*, Harvard University Press, 1934 (TED).

Schumpeter, Joseph, *Business Cycles: A Theoretical, Historical, and Statistical Analysis of the Capitalist Process*, McGraw-Hill, 1939 (BC).

Schumpeter, Joseph, *Capitalism, Socialism and Democracy*, Harper, 1950 (CSD).

Schumpeter, Joseph (Richard Clemence ed.), *Essays of J. A. Schumpeter*, Addison-Wesley Press, 1951 (EJAS).

Schumpeter, Joseph, "The Instability of Capitalism", in Richard Clemence (ed.), *Essays of J. A. Schumpeter*, Addison-Wesley Press, 1951, pp. 47–72.

Schumpeter, Joseph, *Ten Great Economists, From Marx to Keynes*, Oxford University Press, 1951 (TGE).

Schumpeter, Joseph, "Keynes, the Economist", in *Three Views of Keynes the Economist*, Kessinger, 2010, pp. 73–101.

Schumpeter, Joseph, *Economic Doctrine and Method: An Historical Sketch*, Allen & Unwin, 1954.

Schumpeter, Joseph, *History of Economic Analysis*, Oxford University Press, 1954 (HEA).

Schumpeter, Joseph, "Money and the Social Product", *International Economic Papers*, 6 (1956), pp. 148–211.

Schumpeter, Joseph (Richard Clemence ed.), *Essays on Entrepreneurs, Innovations, Business Cycles, and the Evolution of Capitalism*, Transaction, 1989 (EEIBC).

Schumpeter, Joseph (Richard Swedberg ed.), *Joseph A. Schumpeter: The Economics and Sociology of Capitalism*, Princeton University Press, 1991 (ESC).

Schumpeter, Joseph, "The Meaning of Rationality in the Social Sciences", (Richard Swedberg ed.), *Joseph A. Schumpeter: The Economics and Sociology of Capitalism*, Princeton University Press, 1991, pp. 316–38.

Schumpeter, Joseph, *The Nature and Essence of Economic Theory*, Transaction, 2010.

Seidl, Christian (ed.), *Lectures on Schumpeterian Economics: Schumpeter Centenary Memorial Lectures*, Springer-Verlag, 1984.

Seidl, Christian, "Schumpeter Versus Keynes: Supply Side Economics or Demand Management?", in Christian Seidl (ed.), *Lectures on Schumpeterian Economics: Schumpeter Centenary Memorial Lectures*, Springer-Verlag, 1984.

Senn, Peter, "The Influence of Schumpeter's German Writings on Mainstream Economic Literature in English", in Jürgen Backhaus (ed.), *Joseph Schumpeter: Entrepreneurship, Style and Vision*, Kluwer, 2003, pp. 141–62.

Service, Robert, *A History of Twentieth-Century Russia*, Harvard University Press, 1998.

Shiller, Robert, *Finance and the Good Society*, Princeton University Press, 2012.

Shionoya, Yuichi, "Schumpeter on Schmoller and Weber: A Methodology of Economic Sociology", *History of Political Economy* 23.2 (1991), pp. 193–219.

Shionoya, Yuichi (ed.), *Innovation in Technology, Industries, and Institutions: Studies in Schumpeterian Perspectives*, University of Michigan Press, 1994.

Shionoya, Yuichi, *Schumpeter in the History of Ideas*, University of Michigan Press, 1994.

Shionoya, Yuichi, *Schumpeter and the Idea of Social Science: A Metatheoretical Study*, Cambridge University Press, 1997.

Shionoya, Yuichi, *The Soul of the German Historical School: Methodological Essays on Schmoller, Weber, and Schumpeter*, Springer, 2005.

Shonfield, Andrew, *Modern Capitalism: The Changing Balance of Public and Private Power*, Oxford University Press, 1965.

Shonfield, Andrew, "The Politics of the Mixed Economy in the International System of the 1970s", *International Affairs* 56, January (1980), pp. 1–14.

Shonfield, Andrew, and Zuzanna Shonfield, *In Defence of the Mixed Economy*, Oxford University Press, 1984.

Sica, Alan, *Weber, Irrationality, and Social Order*, University of California Press, 1988.

Simmel, Georg, *The Philosophy of Money*, Routledge, 1978.

Smelser, Neil J., and Richard Swedberg, *The Handbook of Economic Sociology*, Princeton University Press, 1994.

Smithies, Arthur, "Schumpeter and Keynes", in Seymour Edwin Harris (ed.), *Schumpeter, Social Scientist*, Harvard University Press, 1951, p. 5.

Smithies, Arthur, "Schumpeter's Predictions", in Arnold Heerjie (ed.), *Schumpeter's Vision*, Praeger, 1981, pp. 130–49.

Sombart, Werner, *The Jews and Modern Capitalism*, Collier, 1962.

Sraffa, Piero, "The Laws of Returns under Competitive Conditions", *Economic Journal* 36.144 (1926), pp. 535–50.

Staley, Charles, "Schumpeter's Business Cycles", *New York Economic Review*, Spring (1986).

Stolper, Wolfgang, "Aspects of Schumpeter's Theory of Evolution", Arnold Heerjie (ed.), *Schumpeterian Economics*, Praeger, 1981.

Swatos, William H., and Lutz Kaelber, *The Protestant Ethic Turns 100: Essays on the Centenary of the Weber Thesis*, Paradigm Publishers, 2005.

Swedberg, Richard, "Introduction" to Richard Swedberg (ed.), *Joseph A. Schumpeter: The Economics and Sociology of Capitalism*, Princeton University Press, 1991, pp. 3–98.

Swedberg, Richard, *Schumpeter: A Biography*, Princeton University Press, 1991.

Swedberg, Richard, "Can Capitalism Survive? Schumpeter's Answer and Its Relevance for New Institutional Economics", *Archives Europennes de Sociologie* 33 (1992), pp. 350–80.

Swedberg, Richard, *Explorations in Economic Sociology*, Sage Foundation, 1993.

Swedberg, Richard, *Max Weber and the Idea of Economic Sociology*, Princeton University Press, 1998.

Swedberg, Richard, "Afterword: The Role of the Market in Max Weber's Work", *Theory and Society* 29 (2000), pp. 373–84.
Swedberg, Richard, "Max Weber's *Economy and Society*: The Centerpiece of Economy and Society?", in Charles Camic, Philip S. Gorski, and David M. Trubek (eds.), *Max Weber's Economy and Society: A Critical Companion*, Stanford University Press, 2005, pp. 127–42.
Swoboda, Peter, "Schumpeter's Entrepreneur in Modern Economic Theory", in Christian Seidl (ed.), *Lectures on Schumpeterian Economics: Schumpeter Centenary Memorial Lectures*, Springer-Verlag, 1984.
Taylor, James, *Creating Capitalism: Joint-Stock Enterprise in British Politics and Culture, 1800–1870*, Royal Historical Society, 2014.
Temin, Peter, *The Roman Market Economy*, Princeton University Press, 2013.
Tenbruck, Friedrich H., "The Problem of Thematic Unity in the Works of Max Weber", in Keith Tribe (ed.), *Reading Weber*, Routledge, 1989, pp. 42–84.
Tichy, Gunther. "Schumpeter's Business Cycle Theory: Its Importance for Our Time", in Christian Seidl (ed.), *Lectures on Schumpeterian Economics: Schumpeter Centenary Memorial Lectures*, Springer-Verlag, 1984, pp. 77–88.
Tribe, Keith, *Reading Weber*, Routledge, 1989.
Trubeck, David, "Max Weber on Law and the Rise of Capitalism", *Wisconsin Law Review* 3, (1973), pp. 720–53.
Tsuru, Shigeto, *Japan's Capitalism: Creative Defeat and Beyond*, Cambridge University Press, 1993.
Tucker, R. (ed.), *The Marx-Engels Reader*, Norton, 1972.
Turner, Bryan S., *Max Weber on Economy and Society*, Taylor and Francis, 2010.
Turner, Stephen P., "Explaining Capitalism: Weber on and against Marx", in Robert Antonio and Ronald Glassman (eds.), *A Weber-Marx Dialogue*, University Press of Kansas, 1985.
Turner, Stephen P., and Regis A. Factor, *Max Weber: The Lawyer as Social Thinker*, Routledge, 1994.
Turner, Stephen P. (ed.), *The Cambridge Companion to Weber*, Cambridge University Press, 2000.
Usher, Abbott Payson, *A History of Mechanical Inventions*, Harvard University Press, 1954.
Varese, Federico, *The Russian Mafia: Private Protection in a New Market Economy*, Oxford University Press, 2001.
Viner, Jacob, Jacques Melitz, and Donald Winch, *Religious Thought and Economic Society: Four Chapters of an Unfinished Work*, Duke University Press, 1978.
Vogl, Joseph, *The Spectre of Capital: Cultural Memory in the Present*, Stanford University Press, 2010.
Walker, Donald (ed.), *William Jaffé's Essays on Walras*, Cambridge University Press, 1983.
Wallerstein, Immanuel Maurice, *The Modern World System: Capitalist Agriculture and the Origins of the European World-Economy in the Sixteenth Century*, Academic Press, 1974.
Walras, Léon, *Elements of Pure Economics; or, the Theory of Social Wealth*, Allen & Unwin, 1954.
Walter, Carl, and Howie, Fraser, *Red Capitalism: The Fragile Financial Foundation of China's Extraordinary Rise*, Wiley, 2011.
Warriner, Doreen, "Schumpeter and the Conception of Static Equilibrium", *Economic Journal* 40, March (1931), pp. 38–50.
Weber, Marianne, and Harry Zohn, *Max Weber: A Biography*, Wiley, 1975.

Weber, Max, *The Protestant Ethic and the Spirit of Capitalism*, Unwin, 1930 (PE).
Weber, Max, *The Methodology of the Social Sciences*, Free Press, 1949 (MSS).
Weber, Max, *The Religion of China: Confucianism and Taoism*, Free Press, 1951.
Weber, Max, *Ancient Judaism*, Free Press, 1952.
Weber, Max, *The Religion of India: The Sociology of Hinduism and Buddhism*, Free Press, 1958.
Weber, Max, *Economy and Society: An Outline of Interpretive Sociology*, Bedminster Press, 1968 (ES).
Weber, Max, "Marginal Utility Theory and 'The Fundamental Law of Psychophysics'", *Social Science Quarterly* 56.1 (1975), pp. 21–36.
Weber, Max, *Roscher and Knies: The Logical Problems of Historical Economics*, Free Press, 1975.
Weber, Max, "Developmental Tendencies in the Situation of the East Elbian Rural Labourers", in Keith Tribe (ed.), *Reading Weber*, Routledge, 1992, pp. 158–87.
Weber, Max, "The Nation State and Economic Policy", in Keith Tribe (ed.), *Reading Weber*, Routledge, 1992, pp. 188–209.
Weber, Max, *Critique of Stammler*, The Free Press, 1977.
Weber, Max (Walter Runciman ed.), *Weber: Selections in Translation*, Cambridge University Press, 1978.
Weber, Max, *General Economic History*, Transaction Books, 1981 (GEH).
Weber, Max, "The Nation State and Economic Policy", in Peter Lassman and Ronald Speirs (eds.), *Weber: Political Writings*, Cambridge University Press, 1994.
Weber, Max, *The Agrarian Sociology of Ancient Civilizations*, Verso, 1988.
Weber, Max, *From Max Weber: Essays in Sociology*, Routledge, 1991 (FMW).
Weber, Max, "Socialism", in Peter Lassman, and Ronald Spiers (eds.), *Max Weber's Political Writings*, Cambridge University Press, 1994.
Weber, Max, *The Russian Revolutions*, Cornell University Press, 1995.
Weber, Max, "The Protestant Sects and the Spirit of Capitalism", in Hans Gerth and Writght Mills (eds.), *From Max Weber*, Routledge, 1991, pp. 302–22.
Weber, Max, "The Social Psychology of the World Religions", in Hans Gerth and Writght Mills (eds.), *From Max Weber*, Routledge, 1991, pp. 267–301.
Weber, Max, "Commerce on the Stock and Commodity Exchanges [Die Borsenverkehr]", *Theory and Society* 29.3 (2000), pp. 339–71.
Weber, Max, "Stock and Commodity Exchanges [Die Borse(1894)]", *Theory and Society* 29.3 (2000), pp. 305–38.
Weber, Max, "Weber's First Reply to Fischer, 1907", "Weber's Second Reply to Fisher, 1908", Weber's First Reply to Rachfahl, 1910", "Weber's Second Reply to Rachfahl, 1910", in David Chalcraft and Austin Harrington (eds.), *The Protestant Ethic Debate: Max Weber's Replies to His Critics, 1907–1910*, Liverpool University Press, 2001, pp. 31–40, 43–54, 61–88, 93–132.
Weber, Max, and Lutz Kaelber, *The History of Commercial Partnerships in the Middle Ages*, Rowman & Littlefileld, 2003.
Weber, Max, *Roman Agrarian History in Its Relation to Roman Public and Civil Law*, Regina Books, 2008.
Weber, Max, *Collected Methodological Writings*, Routledge, 2012.
Weintraub, Roy, "On the Existence of a Competitive Equilibrium", *Journal of Economic Literature* 21.1 (1954), pp. 1–39.
Westra, Richard, *Confronting Global Neoliberalism: Third World Resistance and Development Strategies*, Clarity, 2010.

Westra, Richard, *The Evil Axis of Finance: The US-Japan-China Stranglehold on the Global Future*, Clarity, 2012.
Wicksell, Knut, *Selected Papers on Economic Theory*, Harvard University Press, 1958.
Wicksell, Knut, *Value, Capital and Rent*, Kelley, 1970.
Wicksell, Knut, *Selected Essays in Economics*, Routledge, 1999.
Wieser, Friedich, *Natural Value*, Macmillan, 1893.
Wieser, Friedich, *Social Economics*, 1927.
Wieser, Friedrich, "The Austrian School and the Theory of Value", Chapter 9 in Israel Kirzner (ed.), *Classics in Austrian Economics*, Vol. 1, Pickering, 1994.
Wieser, Friedrich, "On the Relationship of Costs to Value", Chapter 8 in Israel Kirzner (ed.), *Classics in Austrian Economics*, Vol. 1, Pickering, 1994.
Williamson, Judith, *Consuming Passions: The Dynamics of Popular Culture*, Marion Boyars, 1986.
Williamson, Oliver, *The Economic Institutions of Capitalism*, Free Press, 1985.
Williamson, Oliver, and Sidney Winter (eds.), *The Nature of the Firm: Origins, Evolution and Development*, Oxford University Press, 1993.
Wright, Erik Olin, "The Shadow of Exploitation in Weber's Class Analysis", in Charles Camic, Philip S. Gorski, and David M. Trubek (eds.), *Max Weber's Economy and Society: A Critical Companion*, Stanford University Press, 2005, pp. 204–36.
Wood, John Cunningham, *J.A. Schumpeter: Critical Assessments*, Routledge, 1991.
Woodruff, David, *Money Unmade: Barter and the Fate of Russian Capitalism*, Cornell University Press, 1999.
Wrong, Dennis Hume, *Max Weber*, Prentice-Hall, 1970.
Zarnowitz, Victor, "Recent Work on Business Cycles in Historical Perspective: A Review of Theories and Evidence", *Journal of Economic Literature* 33, June (1985), pp. 523–80.

Index